THE BOOK OF NEW UNIVERSALISM

THE BOOK OF NEW UNIVERSALISM

BRANDON ARROUES

Acknowledgment to Earth, Humanity, and Wisdom across Ages

Contents

Preface

Welcome to *The Book of New Universalism*, a text crafted to guide you on a path toward a life of meaning, ethical responsibility, and spiritual unity. This book was born from a vision of interconnected wisdom, where the truths of the universe reveal themselves through reason, shared human experience, and a reverence for all that surrounds us. At its heart, New Universalism calls us to honor life in its many forms and to live with integrity, compassion, and purpose.

As you engage with this book, you will find it serves multiple roles: it is a structured guide, offering teachings and practices for personal and communal growth, and it is also a companion to return to—whether in times of joy, challenge, or quiet contemplation. Here, you may discover practices for individual reflection, learn rituals to share within a community, and find inspiration to guide you in daily living.

The Book of New Universalism honors the idea that spiritual truth and enlightenment do not belong to any one faith or philosophy but are found across many paths. From Indigenous wisdom, with its deep-rooted connection to the Earth, to Eastern philosophies that teach compassion and mindfulness, and Western traditions that emphasize justice and charity—each tradition offers valuable insights. New Universalism embraces these universal truths, drawing from diverse teachings to form a holistic and inclusive faith.

Whether you come to this book as a spiritual seeker, a lifelong practitioner, a skeptic, or someone simply curious about New Universalism, you are welcomed here. This book is for those who wish to explore, connect, and contribute to a shared world founded on respect, stewardship, and kindness. Together, may we embark on a journey toward understanding and unity, grounded in the knowledge that each of us is part of a greater whole.

Section I: Foundations of New Universalism

1

The Proclamation of Faith

Origins and Vision

Introduction to New Universalism

In a world as vast and diverse as ours, humankind has always sought connection—to each other, to the mysteries of existence, and to the world that sustains us. *The Book of New Universalism* was born from a shared yearning to bridge these connections, offering a path that respects individual perspectives while embracing the universal truths that unite us all. New Universalism was founded on the belief that spiritual insight, reason, and compassion need not be confined to any one faith or culture; instead, they can be drawn together to form a greater understanding that transcends division. Here, we recognize that while each path offers its own unique insights, many lead to the same essential truths, and these truths form the bedrock of our faith.

The vision of New Universalism is grounded in three core principles: inclusivity, reason, and reverence for the Earth. In inclusivity, we find our call to see all people as part of one human family. This is not simply a matter of tolerance or acceptance, but a deep, active embrace of diversity—a celebration of the variety that enriches human experience. New Universalism encourages us to see beyond labels and differences, to connect with the inherent dignity that resides in each person. Inclusivity here is both an ideal to strive toward and a way of life to practice. It reminds us that every individual, regardless of identity, background, or beliefs, deserves respect, compassion, and understanding. In our communities and in our relationships, inclusivity becomes an everyday practice that helps dissolve the barriers that divide us.

Reason is equally essential to New Universalism, serving as a guiding light on the path to understanding and growth. Where some may view faith and reason as opposites, New Universalism sees them as partners in the search for truth. We are invited to approach life with curiosity and discernment, to ask questions, and to value the insights gained through experience and thoughtful reflection. Reason encourages us to explore not just through belief but through inquiry, to seek meaning in the world around us, and to welcome wisdom from multiple perspectives. In this way,

New Universalism honors the intellect as a vital part of the spiritual journey, one that complements the heart's yearning for connection and the soul's desire for growth.

Above all, New Universalism reveres the Earth, seeing it not merely as our habitat but as a sacred presence woven into our very existence. The natural world, with its rhythms and cycles, offers endless lessons in patience, resilience, and renewal. We look to the Earth's seasons, the rise and fall of the sun, the growth and decay that sustain life, as reflections of our own lives and spiritual paths. In spring's rebirth, we see hope; in summer's abundance, gratitude; in autumn's harvest, reflection; and in winter's stillness, rest. These cycles teach us to honor life's natural ebb and flow and to live in harmony with the world that sustains us. Earth reverence in New Universalism is not merely a value; it is a call to action, inviting us to care for the planet with the same dedication we extend to one another. Earth Stewardship thus becomes both a personal and collective responsibility, a way of living that recognizes the Earth as both teacher and sustainer.

While New Universalism honors the wisdom of many traditions, it is also a faith uniquely its own. Our respect for inclusivity echoes the teachings of Islam and Christianity, where compassion and care for one's neighbor are central. In our dedication to reason, we align with Buddhism's encouragement of questioning and discernment, and with Western philosophy's reverence for critical inquiry and exploration. Our reverence for the Earth finds resonance in Indigenous and Earth-based spiritualities, where the natural world is seen as sacred, alive with spirit and wisdom. And like Confucianism, we value family and community as essential to personal and social harmony, honoring the bonds that connect us across generations. Yet New Universalism does not seek to replicate or supplant these beliefs. Instead, it draws upon the collective wisdom of humankind, finding unity in diversity, and offering a path that is both ancient and new.

This may invite a comparison with Unitarian Universalism, which similarly upholds principles of inclusivity and respect for individual paths. However, New Universalism is distinct in its foundation on Earth-centered spirituality and the Four Pillars: Reason, Earth Stewardship, Social Responsibility, and Filial Piety. While Unitarian Universalism emphasizes open exploration and tolerance, New Universalism is grounded in the belief that the Earth itself is a sacred source of wisdom and that reverence for its cycles forms the basis of spiritual understanding. Our commitment to human rights extends beyond the philosophical to a spiritual mandate, calling for both personal integrity and social responsibility as reflections of the interconnectedness of all beings. These elements position New Universalism not merely as an interfaith tradition but as a faith in its own right, one that calls for a return to our roots in the natural world, embodying ancient reverence with a modern commitment to inclusivity and justice.

In New Universalism, we are reminded that our faith journey is not only personal but also communal. As individuals, we seek to understand, to grow, and to live in alignment with the values of inclusivity, reason, and Earth reverence. Together, we aim to create communities where these values flourish, where each person's unique gifts are honored, and where the Earth is respected and protected. This is a faith that sees each of us as a part of something larger, a single thread woven into the vast tapestry of existence.

New Universalism invites all who are drawn to these principles—whether spiritual seekers, interfaith practitioners, secular explorers, or those simply curious about the path. As you journey through *The Book of New Universalism*, may you find a welcoming space for your questions, reflections, and hopes. May this book serve as a compass, guiding you toward a life of meaning, unity, and shared purpose. Together, let us embark on a path that honors both the unique and the universal, recognizing that while our individual journeys may differ, we are all part of one sacred whole.

Roots in Earth-Based Spirituality

At the core of New Universalism is a profound reverence for the Earth—a recognition that the natural world is not simply a backdrop for human existence but a living, sacred presence that pulses with wisdom and beauty. The Earth, in all its complexity, diversity, and interconnectedness, is seen as both a divine presence and an active partner in the spiritual journey. To follow New Universalism is to walk in step with the natural rhythms of the world around us, to see life's lessons reflected in the turning of the seasons, and to understand our lives as part of a vast and intricate web of life. Here, the Earth is our teacher, our guide, and our inspiration, revealing universal truths that shape our values, actions, and understanding of the divine.

New Universalism draws inspiration from the wisdom and practices of Earth-based spiritual traditions, including Neo-Paganism, Indigenous teachings, and other nature-centered philosophies. These traditions remind us that the Earth itself is sacred, that its cycles mirror our own, and that life's meaning can often be found in the quiet communion with nature. By integrating these practices, New Universalism aims to cultivate a spirituality that is grounded, inclusive, and deeply respectful of the world that sustains us. Earth-centered spirituality in New Universalism is not an abstract ideal but a lived reality—an invitation to experience the divine through direct engagement with the natural world, to find solace in its cycles, and to see our lives reflected in its rhythms.

Neo-Paganism has provided New Universalism with invaluable insights into the practice of honoring nature's cycles, particularly through the Wheel of the Year. The Wheel of the Year marks the cyclical transitions of the seasons, celebrated through eight festivals that correspond to natural events, such as solstices, equinoxes, and the midpoints in between. Each of these festivals has a distinct character and meaning, reflecting both the tangible changes in the environment and the symbolic stages of human growth. For example, Autumn Festival, the festival at the end of the harvest season, is a time for honoring ancestors, reflecting on the cycle of life and death, and acknowledging the quieting of the Earth as it prepares for winter's stillness. In New Universalism, the Wheel of the Year is more than a calendar of seasonal changes; it is a spiritual framework that guides us in understanding the balance between abundance and rest, light and dark, life and death.

Through these observances, followers of New Universalism are invited to actively participate in the natural world, not only observing but engaging in rituals that honor the Earth's transitions. Each festival becomes an opportunity for reflection and renewal. During the Spring Equinox, a time when light and darkness stand in balance, rituals may involve planting seeds as a physical and symbolic gesture of new beginnings. At the Summer Solstice, the longest day of the year, communities may gather outdoors, celebrating the sun's warmth and the abundance of life. These practices are not only metaphors for growth but deeply experiential acts that encourage participants to feel their connection to the land, the seasons, and the cycles that govern life.

In addition to Neo-Pagan influences, **Indigenous wisdom** deeply informs New Universalism, particularly in its understanding of the interconnectedness of all life. Many Indigenous cultures view the Earth as a living, sentient being—a mother, ancestor, and provider who nourishes and sustains. The teachings of these traditions often include a profound sense of reciprocity: the Earth gives generously, and in return, we are called to care for it with respect and gratitude. This relationship is built on a foundation of mutual dependence and responsibility, where humanity's well-being is inseparable from the health of the land, water, air, and all living beings. Indigenous practices such as offering thanks before taking from the land, recognizing the spirits within nature, and honoring each element's unique role inspire New Universalism's emphasis on Earth Stewardship and ethical living.

In New Universalism, the concept of reciprocity with nature is not symbolic but a lived commitment. Followers are encouraged to view every action—whether gathering resources, tending a garden, or simply walking in the forest—as part of a sacred exchange with the Earth. To take from nature without giving back disrupts the balance upon which life depends. Through practices such as making offerings, practicing conservation, and engaging in ecological restoration, New Universalism promotes a worldview where humanity is not above nature but within it, guided by the same cycles and bound by the same responsibilities. This perspective teaches humility and gratitude, recognizing that just as the Earth sustains us, we must, in turn, act as its caretakers.

The cycles of nature—from the changing seasons to the phases of the moon and the movements of celestial bodies—are central to New Universalism, serving as both metaphors for spiritual growth and structures for communal worship. Each season carries with it themes that reflect the phases of human life and personal transformation. Spring, with its blossoms and fresh growth, represents renewal, hope, and new beginnings. Summer, abundant and warm, invites celebration and gratitude, reminding us to enjoy life's fullness. Autumn, with its harvest and golden light, calls for reflection, inviting us to honor what we have gathered and to prepare for the leaner times ahead. Winter, cold and quiet, encourages introspection and rest, a time to find strength in stillness and prepare for renewal.

These natural cycles teach us that growth, like the seasons, is not linear but cyclical. In New Universalism, followers are encouraged to align their spiritual practices with these rhythms, seeing in each season an opportunity to deepen their understanding of life's patterns. Seasonal rituals become a central part of worship, with each celebration marking a new chapter in the ongoing journey of growth and reflection. During the Winter Solstice, for instance, communities may gather in the evening, lighting candles or fires to symbolize the return of the sun and the light within each of us. This practice invites participants to find warmth, hope, and resilience in times of darkness, knowing that, as in nature, light will return. The Spring Equinox, a time when day and night are balanced, might involve planting seeds or sharing blessings, symbolizing the intentions we plant in our own lives.

The Earth, in all its forms, is understood as a manifestation of the divine—a presence that embodies wisdom, mystery, and power. To engage with the Earth in New Universalism is to engage with the sacred directly. This relationship calls for a mindful and respectful approach to life, where followers are asked to live in harmony with the land, to consume resources thoughtfully, and to support practices that sustain and heal. Earth reverence is not only a spiritual ideal but an ethical imperative, urging each individual to tread lightly, to honor the lives that sustain us, and to contribute to the flourishing of all beings. By fostering practices that restore and protect the Earth, New Universalism seeks to instill a sense of accountability and stewardship in every follower.

In New Universalism, the Earth is more than a landscape; it is a teacher, a divine presence, and a mirror of our own lives. As we walk this path, we are reminded that just as the Earth nurtures and provides, so too are we called to nurture and protect it. This reciprocal relationship forms the foundation of our worship, a continuous cycle of giving and receiving that honors life in all its forms. Through Earth-centered spirituality, New Universalism inspires a life lived in gratitude, humility, and harmony with the world around us—a faith that calls us back to the wisdom of the Earth and invites us to live in alignment with its rhythms and its grace.

Commitment to Universal Human Rights

In the heart of New Universalism lies a deep, unwavering commitment to the dignity and worth of every individual. This commitment is not merely an ideal but a guiding principle that shapes every aspect of our faith, from personal conduct to communal practices. For followers of New Universalism, the recognition of universal human rights is a reflection of our shared humanity—an acknowledgment that each person carries within them a spark of the sacred, deserving of respect, justice, and compassion. This understanding transcends boundaries of culture, religion, nationality, and identity, reminding us that our differences are sources of richness, not division.

New Universalism's dedication to human rights is grounded in both spiritual and ethical imperatives. It reflects the belief that each individual is inherently valuable, not because of what they achieve or how they identify, but simply because they exist. In New Universalism, the protection and promotion of human rights are seen as sacred responsibilities, acts that honor the divine spark within each person. These values resonate with the ideals expressed in the **Universal Declaration of Human Rights** (UDHR), a document that emerged after profound global hardship and which asserts, in its opening lines, that "all human beings are born free and equal in dignity and rights." The UDHR's vision of equality and justice for all people aligns closely with New Universalism's perspective, reinforcing the principle that every person deserves respect, freedom, and a life free from oppression.

This commitment to human rights draws not only from modern frameworks but from the wisdom of diverse spiritual traditions. In **Christianity**, the call to "love your neighbor as yourself" (Mark 12:31) extends beyond religious boundaries, serving as a moral compass that champions kindness, compassion, and justice. Similarly, **Islamic teachings** emphasize the value of mercy and equality, encapsulated in the concept of *tawheed*, which views all life as unified and interdependent under God's creation. In **Buddhism**, the principle of *karuna*, or compassion, guides adherents toward actions that relieve suffering and uphold dignity for all beings. These teachings, each distinct yet deeply interconnected, serve as reminders that human rights are not new ideas but timeless values cherished across cultures and epochs.

Within New Universalism, the commitment to human rights takes shape through specific principles that guide both personal conduct and community life. These principles include equality, freedom, and justice, each of which holds a place within the moral and spiritual framework of our faith.

Equality in New Universalism is a principle that transcends the surface distinctions of identity and background, reaching to the very essence of what it means to be human. To see one another as equals is to see each person as a reflection of the sacred, deserving of respect and inclusion. In daily life, practicing equality involves actively recognizing the inherent worth in everyone we encounter—whether it is through listening without judgment, treating others with kindness, or advocating for those whose voices may be marginalized. This commitment to equality is expressed in community gatherings where all members, regardless of social status, gender, or background, are welcomed and valued as part of a larger family. By honoring equality, we affirm that every individual brings unique gifts to the world and that our diversity is a strength to be celebrated.

Freedom is another cornerstone of New Universalism's approach to human rights, representing the right of each person to live authentically, express themselves openly, and pursue their path without coercion or fear. This principle echoes the words of the **Bhagavad Gita**, which urges individuals to live according to their inner truth: "Better one's own path imperfectly than another's path perfectly" (3:35). Freedom, in this sense, is not only a personal right but a communal responsibility—to create an environment where each person feels safe, valued, and encouraged to live in alignment with their values and beliefs. In practice, this may mean advocating for policies that protect personal freedoms, supporting individuals in their unique journeys, or fostering open dialogues within communities to ensure that all voices are heard and respected.

Justice, the third pillar of New Universalism's commitment to human rights, calls for fairness, accountability, and equity in all aspects of life. Justice is the active pursuit of a society where everyone has the opportunity to thrive, free from oppression and prejudice. It is an ideal that has roots in many traditions; in **Judaism**, the concept of *tzedek* (justice) is not merely a legal principle but a spiritual mandate to pursue righteousness and rectify inequality. Justice in New Universalism translates into practical actions: supporting social causes that promote equity, standing against discrimination, and working within communities to create systems that uplift rather than marginalize. In daily life, justice may mean advocating for fair treatment in the workplace, standing in solidarity with those who are oppressed, or engaging in charitable work that uplifts those who have been denied opportunities.

While these principles provide a moral foundation, New Universalism also emphasizes the active practice of human rights in everyday life. This commitment goes beyond belief, encouraging followers to embody these values in their actions, relationships, and interactions. A simple greeting, a respectful conversation, or a gesture of kindness becomes an expression of this faith. We are reminded that each interaction holds within it the potential to affirm the dignity of others and to contribute to a world where human rights are not merely ideals but lived realities.

In New Universalism, human rights are seen as an ongoing, active responsibility—a call to not only respect but to protect the rights and freedoms of all beings. This commitment asks each follower to move beyond words and intentions, stepping into the role of an advocate, a protector, and a steward of justice. It is a reminder that in upholding the rights of others, we honor the sacredness of life itself, recognizing that each person's freedom and dignity are inextricably linked to our own.

As we reflect on these principles, New Universalism calls upon each of us to consider how we might embody them in our own lives. How do we treat those around us? Do we offer compassion to those who may think or look differently than we do? Are we willing to stand against injustice, even when it is uncomfortable? These questions are not easy, but they invite us to live with intention, to see ourselves as part of a greater effort to create a world where each person's inherent worth is respected and celebrated.

New Universalism, in its dedication to human rights, extends an invitation to all who seek a just and compassionate world. It asks us to see ourselves as part of an interconnected family, where the rights of one are the rights of all, and where every act of kindness, justice, and respect strengthens the fabric of our shared humanity. This is a path that calls us to recognize and celebrate our differences, to seek unity without erasure, and to remember that true peace can only come when each person's dignity is upheld. Together, we move forward, guided by a commitment to human rights that honors the divine within each of us and seeks to create a world that reflects the values of equality, freedom, and justice.

The Four Pillars of Faith

Pillar 1: Reason and Universal Truth

In New Universalism, reason is honored not only as a tool for understanding but as a guiding light that complements the spiritual journey. Far from being in conflict with faith, reason serves as a means of deepening our connection to the sacred, inviting us to explore, question, and grow. In this way, reason is more than a process of logical thought; it is a spiritual practice that brings clarity, discernment, and insight. New Universalism sees reason and faith as partners on the same path, each enriching the other, allowing us to move toward a fuller understanding of universal truths—those principles and ideals that resonate across human experience and form the bedrock of our values.

At its essence, reason is the capacity to think critically, to ask questions, and to seek answers. This drive toward understanding is woven into the fabric of humanity, appearing in countless cultures and philosophical traditions throughout history. In the words of the ancient Greek philosopher **Aristotle**, "All men by nature desire to know." This impulse to know, to understand, and to connect with deeper truths is not simply an intellectual exercise; it is a spiritual calling. Through reason, we seek to comprehend the mysteries of life, the nature of existence, and our place within the world.

For New Universalism, reason is both a discipline and a gift. It grounds us in the here and now, enabling us to approach faith with both reverence and critical thought. This balance between reason and faith is reflected in many spiritual and philosophical traditions. **Buddhism**, for instance, encourages followers not to accept teachings blindly but to test them against their own experiences and reason. The Buddha himself taught, "Do not believe in anything simply because you have heard it. But after observation and analysis, when you find that anything agrees with reason and is conducive to the good and benefit of all, then accept it and live up to it." This encouragement to think critically and reflect deeply aligns closely with New Universalism's vision, which invites each follower to engage actively in their spiritual journey through inquiry and reflection.

Islamic philosophy offers another example of this harmony between faith and reason, particularly through the teachings of scholars such as **Al-Ghazali** and **Ibn Rushd** (Averroes). Al-Ghazali spoke of reason as a light that guides the seeker toward greater understanding, emphasizing that one's spiritual practice should be both heartfelt and intellectually sound. Ibn Rushd, in his defense of rational thought, argued that reason and faith are two paths leading to the same truth. This synthesis of intellect and spirit reflects New Universalism's own belief that reason does not diminish faith but enriches it, leading us to a deeper connection with the sacred.

In New Universalism, reason is a pathway to universal truths—those timeless principles and ideals that echo through diverse cultures and spiritual traditions, connecting us to the shared wisdom of humanity. These truths resonate because they reflect the deepest aspects of human experience: the yearning for peace, the desire for justice, the reverence for life, and the pursuit of harmony. These are not beliefs confined to any one faith; they are ideals that transcend borders and bind us together as a human family. They are the aspirations that, despite cultural differences, continue to surface in every corner of the world.

For instance, **the Golden Rule**, "Do unto others as you would have them do unto you," appears in some form across major world religions, from Christianity's teachings of compassion and forgiveness to **Confucianism's** principle of reciprocity. This rule reflects a universal truth: that kindness and empathy are essential to human flourishing. In New Universalism, the Golden Rule serves as a foundation for how we interact with others, reminding us that each person's dignity and worth must be honored.

Another example of universal truth is the concept of **unity** and interconnectedness found in many traditions. In **Hinduism**, the idea of *Atman* (the individual soul) and *Brahman* (the universal soul) reflects the belief that all beings are part of a greater whole. Similarly, **Indigenous wisdom** often speaks of the Earth and all its inhabitants as interconnected, each life forming part of a web that is sacred and indivisible. These perspectives resonate with New Universalism's view of humanity as part of a shared world, each individual contributing to the greater good. Reason helps us understand this interconnectedness, allowing us to see that actions taken for the benefit of others ultimately benefit us all.

Yet reason in New Universalism is not limited to the intellect alone; it is a balanced partner with spiritual intuition. Just as we use reason to explore life's mysteries, we also turn inward, trusting the insights that arise from within. This partnership allows for a holistic approach to understanding, where both the mind and the spirit are engaged in the search for truth. When reason and intuition work in harmony, they help us recognize and affirm universal truths in both ourselves and the world around us.

As we encounter these universal truths, reason encourages us not only to understand them but to live by them. For example, the recognition of human dignity is a truth that emerges across multiple traditions. From the **humanist teachings** of the Renaissance to the **Universal Declaration of Human Rights**, which states, "All human beings are born free and equal in dignity and rights," the principle of human dignity is universally valued. In New Universalism, reason asks us to reflect on this truth and to embody it in our actions, whether by treating others with kindness, supporting justice, or standing against prejudice.

The practice of reason as a spiritual discipline also requires humility—the willingness to acknowledge that we do not have all the answers and that our understanding will continue to grow. In **Socratic philosophy**, Socrates famously claimed to know only that he knew nothing, emphasizing the importance of intellectual humility. This openness to learning and growth is central to New Universalism, where followers are encouraged to approach life as an ongoing journey of discovery. By embracing reason with humility, we remain open to new insights, welcoming the wisdom of others as we deepen our understanding.

In New Universalism, reason is not an end in itself but a means to greater awareness, compassion, and unity. It is a tool that guides us toward universal truths, helping us see beyond the surface of life and into its deeper connections. By fostering a spirit of inquiry, reflection, and discernment, reason allows us to explore the mysteries of existence with both awe and understanding. It reminds us that faith and intellect are not separate, but woven together, each strengthening the other.

Through reason, we find a path that is both personal and universal, one that respects the insights of every individual while grounding us in shared wisdom. This journey toward understanding is one we walk together, guided by principles that connect us across generations, cultures, and faiths. In New Universalism, reason is both a light and a mirror—illuminating the way forward while reflecting the timeless truths that lie within each of us.

Pillar 2: Earth Stewardship

For New Universalism, the Earth is more than a resource—it is a sacred presence, a divine gift, and a living testament to the beauty and mystery of existence. Our relationship with the natural world forms the foundation of New Universalism, where Earth Stewardship is both a spiritual responsibility and a guiding principle for daily life. The call to care for the Earth is timeless, woven into the teachings of ancient traditions and renewed with urgency in the face of contemporary environmental challenges. Earth Stewardship asks us to honor the planet as a source of life, wisdom, and renewal, embracing our role as caretakers with humility and dedication.

Earth Stewardship in New Universalism is not merely an environmental ethic; it is a spiritual calling that reflects the interconnectedness of all life. We are bound to the Earth in a cycle of giving and receiving, a relationship that reminds us that every action has an impact and that our lives are inextricably linked to the health of the world around us. As stewards, we are asked to walk gently upon the Earth, to take only what we need, and to give back through practices that sustain and nurture life. This principle finds resonance in many Indigenous and Earth-centered spiritual traditions, where the land is seen as sacred and humanity as a partner in maintaining its balance. Within New Universalism, Earth Stewardship is a reminder that to honor the Earth is to honor the divine, and that our responsibility to protect the natural world is both ancient and enduring.

The call to stewardship is grounded in respect for the Earth's rhythms and cycles, which teach us to live with patience, humility, and reverence. In New Universalism, these cycles are reflected in the **Wheel of the Year**, a sacred concept that embodies the Earth's natural rhythms and invites us to align our lives with its seasons. The Wheel of the Year serves as a spiritual calendar, marking the cycles of life, growth, harvest, and rest. Each turn of the Wheel is an opportunity to honor the Earth's abundance, to reflect on our relationship with the natural world, and to renew our commitment to stewardship. Followers of New Universalism celebrate these cycles through seasonal festivals that reinforce the principles of Earth Stewardship, reminding us that we are part of an eternal rhythm of life and that our role as stewards is ongoing.

For example, during the **Spring Equinox**, a time of renewal and balance, communities may gather to plant seeds, both literal and symbolic, representing new beginnings and a commitment to growth. This act of planting serves as a reminder of our responsibility to nurture life and to support the Earth's ability to sustain itself. At the **Autumn Equinox**, a festival of harvest and gratitude, followers may come together to give thanks for the Earth's gifts, sharing food and offerings as a gesture of reciprocity. These gatherings are not only celebrations of nature's abundance but affirmations of our role as caretakers, each festival marking a moment in the cycle where we reflect on our impact and renew our dedication to stewardship.

In addition to these seasonal observances, Earth Stewardship in New Universalism encompasses specific responsibilities that guide both individual and communal practices. **Sustainable living** is encouraged as a way to honor the Earth's resources, reminding us to use only what we need and to minimize waste. Followers are encouraged to adopt practices that reduce their ecological footprint, from choosing environmentally friendly products to conserving water and energy. In New Universalist communities, these practices extend to collective efforts, such as organizing community gardens, supporting local agriculture, or engaging in habitat restoration projects. These actions serve as living expressions of our commitment to sustainability, each effort contributing to the health and vitality of the Earth.

Conservation is another key responsibility under Earth Stewardship, rooted in the recognition that the Earth's resources are finite and that our role as stewards includes protecting these resources for future generations. Conservation involves more than the preservation of land and water; it is an expression of respect for all life. By preserving natural habitats, we protect the diversity of life that enriches our world, from the smallest plants to the most majestic animals. In New Universalism, conservation is seen as a moral imperative, a way to honor the interconnectedness of life and to ensure that the beauty and wisdom of the natural world remain accessible to those who come after us.

Respect for life extends to **biodiversity and wildlife protection**, reminding us that every species is part of the intricate web that sustains our planet. Followers of New Universalism are encouraged to support efforts that protect endangered species, maintain ecosystems, and promote the flourishing of all forms of life. This commitment is not only about preserving nature but about recognizing that we share the Earth with countless other beings, each with its own purpose and place. Just as we rely on the Earth's resources, so too does each species depend on the health of the environment. Our stewardship, therefore, is not limited to human needs but encompasses the welfare of all creatures, reflecting New Universalism's dedication to inclusivity and respect for all life.

While Earth Stewardship is a timeless responsibility, New Universalism recognizes the urgent need to address current environmental challenges, from climate change to deforestation and pollution. These issues threaten not only the planet's ecosystems but the well-being of future generations, underscoring the importance of acting with intention and urgency. Followers are called to engage with these issues actively, to participate in environmental advocacy, to support policies that protect the Earth, and to educate others on the importance of sustainable practices. This commitment to environmental justice is a modern expression of ancient values, a reminder that our role as stewards includes standing up for the Earth and all who depend upon it.

Earth Stewardship in New Universalism is not a passive appreciation of nature; it is an active, lived responsibility that permeates every aspect of our lives. Whether by conserving resources, protecting biodiversity, or engaging in sustainable practices, each action becomes an expression of our faith. We are reminded that to honor the Earth is to honor the divine within it, and that each choice we make contributes to the health and vitality of the world we share. In this way, Earth Stewardship is both a spiritual path and a call to action, inviting us to live with integrity, purpose, and respect for the world that sustains us.

As we walk the path of Earth Stewardship, we are guided by the timeless wisdom of nature's cycles, by the teachings of those who have come before us, and by the urgent call to protect what remains. New Universalism calls each of us to see the Earth not as a possession but as a partner—a sacred presence that nurtures, teaches, and inspires. In caring for the Earth, we care for ourselves, for future generations, and for the countless lives that share this world with us. Earth Stewardship is a reminder that we are part of something greater, a living testament to the interconnectedness of all life and a commitment to the beauty and resilience of our shared home.

Pillar 3: Social Responsibility

In New Universalism, social responsibility is more than a call to kindness; it is a profound commitment to the welfare and dignity of all beings. This principle speaks to our ethical duty to one another and to the collective well-being of society, guiding us to act with compassion, integrity, and a sense of shared purpose. Social responsibility asks us to look beyond our own needs and to consider how we can contribute to the greater good—whether through small acts of kindness, community service, or efforts that reach across borders to foster equity and justice. This commitment is both personal and communal, inviting each of us to live in a way that reflects our interdependence and our responsibility to uplift others.

Social responsibility is a value cherished across many spiritual and philosophical traditions, each offering unique perspectives on our duty to others. **Christianity**, for instance, emphasizes charity and selfless love, with Jesus' teachings calling followers to care for the poor, feed the hungry, and stand in solidarity with the marginalized. "Truly I tell you, whatever you did for one of the least of these brothers and sisters of mine, you did for me" (Matthew 25:40). This passage reflects the understanding that service to others is service to the divine, a sentiment that resonates deeply within New Universalism. In our own faith, caring for others is seen as a reflection of our shared humanity and a sacred act that brings us closer to the divine within each of us.

Islam offers another perspective on social responsibility through the practice of *zakat*, or almsgiving, one of the Five Pillars of Islam. *Zakat* is a requirement for those able to give, ensuring that wealth is redistributed to support those in need. This principle of charitable giving reinforces the idea that we are accountable for one another's welfare and that prosperity is best when shared. In New Universalism, the spirit of *zakat* is embodied in our commitment to charity and mutual support. Followers are encouraged to contribute not only financially but through acts of service and kindness, fostering a community where resources, skills, and support flow freely to those who need them.

Social responsibility in New Universalism extends beyond individual acts of generosity to encompass a broader commitment to justice and equity. **Buddhism** teaches the importance of compassion through the practice of *karuna*, or compassionate action. *Karuna* is not limited to alleviating suffering on a personal level but is understood as a call to reduce suffering in society as a whole. This aligns with New Universalism's vision of a world where fairness and compassion are integral to social systems, and where every individual's dignity is protected. To live with social responsibility in New Universalism is to actively work toward a world where justice is not an ideal but a lived reality, where policies and practices reflect our values of inclusivity and equity.

In practice, social responsibility in New Universalism takes many forms, from small, everyday gestures to sustained efforts that foster change on a larger scale. **Acts of kindness and charity**—such as offering a meal to someone in need, volunteering at a local shelter, or simply listening to someone who is struggling—are seen as sacred acts, expressions of our commitment to compassion. These acts may seem small, yet they create ripples that reach far beyond the immediate moment, contributing to a culture of kindness and support. Followers of New Universalism are encouraged to look for ways to serve others in their daily lives, recognizing that each act of kindness reinforces the bonds that hold communities together.

Beyond personal actions, New Universalism calls its followers to engage in **community service and volunteerism** as a way to give back to society and support the collective well-being. Community service provides a tangible expression of our values, allowing us to make a positive impact in our own neighborhoods and to strengthen the social fabric that sustains us all. Whether through organizing food drives, supporting local education initiatives, or participating in environmental clean-ups, these acts of service reflect our dedication to the welfare of others. By giving our time and energy to these causes, we contribute to a world where support and generosity are woven into the fabric of everyday life.

New Universalism also embraces a commitment to **activism and advocacy**, recognizing that social responsibility includes standing up against injustice and advocating for policies that promote equity and respect. This call to action is aligned with movements for global justice and human rights, echoing the principles found in the **Universal Declaration of Human Rights**. The Declaration affirms that all individuals are entitled to basic rights and freedoms, regardless of race, religion, or background—a belief that New Universalism holds dear. Followers are encouraged to participate in initiatives that promote social justice, whether through supporting equal rights legislation, standing in solidarity with marginalized communities, or working to address systemic inequalities. In this way, our commitment to social responsibility becomes a vehicle for meaningful change, amplifying our values on a societal level.

In addition to these acts of compassion and advocacy, New Universalism emphasizes the importance of **ethical cooperation**—the idea that our actions, individually and collectively, contribute to a shared reality. This principle invites followers to live with integrity, honoring commitments, practicing honesty, and treating others with respect. Ethical cooperation extends to all aspects of life, from our interactions with loved ones to our roles as citizens. In New Universalism, each decision we make, each word we speak, and each relationship we nurture is an opportunity to live in alignment with our values, to contribute positively to the world, and to uphold the dignity of those around us.

Social responsibility in New Universalism is ultimately a vision for a world where compassion, fairness, and justice are the guiding principles of society. It is a vision that recognizes the interconnectedness of all beings, where each person's well-being is linked to the well-being of others. We are encouraged to see ourselves as part of a larger whole, to view our actions not in isolation but as threads in the fabric of humanity. This perspective calls us to act not only for our own benefit but for the collective good, inspiring us to seek harmony in our communities and justice in the world.

As followers of New Universalism, we are invited to reflect on our role in creating a just and compassionate society. How do we contribute to the well-being of others? Are we willing to use our voice for those who cannot speak? Are we prepared to work toward a world where equity and kindness prevail? These questions are not merely theoretical; they are calls to action, reminders that social responsibility is not only a principle to believe in but a path to walk. By living with social responsibility, we honor our shared humanity, we build bridges of understanding, and we create a world that reflects the values of New Universalism.

In the spirit of social responsibility, New Universalism asks each of us to be an agent of compassion, an advocate for justice, and a voice for those in need. Together, we envision a world where no one is left behind, where kindness is abundant, and where fairness and equality are the foundation of our shared existence. Through our actions, great and small, we contribute to this vision, building a future where social responsibility is not an aspiration but a lived reality, and where every life is honored and every voice is heard.

Pillar 4: Filial Piety

Filial Piety is both a sacred duty and a foundation for social harmony. This principle reflects the belief that our lives are interconnected, bound together by relationships that bring both responsibility and profound meaning. Filial Piety invites us to live with respect, understanding, and a sense of duty toward others, honoring the bonds that connect us across generations, communities, and even spiritual realms. Rooted in teachings from many traditions, and significantly inspired by Confucian thought, Filial Piety in New Universalism is an expression of loyalty, care, and integrity. It encourages us to approach all relationships with reverence, recognizing the mutual responsibility that lies at the heart of each bond.

While Confucianism teaches that a child's duty is to respect, honor, and care for their parents, New Universalism expands upon this principle to create a two-way understanding of Filial Piety. Just as a child owes a duty to the parent, so too does the parent hold a sacred responsibility to nurture, guide, and respect the child. This reciprocal view of Filial Piety acknowledges that each relationship is a shared commitment, where both individuals honor one another through acts of kindness, support, and loyalty. This two-way approach extends across all relationships, from family and community to governance and marriage, creating a comprehensive framework for ethical living that honors the dignity of every person.

The Parent-Child Relationship is often considered the heart of Filial Piety. In New Universalism, this bond is viewed as a sacred exchange, where both parent and child are entrusted with duties of care, respect, and understanding. For the child, Filial Piety includes honoring their parents through actions that reflect gratitude, listening to their wisdom, and offering support as they age. This respect is not limited to obedience but is an active, heartfelt reverence that values the sacrifices, guidance, and love that parents provide. In return, the parent's responsibility is to nurture the child with patience, compassion, and respect, guiding them toward independence while honoring their unique identity. The parent is called to embody Filial Piety by being a model of integrity, teaching through example, and fostering an environment of love and acceptance. In this way, Filial Piety in the parent-child relationship becomes a living testament to the balance of giving and receiving, where both individuals grow and learn from one another.

Filial Piety extends beyond the immediate family to encompass the relationship between **Person and Elders**. Elders hold a unique place within New Universalism, valued as keepers of wisdom and tradition. Showing reverence for elders means listening to their experiences, seeking their guidance, and supporting them as they navigate the later stages of life. This respect is not one-sided; elders, too, are encouraged to uphold their role in the community by sharing their wisdom generously, mentoring younger generations, and remaining engaged in communal life. The mutual respect between person and elder creates a bridge across generations, where each learns from the other, honoring the cycle of life and the shared responsibility to care for one another.

The bond between **Person and Ancestors** is another vital aspect of Filial Piety in New Universalism. Ancestors are not only remembered but revered as foundational to our lives and identities. Followers are encouraged to honor their ancestors through rituals, storytelling, and acts of remembrance that acknowledge the lineage and sacrifices that have paved the way for the present. Filial Piety toward ancestors includes expressing gratitude, preserving family traditions, and drawing strength from the lives and values of those who came before us. This relationship is reciprocal in the sense that we, as descendants, carry forward the legacy of our ancestors, living in ways that honor their contributions while shaping a world that future generations will inherit.

In New Universalism, Filial Piety also includes the relationship between **Person and Government**. This bond reflects the belief that civic duty and respect for leadership are essential to societal harmony. Followers are encouraged to engage with governance thoughtfully, honoring laws that uphold justice and contribute to the common good. However, New Universalism emphasizes that this respect is reciprocal; leaders and governments have a duty to serve with integrity, compassion, and a commitment to equity. Filial Piety in this context becomes a two-way responsibility, where citizens support ethical governance and hold leaders accountable to act in the public's best interests. This reciprocal duty fosters a sense of shared responsibility for the welfare of society, creating a foundation for trust, respect, and cooperation between individuals and their governing bodies.

Marital Partnership is also held as a sacred relationship in New Universalism, with Filial Piety extending to the mutual duties between partners. Marriage and committed partnerships are viewed as unions built on love, trust, and shared responsibility. Each partner is called to honor the other's individuality while committing to the well-being of the partnership. Filial Piety here is expressed through acts of support, open communication, and mutual respect. Partners are encouraged to be present for one another, to offer understanding and forgiveness, and to nurture their bond with kindness and dedication. This commitment to Filial Piety within a marital or committed relationship strengthens the partnership, reminding each individual that love is both a gift and a responsibility.

Finally, Filial Piety in New Universalism includes the bond between **Person and Person**, reflecting the belief that all people are connected by a shared humanity. This relationship is expressed through kindness, empathy, and a recognition of each person's inherent dignity. In daily life, Filial Piety toward others may be as simple as offering a smile, lending a helping hand, or listening with compassion. Each act of respect, each gesture of kindness, strengthens the bonds that hold society together. This understanding is reflected in the teachings of many traditions; for example, **Buddhism's principle of compassion**, or *karuna*, emphasizes the duty to alleviate suffering and to act with kindness toward all beings. In New Universalism, Filial Piety in the context of person-to-person relationships serves as a reminder that every interaction is an opportunity to express respect, to uplift others, and to contribute to a community where each individual is valued.

Filial Piety in New Universalism is ultimately a vision of harmony, where each relationship—whether within the family, the community, or society at large—is viewed as an opportunity to practice respect, understanding, and care. This principle is not limited to specific duties but extends to a way of life, encouraging followers to approach all relationships with reverence. By honoring Filial Piety, we contribute to a world where respect is mutual, where love is reciprocal, and where each person's role in the community is recognized and valued.

In embracing Filial Piety, New Universalism calls each of us to reflect on the connections that shape our lives and to honor the individuals who share this journey with us. This principle reminds us that we are not only responsible for ourselves but for each other, that every bond is a commitment, and that every relationship offers a chance to grow in understanding and compassion. Filial Piety, then, is both a duty and a gift, a path that guides us toward a life of meaning, respect, and harmony.

Holy Rites and Ceremonies

Baptism as an Initiation Rite

Baptism is a sacred and transformative act, a commitment to a life guided by reason, compassion, and unity with all existence. This initiation symbolizes both purification and renewal, marking a profound commitment to the principles and values of New Universalism. Through baptism, followers embrace their role as "children of Earth and Starry Heaven," a title that reflects the balance between our connection to the natural world and our place within the cosmos. This phrase, which echoes ancient Greek and other classical wisdom, captures the heart of New Universalism—a faith that honors both earthly existence and the mystery of the infinite.

The rite of baptism has a profound history in spiritual practice, serving as a symbol of rebirth, renewal, and dedication across various cultures and faiths. In New Universalism, this act is both a personal milestone and a spiritual promise, rooted in the belief that true commitment to a life of integrity begins with a declaration of purpose. This commitment is reinforced through water, a powerful symbol universally recognized for its purity and capacity for transformation. Water has long been seen as the source of life, from the ancient rivers of Mesopotamia to the holy waters of the Ganges. Its significance transcends specific religions, appearing across cultures as a symbol of cleansing, rebirth, and the divine flow that connects all beings.

In **Christianity**, baptism is a rite of entry into the faith, representing a washing away of past sins and the embrace of a new life in Christ. This act is seen as a rebirth, aligning the baptized with a community dedicated to love, service, and forgiveness. New Universalism draws from this tradition the understanding that baptism is not just a ritual but a moment of transformation, a declaration that one is entering a life committed to spiritual growth and unity. The water used in New Universalist baptism represents a similar purification—a letting go of past limitations and an opening to a life grounded in compassion, wisdom, and personal integrity.

Similarly, **Buddhist traditions** regard water as a symbol of purity and clarity. In certain rites, such as those practiced in Zen Buddhism, water is used to symbolize the cleansing of the mind and heart, preparing the individual for the practice of mindfulness and inner peace. Baptism in New Universalism mirrors this approach by inviting participants to approach life with an open heart and mind, dedicated to learning, growth, and self-awareness. The water in this context represents clarity, a washing away of ignorance, and an invitation to pursue enlightenment through reasoned inquiry and reflection. By embracing baptism, followers of New Universalism are affirming their commitment to a life that honors both rational thought and spiritual wisdom, seeing both as essential pathways to deeper understanding.

In **Indigenous traditions**, water holds a sacred place as a living entity with its own spirit, representing the continuity of life and the unity of all beings. Indigenous ceremonies often include the use of water in rituals to honor ancestors, connect with the natural world, and bring blessings upon the community. Inspired by this reverence, baptism in New Universalism acknowledges water as a sacred element that not only purifies but also unites us with the Earth. The ritual of submersion serves as a reminder that we are inseparable from the natural world and that our lives are part of a larger cycle of existence. Baptism thus becomes a way to honor our shared home and to commit to the principles of Earth Stewardship, understanding that the health of the planet is intrinsically tied to our own spiritual well-being.

The New Universalist proclamation during baptism, which states, "I am a child of Earth and Starry Heaven," reflects ancient insights into humanity's connection with both the terrestrial and the celestial. The phrase, rooted in **Greek philosophy** and used historically in spiritual contexts, speaks to the duality of our nature as beings both grounded in the physical world and drawn toward the mysteries of the cosmos. In this sense, baptism in New Universalism becomes a profound affirmation of our place in the universe, a reminder that we are bound not only to the Earth but to the greater mysteries of existence. By declaring themselves as children of Earth and Starry Heaven, followers acknowledge their commitment to live in balance with nature while seeking knowledge, understanding, and harmony in all things.

New Universalism respects baptisms performed in other faiths as equally meaningful and valid, recognizing that the search for truth and spiritual renewal is universal. Yet, a baptism within the New Universalist Church holds a distinct significance, inviting individuals to declare their commitment to the pillars of reason, Earth Stewardship, social responsibility, and filial piety. The words of the New Universalist baptismal proclamation serve as a powerful affirmation of these values:

"**I** am a child of Earth and Starry Heaven. I am committed to spiritual truth rooted in reason and the universal human experience. Harming none, I devote myself to personal and spiritual growth, with reverence for the planet and peace and inclusivity for all."

Through this proclamation, individuals affirm their dedication to live with respect, compassion, and awareness, guided by the shared wisdom of humanity. The phrase "Harming none" is a reminder that one's journey is not separate from the welfare of others, calling followers to a life of peaceful intention and mutual respect. This declaration is not only a personal vow but a commitment to the wider community and to the world as a whole, creating a bridge between individual growth and collective harmony.

The inclusive nature of New Universalist baptism allows individuals to undergo this initiation at any stage of life, reflecting the belief that spiritual commitment is a deeply personal journey. Whether in childhood, adulthood, or later in life, followers are welcome to choose baptism when they feel called to embrace New Universalism's values fully. This flexibility acknowledges the unique path each person takes toward spiritual awakening, honoring the understanding that the decision to commit to one's faith is sacred regardless of age or timing.

Baptism ceremonies within New Universalism often take place in natural settings, reinforcing the connection between the individual and the Earth. Bodies of water such as rivers, lakes, or oceans are favored, where the surrounding environment serves as a witness to the rite. For those unable to participate in outdoor settings, sacred water can be used within the community, with the recognition that the essence of the ritual is the connection it creates, not the location itself. This flexibility in setting reflects New Universalism's reverence for nature and its acknowledgment that all water is sacred, carrying with it the life-giving and transformative energy that the act of baptism symbolizes.

In New Universalism, baptism is more than a rite of initiation; it is a pathway to renewal, a deep commitment to living with purpose and integrity. By undergoing baptism, individuals dedicate themselves to a faith that values reasoned inquiry, shared human wisdom, and unity with the natural world. This act reminds followers that they are part of a larger whole, bound not only to their community but to all life. As "children of Earth and Starry Heaven," New Universalists commit to a path that balances personal growth with social responsibility, honoring both their earthly heritage and their spiritual aspirations.

Through baptism, New Universalists embark on a journey of interconnectedness, where each choice and action echoes outward into the world. This rite invites followers to seek a life of compassion, to engage in self-reflection, and to walk a path of peace and understanding. Baptism is a beginning, a moment of dedication that transforms intention into purpose, anchoring each individual in the values that New Universalism holds sacred. In this way, baptism becomes not only an initiation but an enduring reminder of our shared humanity and our sacred bond with all of creation.

Communion as a Shared Bond

The act of communion is a sacred and unifying ritual, a reminder of our connection to the Earth, to one another, and to the divine. Communion is both a symbol of physical sustenance and a ritual of spiritual nourishment, reflecting the balance we seek between body and soul. Through the partaking of bread and water, New Universalists honor the essential gifts of the Earth, recognizing that these elements nourish more than our bodies—they feed our spirits and strengthen our bond with the natural world and with each other. Communion is an invitation to pause, reflect, and renew our commitment to live in harmony with the world around us.

At its heart, communion in New Universalism draws from universal teachings that celebrate the sacredness of sharing food and drink as an expression of unity and gratitude. This ritual echoes the sentiments found in traditions across time and cultures, where the act of breaking bread has symbolized community, peace, and trust. In **Christianity**, the Last Supper serves as an enduring image of communion, where Jesus shared bread and wine with his disciples, urging them to remember and honor his teachings. New Universalism embraces the spirit of this ritual, focusing not on sacrifice but on the shared commitment to a life of compassion, integrity, and interconnectedness. Here, communion serves as a reminder that our lives are intertwined and that each individual's journey is part of a larger, collective experience.

Similarly, many Indigenous traditions regard the act of sharing food as a sacred gesture that honors the Earth's generosity. Food is often seen as a gift from the natural world, carrying within it the energy and life of the land, water, and sun. In this way, communion in New Universalism reflects a deep respect for the Earth as our provider, reminding us that the resources we use for sustenance are gifts to be appreciated and protected. By gathering in communion, New Universalists reaffirm their commitment to Earth Stewardship, recognizing the delicate balance between consumption and conservation. Each bite, each sip becomes an acknowledgment of our responsibility to care for the world that sustains us.

The elements used in communion are also chosen with care and intention. Traditional communion in the New Universalist Church often includes bread wafers and grape juice as symbols of nourishment and unity, though other forms of bread and water may also be blessed by the minister, reverend, or priest conducting the service. In keeping with an inclusive approach, New Universalism refrains from using wine, respecting the diverse needs and practices of its members, including those who abstain for religious, spiritual, or medical reasons. This choice underscores the inclusive nature of communion in New Universalism, affirming that the ritual is meant to welcome all who seek to partake, regardless of personal background or belief.

As each participant partakes in communion, they are invited to reflect on the dual nourishment it provides—feeding both body and spirit. Communion offers a moment of mindfulness, where the simple act of eating and drinking becomes a prayer of gratitude and a reminder of our shared humanity. This reflection aligns with teachings found in **Buddhism**, where the act of eating is often performed with reverence, reminding practitioners to be present and aware of the interconnected web of life that supports them. By bringing this mindfulness into communion, New Universalists are encouraged to see the sacred in the everyday, recognizing that the nourishment of our bodies is intrinsically connected to the nourishment of our spirits and to the well-being of the world around us.

Communion within New Universalism is a flexible and adaptable ritual, offered regularly and as requested to meet the spiritual needs of the community. In alignment with the cyclical nature of the Wheel of the Year, communion is observed during each major festival service, marking the changing seasons and honoring the Earth's rhythms. These festivals—celebrated at solstices, equinoxes, and other seasonal points—serve as touchstones in the communal life of New Universalism, reminding participants of the cycles of growth, harvest, and renewal that govern all life. Additionally, communion is offered monthly, in keeping with the lunar cycle, acknowledging the moon's influence on the natural world and human life alike. This rhythm provides a consistent opportunity for reflection and unity, aligning personal growth with the cycles of nature.

Beyond these regular observances, communion is available to members during significant life events and special ceremonies. For weddings, baptisms, funerals, and memorial services, communion is offered as a way to honor the sacredness of these moments and to connect those present in shared purpose. This flexibility reflects New Universalism's commitment to inclusivity, allowing members to engage with communion in ways that are meaningful and relevant to their own spiritual journeys. By creating spaces for communion both in community gatherings and personal ceremonies, New Universalism encourages followers to seek nourishment—both physical and spiritual—whenever they feel called.

The symbolic act of communion binds individuals to the Earth and to one another, serving as a reminder that we are all part of a larger whole. The sharing of bread and water is not merely a ritual but a profound acknowledgment of our interconnectedness, reinforcing the principle that each person's well-being is linked to the well-being of others. In this sense, communion extends beyond the act itself; it becomes a way to cultivate empathy, understanding, and support within the community. Each time New Universalists come together in communion, they are reminded of the strength that comes from unity, the peace that comes from shared intention, and the reverence that comes from living in harmony with nature.

Through communion, followers of New Universalism find both physical and spiritual sustenance, affirming their commitment to a life of balance, respect, and compassion. As they partake, they are invited to consider the elements before them as symbols of the Earth's bounty and the interconnectedness of all life. Communion, then, becomes an opportunity to reflect on one's place within this web, to give thanks for the nourishment provided by the Earth, and to recommit to living with awareness and intention. In sharing this ritual, New Universalists draw closer to one another, creating bonds that transcend individual differences and unite them in shared purpose and mutual care.

The act of communion in New Universalism is a celebration of the sacred within the simple, a ritual that transforms the ordinary into the divine. As participants partake, they are reminded of the values that New Universalism holds dear: reverence for the Earth, respect for each other, and a commitment to live in harmony with all of existence. Communion becomes more than a moment of reflection; it is an affirmation of the interconnectedness that defines us and a promise to live with compassion, gratitude, and peace.

Wedding & Marriage

Marriage is a sacred bond, a union of souls that transcends societal conventions to embrace the spiritual essence of partnership. This commitment is honored as a journey, a partnership grounded in love, mutual respect, and shared purpose. New Universalism regards marriage as an expression of unity that goes beyond the physical, intertwining the spiritual energies of each partner. Whether celebrated in traditional or non-traditional forms, marriage in New Universalism is a vow to support, uplift, and cherish one another in alignment with the core principles of the faith: inclusivity, reverence for the Earth, and a commitment to integrity and peace.

The wedding ceremony itself is a profound expression of these values, incorporating symbolic rituals that deepen the couple's connection and reflect the universal themes of love and unity. Elements such as vows, hand-fasting, and the pouring of sand are chosen with intention, each representing facets of the commitment being made. Together, these symbolic acts invite the couple and the community to witness a sacred covenant, one that honors the individuality of each partner while celebrating the shared journey they are embarking on.

Vows are central to the New Universalist wedding ceremony, representing not only promises to each other but a shared dedication to live with integrity and compassion. Drawing on teachings from multiple spiritual traditions, vows in New Universalism are seen as sacred commitments that honor the divine within each partner. In **Hindu philosophy**, for instance, the seven vows taken in marriage—*saptapadi*—are pledges that address not only love but mutual responsibility, loyalty, and respect. Inspired by this tradition, New Universalist vows emphasize the holistic nature of partnership, inviting each partner to pledge themselves to a life of shared purpose, continuous growth, and unwavering support. These vows are unique to each couple, reflecting their personal commitments and their alignment with New Universalist values.

The ritual of **hand-fasting**, an ancient Celtic practice, is another symbolic element often included in New Universalist weddings. In hand-fasting, the couple's hands are bound with a cord or ribbon, symbolizing the union of two lives and the merging of two paths. This act represents the strength of their bond, the commitment to support one another, and the resilience required to nurture a lasting partnership. Within New Universalism, hand-fasting is more than a ritual of binding; it is an affirmation that each partner's individual energy and intention are essential to the harmony of the union. The binding of hands reflects the balance and unity that a partnership requires, honoring both the distinctness of each individual and the shared purpose of their journey together.

The **pouring of sand** is another ritual that holds deep meaning in New Universalist weddings, symbolizing the blending of lives, histories, and future paths. In this practice, each partner pours sand from their own vessel into a shared container, creating a unique and inseparable pattern that represents their union. This act, which has roots in Indigenous and Eastern traditions, signifies the merging of identities without the loss of individuality. Each grain of sand contributes to the whole, reflecting the beauty of diversity within unity. In New Universalism, the pouring of sand also connects the couple to the Earth, grounding their union in the natural world and reinforcing the responsibility to care for and nurture the relationship with the same reverence one would offer the Earth itself.

New Universalism embraces and honors a diversity of marital unions, each treated with the same sanctity and reverence. This inclusivity reflects the faith's belief that love transcends definitions and that a sacred union is one based on respect, trust, and commitment to shared values. **Traditional marriage between a man and a woman** is respected as a powerful expression of partnership, a union that reflects balance and mutual support. This form of marriage is celebrated as part of the broader spectrum of relationships, honored for its unique qualities while understood as one of many paths that individuals may choose.

New Universalism also affirms the sacred nature of **same-sex marriage**, recognizing that love and commitment are not confined by gender. This perspective aligns with spiritual teachings that emphasize the value of authenticity and integrity in relationships. **Buddhist teachings** on love, for example, highlight the importance of kindness, compassion, joy, and equanimity—qualities that transcend external definitions of partnership. By honoring same-sex unions, New Universalism affirms that all expressions of love and commitment are worthy of respect, creating a space where every couple can celebrate their union openly and without judgment.

The recognition of **marriage involving transgender individuals** further reflects New Universalism's dedication to honoring the unique identities of each person. New Universalism values the authenticity and courage it takes to live one's truth, and the union of transgender individuals is seen as a testament to the resilience and depth of their love. This respect is grounded in New Universalism's emphasis on autonomy and individual dignity, recognizing that a sacred bond is created not through outward conformity but through shared values and mutual commitment. By embracing marriages involving transgender individuals, New Universalism honors each person's journey toward wholeness and authenticity.

In addition, New Universalism also honors the possibility of **polyamorous unions**, acknowledging the depth and complexity of human relationships that can extend beyond traditional forms. In the New Universalist framework, polyamorous marriage is defined as a primary union between two individuals, with the possibility of a **Consort union** that includes another person(s). In the New Universalist framework, each party of the primary union, with the consent of the other and having undergone pastoral counseling between the minister and all parties of the relationship, may participate in a formal Consort Union Ceremony in that each member may be recognized in formal union in the eyes of the Church. This structure emphasizes ethical relationships, clear communication, and respect for each partner's needs and boundaries. In polyamorous marriages, all partners are encouraged to nurture their connection with honesty and integrity, reinforcing the values of unity and mutual care. This inclusive approach reflects New Universalism's belief in the diversity of love and the understanding that meaningful partnerships can take many forms.

Sexuality and Pre-Marital Relationships

In alignment with its inclusive values, New Universalism holds an open, accepting view of sexuality. Within this faith, sexuality is regarded as both a natural and sacred act—a joining of not only bodies but also souls and energies. Far from being seen as sinful or inherently wrong, sexual intimacy is recognized as a meaningful expression of connection that can enhance emotional and spiritual bonds. However, New Universalism also emphasizes the importance of mindfulness, respect, and responsibility in sexual relationships, recognizing that such connections carry profound significance and should be entered into thoughtfully.

Drawing on teachings from **Tantric philosophy**, New Universalism views sexual intimacy as an exchange of energy that nurtures the spirit as well as the body. In Tantra, sexuality is celebrated as a pathway to spiritual awakening, a means of transcending the self and experiencing a deep connection with the divine within oneself and one's partner. This view resonates with New Universalism's approach to sexuality, which encourages individuals to engage in intimate relationships with reverence, intentionality, and respect. In this context, sexual union is more than a physical act; it is a sacred expression of shared energy, an affirmation of one's own divinity and that of their partner.

New Universalism does not condemn pre-marital sex, acknowledging that the decision to engage in intimate relationships is deeply personal and may vary according to individual beliefs and values. Instead, followers are encouraged to practice **mindfulness** in choosing partners and to consider the emotional and spiritual implications of such connections. New Universalism also strongly advocates for safe-sex practices, underscoring the importance of respect for one's own well-being and that of others. This perspective is rooted in the belief that autonomy, consent, and mutual respect are fundamental to healthy relationships. New Universalism explicitly rejects any form of exploitation or harm, such as child marriages, forced unions, or non-consensual interactions, emphasizing that respect, safety, and autonomy are sacred rights for all individuals.

In all relationships—whether marital or otherwise—New Universalism calls followers to approach intimacy with integrity and awareness, seeing each connection as an opportunity for growth, understanding, and shared joy. This approach invites individuals to honor the sacredness of their own bodies and to treat each partnership with the respect it deserves. In doing so, New Universalism fosters a community where love and connection are celebrated as pathways to both personal and spiritual fulfillment, upheld by values of acceptance, respect, and compassion.

Through these teachings, New Universalism offers a vision of marriage and sexuality that is inclusive, respectful, and grounded in a profound sense of purpose. This faith calls each partner to live with integrity, to uplift one another, and to nurture a bond that reflects the principles of New Universalism. In marriage, individuals find not only a partner but a spiritual companion, a relationship that supports their journey and honors the divine within each person. Together, they build a life that reflects the values of New Universalism—a life of love, understanding, and mutual respect.

Cannabis—Sacred Rite and Medicine

In New Universalism, cannabis is revered as a sacred offering, a gift from both Earth and the Divine. Its use in ceremonial and personal practice is seen as a way to elevate and heal the mind, body, and spirit, bridging the realms of earthly existence and the cosmos. This powerful plant, with roots in both ancient and contemporary healing practices, is recognized not only for its capacity to soothe the physical and mental body but also for its unique ability to expand consciousness and deepen our connection with the divine forces of nature and the universe.

The Spiritual Role of Cannabis: A Gift from Earth and Cosmos

Cannabis holds a special place within New Universalism as a tool of sacred connection. Viewed as a bridge between Earth and the Divine, cannabis invites practitioners into a state of heightened awareness, reflection, and unity. Whether through personal meditation or communal gatherings, the intentional use of cannabis allows New Universalists to transcend the everyday realm, accessing spiritual insights and profound states of connectedness. It is honored as a tool for both personal enlightenment and collective harmony, serving as a conduit for spiritual insight, connection, and healing.

The spiritual use of cannabis in New Universalism draws on practices across history and cultures. Its inclusion in New Universalist rites is not merely an acknowledgment of its psychoactive properties but a reverence for the plant's sacred nature. It is seen as a teacher and healer, one that opens the mind to new perspectives, fosters empathy, and strengthens the bond between self, community, and the natural world.

Ritual and Communal Use of Cannabis

Cannabis is an essential element in certain communal ceremonies within New Universalism. Used with intention and respect, it enhances spiritual gatherings, promotes healing, and fosters unity within the community. In sacred ceremonies—such as seasonal gatherings, spiritual retreats, and rites of passage—the ceremonial use of cannabis can help participants enter a shared state of openness and communion. During these ceremonies, cannabis may be shared in a circle, creating a sense of collective grounding and connection.

Similarly, in spiritual healing rituals, cannabis is revered for its calming and balancing effects, allowing participants to center themselves, release tension, and attune to a higher state of awareness. Through these practices, the community gathers not only to honor the plant itself but also to enter a sacred space where individual and communal healing can occur, connecting more profoundly with one another and the divine essence of life.

In personal practice, cannabis is a powerful ally in meditation, prayer, and ritual. It is used by individuals to deepen their connection with the self, to reflect, and to seek clarity. Whether it is integrated into daily meditation or used during private rituals of healing and reflection, cannabis serves as a sacred medium through which individuals find guidance, grounding, and inner peace.

Ethical Use and Intentionality in Cannabis Practice

In New Universalism, the use of cannabis is approached with mindfulness and respect. To maintain its sacred nature, New Universalists are encouraged to use cannabis in ways that honor its power as both a medicinal and spiritual tool. This involves thoughtful reflection on one's intention, setting an appropriate environment for its use, and respecting personal boundaries and needs.

Guidelines for Sacred Use:

- **Mindfulness and Presence**: Cannabis should be used in states of mindfulness, with a focused intention. Before use, New Universalists are encouraged to set clear intentions—whether for healing, insight, or spiritual connection—allowing the experience to be guided by purpose rather than impulse.
- **Balance and Moderation**: Sacred use emphasizes balance. Practitioners are encouraged to be aware of dosage and frequency, recognizing that overuse may detract from the plant's sacred nature. Through balanced use, cannabis retains its potency as a sacred medicine and an instrument of insight.
- **Respect and Personal Boundaries**: Followers are reminded to use cannabis in ways that respect their own physical, mental, and spiritual limits. Recognizing that cannabis affects each individual differently, practitioners are encouraged to honor their own unique needs, seeking to enhance well-being and self-connection.
- **Respect for Communal Spaces**: In communal settings, the use of cannabis should always prioritize the comfort and autonomy of all participants. This means creating an environ-

ment where everyone feels safe, respected, and free to engage in the experience as they are most comfortable.

Medicinal Use of Cannabis: A Tradition of Healing

As a sacred medicine, cannabis is appreciated in New Universalism for its broad applications in physical and mental health. Honoring both historical uses and modern research, cannabis is recognized as a healing ally for various physical ailments, mental health challenges, and stress relief. Practitioners may use cannabis for its therapeutic benefits, applying it with the same respect and gratitude as a medicine.

In alignment with traditional practices and contemporary insights, New Universalism recognizes the medicinal potential of cannabis for conditions such as chronic pain, anxiety, inflammation, and more. This use is grounded in an understanding that cannabis, like all plant medicines, should be used with intentionality, in respect of its healing properties and guided by a desire to foster wellness.

By approaching cannabis with reverence, mindfulness, and a deep respect for its sacred origins, New Universalists uphold this gift as both a rite and a medicine, recognizing that its power lies not only in its effects but in the thoughtful and intentional way it is used. Through this sacred practice, New Universalists connect more deeply with the natural world, the divine, and the community that shares in these values.

Last Rites

Last Rites are a solemn and sacred ceremony performed by an officiant of the New Universalist Church for individuals nearing the end of their earthly journey. This rite, comprised of holy communion and the sacrament of anointing, honors the individual's passage with reverence, connecting them to the Earth, the cosmos, and the greater mystery of existence. The Last Rites offer a moment of peace and spiritual preparation, allowing the individual to reflect on the continuity of life and to find comfort in the journey that lies beyond.

The Last Rites in New Universalism are distinct from Funeral or Memorial services, as they are performed while the individual is still alive, preparing them to transition with dignity and spiritual support. Administered by an officiant of the New Universalist Church, the rite includes the sharing of holy communion, representing nourishment and unity with the Earth, and the act of anointing, a gesture that symbolizes the sacredness of life and the individual's connection to the divine. These sacraments are reminders that, in New Universalism, each life is both grounded in the physical world and connected to the cosmos—a "child of Earth and Starry Heaven."

Holy Communion within the Last Rites serves as a symbol of nourishment for both body and spirit. Through communion, the individual partakes of blessed bread and water, elements that represent the sustenance provided by the Earth and the unity of all beings. In this context, communion offers comfort and connection, reinforcing the understanding that each life is part of a larger cycle. Communion reflects the teachings of **Indigenous wisdom** on the sacredness of food and sustenance, recognizing that these offerings connect the individual to the world they are leaving behind, even as they prepare for their spiritual transition.

The **anointing** of the individual with holy oil is a sacramental act that honors the sanctity of life and the journey of the soul. The act of anointing is a gesture of blessing, symbolizing the release of earthly burdens and the preparation for a peaceful transition. Anointing is a practice found in many spiritual traditions, including **Christianity**, where it is used to confer grace and peace upon those who are sick or nearing death. In New Universalism, anointing represents a final blessing that affirms the individual's worth, dignity, and unity with the divine. Through this anointing, the officiant honors the individual's journey and offers a sense of peace, grounding them in the connection between body, soul, and the greater mystery of existence.

The following **Last Rite prayer** is recited by the officiant during communion and anointing, offering words of comfort and connection on behalf of the individual:

"**As a child of Earth and Starry Heaven, may you find peace in this transition. You are of the Earth, returning to its embrace, and of the stars, continuing your journey in the cosmos. May your spirit be nourished, your soul be at peace, and your essence find its place among the heavens.**"

This prayer reflects the core beliefs of New Universalism, connecting the individual to both the natural world and the cosmos, offering comfort as they prepare to release their physical form. The prayer affirms that this passage is a continuation, a sacred journey that honors the individual's life and legacy.

Reflections on Continuity and Sacred Transition

Last Rites are a sacred farewell, a ritual that honors the transition from life to death and reflects the belief that death is not an end but a passage. This rite is performed with reverence, grounding the individual in the timeless connection between body, spirit, Earth, and cosmos. As we acknowledge the passing of a loved one, Last Rites serve as a reminder that each life is part of a larger cycle—a cycle that continues beyond the physical realm and connects us to the mysteries of existence. Here, we honor both the earthly journey completed and the sacred journey that continues, affirming that each person's essence, their spirit, remains an eternal part of the universe.

This rite draws on the foundational belief of New Universalism that we are "children of Earth and Starry Heaven," an identity that roots us in the natural world while connecting us to the cosmos. This phrase captures the duality of human existence: we are of the Earth, nourished by its elements, and yet we are also connected to the vast, star-filled heavens that spark awe and wonder. In Last Rites, we affirm that just as life begins in the embrace of the Earth, so too does it return to the Earth upon death. The corporeal form, having been sustained by the Earth, is given back to the soil, completing a cycle that respects the natural order and reflects the continuity of life.

The act of returning to the Earth aligns with spiritual teachings on the impermanence of life, a concept central to **Buddhist philosophy**. In Buddhism, impermanence (*anicca*) teaches us that all things, including life itself, are transient and subject to change. Life and death are seen as natural transitions, each part of the ongoing flow of existence. This understanding encourages acceptance and peace in the face of death, a perspective that New Universalism embraces as part of its approach to Last Rites. By honoring the impermanence of life, we are reminded of the preciousness of each moment, the beauty of each breath, and the continuity that transcends the physical form.

This understanding of continuity finds a parallel in **Indigenous teachings**, which often view death as a sacred journey of the soul. For many Indigenous cultures, the spirit is believed to return to the ancestral realm or to a place within the natural world, where it remains connected to the land, the community, and the cosmos. This belief affirms that the soul does not disappear but transitions into another form, continuing its sacred journey beyond the physical. In New Universalism, this perspective is honored as a reminder that our spirit, our essence, is not confined to the body. It is part of a larger journey that reflects the interconnectedness of all life, a journey that carries us from the Earth and beyond.

New Universalism also draws insight from the **law of thermodynamics**, which states that matter is neither created nor destroyed but transformed. This scientific principle aligns with spiritual teachings on the continuity of life, affirming that while the physical body returns to the Earth, the energy within each of us continues on. Whether we envision this journey as one toward a spiritual afterlife, reincarnation, or a return to the vastness of the cosmos, this concept speaks to a truth that transcends belief—our essence, like all energy in the universe, is eternal. The body nourishes the Earth from which it came, while the spirit or energy that animated it returns to "starry heaven," completing a cycle that is both scientific and spiritual.

Through the rituals and reflections of Last Rites, New Universalism affirms the sacredness of life's transitions and the continuity of the soul's journey. Whether one believes in an afterlife, reincarnation, or simply a return to the elements, this rite offers comfort in the knowledge that each life contributes to the vast web of existence. Each individual, a "child of Earth and Starry Heaven," is remembered not only as they were in life but as part of a greater, enduring whole. In this way, Last Rites become a celebration of life's beauty and the sacred journey that awaits, a reminder that each person's essence remains woven into the fabric of the cosmos.

Through Last Rites, New Universalism offers a way to honor the end of life with respect, understanding, and reverence. The rite holds space for each individual's beliefs and values, allowing them to transition with dignity and peace. By returning to the Earth and releasing the spirit to "starry heaven," we affirm the unity of body, mind, and soul, the eternal connection between Earth and cosmos, and the enduring impact of each individual's life on the community and the world.

Funeral & Memorial Services

Funeral and Memorial services are moments of solemn reverence and warm celebration, honoring the life of the departed and offering support to those who remain. These services are a testament to the continuity of life—a reminder that each individual's essence, their spirit, endures beyond the physical form. Funeral and Memorial services in New Universalism are designed to be both deeply personal and universally inclusive, welcoming diverse perspectives on life's transition and creating a space where all present can find meaning, peace, and comfort. The ceremony honors the memory of the departed, reflects on the beauty of their journey, and reinforces the unity between Earth, community, and cosmos.

New Universalism embraces a spectrum of beliefs about the afterlife, honoring each individual's perspective on what lies beyond. Whether one envisions a reunion with ancestors, reincarnation, a return to the cosmos, or a journey toward spiritual peace, New Universalism upholds the validity of all views. This inclusivity is grounded in the belief that life is continuous, that each existence leaves an imprint on the universe, and that every spirit contributes to the larger tapestry of existence. By honoring this diversity, Funeral and Memorial services become a space where attendees can find meaning and solace in their own beliefs, united by the understanding that life's essence is enduring, resilient, and woven into the fabric of the cosmos.

Standardized Ritual Elements in New Universalist Funeral and Memorial services are designed to ground the ceremony in nature, reflect the cycle of life, and offer emotional and spiritual support. These elements may be combined with personalized rituals to suit the unique wishes of the family or community, allowing for a balance of structure and flexibility that respects each individual's journey.

Lighting of Candles or Lanterns is a central ritual in New Universalist services, representing the light and life of the departed and the warmth they brought to the world. Each flame serves as a beacon, a reminder that even as one journey ends, the light of that life continues to inspire, comfort, and guide. Inspired by the symbolic role of light in many traditions, such as the candle lighting in **Christianity** and the lantern festivals in **Buddhism**, this ritual acknowledges the sacred presence of the departed and invites attendees to reflect on the enduring impact of their life. Each candle lit is a symbol of continuity, reminding all present that the legacy of love and kindness lives on.

Earth-based rituals also play a central role, grounding the ceremony in the New Universalist perspective of unity with nature. One common ritual is the **returning of soil** to the Earth, where family and friends are invited to sprinkle soil upon the grave or around a tree planted in memory of the departed. This act symbolizes the return of the physical body to the Earth that nurtured it, reflecting the belief that life and death are both part of a natural cycle. Drawing from Indigenous teachings on the sacredness of the land and the interconnectedness of all life, this ritual allows attendees to participate actively in the farewell, reinforcing the continuity between the individual, the Earth, and the community.

Another meaningful ritual is the **release of flowers, leaves, or seeds** into a natural setting—often a river, lake, or garden space. This ritual represents the release of the spirit, allowing the memory of the individual to flow into the world around them. Inspired by nature-centered traditions, such as the Japanese custom of floating flowers in water to honor ancestors, this act offers a way to say goodbye while symbolizing the flow of life's journey and the peace of returning to nature. Each flower, leaf, or seed released carries with it the thoughts, prayers, and love of those present, connecting the physical with the spiritual and affirming the individual's ongoing connection with the Earth.

To further honor the diversity within New Universalism, services may include **readings from varied spiritual and philosophical traditions**. Passages from the **Bhagavad Gita** might be chosen to speak to the soul's eternal nature, while excerpts from **Sufi poetry** might offer comfort in the idea of a reunion with the Beloved. An officiant might also read from **Stoic philosophy**, reflecting on the importance of acceptance and the natural course of life. These readings offer comfort, inspire reflection, and create a space where each person present can find resonance, whether through the teachings of Eastern philosophies, Indigenous wisdom, or modern reflections on life and death.

Personalized elements are encouraged within New Universalism to reflect the individuality of the departed and honor the unique wishes of their family and community. Some families may wish to include music that held personal meaning, create a memory-sharing circle, or invite attendees to share stories and reflections. Others may incorporate traditional practices, cultural symbols, or personal mementos. These additions make the ceremony deeply personal, allowing loved ones to celebrate the life of the departed in a way that resonates with their spirit and legacy. This flexibility embodies the New Universalist value of inclusivity, creating a service that is as unique as the life it honors.

Funeral and Memorial services in New Universalism are an opportunity not only to honor the deceased but to support and uplift the community. **Communal reflection** becomes a way to find comfort in one another, to hold space for both grief and celebration, and to reflect on the meaning of life's journey. As the officiant speaks, they may remind those gathered of the New Universalist belief in the enduring nature of each individual's spirit, the "child of Earth and Starry Heaven" who is now returning to the elements and continuing in a new form. This perspective encourages attendees to find peace in the continuity of life, knowing that each person's essence is part of a larger cycle that transcends the limits of physical existence.

In the words of **Rumi**, the Sufi poet, "Goodbyes are only for those who love with their eyes. Because for those who love with heart and soul, there is no such thing as separation." This reflection is often shared in New Universalist services to reinforce the unity between those present and the departed. The belief that love and memory transcend physical separation offers comfort, creating a sense of closeness that continues beyond the ceremony itself. Attendees are encouraged to carry forward the spirit of the departed, embodying their values, remembering their lessons, and allowing their presence to guide them even as life moves forward.

Through these rituals and reflections, Funeral and Memorial services in New Universalism become a celebration of life, a moment to honor the past, and a reminder of the continuity of existence. Each service is a mosaic of community, nature, and remembrance, allowing the New Universalist community to come together in a spirit of respect, unity, and gratitude. By embracing a balanced approach that honors diverse beliefs, New Universalism provides a way to bid farewell that is both deeply personal and universally meaningful, creating a sacred space where all can find peace, comfort, and connection.

Purpose and Role in Community

In New Universalism, sacred rites are more than individual milestones; they are foundational to both personal spiritual growth and the strengthening of communal bonds. Each rite—whether a baptism, communion, marriage, Last Rite, or funeral—reflects the interconnectedness that New Universalism cherishes, a web of relationships that binds individuals to each other, the Earth, and the cosmos. These rites serve as touchstones, inviting each participant to reflect on their values, renew their commitment to the faith, and connect with others on a journey of shared meaning and purpose. Together, these rituals create a rhythm of connection and belonging, grounding both the individual and the community in a shared path of peace, compassion, and unity.

Regular **communal gatherings** play a central role in the New Universalist Church, fostering continuity and shared growth within the community. Weekly religious services, held every Sunday, provide a time for reflection, teaching, and collective worship, reinforcing the shared values that guide New Universalists in daily life. Each service serves as an anchor, offering a sacred space for all to come together, learn, and find strength in one another. Additionally, the eight annual festival services that follow the **Wheel of the Year** celebrate seasonal transitions, reflecting the New Universalist commitment to honor the Earth and the cycles of life. These gatherings mark moments of renewal, gratitude, and unity, inviting the community to pause, reflect, and reconnect with both nature and each other.

Beyond these scheduled services, the New Universalist Church offers rites such as **baptisms**, **weddings**, **Last Rites**, and **funeral or memorial services** as needed. Each of these sacred acts serves a dual purpose: providing personal spiritual support while strengthening communal bonds. The flexibility of these rites reflects the inclusivity at the heart of New Universalism, ensuring that each ceremony is both a personal milestone and a moment of shared reverence. These services adapt to the unique needs of the individual and the community, creating a space where everyone feels seen, valued, and connected.

Additional communal gatherings, such as support groups, study sessions, and pastoral counseling, are offered at the discretion of the New Universalist Church, based on the needs and interests of the immediate community. These gatherings provide an opportunity for deeper engagement, where members can find guidance, companionship, and inspiration as they explore their spiritual journey. Support groups foster solidarity, offering a place to share challenges and celebrate growth, while religious study groups allow for deeper exploration of New Universalist teachings and spiritual insights from other traditions. By offering a diverse range of gatherings, New Universalism provides a flexible framework that supports both personal reflection and collective growth.

The purpose of these rites and gatherings extends beyond ritual to fulfill a deeper spiritual role, one that is grounded in New Universalism's commitment to honor each individual's journey while celebrating the power of unity. The idea that spiritual practice is enriched through shared experience finds resonance in **Indigenous wisdom**, which often emphasizes the collective nature of ritual and the belief that individual well-being is deeply connected to communal health. In many Indigenous cultures, ceremonies such as seasonal festivals and rites of passage are performed not only for the individual but as an affirmation of community bonds, a practice that New Universalism honors by creating spaces where all feel included, respected, and uplifted.

Similarly, **Eastern philosophies** highlight the concept of **interdependence**, the understanding that all beings are interconnected and that each person's actions affect the whole. In **Buddhism**, the practice of Sangha, or community, is seen as an essential part of the spiritual journey, where individuals find strength, wisdom, and encouragement in the company of others. New Universalism embraces this concept, recognizing that spiritual growth is not an isolated pursuit but one that flourishes through collective support and mutual understanding. Each rite and gathering is a reminder that individuals are part of a larger, interconnected reality, and that the presence of others offers both strength and purpose on the path to inner peace.

Philosophical traditions such as **Stoicism** also reinforce the importance of community and shared resilience. The Stoic emphasis on the common good and the belief that individuals should live in harmony with nature align with New Universalist values, encouraging each person to contribute to a compassionate and unified world. In New Universalism, each rite becomes an expression of this commitment to the greater good, reminding individuals of their role in nurturing a world where peace, kindness, and inclusivity prevail. Through shared rituals, followers are reminded that their actions and intentions contribute to the fabric of the community and, by extension, to the harmony of the world.

The rituals of New Universalism thus serve a dual purpose: they nurture the individual's spiritual journey while reinforcing the bonds that hold the community together. Through **baptism**, individuals are welcomed into the faith, joining a family committed to shared values and lifelong growth. Through **communion**, they partake in a ritual that reminds them of the unity of all beings and the nourishment that comes from connection. **Marriage** celebrates the sacred bond between partners, a union that becomes a source of strength and resilience for the community as well. **Last Rites** and **funerals or memorials** provide a space to honor those who have passed, offering comfort to loved ones and reminding the community of life's continuity and the interconnectedness that endures.

These rites and gatherings offer guidance and support for the personal spiritual development of each individual, fostering reflection, peace, and purpose. For the individual, each rite is a moment of affirmation, a reminder of their inherent worth, and a call to live with compassion, integrity, and reverence. Baptism serves as a dedication to personal growth and truth-seeking, while communion strengthens the bond between self and community. Marriage, Last Rites, and funerals honor the various stages of life, offering a framework for reflecting on the beauty of each journey and the impact each life has on others. Through these practices, individuals find not only personal meaning but also the strength that comes from shared commitment.

Together, these rites cultivate a spirit of inclusivity and solidarity that transcends individual differences, creating a New Universalist community grounded in shared purpose. By gathering regularly, honoring life's transitions, and supporting one another through rites of passage, followers of New Universalism build a community that values compassion, empathy, and unity. In this space, each person is both nurtured and nurturer, receiving support from others while offering their own presence, wisdom, and kindness in return.

The purpose and role of these sacred rites in New Universalism is ultimately to foster a community where each person feels valued, connected, and encouraged to grow. By participating in these rituals and gatherings, followers reaffirm their commitment to live in harmony with one another and with the natural world. As each person journeys forward, they carry with them the values that bind them to the community—respect, compassion, and a reverence for the Earth and the cosmos. In this way, the sacred rites of New Universalism become a testament to the power of unity, the beauty of diversity, and the enduring strength of a community built on love and understanding.

The Saints

Definition and Role of Saints in New Universalism

Saints are individuals who have demonstrated an extraordinary commitment to universal virtues and wisdom, embodying the core values that form the foundation of the faith. Saints in New Universalism serve as touchstones for both personal and communal growth, inspiring members to embody virtues such as compassion, wisdom, justice, integrity, and respect for all forms of life. While traditional saints may be recognized primarily within specific religious contexts, New Universalism embraces a broader, inclusive approach, honoring not only established saints from diverse spiritual traditions but also notable philosophers, secular thinkers, and environmental advocates who have lived lives of exceptional integrity and service.

Saints in New Universalism are revered for their contributions to human understanding, advocacy for justice, spiritual insight, and, in many cases, a commitment to Earth-centered wisdom. This Earth-centered perspective aligns with New Universalism's call for environmental stewardship and reverence for the natural world, and it serves as a central criterion for future sainthood within the faith. In recognizing saints, New Universalism honors not only the values that connect us as individuals but also those that unify us with nature and the larger cosmos. These figures act as guides, embodying a holistic perspective that sees the interconnectedness of all beings and the sacred responsibility to nurture and protect life.

The **inclusive approach to sainthood** in New Universalism is multifaceted, embracing the wisdom of established prophets, saints, and sacred figures across time and tradition. Figures such as **Jesus Christ**, revered for his teachings on love, forgiveness, and selfless service; **the Prophet Mohammad**, honored for his compassion, commitment to justice, and community welfare; and **Confucius**, celebrated for his insights on ethics, social harmony, and filial piety, are each recognized as saints in New Universalism. Their teachings, while originating from different contexts, resonate as timeless truths that transcend religious boundaries. Additionally, New Universalism honors influential figures from Indigenous wisdom, Buddhism, and other spiritual or philosophical paths, each contributing unique insights that align with the faith's foundational principles.

Furthermore, New Universalism acknowledges that sainthood is not limited to religious or spiritual figures alone. Secular thinkers, environmental advocates, and humanitarians who have dedicated their lives to universal values are also honored as saints within New Universalism. Figures such as **Mahatma Gandhi** for his unwavering commitment to nonviolence and social justice, **Jane Goodall** for her dedication to wildlife conservation and her insights into humanity's relationship with nature, and **Albert Einstein** for his scientific contributions and philosophical reflections on peace and interconnectedness, are examples of those who embody qualities worthy of sainthood. In this way, New Universalism reflects its inclusive and flexible nature, allowing a space for figures from all backgrounds who embody compassion, reason, and an Earth-centered perspective.

The **role of saints in New Universalism** is both spiritual and practical, offering guidance for daily life and enriching the community's spiritual practice. On a practical level, saints are examples of the virtues that New Universalists strive to embody—figures who exemplify compassion, wisdom, justice, and respect for all life. By reflecting on the lives of the saints, followers are encouraged to incorporate these values into their own lives, building character and nurturing a commitment to the shared ideals of New Universalism. Saints remind individuals that every action, however small, can contribute to a more compassionate, unified, and just world.

Beyond their practical role, the saints also play an essential role in New Universalist **spiritual practice**. Honoring saints is a way to deepen one's connection to the values they represent, to seek guidance, and to foster a sense of spiritual companionship. In both private devotion and community worship, followers may choose to honor specific saints by placing their images or symbols on altars, reflecting their unique contributions to human understanding and their resonance with New Universalist beliefs. Many households or community spaces include a **communal or personal altar** where saints are honored through images, candles, or offerings, creating a sacred space that invites reflection and gratitude.

During various festivals or ceremonies throughout the **Wheel of the Year**, saints may also be honored in a collective setting, with reflections on their teachings, prayers for their intercession, or moments of meditation focused on the virtues they embody. For example, during a festival focused on justice or compassion, followers may honor a saint such as Mahatma Gandhi or Saint Mohammad, reflecting on their lives as sources of inspiration. These observances allow the community to connect with the saints as a way to reinforce shared values and deepen collective spiritual practice.

Additionally, New Universalists may call upon specific **patron saints** in prayer or meditation, particularly during moments of personal need, reflection, or celebration. A follower might turn to Saint Confucius in times when guidance on family or ethical harmony is needed, or call upon Jane Goodall when seeking strength and inspiration for environmental stewardship. In this way, the saints serve as spiritual companions, offering a source of comfort, wisdom, and insight. Through prayer and meditation, individuals can feel a sense of support, guidance, and continuity, drawing strength from the legacy of those who have walked a similar path of compassion and integrity.

In this way, saints in New Universalism offer both a path to spiritual growth and a model of ethical living, their lives and teachings serving as resources for individual study and for ministers in weekly sermons. By contemplating the virtues of these figures and their contributions to humanity, followers are encouraged to incorporate similar qualities into their own lives, enriching their spiritual journey and strengthening their commitment to New Universalist values. As sources of both inspiration and spiritual support, the saints help New Universalists to see their journey as part of a larger story, one woven together by timeless truths, shared wisdom, and a commitment to honoring life in all its forms.

Selection and Recognition of Saints

In New Universalism, sainthood is granted to individuals who exemplify the foundational values of the faith, embodying virtues such as compassion, wisdom, justice, humility, and dedication to service. Saints in New Universalism are revered not only for their personal character but for their impact on humanity, their commitment to universal truths, and their contributions to the understanding of human dignity and interconnectedness. The selection of saints is a process grounded in respect for the diverse traditions and philosophies that enrich New Universalism, honoring figures across major religions, Indigenous practices, secular and philosophical thought, and those whose lives reflect the essence of Earth-centered wisdom.

To qualify for sainthood, individuals must meet specific qualities that align with the principles of New Universalism. These include:

1. **A Life of Exemplary Virtue**: Saints are those whose lives serve as models of New Universalist values, including compassion, integrity, respect for all beings, and a commitment to unity and peace. Their actions must consistently reflect these virtues, inspiring others to pursue lives of ethical purpose and moral clarity.

2. **Service to Humanity**: Saints in New Universalism are recognized for their contributions to the welfare of others. Whether through acts of charity, the pursuit of social justice, or selfless service, they have demonstrated a profound commitment to uplifting humanity and supporting the rights, dignity, and freedom of all people.

3. **Spiritual and Philosophical Insight**: Many saints are also noted for their contributions to spiritual or philosophical thought, offering teachings that expand human understanding and deepen our connection to universal truths. These teachings may emphasize compassion, ethical behavior, and the interconnectedness of all life, supporting the New Universalist vision of a harmonious world.

4. **Respect for the Earth**: While Earth-centered wisdom is not required of historical figures, it is a central consideration for contemporary sainthood. Figures who have demonstrated a deep respect for the natural world, advocated for environmental stewardship, or promoted sustainable practices reflect New Universalism's commitment to Earth stewardship. Those who have served as protectors or advocates for the environment are held in particularly high regard, as their lives align with New Universalism's reverence for the planet.

New Universalism automatically acknowledges **historically recognized figures** as saints, honoring prophets, sages, and spiritual leaders from diverse religious traditions who have left enduring legacies. Figures such as **Jesus Christ**, **the Prophet Mohammad**, and **the Buddha** are celebrated for their teachings on love, compassion, forgiveness, and spiritual enlightenment. These figures offer timeless guidance and are universally respected across New Universalist congregations, reflecting the faith's commitment to inclusivity and interfaith respect. Additionally, figures such as **Confucius**, whose philosophical teachings on ethics, social harmony, and filial piety have shaped Eastern thought, and **Socrates**, whose commitment to truth and reason embodies a philosophical approach to spiritual understanding, are revered as saints within New Universalism.

Saints from **pagan and Indigenous traditions** also hold a prominent place in New Universalism, as these figures embody a respect for the Earth and a reverence for the cycles of nature. Figures such as **Demeter** from ancient Greek traditions, celebrated for her connection to the harvest and the natural cycles of life, and Indigenous wisdom keepers who have protected the environment and taught the sacredness of all life, are honored as saints. These figures serve as reminders of humanity's responsibility to live in harmony with the natural world, reinforcing the Earth-centered principles that are central to New Universalism.

In addition to religious and philosophical figures, New Universalism recognizes **secular thinkers and humanitarians** who have made significant contributions to the well-being of humanity. Figures like **Mahatma Gandhi**, whose advocacy for nonviolence and social justice continues to inspire global movements for peace, and **Albert Einstein**, who combined scientific insight with a deep sense of moral responsibility and a belief in the interconnectedness of all life, are celebrated as saints. By honoring secular figures who embody New Universalist values, the faith emphasizes that sainthood is not limited to religious figures alone but is open to all who have dedicated their lives to truth, compassion, and justice.

Contemporary figures who may be considered for sainthood must embody these foundational values and demonstrate a life committed to universal truths, ethical service, and, preferably, Earth stewardship. While historical figures are automatically acknowledged, the consideration of modern figures involves careful reflection on their contributions to humanity, their alignment with New Universalist principles, and the lasting impact of their work. Figures who exemplify Earth-centered wisdom and environmental advocacy are highly regarded, though those who have demonstrated excellence in other virtues—such as social justice, education, or scientific innovation—are equally eligible for sainthood if their lives reflect the heart of New Universalist teachings.

In New Universalism, saints serve not only as examples but as reminders of the power of individual action to inspire collective change. By honoring saints from diverse backgrounds and traditions, followers are encouraged to see themselves as part of a larger tapestry of values, one that transcends religious, cultural, and philosophical differences. Saints offer guidance, perspective, and a source of spiritual companionship, reminding followers that the path to peace, compassion, and understanding is both universal and attainable. Whether honoring a prophet, a philosopher, or a modern environmentalist, New Universalists find inspiration in these lives, drawing strength from their examples and encouragement for their own journeys

Saints and Patron Saints in New Universalism

Below is a listing of Saints and Patron Saints in New Universalism; however, this is not an exhaustive list as New Universalism respects the more than 10,000 Saints and Patron Saints across various traditions and faiths.

Abrahamic Traditions

1. **Saint Jesus Christ** (Christianity)
   Revered for his teachings on love, forgiveness, and compassion; known as the central figure in Christianity and a universal symbol of peace and self-sacrifice.
2. **Saint Mary, Mother of Jesus** (Christianity)
   Patron saint of mothers, families, and compassion, honored for her role in Christian narratives and her embodiment of gentleness, faith, and nurturing strength.
3. **Saint Peter** (Christianity)
   One of Jesus' apostles, considered the patron saint of fishermen, builders, and the Church itself; symbolizes faith, courage, and resilience.
4. **Prophet Mohammad** (Islam)
   Honored as a prophet in Islam for his teachings on justice, compassion, and community unity; known as a model of humility, dedication, and integrity.
5. **Saint Moses** (Judaism, Christianity)
   Known for his role as a leader and prophet who led his people to freedom; symbolizes justice, resilience, and devotion to faith.
6. **Saint Miriam** (Judaism)
   The sister of Moses, celebrated for her leadership and courage; honored as a patron saint of music and dance, embodying joy and resilience.

Eastern and Asian Philosophical Traditions

1. **Saint Buddha (Siddhartha Gautama)** (Buddhism)
   The founder of Buddhism, revered for his insights on compassion, mindfulness, and the path to enlightenment; a model of self-realization and inner peace.

2. **Saint Confucius** (Confucianism)
   Celebrated for his teachings on ethics, filial piety, and social harmony; known as a patron of educators and advocates for moral integrity.

3. **Saint Laozi** (Taoism)
   The founder of Taoism, honored for his teachings on harmony with nature, balance, and simplicity; patron of natural wisdom and spiritual insight.

4. **Saint Guan Yin** (Buddhism, Chinese folk religion)
   A bodhisattva associated with compassion and mercy; widely honored as a patron saint of those in need and a protector of the suffering.

Indigenous and Earth-Centered Traditions

1. **Saint Black Elk** (Lakota)
   Revered as a holy man and visionary of the Oglala Lakota, known for his wisdom, vision, and commitment to Indigenous rights; a model of unity with nature and spiritual resilience.

2. **Saint Demeter** (Ancient Greek)
   The goddess of harvest and agriculture, celebrated as a patron of farmers and nature; represents the cycles of life and the sacred connection to Earth.

3. **Saint Pachamama** (Andean)
   An Earth mother figure in Andean culture, revered as the goddess of fertility and the land; symbolizes Earth stewardship, abundance, and respect for nature.

4. **Saint Viracocha** (Inca)
   Known as the creator deity in Inca mythology, symbolizing the unity of all life and natural wisdom; a patron of creativity, knowledge, and Earth-centered spirituality.

5. **Saint Brigid of Kildare** (Celtic Pagan and Christian)
   Originally a Celtic goddess, later revered as a Christian saint; patron of healing, fertility, and poetry; embodies Earth-centered wisdom and community care.

African and Afro-Caribbean Traditions

1. **Saint Oshun** (Yoruba, Afro-Caribbean)
   Yoruba goddess of love, fertility, and rivers, celebrated as a patron of creativity and compassion; represents beauty, abundance, and life's flow.
2. **Saint Shango** (Yoruba, Afro-Caribbean)
   Known as the god of thunder, justice, and power in Yoruba spirituality; symbolizes strength, resilience, and the pursuit of justice.
3. **Saint Kateri Tekakwitha** (Catholicism, Native American)
   Patron saint of ecology and the environment, recognized for her dedication to faith and reverence for nature.

Philosophical and Secular Thinkers

1. **Saint Socrates** (Ancient Greek Philosophy)
   Known as a foundational philosopher of ethics and wisdom, celebrated for his commitment to truth and reason; a patron of educators and truth-seekers.
2. **Saint Aristotle** (Ancient Greek Philosophy)
   Revered as a philosopher of ethics, science, and knowledge; known for his contributions to reason, natural philosophy, and ethical living.
3. **Saint Nikola Tesla** (Science)
   Recognized for his scientific insight and dedication to humanity; a patron of inventors, innovation, and the pursuit of knowledge.
4. **Saint Ruth Bader Ginsburg** (Judicial Advocacy)
   Celebrated for her lifelong dedication to justice, equality, and human rights; honored as a patron of justice and advocacy for women's rights.
5. **Saint Jimmy Carter** (Humanitarian Advocacy)
   Former U.S. president honored for his lifelong commitment to peace, human rights, and community service; a model of integrity and compassion.

6. **Saint Albert Einstein** (Science and Philosophy)
   Recognized for his contributions to physics and his philosophical reflections on peace and interconnectedness; a patron of scientific curiosity and ethical responsibility.
7. **Saint Mahatma Gandhi** (Humanitarian)
   Revered for his teachings on nonviolence and social justice; a patron of peace, civil rights, and the quest for social harmony.

Recognized Patrons of Virtue and Specific Causes

1. **Saint Francis of Assisi** (Christianity)
   Known as the patron saint of animals and the environment, celebrated for his love of nature and humility; a symbol of Earth stewardship and compassion for all living beings.
2. **Saint Joan of Arc** (Christianity)
   Patron of soldiers and those seeking courage, celebrated for her bravery and devotion to justice; a model of strength and resilience.
3. **Saint Augustine of Hippo** (Christianity)
   A philosopher and theologian, honored as a patron of those seeking understanding and inner peace; known for his teachings on morality and the pursuit of truth.
4. **Saint Hildegard of Bingen** (Christianity)
   Patron of herbalists and musicians, known for her visionary writings and her connection to nature; represents the unity of spirituality, creativity, and Earth-centered wisdom.
5. **Saint Teresa of Ávila** (Christianity)
   Patron of those seeking spiritual growth and contemplation; known for her teachings on prayer, meditation, and the mystical journey.

Honoring the Saints

Honoring the saints is an act of reverence, reflection, and inspiration. The saints serve as sources of spiritual guidance, exemplars of universal virtues, and companions on the journey of life. Through communal and personal observances, followers are invited to reflect on the lives of these figures, drawing strength and insight from their teachings and contributions. Honoring the saints is a way to deepen one's connection to New Universalist values and to celebrate the shared wisdom that transcends cultural and spiritual boundaries.

Communal Practices for Honoring the Saints

Communal observances offer a space for the community to come together, celebrate shared values, and honor the virtues embodied by the saints. In New Universalism, saints are often honored during specific festivals in the **Wheel of the Year**, with particular focus on All Saints Day, held on **November 1st**. This festival is dedicated to honoring saints from diverse traditions, philosophies, and spiritual paths, and provides an opportunity for the community to celebrate the lives and teachings of those who have inspired humanity toward peace, compassion, and unity.

All Saints Day Observance

On All Saints Day, the New Universalist community gathers to reflect on the saints whose lives resonate with the foundational values of the faith. This day is marked by communal story-telling, in which members share the stories, teachings, and legacies of saints who have influenced their own journeys. The gathering may include readings from sacred texts, poetry, or philosophy that speak to the virtues of compassion, justice, and wisdom. Saints from all traditions are honored, and participants are encouraged to share personal reflections on how these figures have enriched their lives.

The **lighting of candles** is a central ritual for All Saints Day. Each candle represents a saint or virtue, symbolizing the enduring light and inspiration these figures bring to the world. As candles are lit, attendees may offer silent prayers or intentions, connecting with the qualities each saint embodies. This ritual reinforces the idea that each saint's legacy is a source of light, illuminating paths of kindness, resilience, and unity for all.

Festival Observances and Honoring Specific Saints

Throughout the Wheel of the Year, specific saints may be honored during seasonal festivals. These observances are an opportunity to align the teachings of the saints with the themes of each festival, creating a meaningful connection between the natural cycles and spiritual values. Here are suggested links between saints and festivals, with flexibility for communities and individuals to adapt as they feel drawn:

- **Winter Solstice (December 21)**: A time of renewal and hope. Saint Francis of Assisi may be honored for his connection to nature and animals, along with Saint Brigid for her role in bringing light and warmth to the winter season.
- **Spring Festival/Lunar New Year (Late January to Mid-February)**: Celebrates new beginnings and growth. Saints such as Confucius, who taught on social harmony and family values, and Guan Yin, revered for compassion, are honored.
- **Spring Equinox (March 20)**: A celebration of balance and new life. Saint Demeter, the goddess of the harvest, and Saint Buddha, known for his teachings on inner peace and balance, are remembered.
- **Earth Day (April 22)**: Honors Earth stewardship and environmental consciousness. Saints such as Black Elk, a voice for Indigenous wisdom and unity with nature, and Jane Goodall, for her commitment to wildlife conservation, may be celebrated.
- **May Day (May 1)**: Celebrates fertility, joy, and community. Saint Oshun, goddess of love and fertility, and Saint Hildegard of Bingen, known for her writings on nature and healing, may be honored.
- **Summer Solstice/Midsummer Festival (June 21)**: A celebration of abundance and light. Saint Mary, Mother of Jesus, for her nurturing presence, and Saint Augustine, who emphasized inner wisdom, are revered.
- **Harvest Festival (August 1)**: A time to give thanks for the bounty of the Earth. Saint Pachamama, representing the Earth's gifts, and Saint Moses, known for guiding people toward fulfillment, are honored.
- **Autumn Equinox (September 21)**: Celebrates balance and gratitude. Saints such as Saint Teresa of Ávila, who valued contemplation and inner peace, and Socrates, who sought wisdom and integrity, are remembered.
- **All Souls Day (October 31)**: Honoring ancestors and those who have passed, with reflections on mortality and remembrance. Saint Joan of Arc, representing courage, and Saint Miriam, celebrated for resilience, are remembered.

Each festival observance allows the community to integrate the virtues of the saints into their celebrations, creating a rhythm of reflection, gratitude, and inspiration throughout the year.

Weekly Services and Lunar Cycle Observances

Saints may also be honored during regular weekly services or in alignment with the lunar cycle, reflecting New Universalism's flexibility and reverence for natural rhythms. During these observances, ministers may include short reflections or prayers dedicated to a particular saint, connecting their teachings to relevant themes for the community. The lunar cycle offers a gentle reminder to engage in regular reflection and renewal, inviting members to connect with the saints in a way that feels natural and meaningful.

Personal Practices for Honoring the Saints

In addition to communal observances, individuals are encouraged to honor the saints in personal ways that resonate with their own spiritual journeys. Personal practices allow followers to connect deeply with the saints as sources of inspiration, guidance, and support, integrating their virtues into daily life. These practices are flexible, allowing individuals to honor saints as frequently or as occasionally as they feel moved to do so.

Prayer and Meditation

Followers may incorporate the saints into personal prayer or meditation practices, calling upon specific saints for guidance, strength, or insight. For example, one might meditate on the teachings of Saint Confucius when seeking ethical guidance or reflect on Saint Oshun's qualities when in need of compassion and creative inspiration. In this way, saints become spiritual companions, offering support on the journey toward inner peace and moral integrity.

Altar Displays and Symbolic Offerings

Creating a personal or household altar is a meaningful way to honor saints within the home. Individuals may place images, candles, or symbols associated with particular saints on their altar as a visual reminder of their virtues. Offering flowers, leaves, or other natural elements is a gesture of respect and gratitude, reinforcing the connection between personal devotion and the natural world. Altars serve as sacred spaces for reflection, inviting followers to commune with the saints and draw inspiration from their lives.

Journaling and Reflection

Another personal practice for honoring saints involves journaling or reflective writing. By taking time to contemplate a saint's teachings and their relevance to one's own life, individuals deepen their understanding of universal virtues and how they might embody these qualities.

Writing prompts such as, "How can I bring more compassion into my interactions, as Saint Guan Yin did?" or "In what ways can I honor the Earth as Saint Francis did?" encourage followers to integrate these reflections into their own paths of spiritual growth.

Acts of Service and Kindness

Honoring the saints can also be expressed through action. Followers may choose to perform acts of kindness, charity, or environmental stewardship as a way of embodying the values of a particular saint. For example, organizing a community cleanup in honor of Saint Pachamama or volunteering in service to others as an homage to Saint Teresa of Ávila transforms devotion into active practice, reinforcing the New Universalist commitment to compassion and service.

Through both communal and personal practices, honoring the saints in New Universalism becomes a way to actively embody the values of the faith, drawing wisdom from figures across diverse traditions and fostering a spirit of unity, reverence, and purpose. By integrating these observances into the rhythms of the year, followers find a sense of continuity, belonging, and inspiration, united in shared devotion and respect for those who have illuminated the path toward a just, compassionate, and harmonious world.

2

The Wheel of the Year - Seasons and Celebrations

Concepts of the Wheel of the Year

Introduction

The Wheel of the Year is more than a calendar; it is a spiritual framework that honors the continuous cycles of growth, harvest, rest, and renewal that shape both nature and human life. Rooted in Earth-centered spirituality, the Wheel of the Year serves as a reminder of our intrinsic connection to the natural world and the rhythms that govern it. By following these cycles, New Universalism encourages individuals to observe and reflect on the changes in their environment, recognizing that these shifts in nature mirror transformations within themselves.

The Wheel of the Year is celebrated through ten festivals, each marking a specific phase in Earth's cycle and symbolizing a stage in our own spiritual journey. As we observe the shifting seasons, we are invited to journey both outwardly and inwardly, aligning our personal growth with the rhythms of the natural world. These transitions—birth and growth, abundance and harvest, decline and rest—serve as reminders of the interconnectedness of all life and the ongoing cycle of creation and renewal.

At its core, the Wheel of the Year highlights the cyclical nature of existence. Nature's rhythms, such as the return of spring after winter or the harvest in autumn, remind us of the balance between activity and rest, change and continuity. The Wheel serves as a guide, urging us to honor both the beauty of each season and the lessons it offers. For instance, spring's emergence reflects renewal and potential, while winter's stillness invites introspection and quiet strength. By embracing these cycles, we foster a deeper understanding of life's processes and cultivate patience, acceptance, and resilience.

This journey through the Wheel of the Year is both personal and communal, grounding each follower in their own journey while drawing them closer to the larger human family and the world around them. Through each festival, New Universalists celebrate the Earth's transformations and the ways these natural rhythms guide, heal, and restore. In this way, the Wheel of the Year becomes a compass for living, a path that honors the sacredness of both Earth and the personal journey toward spiritual growth.

The Symbolism of Cycles in Nature and Human Life

The Wheel of the Year embodies a sacred rhythm, a constant, quiet pulse that brings life into harmony with the cycles of nature. To follow this Wheel is to engage with a profound spiritual path that leads us back to the Earth, inviting us to see ourselves as part of something vast, beautiful, and interconnected. Every season, every phase of the moon, every change in the natural world reflects the greater journey of life—a journey that all beings share. In New Universalism, this path is both a personal and a communal experience, a practice that aligns our spirits with the steady transformations of the natural world and fosters an understanding of life's cyclical essence.

The **10 major festivals** of the Wheel of the Year act as anchors, marking moments of transition and celebration within the Earth's journey. These festivals are in turn harmonized by the **Lunar Cycles**, which guide monthly observances, adding depth and rhythm to the flow of spiritual life. By honoring these cycles—both the grand and the subtle—New Universalists cultivate an awareness of the delicate balance between growth, rest, transformation, and rebirth. The Wheel of the Year thus becomes a spiritual guide, a reminder that life itself is a circle, without beginning or end, where each moment contributes to a continuous unfolding of wisdom and renewal.

The **circle** is one of the most ancient and powerful symbols in human spirituality. It has been revered in countless cultures as a representation of unity, wholeness, and eternity. In New Universalism, the circle signifies the oneness of all life, the interconnectedness that binds us to the Earth and to one another. Just as the seasons move in a circle, so too do our lives. We are born, we grow, we harvest the fruits of our labor, we rest, and we return to the Earth, only to be reborn in another form. The circle teaches us that every stage of life has purpose, that each transformation is part of a greater whole. In **Indigenous traditions**, the medicine wheel represents this balance and the interconnectedness of all beings; it teaches us to live in harmony with the cycles of life, understanding that everything has its season and that balance is the source of health and wisdom.

Nature, as it turns through the seasons, provides a sacred mirror for our own journeys. In **Taoist philosophy**, the cycle of **yin and yang** reflects the dance of opposites—light and dark, active and passive—that is essential for harmony. In New Universalism, the Wheel of the Year similarly embodies this balance, showing us that both joy and sorrow, growth and retreat, are necessary parts of the journey. The beauty of spring's blossoms is made possible by winter's quiet rest; the abundance of autumn follows the work and warmth of summer. By accepting and embracing each of these phases, we cultivate inner peace and resilience, learning that there is a place for every experience within the circle of life.

The seasons themselves invite us into reflection and transformation. Each season brings its own energy, its own "invitation" for growth and self-discovery. Spring, with its budding life and soft renewal, encourages hope, courage, and potential. Summer, radiant and vibrant, celebrates abundance, vitality, and the joy of community. Autumn, with its harvest and preparation, fosters gratitude, wisdom, and contemplation. Winter, still and introspective, calls for rest, healing, and the deep insights of solitude. In this way, the seasons act as sacred teachers, guiding us through the stages of our lives with grace and purpose. Observing these changes allows us to understand ourselves more fully, to see that every season of our own lives offers unique and valuable lessons.

The **Lunar Cycles** complement these seasonal shifts, providing additional guidance on a more intimate level. Just as the Earth moves through grand cycles, the moon's phases create a monthly rhythm that invites reflection, release, and renewal. The new moon symbolizes beginnings and the planting of intentions; the full moon illuminates our journey, bringing clarity and insight; the waning moon encourages release and gratitude. Together with the seasonal festivals, these monthly rites offer followers a gentle structure, an ongoing reminder of their connection to the world and to the cycles of change within themselves. This balance between the larger seasonal shifts and the more frequent lunar phases enriches the spiritual practice of New Universalism, creating a layered approach to understanding life's ebb and flow.

The teachings of **Buddhism** remind us of the impermanence of all things, a concept that resonates deeply within the Wheel of the Year. Just as each season is temporary, so too are our joys and sorrows, our triumphs and losses. This understanding does not diminish life's beauty; rather, it enhances it. By recognizing the transient nature of existence, we learn to cherish each moment, to find peace in both change and continuity. In New Universalism, the Wheel of the Year becomes a guide to embracing impermanence with gratitude, recognizing that every end is also a beginning and that each phase of life has its own sacred purpose.

Through the Wheel of the Year, New Universalists are reminded that we are part of a larger circle, a vast and sacred interconnectedness that includes all beings. As each season unfolds, we find ourselves drawn closer to one another, bound by the shared rhythms of birth, growth, rest, and renewal. This understanding cultivates compassion and empathy, as we see our own lives reflected in the lives of others and in the cycles of nature. The **circle** thus becomes not only a symbol of unity but a lived experience, a reminder that we are all traveling together along the same path, learning, evolving, and finding our way back to the source.

The Wheel of the Year encourages followers to honor the unique qualities of each season while embracing the cycles of life within themselves. By aligning with these rhythms, we find strength, peace, and a sense of purpose that guides us through both personal growth and communal connection. In New Universalism, each festival and lunar rite becomes a sacred touchpoint, a way of grounding oneself in the wisdom of the Earth and the shared journey of all beings. The Wheel reminds us that we are never alone, that each moment and each cycle brings us closer to a deeper understanding of ourselves and the world around us.

Spiritual Wisdom in Seasonal Change

The Wheel of the Year offers a profound journey of spiritual growth, where each season becomes a chapter in the story of life, inviting us to attune ourselves to nature's wisdom and its timeless lessons. As the Earth turns through cycles of light and darkness, growth and rest, we, too, are invited to turn inward and outward, exploring the rhythms of transformation that shape both our environment and our inner selves. In New Universalism, these seasonal changes are not only markers of time but sacred guides, each season bringing forth its own invitation for renewal, introspection, gratitude, and wisdom.

Each season along the Wheel brings a **unique invitation for self-discovery and spiritual growth**. The seasons invite us to let go of rigid timelines and expectations, and instead, to live in harmony with the natural world. **Winter**, with its quiet rest, calls for reflection and contemplation, offering a space for inner stillness where wisdom can emerge. In the cold and dark, we find the beauty of simplicity, the strength in endurance, and the necessity of rest. Like seeds dormant beneath the Earth, we are reminded that even in moments of stillness, there is preparation and unseen growth. Winter teaches patience, humility, and the resilience that arises from the stillness of waiting.

Spring arrives with an energy of awakening, its tender shoots and blossoms symbolizing the renewal of hope, courage, and potential. It is a season of planting, where we are encouraged to set intentions and pursue the growth we envisioned in winter. Just as the Earth awakens to life, so too are we invited to awaken to our inner calling and to begin anew with optimism. In **Buddhism**, spring's rebirth resonates with the concept of "beginner's mind," an openness and curiosity that sees every day as a new beginning. Spring urges us to release our old beliefs, to view ourselves with fresh eyes, and to nurture the seeds of compassion, creativity, and purpose.

Summer follows, radiant with the warmth and fullness of life. It is a time of abundance, celebration, and community—a season where our efforts begin to bear fruit. The longer days and thriving landscapes remind us to embrace the joy and vitality of the present moment. In New Universalism, summer serves as a time to celebrate not only the physical abundance of nature but the spiritual harvest of our inner work. This season invites us to gather with others, to celebrate our interconnectedness, and to share our gifts with the world. **Indigenous wisdom** often celebrates summer as a time of communal gatherings and shared stories, reinforcing the value of unity, gratitude, and honoring the land. Summer teaches us the joy of community and the strength of relationships, reminding us that we flourish best when we live and celebrate together.

With **Autumn**, the Wheel of the Year turns toward harvest and reflection. It is a season of gathering what has grown, both in the outer world and within ourselves, and of giving thanks for the abundance received. As the leaves fall and the days grow shorter, we are reminded of life's impermanence and the value of gratitude. Autumn calls us to evaluate, to celebrate our accomplishments, and to let go of that which no longer serves us. In this time of harvest, we recognize the balance between effort and surrender, the wisdom of discernment, and the peace that comes from releasing what is complete. In **Stoic philosophy**, there is a focus on understanding what we can control and letting go of the rest. Autumn's letting go is an exercise in humility and grace, showing us that change is a natural and necessary part of life's cycle.

Each seasonal transition within the Wheel of the Year is accompanied by the **Lunar Cycles**, which provide an added rhythm of reflection and renewal throughout the month. The phases of the moon, from new to full and back again, mirror the journey of intention, illumination, release, and rest. The **new moon** is a time for setting intentions, a space for quiet aspiration that complements winter's stillness and spring's planting. The **full moon**—bright and revealing—corresponds to summer's energy, inviting us to celebrate our growth and the clarity that comes with awareness. As the **moon wanes**, it encourages release, aligning with the introspective nature of autumn, guiding us to let go and prepare for the cycle to begin anew. The monthly lunar rites complement the larger seasonal changes, grounding us in the ongoing rhythm of life and reinforcing the wisdom of regular reflection, renewal, and acceptance.

The Wheel of the Year reminds New Universalists to find harmony with these cycles, offering a gentle yet powerful structure for navigating life's transitions. Each season presents an opportunity for **spiritual transformation** that supports growth, self-acceptance, and inner peace. Just as nature moves effortlessly through the stages of life, followers of New Universalism are encouraged to accept change as a sacred part of the journey. The spiritual wisdom of the Wheel is in its invitation to be fully present in each season's unique qualities, understanding that every phase has its own purpose and gifts.

Observing these seasonal changes also teaches reverence for life's diversity and resilience. **Confucian philosophy**, which emphasizes the importance of harmony between humanity and nature, resonates deeply with the Wheel of the Year. In New Universalism, followers are encouraged to cultivate respect for the Earth's cycles, recognizing that every season of life, like every season of the Earth, has value. Through this practice, we learn to see each stage as interconnected and essential, fostering a sense of humility and gratitude for the beauty and complexity of life.

As New Universalists journey through the Wheel of the Year, we are reminded to live with intention, to honor each season's unique teachings, and to celebrate both the blossoming and the falling away. In this way, the Wheel is not only a calendar but a map for spiritual living, a guide that leads us back to the Earth and to the rhythms that sustain us all. By embracing the wisdom of seasonal change, we cultivate resilience, compassion, and an abiding sense of wonder for the world and our place within it.

The Ten Seasonal Festivals

The Wheel of the Year within New Universalism serves as a sacred guide, drawing us into harmony with the Earth's rhythms and offering a framework for both personal and communal reflection. Each of the ten seasonal festivals marks a vital point in Earth's journey—a time when natural transitions are most evident, inviting us to celebrate, contemplate, and align ourselves with these shifts. These festivals are much more than ceremonial observances; they are portals through which we experience the interconnectedness of life, the cycles of growth and rest, and the wisdom of aligning our lives with nature's rhythms.

Each festival within the Wheel of the Year brings its own unique energy, calling forth specific virtues and qualities that encourage growth, gratitude, renewal, and reflection. Through these observances, New Universalists find a structured way to cultivate awareness of both inner and outer landscapes, recognizing that our spiritual journeys mirror the cycles of nature. From the quiet introspection of the Winter Solstice to the vibrant joy of May Day, each festival invites us to pause, take notice, and connect with life's deeper rhythms. Observing these festivals fosters a reverence for the Earth, a reminder of our role as stewards, and a celebration of our bond with the natural world.

The ten festivals are balanced by **Lunar Cycles**, which guide monthly practices and minor rites that support ongoing reflection, renewal, and intention. Together, the seasonal festivals and lunar observances create a dynamic rhythm, grounding followers in the natural cycles of both the Earth and the cosmos. By honoring these cycles, we learn to navigate life's changes with greater acceptance, resilience, and grace.

These seasonal festivals are deeply intertwined with New Universalist principles, embodying the values of **Earth Stewardship** and **Filial Piety**. Each festival invites followers to honor the Earth, to celebrate life's abundance, and to acknowledge the transitions that are integral to our shared existence. Through these observances, we deepen our understanding of Earth Stewardship, learning to care for our environment with respect and gratitude. Likewise, the festivals encourage **Filial Piety**—a reverence for one's ancestors, community, and the natural world that sustains us. By gathering together to mark these sacred times, New Universalists strengthen their bonds with one another and with the generations before and after, fostering unity across both time and tradition.

In the following sections, we will explore each of these ten festivals in detail, delving into the spiritual themes, reflections, and practices that make each observance unique. Each celebration within the Wheel of the Year is an invitation to engage fully with life, to nurture our inner and outer worlds, and to embrace the cyclical beauty of existence. As we journey through these festivals, we are reminded that every season has its purpose, every phase of life has its wisdom, and that we, too, are part of a vast, sacred cycle that connects all beings.

Winter Solstice - December 21

The Winter Solstice marks the longest night of the year, a time when darkness reaches its peak and light begins its return. In New Universalism, this festival symbolizes hope, renewal, and the promise of rebirth. As the Earth pauses on the edge of transformation, followers gather to reflect on the light within, rekindling their inner warmth and welcoming the gradual return of the sun. The Winter Solstice is a time of stillness and introspection, an invitation to go inward and reconnect with the sources of strength and resilience that sustain us through the darker times in life.

The **themes of the Winter Solstice**—inner warmth, community gathering, and the renewal of spirit—encourage followers to cultivate patience, gratitude, and a trust in life's cycles. This festival teaches that even in the quiet and cold of winter, there is a promise of growth and new beginnings. As nature rests and gathers strength, so too are we invited to pause, gather with loved ones, and honor the blessings of both darkness and light.

Spiritual Teachings and Symbolism

The Winter Solstice resonates with spiritual teachings that emphasize resilience, hope, and the interconnectedness of all beings. **Stoic philosophy**, which values inner strength and the cultivation of a steady mind, aligns with the Solstice's themes of endurance and peace in the face of difficulty. In this stillness, we find the strength to continue forward, trusting that light will return even after the darkest nights. **Buddhist teachings on mindfulness and acceptance** also echo the Solstice's call for introspection, reminding us to embrace each moment, finding peace within ourselves.

Saints and Patron Saints associated with the Winter Solstice in New Universalism include **Saint Brigid**, who represents warmth, light, and protection through the cold; and **Saint Francis of Assisi**, known for his humility and closeness to nature. Saint Brigid's symbolic flame is a reminder of the light that can be found even in the darkest times, while Saint Francis's connection to all living beings speaks to the unity and companionship we find within our communities.

Ceremonies, Rites, and Rituals

The Winter Solstice is celebrated through rituals that invoke warmth, light, and the support of community:

1. **Candle Lighting Ceremony**: In a communal setting, followers gather to light candles, symbolizing the return of light and hope. Each participant may light a candle while reflecting on an aspect of their life they wish to rekindle or renew. This simple yet powerful act of lighting a candle serves as a reminder that even a small light can dispel darkness, symbolizing resilience and the quiet strength within.

2. **Circle of Stories**: Winter Solstice gatherings often include storytelling, where individuals share tales of endurance, personal growth, or memories of loved ones. These stories are a way of drawing warmth and connection from each other, honoring both personal and communal histories.

3. **Silent Reflection and Meditation**: For those observing the Solstice individually, a period of silent reflection or meditation can help connect with the themes of the season. Sitting in quiet solitude, followers are encouraged to contemplate the darkness within and around them, finding acceptance and peace in this stillness. Reflective meditation allows individuals to acknowledge their challenges and gently turn toward the light of hope and renewal.

4. **Sharing of Food and Warmth**: A shared meal or the giving of warm drinks symbolizes care and unity within the community. Gathering for a simple feast or preparing food for others reinforces the theme of support and collective resilience. This act of sharing sustenance acknowledges our mutual reliance and strengthens bonds of fellowship during the darkest season.

Guidance for Independent and Communal Observance

For **independent observance**, followers may choose to light a single candle in their home, symbolizing the light within. A personal meditation or journal reflection on the themes of darkness, renewal, and hope can deepen one's connection to the Solstice. Many find meaning in setting intentions for inner growth, noting areas where they seek renewal and resilience in the coming year.

In **communal settings**, Winter Solstice observances encourage participants to gather in a shared space, lighting candles and sharing warmth, stories, and reflection. Ministers may lead a guided meditation or reflection, focusing on themes of hope, unity, and the gradual return of light. Community members are encouraged to share words of gratitude or insights they have gained over the past year, acknowledging both challenges and achievements.

The Winter Solstice encourages New Universalists to embrace the season of darkness not as an end, but as a beginning—a chance to gather strength, seek comfort in community, and prepare for the coming light. This festival reminds us that even in life's darker seasons, there is always hope, warmth, and the quiet promise of renewal

Spring Festival / Lunar New Year - Late January to Mid-February

The Spring Festival, often celebrated in alignment with the Lunar New Year, marks a time when life stirs beneath the surface, preparing to emerge from winter's quiet. This festival is a celebration of new beginnings, personal purification, and the nurturing of inner potential. In New Universalism, the Spring Festival symbolizes the courage to start anew, to set intentions, and to prepare the ground for growth, both literally and spiritually. It is a time to acknowledge the seeds of our hopes and aspirations, honoring the potential they hold as we prepare for the journey ahead.

This festival, positioned between the Winter Solstice and the Spring Equinox, serves as a transitional period, bridging the introspective energy of winter with the vibrant renewal of spring. As the Earth begins its gradual awakening, we, too, are invited to awaken to new possibilities, to cleanse ourselves of past burdens, and to cultivate an open heart and mind.

Spiritual Teachings and Symbolism

The themes of the Spring Festival align closely with teachings of renewal, courage, and self-purification. **Buddhist philosophy** speaks of "beginner's mind," an openness that allows us to approach each moment with fresh curiosity and a willingness to embrace change. Similarly, the **Taoist emphasis on flow and renewal** resonates with this season, encouraging us to release stagnant energies and align with the natural rhythm of transformation.

Saints associated with the Spring Festival in New Universalism include **Saint Guan Yin**, who symbolizes compassion and mercy, guiding us in setting intentions with a loving heart; and **Saint Confucius**, celebrated for his teachings on self-cultivation and the harmony that arises from inner balance. These figures serve as reminders that growth must be nurtured with patience and integrity, and that each beginning is an opportunity to deepen our commitment to compassion and self-awareness.

Ceremonies, Rites, and Rituals

The Spring Festival is observed through practices that emphasize renewal, intention-setting, and the clearing of physical and spiritual space:

1. **Cleansing Ritual**: Followers begin by physically and spiritually cleansing their environments, sweeping away the old to make room for the new. This may involve cleaning homes, clearing out unused items, and symbolically "sweeping away" negative energy. Participants can add meaningful elements, such as sprinkling salt or water infused with herbs, to purify their space and invite fresh energy.

2. **Planting of Seeds**: As a symbol of intention-setting, many followers plant seeds, either in pots or in the ground, representing their aspirations for the coming year. Each seed serves as a metaphor for a personal goal or value they wish to cultivate, reminding them of the care and dedication required for growth.

3. **Intention-Setting and Meditation**: In individual or communal settings, participants may engage in guided meditation focused on renewal and release. During this meditation, followers are encouraged to reflect on what they wish to let go of from the past year and what they hope to cultivate moving forward. Each intention is set with clarity and purpose, aligning with the themes of fresh beginnings and inner cleansing.

4. **Offerings to Nature**: As an expression of gratitude and connection to the Earth, participants may offer natural items like flowers, fruit, or rice to nature. This act honors the Earth as the source of all growth and life, reinforcing the principle of Earth Stewardship central to New Universalism. These offerings can be placed on a communal altar or returned to nature, symbolizing respect for the cycles that sustain us.

Guidance for Independent and Communal Observance

For **independent observance**, followers may start by clearing their personal spaces and reflecting on their intentions for the new year. Lighting a candle or incense can signify the release of old energies and the welcoming of new beginnings. Journaling intentions, aspirations, or areas of life that need renewal helps create a personal connection to the season's themes. Some may choose to write intentions on small slips of paper, symbolically planting them alongside physical seeds in a ritual of commitment to growth.

In **communal settings**, the Spring Festival often begins with a collective space-clearing ritual, followed by shared intention-setting. The group may gather in a circle, with each person sharing their intentions aloud if they feel comfortable. This creates a sense of shared purpose and support, reinforcing the interconnectedness of individual and communal growth. Ministers may lead a group meditation focused on cleansing and renewal, guiding participants through a reflection on what they wish to release and what they seek to cultivate. The gathering often concludes with the planting of seeds, either outdoors if weather permits or in small pots, with each participant nurturing a physical reminder of their intentions throughout the year.

The **Spring Festival's symbolism of renewal and growth** serves as a gentle yet powerful call to nurture one's own potential while honoring the potential in others. By observing this festival, New Universalists reaffirm their commitment to personal and communal growth, drawing strength from the knowledge that every new beginning is part of a larger cycle of transformation.

Spring Equinox - March 20

The Spring Equinox marks a moment of perfect balance, when day and night stand in equal measure, ushering in a season of renewal, creativity, and vibrant growth. This festival in New Universalism symbolizes the harmonious coexistence of light and dark within ourselves and the world around us. At the Equinox, we honor both the beauty and strength of balance, recognizing that growth requires both sun and shadow, action and rest. The Spring Equinox invites us to embrace our potential, celebrate the reawakening of the Earth, and engage with the world in a spirit of creativity and joy.

This festival arrives as the Earth itself comes alive with color, bursting forth with flowers, fresh leaves, and the songs of birds returning to the trees. Just as nature begins to bloom, so too are we encouraged to open ourselves to new possibilities, to honor our growth, and to share our unique gifts with the world. The Spring Equinox embodies the New Universalist ideals of unity and interconnection, reminding us that each being contributes to the beauty and balance of the world.

Spiritual Teachings and Symbolism

The Spring Equinox resonates with teachings on balance, unity, and the sacredness of growth. **Taoist philosophy**, which speaks of the harmony between opposites, aligns with the Equinox's themes of balance and interconnectedness. The concept of **yin and yang** teaches that light and dark, growth and rest, are necessary counterparts that create a harmonious whole. Similarly, **Buddhism's Middle Path** resonates with this festival, encouraging followers to seek balance in their own lives and avoid extremes.

Saints associated with the Spring Equinox in New Universalism include **Saint Demeter**, the ancient Greek goddess of harvest and growth, representing fertility and the nurturing of life, and **Saint Brigid**, who is honored for her role as a protector of life's cycles and as a figure of rebirth. These saints remind us that growth is a sacred process and that nurturing life requires patience, creativity, and balance.

Ceremonies, Rites, and Rituals

The Spring Equinox is observed through rituals that honor life's reawakening, balance, and the beauty of nature:

1. **Flower Planting Ritual**: As a symbol of growth and beauty, followers plant flowers in gardens, pots, or community spaces. Each flower serves as a living tribute to new beginnings, and planting these blooms signifies an intention to cultivate beauty, creativity, and kindness. For many, this ritual also involves offering a prayer or intention for personal growth as they place each seed or flower in the soil.

2. **Egg Decoration and Blessing**: The egg, an ancient symbol of life and potential, is often painted or decorated as a part of Spring Equinox celebrations. Each egg can be inscribed with symbols or words representing personal values or aspirations for the season. Some may choose to bless these eggs with a quiet moment of reflection, holding them as a reminder of the potential within and the beauty of new life.

3. **Equinox Meditation and Balancing Ceremony**: In a communal or individual setting, followers may engage in a guided meditation focused on inner and outer balance. In a group, participants can form a circle, each reflecting on areas of life where balance is needed or where they seek growth. The balancing ceremony may also involve placing symbolic items (such as rocks and feathers) on a central altar, representing the grounding of Earth and the lightness of Air.

4. **Offering to Nature**: In gratitude for the Earth's awakening, many offer small tokens of appreciation, such as grains, herbs, or water poured onto the soil. These offerings symbolize a commitment to Earth Stewardship and an acknowledgment of the interconnectedness be-

tween all beings. This act of giving back honors the Earth's gifts and reinforces the New Universalist value of reciprocity with nature.

Guidance for Independent and Communal Observance

For **independent observance**, followers may start the day with a meditation or reflection on balance, considering ways to nurture harmony within themselves and their surroundings. Planting flowers or tending to a garden provides a hands-on way to connect with the Earth's reawakening and celebrate the beauty of growth. Decorating eggs with meaningful symbols or colors also creates a tangible reminder of personal goals and intentions.

In **communal settings**, the Spring Equinox is celebrated with a gathering that emphasizes creativity and connection to nature. The community may come together to plant flowers in a shared garden, decorate eggs, or hold a balancing ceremony where participants share insights or reflections on finding harmony. Ministers might lead a group meditation focused on balance and interconnection, guiding followers to reflect on ways they can cultivate harmony within themselves and their community. A shared feast featuring seasonal foods and colorful decorations is often enjoyed to celebrate the abundance and joy of spring.

The **Spring Equinox's focus on balance and growth** offers a powerful reminder that life's beauty emerges from a harmonious blending of light and dark, action and reflection. By observing this festival, New Universalists deepen their connection to nature's cycles and to their own potential for growth, unity, and creativity. This celebration encourages followers to see life as a continuous dance of balance, a dynamic interplay that brings depth, richness, and resilience to the journey.

Earth Day - April 22

Earth Day is a sacred occasion in New Universalism, a day to celebrate the Earth and deepen our commitment to its care. Observed on April 22, Earth Day is both a celebration of the planet's beauty and a reminder of our responsibility as stewards. It is a time for reflection on our individual and collective impact on the environment, for raising awareness of ecological challenges, and for taking actionable steps to preserve and restore the natural world. In New Universalism, Earth

Day embodies the principle of Earth Stewardship, encouraging followers to live with reverence for the planet and to recognize the interconnectedness of all life.

The observance of Earth Day within New Universalism highlights the essential role of the Earth as both a home and a sacred partner in our spiritual journey. Just as the Earth sustains us, we, too, are called to protect and nurture its well-being. This festival serves as a reminder that caring for the planet is a moral responsibility, one that transcends generations and requires unity, action, and reverence.

Spiritual Teachings and Symbolism

Earth Day resonates with spiritual teachings that emphasize respect, reciprocity, and responsibility. **Indigenous wisdom**, which speaks of living in harmony with nature and honoring the Earth as a source of life, closely aligns with the values of this day. In many Indigenous traditions, the Earth is seen as a living being, deserving of respect and gratitude. This perspective resonates with New Universalism's commitment to viewing the planet as sacred, honoring both its beauty and its limitations.

Saints and Patron Saints associated with Earth Day in New Universalism include **Saint Francis of Assisi**, revered for his profound connection to nature and animals, and **Saint Kateri Tekakwitha**, the patron saint of ecology, known for her dedication to protecting the land and honoring its gifts. These figures embody the virtues of humility, compassion, and respect for the Earth, serving as guides for those seeking to live in harmony with nature and to protect the environment.

Ceremonies, Rites, and Rituals

Earth Day is observed through rituals that emphasize gratitude for the Earth, active conservation, and the renewal of our commitment to ecological responsibility:

1. **Tree Planting and Habitat Restoration**: Planting trees, shrubs, or flowers is a meaningful way to give back to the Earth and contribute to environmental health. Communities may organize tree-planting events, or individuals can plant a tree in a personal space as a symbol of renewal and life. Many followers also participate in habitat restoration projects, such as cleaning local parks, beaches, or nature reserves, symbolizing a collective effort to restore the Earth's beauty.

2. **Circle of Gratitude for the Earth**: In communal gatherings, followers may form a circle, with each participant expressing gratitude for a specific aspect of the Earth (such as clean

water, fresh air, forests, or oceans). This ritual fosters a sense of shared appreciation and deepens the connection between participants and the natural world. To close the circle, individuals may offer a small token to the Earth, such as flowers, stones, or herbs, symbolizing a commitment to honor and protect these natural elements.

3. **Sacred Walk or Pilgrimage in Nature**: Walking in nature, either alone or with a group, is a powerful way to connect with the Earth and appreciate its gifts. As part of Earth Day observances, followers may take a "sacred walk" through forests, parks, or other natural settings, pausing to observe and reflect on the beauty around them. This ritual encourages mindfulness, helping followers reconnect with the land and recognize the intricate web of life that sustains them.

4. **Commitment to Sustainability**: During Earth Day observances, participants are encouraged to make personal or communal commitments to sustainable practices. These commitments may include reducing waste, conserving energy, supporting local and eco-friendly businesses, or actively participating in environmental advocacy. By making these promises, followers honor the Earth through tangible actions, reinforcing New Universalism's principle of Earth Stewardship.

Guidance for Independent and Communal Observance

For **independent observance**, followers might begin the day with a moment of silent gratitude for the Earth, offering thanks for its gifts and contemplating ways to lessen their ecological footprint. Personal commitments to sustainable practices, such as reducing single-use plastics or planting pollinator-friendly flowers, can serve as daily reminders of one's dedication to Earth Stewardship. A mindful walk in nature allows individuals to witness the beauty and resilience of the Earth firsthand, fostering a sense of unity and responsibility.

In **communal settings**, Earth Day observances may begin with a collective reflection or meditation on the themes of gratitude and stewardship. Ministers might lead a group in the Circle of Gratitude, inviting each participant to share an aspect of the Earth for which they are thankful. The group may then proceed to plant trees or engage in a habitat restoration project, creating a tangible impact that strengthens both the local environment and the community's bond. Communal discussions on sustainable living or environmental issues can further encourage collective action and awareness.

The **celebration of Earth Day in New Universalism** is a reminder of our responsibility to the Earth and to each other. This festival encourages followers to live with mindfulness, respect, and gratitude, honoring the Earth as both a source of life and a sacred trust. By observing Earth Day, New Universalists reaffirm their commitment to protecting and nurturing the planet, embodying the values of reverence, reciprocity, and care for all living things.

May Day - May 1

May Day, celebrated on May 1, marks the height of spring's bloom, a time when the Earth is brimming with life, beauty, and abundance. This festival is a celebration of fertility, joy, and the interconnectedness of all beings. In New Universalism, May Day represents the vibrancy of creation, the warmth of community, and the celebration of life in all its forms. The energy of May Day is one of exuberance and renewal, a time to revel in the beauty of nature, honor our connections with one another, and express gratitude for the abundance that surrounds us.

As the Earth blossoms, followers are invited to reconnect with their own vitality, creativity, and sense of wonder. May Day is an opportunity to honor the bonds that unite us with the natural world and with each other, to celebrate the life force that flows through all beings, and to recognize the sacred joy in simply being alive.

Spiritual Teachings and Symbolism

May Day embodies themes of unity, celebration, and the sacredness of life. **Pagan traditions** celebrate May Day as **Beltane**, a festival that honors the fertility of the Earth and the balance between light and dark, growth and rest. In New Universalism, the spirit of Beltane is embraced, emphasizing the joy of creation, the beauty of interconnectedness, and the importance of celebrating life's abundance. **Indigenous teachings** that honor the Earth as a source of life and community also align with the essence of May Day, encouraging followers to view the natural world as a sacred partner in creation.

Saints and Patron Saints associated with May Day in New Universalism include **Saint Oshun**, the goddess of love, fertility, and rivers in Yoruba spirituality, who embodies beauty, abundance, and the vitality of life; and **Saint Hildegard of Bingen**, known for her reverence for the natural world and her writings on the healing power of nature. These figures remind followers of the sacredness of joy, creation, and the unity that connects all beings in the cycle of life.

Ceremonies, Rites, and Rituals

May Day is celebrated through rituals that honor the beauty of the Earth, the joy of community, and the fertility of life:

1. **Dancing Around the Maypole**: One of the most iconic May Day rituals, dancing around the Maypole is a celebration of life and community. In this joyful dance, participants weave colorful ribbons around a tall pole, creating a vibrant display of unity and connection. The Maypole itself represents the tree of life, symbolizing growth, vitality, and the interconnectedness of all beings.

2. **Flower Crown Weaving**: Followers may create crowns of fresh flowers and greenery to wear during May Day celebrations. This ritual honors the beauty and abundance of nature and serves as a reminder of our unity with the Earth. Each flower crown is unique, symbolizing the individuality and diversity within the community, woven together by the shared joy of celebration.

3. **Offerings to the Earth**: In gratitude for the Earth's abundance, participants may offer flowers, seeds, or other natural items to the land. These offerings symbolize respect for the Earth's gifts and reinforce the New Universalist principle of reciprocity with nature. Some may place these offerings at the base of a tree or in a garden, acknowledging the Earth as a sacred partner in life.

4. **Community Feast and Celebration**: A shared meal, featuring fresh and seasonal foods, is an essential part of May Day celebrations. This communal feast is a way to honor the abundance of the Earth and to strengthen bonds within the community. During the feast, followers may share stories, songs, or expressions of gratitude, deepening their sense of connection and unity.

Guidance for Independent and Communal Observance

For **independent observance**, followers may begin the day by weaving a small flower crown or arranging fresh flowers in their home as a symbol of life's beauty and abundance. A personal meditation on interconnectedness and gratitude can help deepen one's connection to the themes of May Day. Some may choose to walk in nature, appreciating the blooming landscape and offering small tokens, such as flowers or seeds, as a gesture of reverence for the Earth.

In **communal settings**, May Day celebrations often begin with the traditional Maypole dance, bringing participants together in a circle of movement and joy. Ministers may lead the group in creating flower crowns or decorating a communal altar with seasonal flowers and greenery. The community may then share a meal, featuring fresh fruits, vegetables, and other offerings of spring, as a way to honor life's abundance and the nourishment the Earth provides. During this feast, participants may exchange blessings, express gratitude, or share personal reflections on the joy and beauty of life.

The **celebration of May Day** within New Universalism is a reminder of the sacredness of joy, community, and life's interconnectedness. By observing this festival, followers reaffirm their commitment to live with gratitude, unity, and a sense of wonder, honoring the beauty of the Earth and the bonds that connect all beings. May Day encourages New Universalists to celebrate life's abundance, to embrace the vitality of the season, and to recognize the sacred joy that flows through all creation.

Summer Solstice (Midsummer) - June 21

The Summer Solstice, celebrated on June 21, marks the peak of sunlight and the longest day of the year. Known as Midsummer in many traditions, this festival is a time for honoring life's fullness, expressing gratitude for the gifts of the Earth, and reflecting on personal growth and achievement. In New Universalism, the Summer Solstice symbolizes the vibrancy and abundance of life, a celebration of both the external light of the sun and the internal light within each individual. It is a time to gather in joy, to honor the vitality that summer brings, and to acknowledge the blessings and progress made throughout the year.

As the Earth reaches the height of its energy, followers are encouraged to embrace their own moments of flourishing, to celebrate achievements, and to nurture connections within their communities. The Summer Solstice invites us to recognize the beauty and abundance around us, and to pause in gratitude for life's richness.

Spiritual Teachings and Symbolism

The Summer Solstice resonates with teachings of gratitude, joy, and celebration. **Pagan traditions** often observe Midsummer as a time to honor the sun's strength, emphasizing the themes of light, life, and communal celebration. In **Buddhism**, the concept of "mindful joy" aligns with the Solstice, encouraging followers to fully experience and appreciate the present moment. The Solstice calls us to find joy in life's brightness and to acknowledge the ways in which we contribute to and benefit from the greater community.

Saints associated with the Summer Solstice in New Universalism include **Saint Mary**, revered for her nurturing and sustaining qualities, symbolizing the abundance of life; and **Saint Augustine**, who emphasized inner wisdom and the pursuit of truth. These figures remind followers to seek fulfillment both within themselves and in connection with others, nurturing a balance between inner reflection and outward joy.

Ceremonies, Rites, and Rituals

The Summer Solstice is celebrated through rituals that honor light, gratitude, and communal joy:

1. **Sunrise or Sunset Gathering**: Followers may gather at dawn or dusk to honor the sun and the gift of light. These gatherings provide a space for reflection on personal growth, community, and the blessings of life. At sunrise, participants may offer words of gratitude as they watch the sun rise, symbolizing hope, vitality, and renewal. At sunset, followers may share reflections on achievements and joys, acknowledging the day's fullness and life's beauty.

2. **Flower and Herb Gathering**: A traditional Solstice ritual involves gathering flowers, herbs, or other natural elements, often used in wreaths or decorations. Followers may collect local, seasonal blooms as symbols of life's abundance and beauty. These wreaths or garlands are worn or placed on altars, celebrating the richness of the Earth and the vibrancy of summer.

3. **Bonfire Ceremony**: In communal settings, the Solstice is often marked by a bonfire, symbolizing the strength and warmth of the sun. Participants gather around the fire, sharing stories, songs, or reflections on their blessings and achievements. As the fire crackles, followers may offer intentions or expressions of gratitude, connecting with one another and with the energy of the season.

4. **Reflection on Personal Goals and Achievements**: For some, the Summer Solstice serves as a midpoint for evaluating personal goals set earlier in the year. This may include journal reflections, discussions, or meditative practices, allowing followers to acknowledge progress, make adjustments, and celebrate the ways they have grown. This ritual of self-reflection aligns with New Universalism's emphasis on personal growth, reminding followers that inner light shines brightest when nurtured with mindfulness and intention.

Guidance for Independent and Communal Observance

For **independent observance**, followers may begin the day with a moment of gratitude, reflecting on the abundance and beauty of the season. Watching the sunrise or sunset serves as a simple but powerful practice to connect with the energy of the sun and the fullness of life. Creating a flower wreath or arranging fresh herbs and flowers in the home can also bring the vibrant energy of the season into one's personal space, symbolizing both gratitude and the celebration of nature's gifts.

In **communal settings**, the Summer Solstice may begin with a sunrise or sunset gathering, where participants share reflections on personal growth and gratitude. Ministers may lead a meditation focused on light, joy, and inner fulfillment, guiding followers to honor both personal and communal achievements. The group may then proceed to light a bonfire or arrange a communal altar with seasonal flowers, creating a visual representation of life's abundance and connection. A shared meal featuring fresh, colorful foods can enhance the sense of celebration, reinforcing the theme of gratitude for life's richness.

The **celebration of the Summer Solstice in New Universalism** is a reminder to appreciate life's blessings, to honor personal and communal achievements, and to recognize the beauty of the present moment. This festival encourages followers to live with joy and gratitude, embracing the fullness of life and celebrating the light within themselves and the world around them. By observing the Summer Solstice, New Universalists deepen their connection to the rhythms of nature, finding strength and inspiration in the abundance of the Earth and in the shared journey of life

Harvest Festival - August 1

The Harvest Festival, observed on August 1, is a time of gratitude, reflection, and communal sharing. This festival celebrates the first harvest of the season, acknowledging the fruits of one's labor, the abundance of the Earth, and the strength of community bonds. In New Universalism, the Harvest Festival is an invitation to recognize both individual and collective contributions, to express gratitude for the blessings in our lives, and to share these gifts with others. It is a time for appreciating the cycles of giving and receiving, reinforcing the values of generosity, unity, and sustenance.

The Harvest Festival marks the beginning of the transition from the vibrancy of summer to the quiet preparation of autumn. As the Earth offers its bounty, followers are encouraged to reflect on the importance of gathering, sharing, and honoring the journey that led to this abundance. This celebration reinforces the New Universalist principles of Earth Stewardship and social responsibility, emphasizing that we are all nourished by the same land, and we have a shared responsibility to care for one another.

Spiritual Teachings and Symbolism

The Harvest Festival resonates with teachings on gratitude, community, and the balance of giving and receiving. **Stoic philosophy**, which emphasizes the virtue of gratitude and the acceptance of life's blessings, aligns with the Harvest Festival's focus on appreciation and contentment. This philosophy teaches that true abundance lies not in what we possess, but in our capacity to appreciate what we have and to share it generously with others.

Saints associated with the Harvest Festival in New Universalism include **Saint Pachamama**, the Andean Earth Mother revered for her role as a provider and sustainer of life, symbolizing the generosity and nurturing power of nature; and **Saint Moses**, known for his guidance and leadership, who represents the strength found in unity and communal support. These figures remind followers of the importance of giving thanks, supporting one another, and recognizing the interconnectedness of all life.

Ceremonies, Rites, and Rituals

The Harvest Festival is celebrated through rituals that honor the Earth's abundance, the blessings of community, and the practice of gratitude:

1. **Gratitude Circle**: In communal settings, followers may form a gratitude circle, where each participant shares something they are thankful for from the past season. This ritual fosters a sense of unity and appreciation, allowing individuals to express their gratitude and to recognize the blessings that sustain them. The circle concludes with a collective offering of thanks to the Earth, acknowledging the role of nature in providing for the community.

2. **Harvest Sharing and Communal Feast**: The Harvest Festival is often marked by a shared meal, featuring fresh, seasonal foods. Each person or family is invited to bring a dish made from local ingredients, symbolizing the collective abundance of the harvest. This communal feast reinforces the value of sharing and gratitude, as participants break bread together, recognizing that they are nourished not only by the food but by the bonds of community.

3. **Creation of an Altar or Offering Space**: Followers may create a temporary altar or offering space, decorated with seasonal fruits, grains, flowers, and herbs. Each item represents the blessings of the Earth and serves as a visual expression of gratitude. Some may choose to place written notes of appreciation or small tokens of intention on the altar, symbolizing their thanks for the gifts of the season. The altar is often dismantled at the end of the festival, with items shared, composted, or returned to nature as a final act of reciprocity.

4. **Acts of Service and Charity**: In alignment with the themes of sharing and support, followers are encouraged to give back to their communities through acts of service or charity. This might include volunteering, donating food or resources, or assisting those in need. By engaging in acts of kindness, followers honor the festival's values and reinforce the New Universalist commitment to social responsibility and compassion.

Guidance for Independent and Communal Observance

For **independent observance**, followers may begin by creating a small altar or offering space in their home, arranging seasonal fruits, grains, or flowers as a gesture of gratitude. Personal reflections on gratitude, written in a journal or expressed through silent contemplation, allow individuals to connect deeply with the theme of the season. Many choose to perform a simple ritual of thanks, perhaps by lighting a candle or offering a token to the Earth, to acknowledge the blessings they have received.

In **communal settings**, the Harvest Festival is celebrated with a shared meal, gratitude circle, and communal offerings. Ministers may lead a reflection on the theme of abundance, guiding participants in recognizing the ways they have been blessed and encouraging acts of generosity toward others. The group may conclude with a service activity, such as preparing food for a local shelter or organizing a community donation, reinforcing the values of sharing and support.

The **celebration of the Harvest Festival** in New Universalism is a time for giving thanks, honoring the Earth, and strengthening community bonds. This festival encourages followers to embrace a spirit of generosity, to recognize the abundance in their lives, and to share these blessings with others. By observing the Harvest Festival, New Universalists reaffirm their commitment to gratitude, reciprocity, and communal care, nurturing a sense of fulfillment that comes not from accumulation, but from the willingness to give and to serve.

Autumn Equinox - September 21

The Autumn Equinox, observed on September 21, marks a point of balance when day and night are of equal length, ushering in a season of reflection, gratitude, and inner preparation. As the Earth transitions from the fullness of summer to the quiet of winter, followers of New Universalism are invited to pause and reflect on their own journey, honoring the year's blessings and acknowledging the changes to come. The Equinox symbolizes balance and acceptance, a time to let go of what is complete and to focus inward, preparing for the introspection of winter.

The Autumn Equinox is a time of "inner harvest," a chance to celebrate personal and communal growth while letting go of what no longer serves us. In New Universalism, this festival emphasizes the value of gratitude, self-reflection, and embracing life's transitions with grace. Just as the trees release their leaves, we, too, are encouraged to release, simplify, and find peace in the balance between light and dark, action and rest.

Spiritual Teachings and Symbolism

The Autumn Equinox aligns with teachings on balance, transition, and the acceptance of change. **Confucian philosophy**, which values harmony and the wisdom of nature, resonates with the Equinox's themes of reflection and inner balance. The teachings of **Buddhism**, with its focus on impermanence and the art of letting go, also align with this season, encouraging followers to release attachments and embrace the natural flow of life.

Saints associated with the Autumn Equinox in New Universalism include **Saint Francis of Assisi**, who exemplifies humility, gratitude, and respect for nature, and **Saint Teresa of Avila**, known for her emphasis on inner peace, contemplation, and simplicity. These figures serve as guides for those seeking to find balance, humility, and spiritual depth as they enter the quiet season.

Ceremonies, Rites, and Rituals

The Autumn Equinox is observed through rituals that emphasize gratitude, balance, and the gentle release of what is no longer needed:

1. **Creation of a Gratitude Altar**: Followers may create an altar decorated with seasonal fruits, nuts, leaves, and symbols of the harvest. Each item represents a blessing or accomplishment from the past year. During the ritual, individuals place objects or notes on the altar to symbolize what they are grateful for, grounding themselves in appreciation and honoring the abundance of their lives.

2. **Balancing Ritual**: In communal settings, participants may engage in a balancing ritual where they reflect on areas of their lives that need harmony. This could involve lighting two candles—one for light and one for dark—or placing objects representing opposing qualities (such as stones and feathers) on a central altar. This ritual serves as a visual reminder of the beauty and necessity of balance, encouraging followers to embrace both the joys and challenges of life.

3. **Meditative Walk in Nature**: A walk through nature during the Equinox allows followers to witness the beauty of transition firsthand. This meditative practice encourages mindfulness and acceptance, as individuals observe the falling leaves, the cooling air, and the gradual shift in light. This walk can be performed individually or as a group, with participants encouraged to reflect on what they are releasing and what they wish to carry forward.

4. **Release Ceremony**: In alignment with the Equinox's themes of letting go, a release ceremony allows followers to symbolically release what is complete. This may involve writing down fears, regrets, or attachments on slips of paper and then burning them or burying them in the Earth. This ritual fosters a sense of closure and renewal, creating space for introspection and the quiet growth that winter brings.

Guidance for Independent and Communal Observance

For **independent observance**, followers may start by creating a personal gratitude altar, arranging autumn leaves, fruits, or other seasonal items as symbols of appreciation. A journal reflection on balance and transition allows individuals to explore the areas of their lives where they seek harmony and peace. Some may choose to perform a release ceremony, letting go of old habits or attachments to prepare for the introspective season ahead.

In **communal settings**, the Autumn Equinox may begin with the creation of a shared altar, where each participant contributes a token of gratitude. Ministers may lead a guided meditation or balancing ritual, encouraging participants to reflect on themes of release, acceptance, and preparation for winter. A nature walk as a group, followed by a release ceremony, allows the community to bond through shared reflection, creating a sense of unity in the journey through life's cycles.

The **celebration of the Autumn Equinox** in New Universalism is a time to honor both abundance and transition, to celebrate the balance of life, and to embrace the wisdom of letting go. By observing this festival, followers are reminded of the beauty of harmony, the value of reflection, and the importance of accepting change with grace. The Autumn Equinox encourages New Universalists to find peace within themselves, to embrace life's transitions, and to prepare for the inward journey of winter

All Souls Day - October 31

All Souls Day, observed on October 31, marks the end of the harvest season and the beginning of winter's quiet descent. In New Universalism, this festival is a sacred day for honoring ancestors, remembering loved ones who have passed, and embracing the mystery and beauty of life's cyclical nature. As the natural world shifts into a season of rest, All Souls Day invites followers to connect deeply with their roots, celebrate their heritage, and acknowledge the presence of those who have shaped their lives. This day reflects a blending of practices from traditions such as Samhain, Halloween, the Day of the Dead, and Tomb Sweeping Day, creating a time for both reverence and celebration.

The night of All Souls Day is believed to be a time when the veil between the physical world and the spirit world is at its thinnest, allowing the living and departed to share a moment of connection. In New Universalism, this festival holds dual themes of honoring our ancestors and celebrating the journey of the soul. Through rituals, offerings, costumes, and shared stories, followers recognize the influence of those who came before, express gratitude for their legacy, and prepare to journey together through the season of reflection and inner growth.

Spiritual Teachings and Symbolism

All Souls Day resonates with teachings on remembrance, ancestral reverence, and the cycles of life and death. **Buddhist philosophy** on impermanence encourages followers to embrace mortality with acceptance, viewing death as a natural part of life's cycle. Similarly, **Indigenous and African traditions** that emphasize ancestral wisdom inspire New Universalists to honor and remember the past, recognizing the strength and guidance of those who have paved the way.

Saints associated with All Souls Day include **Saint Lazarus**, who symbolizes renewal and transformation beyond death, and **Saint Dymphna**, the patron of mental and emotional healing, offering comfort to those in mourning or reflection. These figures remind followers that memory and legacy continue to nourish us, even as we honor those who have passed from the physical realm.

Ceremonies, Rites, and Rituals

All Souls Day is observed through a range of rituals that honor ancestors, celebrate life, and allow followers to connect with their heritage and loved ones:

1. **Ancestral Altar and Offerings**: Followers may create an altar dedicated to their ancestors, adorned with photos, keepsakes, seasonal fruits, candles, and symbolic offerings of food and drink. Each item on the altar serves as an expression of gratitude and remembrance, creating a space where the living can commune with the departed. Small portions of favorite foods or traditional dishes may be placed on the altar as an offering, symbolizing nourishment for the spirit and the belief that those we honor continue to live within and around us.

2. **Lighting a Candle for Ancestral Guidance**: In keeping with the tradition of leaving a light for wandering souls, followers light candles in honor of their ancestors. This candle is often placed on a window ledge or the ancestral altar, symbolizing guidance for the spirits' journey and a welcome invitation for them to join in the celebration. The candlelight represents the continuity of life, memory, and the lasting connection between past and present.

3. **Costume and Mask Traditions**: Reflecting the historical roots of wearing costumes as a way to honor spirits and the mysteries of the otherworld, many New Universalists dress in costumes on All Souls Day. Costumes can represent an aspect of one's heritage, embody a specific virtue or ancestor, or honor the transformative power of the soul's journey. Some may wear masks to symbolize the unity of all beings, both living and departed, and to remind us that life and death are intertwined.

4. **Gravesite Visits and Tomb Sweeping**: For those with access to ancestral graves, visiting these sites is a traditional way to honor the departed. Followers may clean and decorate the graves with flowers, candles, or symbolic offerings, taking a moment to reflect on the legacy of those who rest there. This ritual, inspired by Tomb Sweeping Day, is both an act of respect and a reminder of the sacred continuity that binds all generations.

5. **Storytelling and Remembrance Circles**: In communal settings, followers gather to share stories, memories, or reflections about loved ones who have passed. This circle of remembrance allows individuals to celebrate the lives of those they honor, to offer comfort and solidarity to one another, and to recognize the shared journey of life and death. Through storytelling, participants bring the memories of their loved ones into the present, reinforcing the connection between past and future generations.

Guidance for Independent and Communal Observance

For **independent observance**, followers may create a small ancestral altar in their homes, arranging photos, candles, or other meaningful items as symbols of connection and gratitude. Lighting a candle and spending a few moments in quiet reflection allows individuals to honor their ancestors and to contemplate their own journey within life's cycle. Some may prepare a small offering of food or drink, placed on the altar as a gesture of unity and respect, symbolizing the nourishment of memory and the soul.

In **communal settings**, All Souls Day often begins with a candle-lighting ceremony to honor the departed, with each participant lighting a candle for their loved ones or ancestors. Ministers may lead a guided meditation or reflection on the themes of mortality, continuity, and the beauty of life's transitions. The community may gather in a remembrance circle, sharing stories, memories, or words of appreciation for those who have passed. Some communities may hold a shared meal, featuring foods that are traditional to each participant's family or culture, deepening the connection to heritage and honoring the ongoing legacy of the departed.

The **celebration of All Souls Day in New Universalism** blends the solemnity of remembrance with the warmth of celebration, inviting followers to reflect on the wisdom and presence of those who have shaped them. By observing this festival, New Universalists honor their ancestors, recognize the beauty and mystery of life's transitions, and strengthen their connection to the past, present, and future. All Souls Day serves as a reminder that our stories and lives are part of a greater cycle, and that the love, memory, and wisdom of those who have passed continue to illuminate our journey.

All Saints Day - November 1

All Saints Day, celebrated on November 1, is a festival dedicated to honoring humanity's collective spiritual heritage. In New Universalism, this day is a celebration of individuals across time, faiths, and philosophies who have embodied universal virtues—such as compassion, wisdom, justice, and humility. All Saints Day honors saints, prophets, philosophers, and other notable figures from diverse traditions who have devoted their lives to serving humanity, advancing spiritual understanding, and upholding values that resonate with New Universalist principles.

This day offers followers a chance to reflect on the interconnectedness of all spiritual traditions, recognizing that wisdom and virtue are universal threads woven across cultures and histories. All Saints Day reinforces New Universalism's commitment to inclusivity and respect for all spiritual paths, encouraging followers to find inspiration in a broad array of teachings and lives. By celebrating saints from diverse backgrounds, followers are invited to honor the lives and legacies that uplift humanity and to embody similar virtues in their own lives.

Spiritual Teachings and Symbolism

All Saints Day embodies inclusivity, unity, and respect for diverse spiritual perspectives. **Sikh teachings** on equality and selfless service resonate with the inclusive spirit of this festival, while **Taoist philosophy** on the harmony of all beings aligns with the interwoven nature of diverse spiritual insights. By honoring saints from various backgrounds, New Universalists affirm the belief that spiritual truth exists in all traditions and that wisdom transcends cultural boundaries.

A varied selection of saints honored on All Saints Day in New Universalism may include figures such as **Saint Sor Juana Inés de la Cruz**, a Mexican nun and scholar celebrated for her contributions to knowledge, spirituality, and women's rights; **Saint Nicholas of Myra**, revered for his acts of kindness and generosity toward children and the less fortunate; **Saint Hakuin Ekaku**, a Japanese Zen monk known for his profound teachings on enlightenment and compassion; and **Sojourner Truth**, an abolitionist and advocate for human rights who exemplifies courage, resilience, and dedication to justice. These figures, along with countless others, remind followers of the universality of virtue and the shared journey toward spiritual growth.

Followers are also encouraged to personalize their recognition of saints, honoring individuals who resonate with their unique spiritual path and values. By selecting saints and patron saints who inspire them personally, New Universalists foster a meaningful and individualized approach to this celebration.

Ceremonies, Rites, and Rituals

All Saints Day is observed through rituals that honor diversity, encourage unity, and inspire followers to live by universal values:

1. **Creation of a Multifaith Altar**: Followers may create an altar that includes symbols, images, or writings from various spiritual traditions. Items representing saints, philosophers, and notable figures from diverse backgrounds are placed together, symbolizing the unity of spiritual values across cultures. This altar serves as a space for reflection, inviting followers to connect with the teachings and virtues of these figures and find inspiration for their own spiritual journeys.

2. **Reading and Reflection on Sacred Texts**: In both communal and individual settings, followers may read passages from sacred texts, philosophical writings, or poetry that reflect themes of unity, compassion, and wisdom. Each reading reminds participants of humanity's shared pursuit of truth and understanding. After each reading, followers may take a moment for reflection, allowing the words to deepen their commitment to universal values and personal growth.

3. **Lighting of Candles for Universal Virtues**: A ritual of candle lighting can be held, with each candle representing a different virtue, such as compassion, humility, courage, and wisdom. As each candle is lit, participants reflect on the lives of saints who have embodied these

qualities. This ritual reinforces the belief that these virtues are universal and encourages each person to strive to live in alignment with them.

4. **Personal Dedication or Commitment**: All Saints Day is also a time for followers to reflect on their own values and consider how they can embody the virtues they admire. In communal settings, this may involve a quiet moment where each participant makes a personal commitment to uphold a specific value, inspired by the saints and figures they honor. This dedication serves as a renewal of one's commitment to live with integrity and compassion.

Guidance for Independent and Communal Observance

For **independent observance**, followers may create a small multifaith altar at home, arranging symbols, writings, or images that represent saints or figures they feel personally connected to. A period of meditation or reflection on the lives and teachings of these individuals can help deepen one's sense of purpose and connection to universal values. Lighting candles, each representing a virtue or figure, provides a meaningful way to internalize the day's themes, and personal journaling can offer a space to express gratitude for the inspiration these figures provide.

In **communal settings**, All Saints Day may begin with the creation of a shared altar where each participant contributes a symbol, image, or passage that represents a saint or figure they wish to honor. Ministers may lead a series of readings from diverse sacred texts or philosophical writings, each followed by a moment of reflection. Participants may then light candles for universal virtues, with each person sharing a brief reflection on a figure who embodies a particular quality. The communal observance often concludes with a moment of silence or a group affirmation, encouraging all present to carry forward the inspiration of the day into their lives.

The **celebration of All Saints Day in New Universalism** is a testament to the richness and diversity of human wisdom. By honoring saints and notable figures from all backgrounds, followers are reminded of the interconnectedness of spiritual truth and the shared values that unite humanity. This festival encourages New Universalists to find guidance in the lives of those who have come before, to celebrate the beauty of diverse traditions, and to live in harmony with values that transcend individual paths. All Saints Day serves as a source of inspiration, reminding followers that each person has the potential to embody virtues that uplift and unite all beings.

The Significance of Observances in New Universalism

The Wheel of the Year is more than a series of seasonal celebrations—it is a living expression of New Universalism's core values and an invitation to engage with life's rhythms in a way that fosters personal growth, communal unity, and deep reverence for the Earth. Each festival represents a distinct aspect of the human experience, encouraging followers to reconnect with nature, honor shared values, and explore spiritual truths with Reasoned Inquiry as the foundation of this journey.

At the heart of New Universalism is the principle of **Reasoned Inquiry**—the belief that reason guides the search for truth and spiritual meaning, which can be found in all faiths, philosophies, and human experiences. This principle forms the theological foundation of New Universalism, guiding followers to explore each observance thoughtfully and to draw meaning from diverse sources. Rooted in this principle, the Wheel of the Year invites followers to approach each celebration with reflection, curiosity, and openness to universal wisdom.

Through these observances, New Universalists are encouraged to practice **Earth Stewardship**, **Filial Piety**, and **Social Responsibility**, fostering connections to nature, community, and humanity. Each festival becomes an opportunity to deepen awareness of the natural world, nurture communal bonds, and explore spiritual truths through a lens of reason and universal inquiry.

Embodiment of New Universalism's Core Values

Each festival within the Wheel of the Year reflects New Universalism's core values in unique ways, reinforcing a commitment to living with gratitude, integrity, and compassion. Observances such as **Earth Day** and the **Harvest Festival** embody Earth Stewardship, calling followers to honor the planet and engage in sustainable practices. Festivals like **All Souls Day** and **All Saints Day** reinforce Filial Piety, encouraging followers to honor their ancestors and uphold traditions of respect for those who came before.

Social Responsibility is interwoven throughout the Wheel of the Year, fostering a sense of collective care and service. Celebrations such as the **Harvest Festival**, where communal feasts emphasize sharing and support, and **May Day**, with its joyful celebration of life's interconnectedness, encourage followers to live with compassion and to engage actively in their communities. By participating in these festivals, followers not only honor these values but also reinforce the understanding that we each hold a role in creating a just and inclusive world.

At each observance, followers are encouraged to apply **Reasoned Inquiry**—approaching their celebrations thoughtfully, reflecting on teachings from diverse traditions, and allowing new insights to emerge. By practicing reflection and curiosity, followers can deepen their understanding of these values and gain insights that resonate with their personal and communal journeys.

Supporting Personal Growth and Community Unity

The festivals of the Wheel of the Year serve as both personal milestones and communal experiences, fostering unity, shared purpose, and growth. Individually, followers use the festivals as markers for self-reflection, contemplating their lives in relation to the themes of each season. Whether setting intentions at the **Spring Festival** or expressing gratitude at the **Autumn Equinox**, followers are invited to align their actions with the highest values of New Universalism.

In communal settings, the festivals strengthen bonds and celebrate the power of shared rituals. Through group meditations, feasts, dance, and acts of service, followers nurture a collective understanding that connects each individual to a larger, interwoven community. The shared experiences of each festival create spaces of mutual respect, support, and inspiration, reinforcing the commitment to values that uplift and unify all.

Encouraging Earth Stewardship, Filial Piety, and Social Responsibility

The observances of the Wheel of the Year remind New Universalists of their responsibility to the Earth, to each other, and to the broader community. **Earth Stewardship** is woven into every festival, inviting followers to honor the land, live sustainably, and acknowledge their role as caretakers of the planet. Whether planting trees on Earth Day or offering seasonal fruits to the land during the Harvest Festival, followers practice reciprocity with nature and affirm their commitment to protect and sustain it.

Filial Piety, the respect for one's elders, ancestors, and community, is deeply connected to these observances. Through rituals honoring the departed on **All Souls Day** or celebrating the legacy of saints on **All Saints Day**, followers uphold traditions of reverence, gratitude, and care. These practices honor the past and strengthen bonds within families and communities, reinforcing an understanding of each person's place within the greater whole.

Social Responsibility extends the values of care and reciprocity to all beings, fostering ethical cooperation and a commitment to justice. New Universalist observances encourage acts of kindness, volunteerism, and support for community needs. By engaging in collective practices and communal gatherings, followers reinforce the belief that humanity's welfare is intertwined with their own, and that living in alignment with social responsibility creates a foundation for peace and equity.

Nurturing a Harmonious Relationship with Nature's Cycles

The Wheel of the Year invites followers to nurture harmony with the cycles of nature, celebrating the balance of light and dark, growth and rest, abundance and simplicity. Each festival reminds followers that life is a cycle, each season offering its own lessons and guidance. The **Summer Solstice** may inspire gratitude for life's fullness, while the **Winter Solstice** encourages reflection and quiet renewal. This seasonal approach fosters resilience, adaptability, and peace as followers learn to live in sync with nature's enduring rhythms.

By aligning their lives with the Earth's cycles, New Universalists cultivate a deep sense of connection to the world and its patterns. This cyclical approach encourages followers to embrace both change and continuity, finding inspiration in the beauty of each season and recognizing their place within life's larger tapestry. The Wheel of the Year becomes a spiritual map that guides followers to live with reverence, reason, and respect for all beings.

Ritual in Earth-Based Faith

The Role of Ritual in Earth-Based Faith

In New Universalism, ritual is a sacred practice that strengthens our connection to nature, celebrates the cycles of life, and reinforces our spiritual values. Through simple, intentional acts, followers engage with the natural world in ways that bring meaning, reflection, and unity to their lives. Rituals, whether personal or communal, are deliberate actions that draw followers into deeper alignment with Earth's rhythms and encourage mindfulness, gratitude, and presence.

Rituals in New Universalism are not only acts of devotion but also expressions of our core values, transforming beliefs into lived experiences. Each ritual—whether a small gesture of lighting a candle or a community gathering to celebrate the harvest—brings followers into communion with the sacred, making spirituality an active, lived experience that honors both the self and the world.

Understanding Ritual as a Sacred Practice

Ritual in New Universalism is a conscious, embodied practice. It is an invitation to enter the present moment with intention, to become fully aware of one's surroundings, and to honor the larger natural world. A simple ritual, such as pausing to observe a sunrise or placing a small offering on a seasonal altar, transforms the ordinary into the sacred. By engaging in rituals aligned with nature's cycles, followers find new layers of connection with the Earth and cultivate an awareness of the beauty in each moment.

In New Universalism, rituals are also **physical expressions of spiritual values**. By intentionally performing acts that reflect beliefs—such as gathering to plant trees, offering prayers for the Earth, or celebrating the seasons—followers ground their values in action. These practices reinforce New Universalism's emphasis on Earth Stewardship, Filial Piety, Social Responsibility, and Reasoned Inquiry, allowing followers to embody these values in ways that are both meaningful and practical.

Purpose and Benefits of Ritual in New Universalism

Rituals within New Universalism serve many purposes, each of which supports individual growth, community connection, and environmental awareness:

- **Reconnecting with Nature**: Rituals draw followers closer to the natural world, inviting them to observe and honor Earth's rhythms. Small acts of reverence, like setting intentions with the lunar cycles or creating seasonal offerings, help followers recognize their role as part of a larger, interconnected world. This practice nurtures the values of Earth Stewardship by fostering appreciation and care for the planet.
- **Fostering Community Unity**: In communal settings, rituals become acts of solidarity, cooperation, and shared purpose. Celebrating seasonal festivals, sharing meals, and performing symbolic acts together remind followers that they are part of a larger whole. Communal rituals create bonds of trust, mutual respect, and collective joy, reinforcing the New Universalist commitment to Social Responsibility.
- **Guiding Self-Reflection and Growth**: Personal rituals offer a space for self-reflection, introspection, and spiritual growth. By aligning with the teachings of each season, followers use these rituals as touchstones for personal development. A winter ritual may inspire contemplation, while a spring ritual might focus on renewal and planting intentions. Each ritual becomes a way to internalize the spiritual lessons of the year and to deepen one's commitment to New Universalist values.

Types of Rituals within the Wheel of the Year

In New Universalism, rituals are both personal and communal, ranging from simple, mindful practices to elaborate seasonal celebrations. Each ritual is an opportunity to engage with nature, community, and oneself in meaningful ways, reinforcing the interconnectedness that defines New Universalism.

- **Personal Rituals**: Small, mindful acts that help individuals align with each season's spirit. These rituals can include lighting a candle as a symbol of hope during the Winter Solstice, keeping a gratitude journal at the time of the Harvest Festival, or taking a silent walk during the Autumn Equinox. Personal rituals create space for solitude and reflection, encouraging followers to contemplate the teachings of each season and integrate them into daily life.

- **Communal Rituals**: Group activities that deepen community bonds and celebrate shared values. Communal rituals might include feasting together, sharing stories that reflect the season's themes, or engaging in symbolic acts such as planting trees, harvesting, or lighting bonfires. These rituals strengthen the connections between followers, fostering a sense of unity, purpose, and mutual support.
- **Seasonal Altars and Offerings**: Creating seasonal altars using natural elements like flowers, stones, fruits, and herbs to honor the cycle of life and express gratitude. These altars serve as focal points for reflection and prayer, changing with each season to mirror Earth's own transformations. Placing offerings on these altars—such as seeds in spring, fruits in summer, and leaves in autumn—becomes a symbolic act of reciprocity and respect for the Earth.
- **Meditative Practices**: Reflective practices that attune practitioners to the wisdom of each season. Meditative rituals, such as silent walks, moon-gazing, or seasonal meditations, provide space for followers to listen to nature's quiet lessons. By practicing stillness and mindfulness, followers cultivate inner peace and awareness, learning to observe the cycles of life with acceptance and patience.

Aligning with Earth's Rhythms through Ritual

Rituals in New Universalism encourage followers to slow down, to be present, and to find harmony with the cycles of nature. By observing and honoring Earth's rhythms, followers reconnect with life's inherent continuity and resilience. These rituals invite followers to step away from the rush of daily life and embrace the steady, grounding presence of nature.

Each ritual serves as a reminder that we are deeply connected to the Earth, and that by aligning with its rhythms, we can cultivate a sense of inner harmony and balance. In winter, rituals of stillness and contemplation help followers enter a quiet space within, preparing for renewal. In spring, acts of planting and creation encourage new beginnings, reflecting the energy of growth and transformation. By observing these patterns, followers find strength, peace, and resilience, embodying the values of New Universalism through simple, sacred practices.

Universal Truths and Wisdom

Across Faiths and Philosophies

3

Truth through Reason and Experience

The Role of Reason in Faith

New Universalism is founded on the belief that reason is not an obstacle to faith but a pathway to deeper understanding. Within New Universalist theology, reason is valued as a sacred tool—a means of exploring spiritual truths, discerning ethical choices, and finding connection with others across diverse beliefs. In this view, reason is not intended to replace faith but to enrich it, guiding followers toward wisdom, empathy, and unity.

Reason as a Pathway

In New Universalism, reason is defined as the faculty that enables individuals to reflect, question, and seek truth. It is an essential aspect of spiritual exploration, moving beyond blind belief to a conscious, thoughtful engagement with one's faith. **Reason within the context of faith** means using discernment to examine beliefs, to weigh ethical choices, and to seek greater clarity about life's mysteries. This approach encourages followers to bring a spirit of inquiry into their practice, exploring questions that illuminate both personal values and universal truths.

Reason is also a **common language** shared across diverse cultures, religions, and philosophies. Throughout history, reasoned inquiry has united humanity in the search for truth, encouraging dialogue and understanding among people with different backgrounds and beliefs. From the teachings of Socratic questioning in Greek philosophy to the critical analysis promoted by Islamic scholars, reason has served as a bridge for meaningful exchange and mutual respect. In New Universalism, reason is seen as a means of expanding empathy, as it allows individuals to connect with others' perspectives, recognizing shared values such as compassion, justice, and love.

In essence, New Universalism teaches that reason and faith are not opposites; rather, they are complementary forces. While faith provides the inner sense of connection to the divine and to the mysteries of existence, reason offers a way to explore these connections thoughtfully and respectfully. This dual approach fosters a faith that is alive, adaptable, and capable of growth—one that resonates not only with personal experience but also with the collective wisdom of humanity.

Reason as a Bridge Across Faiths and Philosophies

In New Universalism, reason is celebrated not only as a personal tool for discernment but as a bridge that connects people across different faiths, philosophies, and cultures. Reasoned inquiry—the practice of questioning, reflecting, and exploring ideas critically—has been central to many spiritual and philosophical traditions throughout history. This shared emphasis on reason underscores the belief that wisdom and understanding are universal pursuits, accessible to all who seek them with an open mind.

By fostering an environment where reason is valued, New Universalism encourages followers to engage with the teachings of varied traditions. This approach not only strengthens individual faith but also builds empathy and respect for others' beliefs, recognizing that many paths lead to shared values and insights about the human condition.

Examples of Reasoned Inquiry Across Traditions

1. **Buddhist Tradition and the Spirit of Inquiry**
   In Buddhism, the Buddha himself encouraged his followers to question all teachings, including his own, and to seek answers through direct experience. This principle, known as the **Kalama Sutta**, teaches that spiritual truths should not be accepted blindly but should be examined, tested, and validated through personal understanding. The Buddha's emphasis on inquiry encourages followers to trust their inner discernment, fostering a faith that is rooted in awareness and personal growth rather than dogma. In New Universalism, this spirit of questioning aligns with the view that reason enhances spiritual exploration, helping individuals find truth through self-reflection and open inquiry.

2. **Greek Philosophy and the Socratic Method**
   Greek philosophy, particularly through the teachings of Socrates, holds reason as a central path to ethical understanding. The **Socratic method**—a process of questioning aimed at uncovering underlying truths and values—has influenced generations of thinkers and remains a model for reasoned inquiry today. Socrates believed that knowledge and virtue were interconnected, teaching that a well-examined life leads to greater wisdom and moral clarity. By encouraging followers to ask questions and explore ideas deeply, New Universalism upholds the Socratic belief that reason can guide individuals to a more compassionate, just, and harmonious life.

3. **Islamic Philosophy and the Harmony of Faith and Reason**

   Within Islamic philosophy, reason is celebrated as a means to understand and deepen one's faith. Prominent Islamic thinkers like **Al-Farabi** and **Averroes** (Ibn Rushd) explored the compatibility between faith and rational inquiry, arguing that true wisdom arises from the integration of spiritual insight with intellectual exploration. In the Islamic tradition, reason is seen as a gift that allows humans to comprehend divine teachings and ethical principles. This perspective is echoed in New Universalism's belief that reason and faith are complementary, each enhancing the other in the pursuit of truth.

4. **Jewish Tradition and the Value of Debate and Interpretation**

   Jewish teachings also honor reason as a path to wisdom, especially within the tradition of **Talmudic study**, where questioning, debating, and interpreting sacred texts are essential practices. This tradition encourages followers to engage actively with teachings, interpreting and reinterpreting them in light of contemporary experiences. The act of engaging in dialogue and debate fosters a vibrant faith that grows and adapts over time. For New Universalists, this approach to study and interpretation mirrors the value placed on reasoned inquiry, allowing beliefs to evolve and adapt while remaining rooted in core values.

5. **Hindu Philosophy and the Path of Knowledge**

   In Hindu philosophy, reason is central to **Jnana Yoga**, the path of knowledge, which emphasizes self-inquiry as a means to reach spiritual enlightenment. Followers of Jnana Yoga are encouraged to question their perceptions, beliefs, and assumptions in order to arrive at a deeper understanding of reality and self. By valuing reason as a tool for self-discovery, Hindu philosophy aligns with New Universalism's view that questioning is not an obstacle to faith but a means of deepening it.

Reason as a Path to Universal Values

Through reasoned inquiry, followers of New Universalism are encouraged to seek understanding and to recognize values that resonate across traditions—concepts like compassion, justice, and humility. When individuals engage in thoughtful questioning, they often find that universal truths emerge, linking their experiences with those of people from other cultures and times. For example, exploring the concept of **compassion** reveals its importance in nearly every spiritual tradition, from the Buddhist teaching of **metta** (loving-kindness) to the Christian ethic of **agape** (unconditional love).

In New Universalism, reasoned inquiry is used not to break down spiritual beliefs but to illuminate them, making room for interpretations that respect the diversity of human experience. By examining shared values through reason, followers are able to approach teachings with clarity, allowing these values to inform their daily actions and relationships.

Aligning Faith with Universal Human Experience

In New Universalism, faith is not an isolated or abstract concept—it is grounded in universal human experience and connected to the realities of everyday life. Through reason, followers are encouraged to examine their beliefs and practices in light of shared human values and insights that resonate across cultures and times. By rooting faith in experiences common to all people—such as love, suffering, compassion, and joy—New Universalists cultivate a spirituality that is both inclusive and deeply personal.

Reason as a Means of Connecting Faith with Daily Life

Reason offers a pathway to understanding how spiritual beliefs align with and support everyday experiences. In New Universalism, faith is not confined to sacred texts or rituals but is seen as a living practice, woven into the fabric of daily life. Through reasoned inquiry, followers reflect on how their beliefs inform their actions, relationships, and choices, ensuring that spirituality remains both practical and transformative.

For instance, the universal value of **compassion** finds expression not only in acts of kindness but also in the understanding that compassion is an essential part of a just society. Followers of New Universalism may reflect on this value in various contexts—whether in personal relationships, community work, or advocacy—seeking ways to live compassionately. By applying reason to these reflections, followers develop a more nuanced understanding of compassion, finding ways to embody it in their own unique lives.

Faith and Reason as Complementary Forces

New Universalism teaches that faith and reason are not opposing forces but mutually enriching aspects of a full spiritual life. Faith provides a sense of connection, meaning, and openness to the unknown, while reason offers clarity, structure, and a means of exploring these connections thoughtfully. Together, faith and reason create a balanced approach to spirituality, where beliefs are both heartfelt and well-considered.

This relationship between faith and reason is exemplified in **the teachings of Confucianism**, where a sense of duty and respect is balanced by a deep commitment to rational thought and ethical discernment. Similarly, in **Taoism**, followers are encouraged to observe nature and draw wisdom from its patterns, using both intuition and logic to understand life's flow. These examples reflect New Universalism's belief that a truly meaningful faith is one that values both conviction and reflection.

By holding faith and reason in harmony, New Universalists can approach their spirituality with confidence, curiosity, and openness to new insights. This balance helps followers navigate the complexities of life, providing a framework for understanding not only the joys of connection and love but also the challenges of suffering, change, and loss.

Shared Human Experiences as Pathways to Spiritual Truths

New Universalism emphasizes that the search for spiritual truth is not limited to any single doctrine or tradition. Instead, spiritual truths are found in the common experiences that unite all people. Reason allows followers to reflect on these shared experiences and recognize the values and insights they contain.

For example, **forgiveness** is a concept that appears in many religious and philosophical traditions, from the Christian teaching of forgiving others as a path to healing, to the Buddhist practice of releasing anger for inner peace. By reflecting on the experience of forgiveness, New Universalists can see it as both a personal and a universal truth—an act that not only heals relationships but also fosters inner freedom and growth.

Similarly, **the concept of justice** resonates across cultures, whether it's the Jewish call to pursue justice (tzedakah) or the Islamic principle of fairness (adl). Reason allows followers to explore these teachings in ways that are applicable to their own lives and communities, encouraging them to contribute to a more equitable world. In New Universalism, these shared values are viewed as sacred, representing humanity's ongoing commitment to compassion, integrity, and mutual respect.

The Journey of Faith as a Reflection of Life's Cycles

New Universalism encourages followers to view their spiritual journey as a reflection of the cycles found in nature and life itself. By observing these rhythms—such as growth, harvest, rest, and renewal—followers find inspiration and guidance for their own journey. Reason allows followers to see patterns within their experiences, drawing wisdom from life's natural cycles and recognizing the continuity of growth and transformation.

In this way, faith becomes a dynamic journey that mirrors life itself, marked by questions, discoveries, setbacks, and renewals. New Universalists are invited to explore their beliefs through reason, discovering new insights that enrich their faith and bring clarity to their lives. Each festival, ritual, or personal reflection becomes an opportunity to align with the Earth's rhythms, fostering resilience and adaptability in the face of life's changes.

Through reason, followers find strength and inspiration in these shared human experiences, recognizing that each person's journey contributes to a larger, universal story. This perspective creates a sense of belonging, purpose, and unity, affirming that, despite our differences, we all participate in the same unfolding journey of life.

Living a Balanced Faith Rooted in Reason

New Universalism teaches that a balanced faith, rooted in reason, is one that honors both the head and the heart. Through reasoned inquiry, followers find ways to apply their beliefs to real-world challenges, using their faith to inspire action, resilience, and compassion. This approach makes faith a lived experience, encouraging followers to question, reflect, and grow in alignment with universal truths and shared human values.

In this way, reason and faith together create a spirituality that is as dynamic and adaptable as life itself. New Universalists are called to embrace both the mystery and the clarity of their beliefs, to question and to trust, to learn and to grow. By engaging with faith through reason, followers cultivate a spirituality that evolves with them, providing strength and insight for each stage of life's journey.

Universal Wisdom in Human Experience

Wisdom is not confined to any single tradition but is recognized as a gift shared across cultures and ages. This universal wisdom is woven into humanity's shared values, reflecting common aspirations for compassion, integrity, humility, and respect. By embracing these values, New Universalists honor a rich inheritance of insight and strive to embody a faith rooted in both reverence and reason.

Introduction to Universal Values

At the heart of New Universalism lies the belief in **universal values**—core principles such as compassion, humility, kindness, and integrity that have emerged across cultures and philosophies as essential elements of human flourishing. These values are not only ethical guides; they represent the collective wisdom of humanity, responding to the needs, challenges, and joys of life. Through these values, people find a shared language of care, resilience, and responsibility, illuminating pathways toward a more harmonious world.

Universal values reflect humanity's innate capacity for empathy and the desire for connection. **Compassion**, for example, is a value that appears in countless forms and expressions, from religious teachings to secular philosophies. This shared reverence for compassion teaches followers to see the divine in each other, fostering social bonds that sustain communities. **Humility**, another deeply respected value, teaches openness and self-awareness, allowing individuals to recognize their place within a larger whole. By cultivating humility, New Universalists are reminded of their connection to each other and to the natural world, encouraging a life of respect and balance.

These values are as relevant today as they were in ancient times, guiding New Universalists to align their actions with the needs of their communities and the Earth. **Integrity**—the commitment to act in alignment with one's values and responsibilities—teaches accountability and respect for others. Integrity calls New Universalists to live with honor, to uphold their commitments, and to treat all beings with dignity and fairness.

In New Universalism, these values serve as **pillars of ethical guidance and spiritual practice**, bringing followers into alignment with both human and ecological relationships. They create a framework of understanding and action that transcends differences in culture or belief, allowing followers to recognize themselves as part of a global community. Through embracing universal wisdom, New Universalists find a path to spiritual fulfillment that is deeply rooted in common human experience and oriented toward the well-being of all.

The Role of Compassion in Universal Teachings

Compassion is a value that transcends individual belief systems, woven into the teachings of diverse religions, philosophies, and cultures. In New Universalism, compassion is considered both a spiritual imperative and a practical guide for living harmoniously. By embracing compassion, followers connect with the heart of humanity, finding shared purpose in the pursuit of kindness, understanding, and justice. Compassion is not simply an emotion; it is a commitment to see and honor the inherent worth in others, responding to suffering with empathy and active care.

Compassion Across Traditions: A Shared Value

Across spiritual traditions, compassion emerges as a central teaching, reminding followers of the bond that unites all beings. The value of compassion is especially profound because it urges individuals to transcend self-interest, cultivating a sense of interconnectedness that forms the basis for social harmony. In **Christianity**, the commandment to "love your neighbor as yourself" (Mark 12:31) reflects compassion's role in fostering community. Jesus's teachings emphasize mercy, kindness, and forgiveness, inspiring followers to practice compassion as a way to honor the divine presence within each person.

Buddhism further reinforces compassion through the practice of **karuna**, a commitment to relieve the suffering of others. In Buddhist teachings, compassion is inseparable from wisdom, as understanding the interconnectedness of life naturally gives rise to empathy. Followers of Buddhism are encouraged to cultivate **metta**, or loving-kindness, toward all beings, viewing compassion as both an ethical duty and a pathway to enlightenment. This teaching resonates with New Universalism's view of compassion as a bridge between individuals, fostering a sense of shared purpose and collective well-being.

In **Hinduism** and **Jainism**, the principle of **ahimsa**, or non-violence, underscores the importance of compassion as a guiding force. Ahimsa teaches followers to avoid harm in thought, word, and action, embracing compassion as a means of respecting the sanctity of all life. This commitment to non-violence extends beyond physical actions, encouraging followers to cultivate compassion as a way to honor the divine within each being. New Universalism draws upon this perspective, recognizing that compassion is both an internal and external practice, shaping how followers interact with themselves, others, and the Earth.

In **Islam**, compassion is a fundamental attribute of Allah, reflected in the name **Ar-Rahman** (The Compassionate). The teachings of the Quran encourage followers to embody this divine attribute, practicing mercy and kindness in their interactions. Islamic ethics emphasize generosity, charity, and empathy, urging followers to care for those in need as a reflection of divine compassion. Through this lens, compassion becomes a means of spiritual growth and service, inspiring New Universalists to approach others with an open heart, seeking unity through empathy.

Secular philosophies also recognize the transformative power of compassion. In the **writings of Confucius**, compassion, or **ren**, is considered essential to the cultivation of virtuous character. Confucius taught that compassion is the root of harmony within families, communities, and societies, reflecting the interconnectedness of all people. **Humanist philosophy** similarly upholds compassion as a moral imperative, viewing empathy as the foundation of ethical behavior and social justice. New Universalism draws from these secular teachings, recognizing that compassion unites people beyond religious boundaries, serving as a universal call to honor each other's dignity.

The Transformative Impact of Compassion

Compassion, as understood in New Universalism, is a practice that transforms both the individual and the community. By choosing compassion, followers align themselves with a spirit of generosity and understanding that nurtures collective well-being. Compassion encourages acts of kindness and selflessness, teaching that by caring for others, individuals find fulfillment and purpose. In many ways, compassion serves as a guide for social responsibility, inspiring New Universalists to engage in acts of service, to advocate for justice, and to offer support where it is needed.

The impact of compassion extends beyond personal interactions. Compassionate communities are marked by mutual respect, active support, and a commitment to the welfare of all. In societies where compassion is valued, social bonds are strengthened, and conflicts are approached with a willingness to understand rather than condemn. New Universalists are encouraged to contribute to compassionate communities by embodying the values of respect, patience, and empathy, viewing each person as an essential part of the whole.

In addition to its social effects, compassion fosters personal growth, allowing individuals to cultivate resilience and inner peace. When followers approach challenges and suffering with compassion, they gain the ability to respond rather than react, finding strength in gentleness. By practicing compassion toward oneself, individuals learn to forgive their mistakes, to honor their journeys, and to approach life with kindness and grace. This self-compassion is as essential as compassion for others, as it builds a foundation of self-respect and inner harmony.

Compassion as a Core Principle in New Universalist Theology

In New Universalist theology, compassion is recognized as a sacred practice—a way of living that honors the unity and dignity of all life. Compassion is more than an ideal; it is a conscious choice to act with kindness, to listen with empathy, and to care for others as an expression of shared humanity. New Universalists view compassion as an active commitment to uphold the well-being of all beings, recognizing that every person's journey is interconnected.

Through compassion, followers experience a profound sense of connection that transcends differences in belief, culture, and background. This connection becomes a source of spiritual strength, providing guidance and purpose for those who seek to live in harmony with New Universalist values. As a core principle, compassion encourages followers to cultivate relationships that are built on respect, integrity, and genuine care.

In practice, New Universalists are called to make compassion a part of their daily lives. Acts of kindness, listening without judgment, offering support to those in need, and treating others with respect are ways in which compassion becomes a living force within the community. This commitment to compassion reflects New Universalism's aspiration to create a world that is inclusive, peaceful, and just.

Humility and Self-Understanding Across Cultures

Humility is valued as a practice of self-awareness, respect, and openness. Humility allows followers to see themselves clearly, acknowledging their strengths as well as their limitations, and recognizing their place within a larger whole. Humility is not only about modesty; it is a way of being that fosters personal growth, enhances empathy, and nurtures an openness to wisdom from others. Across diverse cultures and spiritual traditions, humility has been upheld as an essential virtue, guiding individuals toward a balanced and harmonious life.

Humility as a Path to Self-Understanding

Humility encourages followers to approach life with a sense of reverence, acknowledging that there is always more to learn and discover. In New Universalist theology, humility is a pathway to self-understanding, a means of deepening one's awareness of both the inner and outer worlds. By cultivating humility, followers are reminded of the limitations of personal knowledge, fostering an openness to new insights and experiences.

Humility teaches individuals to look beyond the self, recognizing that each person is part of a larger, interconnected world. In many ways, humility frees followers from the need for constant validation, allowing them to live with authenticity and to act from a place of integrity. New Universalism sees humility as a way of aligning with life's natural rhythms, inviting individuals to embrace the ebb and flow of existence without the need for control or dominance.

Teachings of Humility Across Traditions

1. **Buddhist Practice of Self-Restraint**

   In Buddhism, humility is deeply connected to the practice of **self-restraint** and the reduction of ego. By cultivating humility, followers learn to let go of attachment to personal desires and identity, finding peace in selflessness. The Buddhist teachings of **anatta** (no-self) encourage practitioners to see beyond individual ego, recognizing the impermanent and interconnected nature of life. This humility allows individuals to approach others with kindness and openness, seeing themselves as part of the same flow of existence.

2. **Christian Emphasis on Humility before God and Others**

   In Christianity, humility is often expressed as an attitude of reverence toward God and service to others. The teaching to "humble yourselves before the Lord" (James 4:10) reflects humility as a means of surrendering pride and accepting divine guidance. Jesus's life is often cited as a model of humility, showing compassion, kindness, and a willingness to serve. For New Universalists, this humility teaches the importance of placing service to others above self-interest, fostering a community that values cooperation and empathy.

3. **Islamic Teaching of Humility and Submission**

   In Islam, humility is essential to the concept of **submission** (Islam itself means "submission to God's will"). Muslims are encouraged to act with humility toward both God and their fellow beings, recognizing that human knowledge and power are limited. The Prophet Muhammad is quoted as saying, "Whoever has an atom's weight of pride in his heart will not enter Paradise," underscoring the importance of humility in spiritual practice. This teaching aligns with New Universalist values by promoting self-restraint, respect for others, and the willingness to serve a purpose beyond the self.

4. **Taoist Wisdom of Yielding and Balance**

   In Taoism, humility is viewed as an expression of alignment with the **Tao**, or the natural flow of life. Taoist teachings encourage followers to embrace **wu wei** (effortless action), which emphasizes yielding, adapting, and letting go of the need to control. Humility is seen as a means of finding balance, recognizing that true strength often comes from softness and flexibility. This perspective teaches New Universalists to approach life with openness and adaptability, cultivating humility as a means of finding harmony within oneself and with the world.

5. **Secular and Indigenous Perspectives on Humility and Connection**

   In many Indigenous cultures, humility is regarded as a recognition of one's role within the community and the natural world. Indigenous teachings often emphasize the importance of honoring the Earth, respecting one's ancestors, and acting with humility in relation to the environment. Humility is expressed as an understanding that all beings are interconnected and that humans are part of, not above, the natural world. This resonates with New Universalist values, encouraging followers to approach the Earth with reverence and to see themselves as caretakers within a larger web of life.

In secular philosophy, humility is also recognized as a virtue that enables individuals to cultivate ethical relationships. Thinkers such as **Albert Schweitzer** emphasized "reverence for life" as a guiding principle, teaching that humility fosters respect and empathy toward all beings. **Humanism** further upholds humility as a means of living with integrity, promoting self-awareness, respect for others' perspectives, and a commitment to the common good.

How Humility Nurtures Personal Growth and Community Harmony

In New Universalism, humility is understood as a practice that nurtures both personal growth and harmonious relationships within the community. By cultivating humility, followers open themselves to learning, growth, and transformation, recognizing that wisdom is found in a multitude of voices and experiences. Humility teaches patience and acceptance, allowing individuals to engage in dialogue, embrace differences, and approach others with respect.

Personal growth is rooted in the willingness to acknowledge one's own limitations and to seek improvement. Humility encourages followers to look inward with honesty, seeing both strengths and areas for growth. This self-reflection fosters a deeper understanding of one's role and responsibilities, creating a foundation for ethical action and self-improvement.

Within the community, humility serves as a basis for unity and cooperation. A humble community is one that values each member's contributions, respects differing perspectives, and upholds the common good over individual gain. By practicing humility, New Universalists create an environment of trust, mutual support, and shared purpose, where individuals are free to express themselves while remaining mindful of the needs of others.

Humility as a Path to Openness and Learning

Humility in New Universalism is seen not as self-deprecation, but as a path to openness. It teaches followers to approach each interaction with a willingness to learn, embracing the understanding that every person holds unique insights. By cultivating humility, individuals become receptive to wisdom in all its forms—whether from nature, traditions, or personal experience.

This openness fosters a lifelong commitment to growth, encouraging followers to remain curious, adaptable, and open to change. Humility, as a guiding principle, strengthens the New Universalist commitment to Reasoned Inquiry, as it reminds followers that truth is vast, evolving, and accessible to those who seek it with an open heart and mind.

In practice, humility empowers followers to recognize the beauty and strength in vulnerability, the potential for learning in each experience, and the sacredness of each person's journey. By cultivating humility, New Universalists honor their place within the world, recognizing that each individual is part of a greater, interconnected whole.

Understanding Through Shared Human Experience

Shared human experience is seen as a profound source of wisdom, connecting people across cultures, backgrounds, and beliefs. Through values such as interconnectedness, integrity, and kindness, humanity finds common ground in the pursuit of understanding, equity, and respect. These universal values resonate deeply within New Universalist theology, guiding followers to honor the sacredness of life, embrace diversity, and cultivate compassion.

Interconnectedness: Recognizing the Web of Life

Interconnectedness is a value that lies at the heart of many Indigenous and Earth-centered traditions, teaching that all beings—humans, animals, plants, and the elements—are woven into the same sacred web of life. In Indigenous teachings, the Earth is viewed not merely as a resource but as a living entity, deserving of respect and care. **The Lakota concept of "Mitákuye Oyás'iŋ"** (All My Relations) expresses this worldview, reminding followers of their interconnectedness with all that exists.

In New Universalism, interconnectedness is seen as both a spiritual truth and a call to action. Recognizing that each person is part of a larger whole, followers are encouraged to approach all beings with respect, kindness, and reverence. Interconnectedness fosters an understanding that one's actions ripple outward, affecting the environment, communities, and future generations. By embracing this value, New Universalists cultivate empathy, recognizing that harm to one part of the world impacts all parts, and care for others becomes care for oneself.

From a secular perspective, **systems theory** reinforces the concept of interconnectedness, showing how ecosystems and societies function as interconnected networks. This perspective encourages followers to understand that all parts of life are interdependent, strengthening the New Universalist commitment to Earth Stewardship and social responsibility. By honoring interconnectedness, followers deepen their relationship with the world, finding unity in diversity and harmony in nature's rhythms.

Integrity: Living with Honesty and Accountability

Integrity, as a universal value, is the practice of living in alignment with one's principles, maintaining honesty, accountability, and respect in all interactions. Integrity fosters trust within communities and enables individuals to act with authenticity and clarity. In New Universalism, integrity is seen as an essential aspect of spiritual practice, connecting one's beliefs with actions and ensuring that values are lived rather than simply professed.

Across various cultures, integrity is upheld as a core principle of ethical living. **Confucianism**, for example, places a strong emphasis on integrity, or **yi** (righteousness), as a means of achieving harmony in personal and social relationships. Confucian teachings encourage individuals to uphold their commitments, act with sincerity, and prioritize the common good over personal gain. This understanding of integrity aligns with New Universalist values, reinforcing the idea that ethical actions contribute to communal well-being.

In Indigenous teachings, integrity is closely linked to respect for the Earth and one's community. Indigenous practices often include oaths or ceremonies that bind individuals to their responsibilities, encouraging followers to uphold their commitments to future generations. For New Universalists, this understanding of integrity as accountability to both people and the planet encourages followers to act with honor, to take responsibility for their actions, and to protect the environment for the welfare of all.

In secular thought, **humanist philosophy** views integrity as the foundation of ethical behavior, supporting the idea that honesty and accountability strengthen both personal character and community bonds. This perspective resonates within New Universalism, where integrity is viewed as a sacred commitment to act in alignment with one's values, fostering trust and mutual respect. By practicing integrity, followers contribute to a community that values honesty, fairness, and cooperation.

Kindness: A Universal Language of Respect and Empathy

Kindness is a value that transcends cultural boundaries, expressing the universal desire for connection, compassion, and understanding. In New Universalism, kindness is more than a personal virtue—it is an active commitment to treat others with respect and empathy. By practicing kindness, followers cultivate a spirit of openness, recognizing the divine in every being and responding to others with warmth and generosity.

Buddhist teachings emphasize kindness through the practice of **metta**, or loving-kindness, which encourages followers to extend compassion to all beings without distinction. In Buddhism, metta is seen as a way to purify the mind, transforming negative thoughts into positive intentions and fostering inner peace. This practice of loving-kindness reflects New Universalism's belief in the power of kindness to heal, uplift, and create unity.

In **Islam**, kindness is reflected in the Prophet Muhammad's teaching that "the best among you are those who are best to their family" and in the broader concept of **ihsan** (benevolence). Islamic teachings encourage followers to act with compassion and generosity, embodying kindness as a reflection of divine mercy. For New Universalists, kindness becomes a spiritual practice that nurtures harmony within families, communities, and societies, serving as a foundation for social responsibility and peace.

Secular philosophies, too, recognize kindness as a universal value essential to ethical living. **Humanitarian philosophy**, as seen in the work of figures like **Albert Schweitzer**, emphasizes "reverence for life" as an expression of kindness, encouraging individuals to treat all beings with care. New Universalism embraces this understanding, seeing kindness as a way to honor the sacredness of life and to foster a culture of respect and empathy.

Promoting Global Understanding, Equity, and Respect

New Universalism teaches that interconnectedness, integrity, and kindness are not only personal virtues but also pathways to global understanding, equity, and respect. By practicing these values, followers create a foundation for peace and cooperation, contributing to a world that values inclusivity and fairness. These values guide followers in their relationships with others, their interactions with the environment, and their engagement in social issues, creating a balanced and ethical way of life.

Interconnectedness teaches followers to see themselves as part of a larger whole, encouraging empathy and care for all beings. Integrity provides the moral compass that ensures actions are aligned with principles, fostering trust and accountability within communities. Kindness creates bridges of understanding and compassion, enabling followers to approach others with openness and respect.

Through these values, New Universalists find common ground with people of all backgrounds, creating a shared space for dialogue, cooperation, and healing. In a world often divided by differences, these universal values offer a unifying language, reminding followers that beneath the surface, we are all part of the same human family, striving for connection, understanding, and peace.

Honoring Nature and Humanity Through Shared Values

In New Universalism, understanding through shared human experience extends beyond human relationships to include the Earth and all its inhabitants. Followers are encouraged to see the world as a sacred community, where every being has intrinsic worth and a unique role. By honoring values such as interconnectedness, integrity, and kindness, New Universalists affirm their commitment to Earth Stewardship, Filial Piety, and Social Responsibility.

These values remind followers that life is interdependent, that ethical living requires accountability, and that kindness is the essence of respect. By embodying these values, New Universalists contribute to a harmonious world, honoring both nature and humanity as sacred parts of the whole.

Universal Wisdom in Human Experience

The universal values such as compassion, humility, interconnectedness, integrity, and kindness are revered as pathways to understanding and harmony. These values are not merely ideals but active commitments that guide followers toward a life of meaning, connection, and service. By grounding their spiritual practice in these shared values, New Universalists engage in a faith that honors humanity's common journey, drawing from the wisdom of many traditions while remaining true to the principles of New Universalist theology.

Compassion teaches followers to care for others and to approach all beings with respect, fostering unity through empathy and understanding. Humility cultivates self-awareness and openness, encouraging followers to seek wisdom in all aspects of life and to honor the diverse perspectives that enrich their journey. Interconnectedness reveals the bonds that unite all beings, calling New Universalists to recognize their place within the larger web of life and to act in ways that nurture harmony and resilience.

Integrity and kindness further deepen this commitment, offering a moral compass that aligns beliefs with actions. Integrity empowers followers to live with authenticity and accountability, while kindness serves as a universal language of respect, creating connections that transcend differences in culture, background, and belief.

Together, these values form the heart of New Universalism, guiding followers to live in alignment with Earth Stewardship, Filial Piety, and Social Responsibility. They create a unifying framework for spiritual growth, inviting followers to explore the wisdom of humanity's shared experiences and to embody these insights in their daily lives. Through these values, New Universalists find both strength and purpose, contributing to a world where inclusivity, peace, and justice are the natural expressions of a faith rooted in reason, compassion, and universal wisdom.

In embracing these values, New Universalists affirm their role in a global community of seekers, united by a commitment to honoring the sacredness of life and the interconnectedness of all beings. By living these values, they not only deepen their understanding of self and others but also contribute to a more harmonious, compassionate, and sustainable world—a legacy of wisdom for future generations and a testament to the enduring power of universal truths.

Parables and Analogies

Parables and analogies are timeless teaching tools, drawing upon simple, symbolic stories to convey profound truths. In New Universalism, parables hold a sacred place as they speak directly to the heart of our shared humanity, bridging cultural and spiritual divides to reveal universal values. Through these stories, followers of New Universalism find insight into ethical and spiritual truths, which guide them in living with compassion, humility, integrity, and interconnectedness.

Introduction to Parables as Vehicles for Universal Values

Parables have been used across cultures and religions for centuries to communicate values and ethics that are universally accessible. These stories distill complex ideas into relatable narratives, allowing individuals to draw wisdom and meaning from them regardless of background or belief. In New Universalism, parables are seen as sacred vehicles, holding universal truths that are relevant across time and place. By sharing simple yet powerful stories, parables invite followers into a dialogue with the human experience, encouraging reflection, empathy, and ethical living.

In New Universalist theology, parables serve two primary functions. First, they provide a **framework for understanding core values** like compassion, resilience, humility, and justice. Parables often reveal these values through example, showing characters who embody or struggle with virtues that guide the listener toward self-reflection. Second, parables bridge diverse cultures and traditions, bringing followers into contact with insights that resonate across humanity. For example, the teaching to "love one's neighbor" appears in multiple forms across Christianity, Confucianism, and Indigenous traditions. This universality reinforces the New Universalist belief that spiritual wisdom is woven throughout the human experience.

Parables allow followers to explore ethical questions, often prompting them to consider how their actions affect others and the world around them. In stories like the **Parable of the Good Samaritan** or **Indra's Net**, followers are reminded that kindness, compassion, and interconnectedness are qualities that transcend cultural or religious boundaries. By engaging with parables,

New Universalists are invited to see themselves as part of a larger whole, responsible for the well-being of both their community and the Earth.

In addition to parables, New Universalism draws upon **analogies from nature** to illustrate its core values. Simple metaphors, such as "we are all leaves on the same tree," provide a clear and relatable way of understanding unity and interconnectedness. Analogies rooted in nature resonate deeply within New Universalist theology, reflecting the belief that the natural world offers wisdom and guidance for living in harmony. Just as a forest thrives through the interconnected roots of its trees, so too does a community flourish through mutual support and shared purpose.

Through these parables and analogies, New Universalists find inspiration to lead lives of integrity, humility, and kindness. The following stories and interpretations offer pathways for reflection, helping followers apply these values to contemporary life. As New Universalists encounter these stories, they are encouraged to look inward, asking themselves how they can embody these timeless truths in their own relationships, actions, and spiritual journeys.

Parables from Various Traditions

Parables have been told across generations to illuminate timeless truths. In New Universalism, parables are honored as windows into the universal values that guide compassionate and ethical living. Each parable included here has been selected for the insights it offers into New Universalist theology, reflecting values that unite followers in a shared journey toward understanding, kindness, and integrity.

Compassion: The Parable of the Good Samaritan

A man was traveling from Jerusalem to Jericho when he was attacked by robbers. They stripped him of his clothes, beat him, and went away, leaving him half dead. A priest happened to be going down the same road, and when he saw the man, he passed by on the other side. So too, a Levite, when he came to the place and saw him, passed by on the other side. But a Samaritan, as he traveled, came where the man was, and when he saw him, he took pity on him. He went to him, bandaged his wounds, poured oil and wine on them, and then placed the man on his own donkey.

He took him to an inn and cared for him. The next day, he gave two denarii to the innkeeper and said, "Take care of him; when I return, I will reimburse you for any extra expense you may have."

New Universalist Interpretation

In New Universalism, compassion is seen as a sacred commitment to uphold the dignity and well-being of all beings. The Samaritan's choice to stop and help, even though others had passed by, illustrates compassion as an active and deliberate act, a choice made without expectation of reward. The Samaritan transcends social, religious, and cultural divisions to respond to another's suffering, demonstrating that true compassion extends beyond personal identity or affiliation.

For New Universalists, compassion is both a responsibility and an expression of grace—a generous and unconditional kindness. This parable serves as a reminder that each act of compassion, no matter how small, has the power to affirm our shared humanity. Followers are encouraged to see each person as a reflection of the divine, deserving of empathy and care. The Parable of the Good Samaritan illustrates that compassion is not a feeling alone but a practice, something to be expressed through service, listening, and selfless action.

Practical Applications and Reflections

In New Universalism, compassion is a guiding principle for daily life, inviting each person to approach others with openness and empathy. This parable encourages everyone to look for opportunities to extend kindness and care, even when it is challenging or inconvenient. For example:

- **When encountering those in need, seek ways to help directly or connect them to resources.** Compassion can be as simple as a listening ear, an offer of support, or the act of sharing what we have.
- **Extend kindness across boundaries**—to strangers, neighbors, and those who might hold different beliefs. Compassion in New Universalism recognizes no cultural, religious, or personal divisions, and calls each person to care without judgment.
- **Reflect on the impact of small acts of compassion**, such as offering encouragement or acknowledging others. These simple actions serve as reminders that we are all part of a shared human experience.

Through these actions, compassion becomes a living expression of New Universalist values, creating a ripple effect that strengthens community and reinforces the bonds that connect all beings.

Reflection questions:

- How can I extend compassion to those around me, even when it is difficult or inconvenient?
- In what ways can I embody the spirit of the Good Samaritan in my community?
- How does practicing compassion help me understand my connection to others and my role within the larger community?

By reflecting on these questions, we deepen our understanding of compassion as a core value, allowing it to guide their interactions and choices. The Parable of the Good Samaritan thus becomes not only a story of kindness but a reminder of each person's responsibility to uphold the well-being of all.

Compassion: The Parable of the Lotus in the Mud

In a tranquil pond, there lay thick mud at the bottom, dark and cold, seemingly lifeless. Yet from this mud, a lotus began to grow. Slowly, it pushed its way through the darkness, seeking the light above. As it rose, it spread its roots wide, stabilizing itself in the dense mud. Eventually, the lotus broke the water's surface and blossomed into a flower of stunning beauty, untouched by the mud from which it came.

One day, a traveler stopped by the pond, gazing at the lotus in admiration. "How can such beauty come from darkness?" he asked. A monk, who was passing by, responded, "The lotus grows out of the mud because it finds strength within itself to seek the light. Likewise, true compassion blooms when we find the courage to embrace life's suffering and transform it into kindness."

(Source: Parable inspired by Buddhist and Eastern teachings)
New Universalist Interpretation

In New Universalism, compassion is an active, transformative force that emerges from empathy and an understanding of shared suffering. The Parable of the Lotus in the Mud teaches that just as the lotus rises above the mud to become a beautiful flower, compassion arises from a willingness to acknowledge and confront pain and difficulty, both in ourselves and in others. Compassion in this sense is not about avoidance but about fully engaging with life's challenges, offering kindness, and uplifting others from a place of understanding.

This parable reminds us that compassion is deeply rooted in empathy, self-awareness, and a commitment to alleviating suffering. Just as the lotus draws strength from its roots in the mud, individuals can cultivate compassion by connecting with their own experiences of struggle and using them to offer support and kindness to others. In doing so, they help nurture beauty, resilience, and hope within their communities.

Practical Applications and Reflections

The Parable of the Lotus in the Mud invites us to practice compassion by embracing life's challenges with empathy and a commitment to growth:

- **Acknowledge your own struggles** and use them as a source of strength and understanding when offering compassion to others. Recognizing shared experiences of hardship fosters deeper empathy and genuine kindness.
- **Approach others with nonjudgmental support,** understanding that everyone has their own "mud" they're working through. By offering kindness without expectations, followers help others rise and blossom, just as the lotus emerges from the mud.
- **Use compassion to create spaces for healing** within the community, welcoming people with open hearts and fostering a sense of belonging and support.

Reflection Questions:

- How can I draw on my own experiences of struggle to offer genuine compassion to those around me?
- In what ways does understanding others' suffering deepen my capacity for kindness and empathy?

- How can I practice nonjudgmental compassion in my community, creating a welcoming environment for all?

The Parable of the Lotus in the Mud teaches us that compassion is a transformative force, rooted in empathy and acceptance. By embracing life's difficulties and choosing to respond with kindness, we embody the beauty and resilience of the lotus, contributing to a community grounded in understanding and compassion.

Humility: The Parable of the Two Wolves

An old Cherokee chief was teaching his grandson about life. "A fight is going on inside me," he said to the boy. "It is a terrible fight, and it is between two wolves. One is evil—anger, envy, sorrow, regret, greed, arrogance, self-pity, guilt, resentment, inferiority, lies, false pride, and ego." He continued, "The other is good—joy, peace, love, hope, serenity, humility, kindness, empathy, generosity, truth, compassion, and faith." The grandson thought about it for a moment and then asked his grandfather, "Which wolf will win?" The old chief simply replied, "The one you feed." *(Traditional Native American parable, commonly attributed to the Cherokee people)*

New Universalist Interpretation

In New Universalism, humility is understood as a practice that allows followers to observe their inner world with honesty and openness. This parable, passed down through Native American wisdom, teaches that each person holds both light and shadow within them. The "two wolves" represent opposing qualities—one embodying pride and anger, the other humility and compassion. The story encourages followers to recognize their own potential for both growth and error, highlighting the importance of choice in shaping one's character.

In this story, humility is not merely a feeling; it is an active commitment to feed the qualities of kindness, empathy, and humility over pride and resentment. The choice to "feed" humility is a choice to seek self-awareness, to understand one's limitations, and to cultivate inner strength through gentleness. In New Universalism, this parable encourages followers to approach life with a humble heart, aware of their influence on others and committed to fostering harmony both within and beyond themselves.

Practical Applications and Reflections

Humility as practiced in New Universalism is a way of living that respects both the self and others, fostering a balanced, harmonious life. The Parable of the Two Wolves offers insights into nurturing humility in everyday interactions:

- **Reflect on daily choices that "feed" humility**, such as speaking honestly, listening openly, and avoiding judgment. Practicing humility invites each person to approach life as a learner, seeing every experience as a source of growth.
- **Acknowledge both strengths and limitations**, understanding that humility does not mean diminishing oneself but recognizing that all beings have something valuable to contribute.
- **Cultivate an openness to learning from others**, regardless of background, age, or belief. Humility in New Universalism encourages dialogue and exchange, seeing each interaction as an opportunity for shared wisdom.

Reflection Questions:

- What qualities do I "feed" in my daily life, and how do they shape my interactions with others?
- How can I balance confidence in my own knowledge with humility and openness to learning from others?
- In what ways does practicing humility bring me closer to understanding New Universalist values of interconnectedness and respect for all beings?

By feeding the "good wolf," we learn to embody humility in thought and action, creating space for understanding, respect, and mutual support within their communities and in their personal lives.

Humility: The Parable of the Empty Cup

A wise master once welcomed a visiting scholar who wished to learn from him. The scholar spoke at length about his knowledge, theories, and opinions, eager to impress the master. The master listened patiently, then offered the scholar a cup of tea. He began to pour, filling the cup until it overflowed, spilling tea onto the table. The scholar cried, "Stop! The cup is full. It can't hold any more."

The master set down the teapot and said, "Just like this cup, you are full of your own ideas and knowledge. How can I teach you unless you first empty your cup?" Only then did the scholar understand that to truly learn, he needed to approach with an open mind, letting go of preconceptions and pride.

(Source: Traditional Zen Buddhist parable)

New Universalist Interpretation

In New Universalism, humility is seen as a foundational value that invites openness, self-reflection, and respect for the wisdom beyond one's own understanding. The Parable of the Empty Cup teaches that humility is necessary for true learning and growth. The scholar's initial confidence in his own knowledge prevented him from receiving new insights, illustrating how humility allows individuals to expand their perspective and connect with others' experiences.

Humility is not self-deprecation but a recognition that each person has limitations and blind spots. By remaining open to learning from others, we practice humility as a path to wisdom and self-awareness. This parable encourages us to "empty our cups," setting aside ego and pride to approach each moment and interaction as an opportunity to grow.

Practical Applications and Reflections

The Parable of the Empty Cup invites us to cultivate humility through open-mindedness, respect for others' insights, and a willingness to embrace continuous learning:

- **Approach each experience with an open mind,** recognizing that each person, situation, and challenge offers a chance to learn. Humility in New Universalism is about seeing every encounter as an opportunity for growth and understanding.

- **Listen deeply to others,** allowing their perspectives and wisdom to enrich one's own understanding. Practicing humility means respecting the diversity of experiences and viewpoints, fostering mutual respect and connection.
- **Embrace humility in one's own limitations,** acknowledging that no one has all the answers. This awareness fosters empathy, patience, and a genuine openness to learning, supporting a lifelong journey of growth.

Reflection Questions:

- In what areas of my life can I practice "emptying my cup," letting go of my own preconceptions and judgments?
- How can humility help me appreciate the unique insights and experiences of others?
- How does approaching life with humility allow me to grow, connect, and deepen my understanding?

The Parable of the Empty Cup reminds us that humility is essential for wisdom and growth. By setting aside pride and remaining open to new insights, we cultivate a spirit of respect, learning, and connection, honoring the diversity of wisdom within the community and the world.

Interconnectedness: The Parable of Indra's Net

In ancient Hindu and Buddhist cosmology, the image of **Indra's Net** is used to illustrate the vast interconnectedness of all life. Indra, the god of storms and ruler of the heavens, is said to have stretched an enormous, infinitely large net across the entire cosmos. At each crossing point of the net lies a radiant, multifaceted jewel. Each jewel reflects the light of all other jewels, mirroring one another endlessly so that when one jewel is moved, touched, or even simply illuminated, the effects ripple outward, subtly altering every jewel in the net.

The meaning of Indra's Net extends beyond physical imagery. This story is often interpreted as a profound symbol of the **interconnectedness of all beings and actions**—an expression of the belief that each individual, thought, and action is woven into the greater whole. In **Buddhism**, Indra's Net has come to symbolize the idea of **"dependent origination"** or **"inter-being,"** a teaching that suggests nothing exists in isolation. All things arise in connection with and dependence on all other things. As Buddhist scholar Francis H. Cook describes, "Each jewel in Indra's Net exists only as a reflection of all the others, and hence the whole universe is contained within each jewel." (*Cook, "Hua-yen Buddhism: The Jewel Net of Indra"*)

In the **Hua-yen school of Chinese Buddhism**, this concept of Indra's Net is used to teach that each individual moment, being, or element of life is interdependent with all others. Every thought and action sends ripples into the world, affecting all other beings, just as each jewel in the net reflects and influences the others. The story of Indra's Net thus offers a cosmic view of existence, urging followers to understand that they are part of an intricate, sacred web that connects all beings.

New Universalist Interpretation

In New Universalism, interconnectedness is seen as a spiritual truth and a reminder of each person's sacred place within the greater whole. The parable of Indra's Net illustrates this understanding by revealing that each person, thought, and action contributes to the harmony or disharmony of the entire world. Like the jewels in Indra's Net, each individual reflects and is reflected by others, forming a unified, interdependent network that sustains all of life.

For New Universalists, interconnectedness is not only a truth to be understood but a responsibility to be practiced. This parable teaches that each person's actions influence the well-being of others, creating a ripple effect that reaches across time, space, and culture. By recognizing this profound connection, followers are encouraged to live with compassion, care, and awareness, understanding that their choices impact the lives of those around them and the health of the Earth itself.

The image of Indra's Net reminds followers to see themselves as both unique and integral to the larger web of existence. Each person is a jewel within the net, valuable and luminous on their own yet inseparable from the whole. This understanding fosters a deep reverence for all beings, encouraging New Universalists to honor diversity while recognizing the unity that binds all life together.

Practical Applications and Reflections

The lessons of Indra's Net inspire New Universalists to cultivate awareness of how their actions affect others and to embody interconnectedness through compassionate and mindful living:

- **Engage in acts of kindness and service**, knowing that each positive action adds to the harmony of the whole. For example, contributing to the well-being of others—whether through volunteering, supporting friends, or caring for the environment—strengthens the entire community.
- **Approach relationships with empathy and openness**, remembering that each person, like a jewel in Indra's Net, reflects and is connected to all others. Practicing active listening, patience, and compassion deepens these connections.
- **Take time to reflect on how personal habits, consumption, and communication contribute to the broader world.** Followers are encouraged to make conscious choices, recognizing that small, intentional acts shape the collective experience.

Reflection Questions:

- How does understanding interconnectedness change the way I view my relationships and responsibilities?
- In what ways can I honor the sacred connections I share with all beings, both human and non-human?
- How can I apply the image of Indra's Net in my community to create a positive ripple effect?

Through the teachings of Indra's Net, we find inspiration to live in harmony with all of life, seeing their choices and actions as reflections within a vast, sacred web. This parable invites each of us to embrace their role in sustaining the beauty, balance, and unity of the world.

Interconnectedness: The Parable of the Geese in Flight

A flock of geese was seen flying south for the winter, forming a graceful "V" in the sky. Observing them, a farmer noticed something curious: as the geese flew together, each bird flapped its wings, creating an uplift for the bird behind it. This teamwork allowed the entire flock to fly faster and farther than any one bird could on its own.

From time to time, the lead goose would tire and fall back, letting another take its place at the head of the formation. In this way, the flock shared the burden of leadership, ensuring that each bird could rest and the journey could continue without interruption.

When one goose fell ill or became too tired to keep up, two other geese would leave the formation and follow their fallen companion to provide support and protection. They would stay together until the ailing goose recovered or passed, and then they would continue their journey as a group.

(Source: Traditional teaching inspired by Indigenous wisdom and natural observation)

New Universalist Interpretation

In New Universalism, interconnectedness is viewed as a sacred unity and mutual responsibility, where each individual's strength supports the whole. The Parable of the Geese in Flight teaches that, just as each goose contributes to the flock's success, each person plays a vital role in their community. This story reflects the belief that no one person can truly thrive in isolation; we are all part of a larger "flock" that depends on shared effort, support, and compassion.

The actions of the geese illustrate how interconnectedness requires both individual commitment and collective responsibility. Each bird's willingness to take turns leading and resting symbolizes the power of cooperation, while the instinct to stay behind with an injured companion embodies the spirit of compassion and solidarity. This parable serves as a reminder that by supporting one another, each individual contributes to the health and harmony of the community.

Practical Applications and Reflections

The Parable of the Geese in Flight encourages us to practice interconnectedness by valuing unity, supporting one another, and embracing shared responsibility:

- **Contribute to the community with consistent effort,** recognizing that each person's strengths uplift the whole. Like the geese, followers can practice interconnectedness by working together to reach common goals, honoring the mutual support that sustains the community.
- **Offer support to those who are struggling,** providing companionship and compassion to those in need. Just as the geese stay with an ailing companion, followers are encouraged to offer help, understanding that interconnectedness includes supporting one another through life's challenges.

- **Take turns in roles of leadership and service,** appreciating that interconnectedness involves both guiding and being guided. By sharing responsibilities, followers create a balanced community where all members contribute and receive in equal measure.

Reflection Questions:

- How can I contribute to my community's wellbeing, recognizing that my actions support the whole?
- In what ways can I practice compassion and solidarity, supporting those who may be facing challenges?
- How does taking turns in roles of leadership and service deepen my understanding of interconnectedness and shared responsibility?

The Parable of the Geese in Flight teaches us that interconnectedness is a blend of shared effort, mutual support, and compassionate unity. By embracing the principles of cooperation and care, we foster a community that thrives on interdependence, resilience, and collective strength.

Earth-Stewardship: The Parable of the Sacred Tree

In a Native American tradition, there is a story of a **Sacred Tree** that stands in the heart of the land. The tree's roots reach deep into the Earth, and its branches stretch wide into the sky, providing shelter, nourishment, and life for all beings who come to it. Animals find protection under its canopy, birds build their nests among its branches, and people gather around it for guidance, sustenance, and wisdom. The tree is respected by all, for it sustains and unites the community. But as time goes on, some begin to take from the tree without giving back. They cut its branches, strip its bark, and take its fruit without respect or gratitude. Eventually, the tree withers, and with it, the land begins to suffer, losing its beauty and vitality.

Elders teach that only by honoring the tree—giving thanks, protecting its roots, and taking only what is needed—can the community ensure that it thrives and continues to sustain life for future generations. The tree is sacred, a reminder that all of life is interconnected and that humanity has a responsibility to care for the Earth, as it cares for them.

(Source: Traditional Native American wisdom on the Sacred Tree)

New Universalist Interpretation

In New Universalism, the value of earth-stewardship is rooted in the understanding that the Earth itself is sacred, deserving of respect, care, and protection. The Parable of the Sacred Tree reflects this belief, teaching that humanity's relationship with the Earth is one of reciprocity, not exploitation. Like the tree in the story, the natural world provides nourishment, shelter, and beauty, sustaining all beings and reminding them of their place within a larger whole.

This parable conveys that the Earth is not simply a resource to be used but a living entity to be honored. When followers of New Universalism recognize this, they are encouraged to act as stewards rather than mere consumers, understanding that the well-being of the planet and future generations depends on their care and respect for the natural world. This sense of reverence cultivates gratitude, reminding followers that their actions, large and small, shape the health and harmony of the Earth.

Practical Applications and Reflections

The lessons of the Sacred Tree inspire New Universalists to actively protect and sustain the environment, integrating earth-stewardship into their daily lives and spiritual practices:

- **Practice mindful consumption** by taking only what is necessary and giving thanks for the resources used. Simple acts, like reducing waste, choosing sustainable products, and recycling, become acts of gratitude and respect for the Earth's offerings.
- **Engage in community projects** that protect and restore the environment, such as tree planting, habitat restoration, or beach clean-ups. By actively contributing to the health of the planet, followers embody the reciprocal relationship that sustains life.
- **Incorporate nature-based rituals into worship** to reinforce the bond with the Earth. Creating seasonal altars with natural elements, offering blessings to rivers, or holding ceremonies in natural settings connect followers with the spirit of the land and renew their commitment to earth-stewardship.

Reflection Questions:

- How can I express gratitude for the Earth's gifts in my daily life and choices?
- What steps can I take to protect and nurture the natural world around me, ensuring its beauty and resources endure for future generations?
- In what ways can I see the Earth as a sacred presence, recognizing my role as a caretaker rather than a consumer?

The Parable of the Sacred Tree serves as a reminder that earth-stewardship is a sacred responsibility in New Universalism. By honoring the natural world and acting as stewards of the Earth, followers sustain the sacred balance that nurtures life and connect with the divine presence that lives within the land.

Earth-Stewardship: The Parable of the Hummingbird and the Forest Fire

One day, a great forest fire broke out, consuming the trees and threatening the lives of countless creatures. As the animals fled to safety, they stopped at the edge of the forest, watching helplessly as the flames raged on. But amidst the chaos, a small hummingbird darted toward the river, dipping its beak into the water and flying back toward the fire. The bird dropped a single droplet onto the flames, then flew back to the river to repeat the task.

A large animal called out, "Hummingbird, what are you doing? You're too small to put out this fire."

The hummingbird paused only briefly and replied, "I am doing what I can."

Moved by the hummingbird's dedication, other animals began to join in, carrying water from the river to the flames. Together, they worked tirelessly, each doing their part to protect their home. Though small, each effort became part of a larger movement, and slowly, the fire began to subside.

(Source: Indigenous parable shared in various forms)

New Universalist Interpretation

In New Universalism, earth-stewardship is understood as a shared responsibility to protect, preserve, and nurture the natural world. The Parable of the Hummingbird and the Forest Fire teaches that even the smallest actions, when united in purpose, have the power to create meaningful change. The hummingbird's willingness to "do what it can" reflects an ethic of stewardship that does not rely on grand gestures alone but values each effort, no matter how small, as essential to the collective wellbeing.

This parable reminds us that caring for the Earth is not an individual effort, but a communal one. Each person has a role to play, whether through mindful consumption, conservation, or advocacy. The actions of one may seem insignificant, but together, they form a powerful movement for the healing and restoration of the planet. The hummingbird's courage and commitment inspire followers to take ownership of their responsibility to the Earth, knowing that their efforts contribute to the wellbeing of all life.

Practical Applications and Reflections

The Parable of the Hummingbird and the Forest Fire invites us to practice earth-stewardship by taking conscious, intentional actions that reflect care and respect for the natural world:

- **Make mindful choices in daily life** that reflect a commitment to sustainability, such as reducing waste, conserving energy, and supporting eco-friendly practices. Each small act contributes to the health of the planet.
- **Join in community efforts to protect and restore nature,** understanding that earth-stewardship is a collective responsibility. Working with others amplifies each individual's contribution, strengthening the movement for environmental care.
- **Cultivate a spirit of courage and resilience,** recognizing that meaningful change often begins with a single action. Like the hummingbird, followers are encouraged to take initiative, knowing that their actions, however small, matter.

Reflection Questions:

- What small, consistent actions can I take to care for the Earth and promote environmental wellbeing?
- How can I encourage others in my community to join in the work of earth-stewardship, creating a collective impact?
- In what ways can I embody the resilience and dedication of the hummingbird, honoring my responsibility to the natural world?

The Parable of the Hummingbird and the Forest Fire reminds us that every effort counts in the journey of earth-stewardship. By working together and honoring their shared duty to the planet, followers contribute to a community of care, resilience, and lasting environmental harmony.

Reasoned Inquiry: The Parable of the Blind Men and the Elephant

In an ancient Indian story, a group of blind men encounters an elephant for the first time. Each man touches a different part of the animal, trying to understand what it is. One man touches the elephant's trunk and says, "An elephant is like a thick snake." Another touches its leg and declares, "No, an elephant is like a sturdy tree." Another feels its side and concludes, "An elephant is like a wall." Each man is convinced of his perception, yet none of them has grasped the entirety of the elephant. They begin to argue, each holding onto his limited understanding, certain he is correct.

A wise man who overhears the argument steps in and explains, "Each of you touched only one part of the elephant, yet the truth of what an elephant is goes beyond any single part. Only by listening to each other and combining your insights can you approach a fuller understanding." This story reminds us that **truth often requires multiple perspectives** and that rigid certainty can obscure deeper insight.

(Source: Ancient Indian parable, found in Jain, Hindu, and Buddhist teachings)

New Universalist Interpretation

In New Universalism, reasoned inquiry is a pathway to understanding, allowing followers to seek truth by embracing diverse perspectives. The Parable of the Blind Men and the Elephant illustrates that knowledge is often limited when viewed from a single vantage point, and that openness to various perspectives is essential for a more complete understanding. Each man in the parable grasps only one aspect of the elephant, yet by listening to one another and questioning their own assumptions, they can begin to see beyond their individual experiences.

This parable reminds us that reasoned inquiry is not a process of proving oneself "right," but rather an ongoing, humble search for truth. We are encouraged to approach spiritual, ethical, and philosophical questions with open minds, understanding that different traditions, experiences, and insights contribute to a greater whole. By engaging in reasoned inquiry, New Universalists cultivate both wisdom and compassion, recognizing the importance of dialogue, empathy, and thoughtful reflection.

Practical Applications and Reflections

The Parable of the Blind Men and the Elephant offers valuable guidance for practicing reasoned inquiry in daily life. In New Universalism, reasoned inquiry calls each person to seek understanding with humility, openness, and a willingness to grow:

- **Embrace diverse viewpoints** by engaging in dialogue with others from different backgrounds, beliefs, or experiences. By actively listening to others, followers broaden their understanding and challenge their assumptions, leading to richer insights.
- **Reflect on personal beliefs and assumptions**, asking questions that encourage deeper exploration. Recognize that learning and growth are continuous processes that involve questioning one's own ideas and remaining open to new information.
- **Seek out wisdom from multiple traditions** to gain a holistic view of spiritual and ethical questions. Reading texts, studying teachings, or listening to stories from various cultures allows followers to see universal truths through multiple lenses.

Reflection Questions:

- In what areas of my life might I be holding onto only one "part of the elephant," missing the broader truth?
- How can I cultivate a spirit of inquiry, allowing myself to question and expand my understanding without judgment or fear?
- What steps can I take to learn from others and integrate diverse perspectives into my spiritual journey?

Through the lessons of the Blind Men and the Elephant, we are reminded that truth is multifaceted and that reasoned inquiry is a journey rather than a destination. By embracing openness and humility, we deepen our understanding and embody the values of empathy, respect, and wisdom.

Reasoned Inquiry: The Parable of the Seeds and the Farmer

A wise farmer gathered his children and gave each of them a handful of seeds, saying, "These seeds hold great potential, but each will grow differently depending on where and how it is planted. Take your seeds, plant them, and observe closely. Learn from what you see and do not be afraid to make changes along the way."

The children went their separate ways and planted the seeds. One child placed the seeds in rich soil, watering them carefully and ensuring they received ample sunlight. Another child planted the seeds in shallow, rocky soil, eager for quick results. A third child questioned the best way to plant and experimented with different techniques, adjusting the water and soil as they observed the plants' responses.

Over time, the first child's seeds grew well, though some plants became crowded, needing more space. The seeds planted in rocky soil struggled, their roots unable to reach deep. Meanwhile, the third child's seeds thrived as they continued to adapt and refine their methods, learning from both success and setback.

When they returned to the farmer, each child had learned unique lessons about growth. The farmer smiled and said, "Those who ask questions and remain open to change will see their understanding deepen and their wisdom grow."

(Source: Inspired by parables on learning and experimentation)

New Universalist Interpretation

In New Universalism, reasoned inquiry is celebrated as a pathway to truth and personal growth. The Parable of the Seeds and the Farmer teaches that learning is an ongoing process that requires observation, questioning, and the courage to adapt. Just as the third child learned through experimentation and adjustment, followers are encouraged to seek understanding by engaging in thoughtful inquiry rather than relying solely on established answers.

This parable reminds us that reasoned inquiry is a dynamic journey. Faith in New Universalism is not about accepting ideas unexamined, but about nurturing a spirit of curiosity and open-mindedness. By observing and questioning the world around us, we deepen our understanding of both ourselves and the greater truths that guide our lives.

Practical Applications and Reflections

The Parable of the Seeds and the Farmer encourages us to embrace reasoned inquiry as a tool for growth, understanding, and wisdom:

- **Question assumptions and seek understanding,** approaching life with an open mind. Reasoned inquiry is an active process of exploration, empowering followers to find insights through personal experience and thoughtful reflection.
- **Be willing to adapt and change course** as new information or insights arise. Just as the third child adjusted their planting methods, followers are encouraged to remain flexible and open to growth, recognizing that truth often emerges over time.
- **Embrace a spirit of experimentation,** viewing setbacks as opportunities to learn and grow. Reasoned inquiry means that every experience, whether successful or challenging, adds depth and wisdom to one's journey.

Reflection Questions:

- How can I cultivate a spirit of reasoned inquiry, embracing curiosity and the willingness to question?
- In what areas of my life can I apply observation and experimentation, allowing new insights to emerge?
- How does remaining open to change enhance my understanding of myself and the world around me?

The Parable of the Seeds and the Farmer teaches us that reasoned inquiry is a path of growth, exploration, and transformation. By remaining open to learning and seeking understanding, we cultivate wisdom, humility, and a deeper connection to truth

Filial Piety: The Parable of the Bamboo and the Oak

Once in a forest, an ancient oak tree and a young bamboo shoot grew side by side. The oak was strong and steady, its roots reaching deep into the earth, with branches that spread wide, offering shade and shelter. The bamboo, though young and slender, found strength in its flexibility, swaying gracefully with each breeze. The oak, proud of its resilience, would often say to the bamboo, "I stand strong, unyielding to the winds." The bamboo, respectful and humble, would respond, "I admire your strength, wise Oak. I, too, find my own way to endure."

One day, a fierce storm swept through the forest. The mighty oak stood firm, but as the winds grew stronger, its rigidity became its undoing, and the oak ultimately fell, uprooted by the storm. The bamboo, meanwhile, bent and swayed with the wind, its flexibility allowing it to survive. After the storm passed, the bamboo remained standing, honoring the fallen oak and acknowledging the wisdom it had shared.

The bamboo reflected, "Though I continue to stand, I carry your strength within me, wise Oak. You taught me resilience, and in return, I offer the lessons of adaptability and grace. Together, we honor each other's wisdom, enduring beyond our individual forms."

(Source: Inspired by East Asian folk wisdom on resilience and respect)

New Universalist Interpretation

In New Universalism, filial piety is understood as a two-way, reciprocal responsibility that reflects mutual respect, honor, and gratitude within a variety of relationships—between parent and child, younger and elder, marital partners, individuals and their communities, and citizens and their government. The Parable of the Bamboo and the Oak illustrates this principle by showing that both younger and older generations contribute valuable qualities to one another. The bamboo respects the oak's strength and wisdom, yet the oak, too, recognizes the bamboo's flexibility as a strength essential for survival. This interdependence demonstrates that filial piety involves honoring each other's unique qualities and wisdom, regardless of age or role.

In this expanded view of filial piety, younger generations owe respect, gratitude, and deference to their elders, while elders, in turn, owe the same virtues to the younger. Parents have a responsibility not only to guide and protect their children but also to honor and nurture each child's individuality and potential. Similarly, community leaders and government officials bear an obligation to uphold values of respect and service to the people they lead, while individuals honor these institutions by participating with integrity and respect.

Through this lens, filial piety is not one-sided; it is a balanced relationship of mutual acknowledgment and responsibility. The bamboo and the oak represent different but equally significant aspects of strength, demonstrating that respect, learning, and growth flow in both directions, enriching all members of the community.

Practical Applications and Reflections

The Parable of the Bamboo and the Oak encourages followers of New Universalism to practice filial piety through respect, humility, and reciprocity in all relationships:

- **Honor family and community members** by listening to their stories, respecting their contributions, and offering support when needed. Filial piety is expressed through patience, empathy, and gratitude, regardless of age or role.
- **Uphold mutual respect and honor across generations**, recognizing that younger individuals bring adaptability, creativity, and new perspectives while elders offer wisdom, guidance, and stability. Both perspectives are essential to the health and harmony of the community.
- **Cultivate intergenerational bonds within family, community, and society,** creating spaces for both younger and older individuals to share, teach, and learn from one another. By engaging in dialogue and cooperative activities, followers strengthen bonds that support mutual growth and resilience.

Reflection Questions:

- How can I show respect and gratitude for the wisdom of those who came before me, while also honoring the potential and individuality of those who come after?
- In what ways can I contribute to a balanced, respectful exchange in my relationships, whether with family, partners, community, or society?
- How can I embody the spirit of mutual piety in my interactions, honoring both the wisdom of tradition and the adaptability of the present?

The Parable of the Bamboo and the Oak reveals that filial piety in New Universalism is a sacred commitment to honoring the strengths of all, young and old alike. By recognizing the value each person brings, followers create a legacy of respect, resilience, and mutual support that strengthens family and community alike.

Filial Piety: The Parable of the Old Man and the Young Tree

An old man spent his days tending to a young tree he had planted at the edge of his property. Each morning, he would water the tree, protect it from pests, and make sure it grew strong and healthy. He worked with great patience, year after year, though the tree provided no shade, fruit, or flowers in its early stages.

One day, a traveler passing by asked the old man, "Why do you care so much for this tree when it offers you nothing in return?"

The old man smiled and replied, "When I was young, others planted trees whose shade and fruit I enjoyed. Now, it is my turn to nurture this tree for those who come after me. I may never see it fully grown, but my love and care will live on through it."

Years later, after the old man had passed on, the tree had grown tall and strong. It provided shade for the young and fruit for the hungry, its roots reaching deep into the earth. And in this way, the old man's legacy of love and care continued to bless those who came after him.

(Source: Parable inspired by traditional teachings on respect for elders and generational care)

New Universalist Interpretation

In New Universalism, filial piety is a reciprocal practice of honoring both past generations and nurturing future ones. The Parable of the Old Man and the Young Tree illustrates the value of mutual care, teaching that each generation is both a beneficiary and a caretaker. The old man's dedication to the young tree reflects a commitment to preserving and enhancing the world for others, understanding that every act of love and respect contributes to the community's future wellbeing.

This parable reminds us that filial piety is not only about revering one's elders but also about fulfilling the responsibility to care for those who will come after. By honoring the wisdom and sacrifices of those before and tending to the growth of those to come, we uphold the interconnected nature of life, ensuring that our actions contribute to a legacy of respect, love, and stewardship.

Practical Applications and Reflections

The Parable of the Old Man and the Young Tree encourages us to practice filial piety by honoring the past, nurturing the present, and preparing for the future:

- **Show respect and gratitude for elders** and those who have contributed to the community. This respect acknowledges the foundation upon which followers build their own lives and cultivates a spirit of gratitude and humility.
- **Nurture the younger generation,** offering guidance, support, and care as they grow. Filial piety is an ongoing commitment to fostering the wellbeing of those who come after, creating a community that honors each stage of life.
- **Embrace a sense of responsibility for the legacy left behind,** understanding that every action contributes to a shared future. By acting with love, patience, and care, followers create a lasting impact that benefits all.

Reflection Questions:

- How can I honor and show gratitude for those who have contributed to my growth and wellbeing?
- In what ways can I nurture and support future generations, offering guidance and love as they grow?
- How does practicing mutual care for past and future generations deepen my connection to the New Universalist community?

The Parable of the Old Man and the Young Tree teaches us that filial piety is both a reverence for the past and a responsibility for the future. By tending to this balance, we create a legacy of love, respect, and interconnected care, ensuring that their actions contribute to a harmonious and thriving community.

Grace: The Parable of the Prodigal Son

In a well-known story from the Christian tradition, a man had two sons. One day, the younger son asked his father for his share of the family inheritance. The father, though saddened by this request, honored it and gave the son his portion. The young man then left home and traveled far away, spending his wealth in careless and reckless ways until he found himself with nothing.

Alone, hungry, and desperate, he took work feeding pigs, realizing how low he had fallen and how even his father's servants lived better than he did.

At last, humbled and remorseful, the young man decided to return home, hoping his father would at least allow him to work as a servant. But as he approached, his father saw him from afar, ran to meet him, and embraced him warmly. The father, overjoyed by his son's return, called for a celebration, saying, "This son of mine was dead and is alive again; he was lost and is found." Without reproach or judgment, the father welcomed his son back with grace, healing their relationship and restoring him to the family. *(Source: Christian New Testament, Luke 15:11-32)*

New Universalist Interpretation

In New Universalism, grace is a profound expression of kindness, forgiveness, and understanding that flows from one's awareness of shared humanity. The Parable of the Prodigal Son illustrates grace as an act of unconditional acceptance, freely given without expectation or demand. The father's response to his son's return, filled with joy rather than resentment, represents a boundless compassion that embraces each person's imperfections and mistakes.

For New Universalists, grace is a guiding principle that calls followers to look beyond judgment and extend kindness, especially in moments of vulnerability. This parable encourages followers to offer forgiveness not only to others but also to themselves, recognizing that growth and understanding arise from accepting one's mistakes as part of the human journey. Grace in New Universalism embodies humility, empathy, and a willingness to see each individual's inherent worth, regardless of their actions or past choices.

Practical Applications and Reflections

The Parable of the Prodigal Son encourages followers to practice grace by embodying forgiveness, kindness, and understanding in their relationships and daily lives:

- **Extend forgiveness and compassion to others**, especially when they seek reconciliation or show remorse. Grace in New Universalism is not contingent on perfection but embraces humanity in its entirety, fostering healing and reconnection.
- **Cultivate self-forgiveness**, accepting one's own past mistakes as stepping stones on the path of growth. Grace begins with oneself, allowing individuals to let go of shame and instead focus on continuous improvement and self-compassion.

- **Practice empathy and patience** in relationships, understanding that each person carries their own challenges and struggles. By responding with kindness, followers nurture a spirit of grace that strengthens their bonds and supports healing in the community.

Reflection Questions:

- How can I extend grace to others, even when it may be challenging or uncomfortable?
- In what ways can I show grace to myself, acknowledging past mistakes without judgment?
- How can grace guide me in building stronger, more understanding relationships within my family, community, and beyond?

The Parable of the Prodigal Son reminds us that grace is a force of renewal, opening the heart to forgiveness, acceptance, and unity. In practicing grace, New Universalism honor the sacred connection they share with others, fostering a spirit of reconciliation and compassion that transcends personal differences.

Grace: The Parable of the Unforgiving Servant

In a kingdom long ago, there was a servant who owed the king a great sum of money. When he could not repay it, the king commanded that he, his family, and all his possessions be sold to settle the debt. The servant fell to his knees, begging, "Have patience with me, and I will repay everything!" Moved by compassion, the king forgave his debt entirely and released him.

However, as the servant left the king's presence, he encountered a fellow servant who owed him a small sum. Grabbing him by the throat, he demanded, "Pay me what you owe!" The fellow servant also fell to his knees, pleading, "Have patience with me, and I will repay you." But the unforgiving servant refused and had his fellow servant thrown into prison until the debt could be paid.

When the king heard what had happened, he called for the unforgiving servant and said, "I showed you mercy and forgave you a great debt. Should you not have had compassion for your fellow servant as well?" And with that, the king withdrew his forgiveness, sending the servant to be held accountable for his own actions.

(Source: Parable from the Christian New Testament, Matthew 18:21-35)

New Universalist Interpretation

In New Universalism, grace is a transformative kindness that goes beyond what is deserved, offering forgiveness and understanding as a pathway to healing and unity. The Parable of the Unforgiving Servant demonstrates that grace is most powerful when it is shared. The king's initial act of forgiveness reflects the compassion that uplifts and liberates; yet the servant's failure to extend that grace to others reveals the need for grace to be freely given, without expectation or reservation.

This parable encourages us to practice grace by releasing grudges, judgment, or retribution. Grace, in this context, is a conscious choice to offer compassion even when it is not owed. By embracing grace, we acknowledge that every person is fallible and deserving of kindness, allowing forgiveness to heal divisions and build understanding. This grace fosters harmony within oneself and strengthens bonds within the community.

Practical Applications and Reflections

The Parable of the Unforgiving Servant invites us to embody grace in their interactions and relationships, creating a culture of forgiveness and compassion:

- **Offer forgiveness freely,** understanding that true grace involves letting go of resentment and choosing compassion. This act of kindness uplifts both the giver and the receiver, creating space for healing and unity.
- **Remember one's own need for grace,** recognizing that everyone has faults and moments of struggle. Practicing self-compassion allows followers to extend grace to others with understanding and empathy.
- **Embrace kindness and patience in relationships,** knowing that grace fosters strong, trusting bonds. By choosing grace over judgment, followers build a community rooted in mutual respect and support.

Reflection Questions:

- In what ways can I practice grace in my life, choosing forgiveness over resentment?
- How can I cultivate compassion for both myself and others, recognizing the shared human need for grace?
- How does offering grace deepen my relationships and strengthen my commitment to New Universalist values?
- The Parable of the Unforgiving Servant reminds us that grace is a sacred act of compassion, freeing both the giver and receiver. By offering grace freely, we cultivate a spirit of unity, healing, and mutual understanding within ourselves and our communities.

Integrity: The Parable of the Honest Woodcutter

In a traditional folk tale, a poor woodcutter was chopping wood by a river when his axe slipped from his hands and fell into the water. The woodcutter, unable to retrieve his only tool, sat down in despair, knowing he could not afford a new axe to earn his living. As he sat there, a water spirit emerged from the river and, seeing the man's sorrow, offered to help.

The spirit dove into the river and soon returned with a shining golden axe, asking, "Is this your axe?" The woodcutter shook his head and replied, "No, that is not mine." The spirit then retrieved a silver axe and asked again, "Is this your axe?" The woodcutter again shook his head, saying, "No, that is not mine either."

Finally, the spirit returned with the woodcutter's own iron axe, and the man's face brightened as he said, "Yes, that one is mine." Impressed by his honesty, the spirit gave him all three axes as a reward, saying, "Your integrity is worth more than gold or silver. Let these be a symbol of the rewards that come from living with honesty." The woodcutter left with gratitude, knowing he had gained more by being truthful than he ever could by deception.

(Source: Traditional folk tale from Greek and other folk traditions)

New Universalist Interpretation

In New Universalism, integrity is seen as a foundational value that aligns actions with one's highest principles, fostering trust, self-respect, and authenticity. The Parable of the Honest Woodcutter illustrates that integrity is not merely about telling the truth, but about choosing honesty even when it might seem easier to benefit from deception. The woodcutter's decision to be truthful, despite his poverty, highlights that true integrity comes from an internal commitment to do what is right, regardless of personal gain.

This parable teaches that integrity strengthens the individual and the community. When we practice integrity, we reinforce the values of trust and authenticity within ourselves and our relationships. In New Universalism, integrity is both an ethical compass and a source of personal strength, guiding us to live in alignment with our beliefs and values. This integrity connects individuals to a deeper sense of purpose, grounding their actions in honesty and respect for the self and others.

Practical Applications and Reflections

The Parable of the Honest Woodcutter offers insights into practicing integrity in daily life and community interactions. In New Universalism, integrity is upheld through consistent, truthful action, building trust and respect within oneself and with others:

- **Commit to honesty in all interactions**, whether with friends, family, or colleagues. Practicing integrity means choosing truthfulness over convenience or personal gain, nurturing authenticity in relationships.
- **Align words with actions**, ensuring that commitments are met and that intentions are communicated clearly. Integrity is reflected not only in words but in follow-through, showing respect for one's own commitments and others' expectations.
- **Hold oneself accountable for mistakes or missteps** without deflecting or hiding from responsibility. Practicing integrity involves humility and self-awareness, recognizing that honesty includes acknowledging imperfections.

Reflection Questions:

- In what ways can I cultivate greater honesty and alignment between my words and actions?
- How does living with integrity strengthen my sense of self and my relationships within my community?
- When have I been tempted to compromise my values, and what can I learn from those moments about practicing integrity in the future?

The Parable of the Honest Woodcutter encourages us to embody integrity as an expression of authenticity and self-respect. By choosing truthfulness, we reinforce the trust and unity that bind our community, living in harmony with our deepest values.

Integrity: The Parable of the Emperor's Seed

An aging emperor, without an heir, decided to find a successor by testing the children of his kingdom. He summoned all the young people and gave each of them a single seed, saying, "Take this seed, plant it, care for it, and return in one year. I will judge each of you by the plant you bring back, and the one with the most beautiful plant will become the next emperor."

A boy named Ling took his seed home and planted it in a pot, tending to it with great care. He watered it every day, ensured it received sunlight, and nurtured it faithfully. But despite his efforts, the seed did not sprout. While others boasted of their growing plants, Ling's pot remained empty.

When the year was up, the children returned to the emperor with their plants, each trying to outshine the others with the beauty and size of their blossoms. Ling, feeling disheartened, brought his empty pot, worried that he had failed. Yet he chose to show the emperor his barren pot, as he had nothing else to offer.

The emperor looked over the plants and, when he saw Ling's empty pot, he smiled. "All of you were given boiled seeds, which cannot grow," he announced. "Yet each of you brought me beautiful plants. Only Ling had the courage to bring me an empty pot, showing honesty and integrity. Therefore, Ling shall be my successor."

(Source: Traditional parable adapted across cultures)

New Universalist Interpretation

In New Universalism, integrity is the foundation of trust, authenticity, and ethical living. The Parable of the Emperor's Seed teaches that integrity is about remaining true to one's values, even when it would be easier to follow others or present a false image. Ling's honesty, despite the pressure to appear successful, reflects a commitment to truth and self-respect. Integrity, in this sense, is not merely about following rules but about being faithful to one's inner principles.

This parable encourages followers of us to live with integrity by embracing honesty and authenticity, recognizing that true strength lies in standing by one's values. Integrity fosters trust within the community and supports personal growth by allowing each individual to act in alignment with their beliefs. Ling's courage and honesty serve as a reminder that integrity is often tested in difficult moments, and choosing truth over appearances strengthens the spirit.

Practical Applications and Reflections

The Parable of the Emperor's Seed invites us to practice integrity in daily life, building trust and authenticity through honest, principled actions:

- **Remain true to your values** even in challenging situations, prioritizing honesty and self-respect. Integrity is a commitment to inner truth, fostering a sense of personal honor and strength.
- **Cultivate authenticity** in relationships, being honest about your intentions and actions. Acting with integrity builds trust, respect, and deeper connections within the community.
- **Have the courage to acknowledge mistakes or limitations,** understanding that integrity is not about perfection but about commitment to one's values. By embracing honesty, followers create a culture of acceptance and mutual respect.

Reflection Questions:

- In what areas of my life can I practice greater integrity, staying true to my values even when it's difficult?
- How does honesty and authenticity in my actions strengthen my connection with others and with New Universalist principles?
- What does it mean to me to "stand by my truth," and how can I honor that commitment each day?

The Parable of the Emperor's Seed teaches us that integrity is about courage, truth, and alignment with one's inner principles. By choosing honesty over appearances, we embody a spirit of trustworthiness, authenticity, and respect, creating a community rooted in shared values.

Kindness: The Parable of the Starfish

One day, a young boy was walking along the shore when he noticed that countless starfish had washed up on the beach, stranded and struggling under the sun. Moved by compassion, the boy began picking up one starfish at a time and tossing it back into the ocean. A man passing by watched the boy and finally approached, saying, "Why are you doing this? There are too many starfish to save, and you can't make a difference."

The boy picked up another starfish, gently threw it into the water, and replied, "It made a difference to that one." Then, he continued his task, one starfish at a time, undeterred by the man's words.

(Source: Parable popularized by Loren Eiseley, "The Star Thrower")

New Universalist Interpretation

In New Universalism, kindness is understood as a powerful, transformative act that reflects both compassion and a sense of shared responsibility. The Parable of the Starfish illustrates that kindness is not about changing the entire world in one act but about bringing relief, comfort, and care to one life at a time. The boy's actions are driven by a heartfelt understanding that each life matters, and even small gestures of kindness have significance.

This story reminds us that kindness, when practiced intentionally and consistently, becomes a form of service that uplifts individuals and contributes to the greater harmony of the community. The boy's simple act of kindness toward the starfish may seem small, yet it reflects a profound truth: that each person has the power to impact others positively, even in situations that seem overwhelming. In New Universalism, kindness is an everyday practice of generosity, empathy, and care that bridges differences, affirms the value of each being, and creates ripple effects of compassion.

Practical Applications and Reflections

The Parable of the Starfish encourages us to practice kindness as an essential part of their daily lives. Acts of kindness are not defined by their scale but by the intention and compassion behind them:

- **Engage in small, thoughtful actions that bring comfort or joy** to others, whether by offering help to a neighbor, listening to a friend, or simply extending a smile. Each small act affirms a connection that contributes to the collective good.
- **Be present and responsive to those in need**, recognizing that kindness often involves noticing and addressing even the smallest needs in one's community. Offering a hand, lending support, or acknowledging others fosters a community built on mutual care.
- **Practice kindness toward oneself,** as self-compassion allows one to give freely and wholeheartedly to others. When followers nurture their own well-being, they are better able to extend kindness to the world around them.

Reflection Questions:

- How can I practice kindness in ways that positively impact even one person's life today?
- In what ways does choosing kindness, even in small actions, align with my values and bring me closer to others?
- How can I extend kindness to myself, ensuring that I have the compassion and energy to serve others fully?

The Parable of the Starfish reminds us that kindness has no requirements of size or recognition. By choosing kindness in everyday moments, we help create a culture of empathy, support, and compassion, nurturing the well-being of both individuals and the community.

Kindness: The Parable of the Cracked Pot

A water bearer had two large pots, each hung on either end of a pole he carried across his neck. One of the pots was perfect and always delivered a full portion of water. The other pot had a crack in it, and by the time they reached the master's house, it was only half full.

The perfect pot took pride in its flawless performance, but the cracked pot felt ashamed, as it was only able to accomplish half of what it was meant to do. One day, it spoke to the water bearer as they walked, saying, "I am sorry that I can't deliver a full load of water. My flaw causes the water to leak out along the way."

The water bearer smiled kindly and replied, "Have you noticed the flowers growing along your side of the path? I planted seeds there because I knew you would water them each day as we walked. Because of your kindness in carrying water, beautiful flowers now line the path."

The cracked pot looked around, seeing the colorful blooms that had grown because of its flaw, and felt a deep sense of peace. It realized that its unique condition had made it a vessel of kindness and beauty, bringing joy to others along the path.

(Source: Traditional parable adapted in various forms)

New Universalist Interpretation

In New Universalism, kindness is recognized as an act that goes beyond perfection and performance. The Parable of the Cracked Pot teaches that kindness is about using one's unique qualities to contribute to the wellbeing of others. The cracked pot's flaw, which it once saw as a limitation, became a source of beauty and nourishment along the path. This story reminds us that kindness does not require perfection but rather an openness to serving others in ways that reflect one's unique strengths and experiences.

This parable encourages us to see kindness as a gift that each individual can offer, regardless of perceived flaws or limitations. Just as the cracked pot's gentle contributions helped flowers bloom, followers are called to act with kindness, knowing that small, consistent acts can bring joy, comfort, and meaning to others. This compassion reflects the New Universalist belief that every person has something to offer, and that acts of kindness create a ripple effect, enriching the community.

Practical Applications and Reflections

The Parable of the Cracked Pot invites us to practice kindness by embracing our own unique qualities and using them to uplift others:

- **Offer kindness without self-judgment,** recognizing that every act of compassion, no matter how small, brings value to others. Just as the cracked pot nourished flowers, each follower can make a difference in their own way.

- **Embrace personal uniqueness** as a source of strength in relationships and community. By appreciating one's own journey, followers cultivate kindness that is genuine, compassionate, and accepting of both self and others.
- **Create opportunities for kindness,** even in everyday moments, understanding that consistent acts of generosity enrich the lives of others and foster a spirit of joy and gratitude.

Reflection Questions:

- How can I embrace my own uniqueness, offering kindness in ways that reflect my personal strengths?
- What small acts of kindness can I cultivate in my daily life, knowing that they contribute to the wellbeing of others?
- In what ways does offering kindness bring meaning and purpose to my own journey, connecting me with New Universalist values?

The Parable of the Cracked Pot reminds us that kindness is a gentle, powerful force that can blossom from every person's unique qualities. By embracing kindness and seeing value in our individuality, we nurture a community that values compassion, acceptance, and mutual joy.

Patience: The Parable of the Chinese Farmer

Once, there was a Chinese farmer who worked his land with patience and dedication. One day, his horse ran away, and upon hearing the news, his neighbors came to console him, saying, "What bad luck!" The farmer simply replied, "Maybe so."

The next day, the horse returned, bringing with it several wild horses. The neighbors came again, this time congratulating him on his good fortune, saying, "What wonderful luck!" The farmer again replied, "Maybe so."

The following day, the farmer's son attempted to ride one of the wild horses. He was thrown off and broke his leg. The neighbors arrived once more, offering their sympathy for the misfortune. "What terrible luck," they said. The farmer's response was again, "Maybe so."

A few days later, soldiers arrived in the village, conscripting all the young men for war. Because of his injury, the farmer's son was spared. The neighbors, marveling at the turn of events, remarked, "What amazing luck!" And, as always, the farmer replied, "Maybe so."

(Source: Traditional Taoist parable)

New Universalist Interpretation

In New Universalism, patience is not simply about waiting but about embracing a deep trust in life's unfolding, allowing events to reveal their meaning over time. The Parable of the Chinese Farmer teaches that true patience involves releasing judgments about what is "good" or "bad" and developing a perspective that honors the unknown. The farmer's quiet responses reflect an inner wisdom, showing that each experience holds its own lessons and that immediate reactions do not capture the entirety of life's journey.

This parable encourages us to approach life's challenges and blessings with openness, understanding that both joy and hardship are part of a greater rhythm. Practicing patience, in this context, means accepting life's unfolding without rushing to conclusions. This patience fosters resilience, balance, and an ability to find meaning in life's unexpected turns. The farmer's attitude illustrates that, while circumstances may shift, there is wisdom in allowing time and experience to provide insight.

Practical Applications and Reflections

The Parable of the Chinese Farmer encourages followers to embody patience by nurturing acceptance, resilience, and a nonjudgmental approach to life's ups and downs:

- **Practice acceptance in challenging times**, trusting that each experience, whether pleasant or painful, has meaning that may not be immediately understood. This form of patience allows followers to remain centered and open to future possibilities.
- **Resist the urge to label events as "good" or "bad,"** recognizing that every experience unfolds over time. By approaching life with an open mind, followers can avoid attachment to specific outcomes, embracing each event as part of their personal growth.
- **Cultivate a sense of calm in moments of uncertainty,** drawing on inner strength to navigate unexpected changes. Patience in this sense becomes a source of stability and wisdom, grounding followers as they move through life's cycles.

Reflection Questions:

- How can I practice patience by accepting both challenges and blessings as part of a larger journey?
- In what ways does letting go of judgments about "good" or "bad" help me find greater peace and resilience?
- How can I cultivate a balanced perspective, allowing time and experience to shape my understanding of events in my life?

The Parable of the Chinese Farmer reminds us that patience is a virtue of trust, acceptance, and inner peace. By refraining from rushing to conclusions, we can experience life's fullness, recognizing the beauty in its unfolding mystery.

Patience: The Parable of the Bamboo and the Fern

A gardener planted a fern and a bamboo seed on the same day. He nurtured both with equal care, ensuring they received sunlight, water, and rich soil. The fern quickly grew tall and lush, spreading its fronds wide in only a few weeks, but the bamboo seed showed no sign of life. The gardener continued to tend to both, faithfully watering and caring for them, even as the seasons passed and still the bamboo did not grow.

By the end of the second year, the bamboo had not sprouted, while the fern flourished. Friends and neighbors questioned why the gardener continued to care for the bamboo, but he simply smiled and continued. By the third and fourth years, the bamboo still showed no signs of growth, yet the gardener persisted, trusting in the bamboo's potential.

Finally, in the fifth year, a small shoot emerged from the soil. Within weeks, the bamboo grew to towering heights, reaching over fifty feet, while the fern remained close to the ground. The gardener knew that, though it had taken years, the bamboo had been growing strong roots, preparing to sustain its rapid growth.

(Source: Traditional parable shared across cultures)
New Universalist Interpretation

In New Universalism, patience is understood as a steady commitment to growth, even when immediate progress is not visible. The Parable of the Bamboo and the Fern illustrates that true patience often requires trust in the unseen, as well as faith in the process. The bamboo's long period of invisible root development reminds us that life's most meaningful growth often happens gradually and unseen, allowing for stability and resilience.

This parable encourages us to cultivate patience, understanding that periods of delay or stillness can be fertile grounds for deep-rooted strength. Just as the gardener trusted in the bamboo's potential, we are called to embrace patience as a virtue that fosters perseverance, resilience, and inner peace. The story of the bamboo and the fern serves as a reminder that each individual grows at their own pace, and that true progress often takes time.

Practical Applications and Reflections

The Parable of the Bamboo and the Fern invites us to practice patience by trusting in life's timing, nurturing growth with dedication, and appreciating the unseen progress:

- **Trust in the unseen progress** that may be happening beneath the surface, knowing that true growth often requires time and foundation-building. Patience allows followers to remain hopeful and resilient, even during times of stillness.
- **Practice persistence in personal and spiritual growth,** understanding that meaningful change develops gradually. Like the gardener, followers are encouraged to continue their efforts with faith, embracing patience as a pathway to fulfillment.
- **Accept different paces of growth** in oneself and others, recognizing that every journey is unique. By honoring both immediate and delayed progress, followers create a community that values patience, support, and mutual encouragement.

Reflection Questions:

- How can I nurture patience in my personal journey, trusting that unseen progress is meaningful?
- In what areas of my life can I practice persistence, embracing patience as I work toward long-term goals?

- How does patience deepen my understanding of growth, allowing me to appreciate the journey rather than the destination?

The Parable of the Bamboo and the Fern reminds us that patience is an active virtue, rooted in trust, resilience, and acceptance. By embracing patience, we foster a spirit of calm persistence, allowing growth to unfold naturally and harmoniously over time.

Baptism: The Parable of the River's Renewal

In a remote village, there was a river that nourished the people, plants, and animals. This river was considered sacred, and villagers would come to it each day, bringing offerings and saying prayers. Over time, however, the river became muddy and polluted. Some villagers turned away, seeking other sources of water, but an elder reminded them, "This river has given us life for generations. We must honor it and help it heal."

The villagers came together, cleansing the banks and removing debris from the waters. As they worked, they sang songs of gratitude and hope. Gradually, the river's waters became clear again, reflecting the blue sky above. Villagers gathered to celebrate its renewal, understanding that the river's cleansing was also their own. For, just as the river had been restored, so too were their hearts renewed with reverence, unity, and purpose.

(Source: Inspired by water renewal and cleansing traditions)

New Universalist Interpretation

In New Universalism, baptism represents a commitment to spiritual truth, renewal, and a life-long journey of growth. The Parable of the River's Renewal illustrates the importance of cleansing and recommitment, both of which are central to the rite of baptism. Just as the villagers gathered to restore the river, New Universalists come together in the act of baptism to renew their commitment to the faith's principles and values, symbolizing a "cleansing" of spirit and a rebirth into a life dedicated to truth, respect, and interconnectedness.

Drawing from global traditions, baptism in New Universalism is inspired by purification and initiation rites found in many cultures, from the water-based rites of Indigenous and Earth-centered spiritualities to the cleansing practices in Eastern traditions. The ritual of water immersion symbolizes both a return to the sacred and a journey toward greater understanding, embodying a purification that is not only physical but also spiritual. Baptism through water represents the "washing away" of the old self and a conscious embrace of New Universalist values rooted in Earth-centered spirituality, reasoned inquiry, and compassion.

Baptism: The Seed in the Soil

Imagine a seed planted deep within the soil. In the darkness, it sheds its outer shell, releasing its potential to grow into a new form. As it begins to sprout, it reaches toward the surface, seeking light and nourishment. In this way, baptism is like the journey of the seed. It is a ritual of rebirth, allowing individuals to shed old beliefs or limitations, awakening their potential as they reach toward spiritual truth and inner growth. The act of baptism in New Universalism reflects this natural transformation, inviting followers to plant the "seeds" of compassion, wisdom, and reverence for all life.

Practical Applications and Reflections

The Parable of the River's Renewal and the analogy of the seed in the soil encourage followers to approach baptism as a meaningful beginning—a commitment to spiritual renewal and unity with the New Universalist community:

- **Honor the act of baptism** as a personal commitment to growth, understanding that it represents a sacred connection to New Universalist values. Just as the river was renewed, baptism calls for a mindful cleansing of intentions and purpose.
- **Embrace baptism as an opportunity for rebirth,** releasing old habits or beliefs that no longer serve, and welcoming a journey grounded in interconnectedness, compassion, and reasoned truth.
- **Reflect on the continuous nature of growth,** recognizing that baptism is the start of an ongoing spiritual journey, like the seed growing toward light. Baptism becomes a living commitment to New Universalist values.

Reflection Questions:

- In what ways does the act of baptism represent a personal commitment to growth and renewal in my life?
- How can I continue to "renew the river" within myself, nurturing compassion, wisdom, and reverence in my journey?
- What beliefs or practices might I release to embrace the principles of New Universalism more fully?

Through the Parable of the River's Renewal and the analogy of the seed, baptism in New Universalism is celebrated as a sacred commitment to spiritual awakening, unity, and compassion. By embracing this rite, we begin a journey of purposeful growth, honoring the spirit of interconnectedness that lies at the heart of their faith.

Communion: The Parable of the Shared Harvest

In a village surrounded by fields, there was a yearly tradition of a shared harvest. Each family grew different crops—wheat, rice, vegetables, and fruits. At harvest time, the villagers would gather in the center of the village, bringing baskets of their bounty to share with one another. Together, they would prepare a grand feast, celebrating the abundance that the Earth had provided them.

One year, the weather had been harsh, and many families struggled to grow enough food. Some feared that they wouldn't have enough to contribute, but they brought what they had nonetheless. When they gathered for the harvest feast, they saw that their combined efforts had created a meal that could nourish everyone. The villagers realized that, through sharing, they found not only sustenance but also unity, gratitude, and connection. They recognized that their survival and joy depended on their willingness to give and receive as one community.

(Source: Parable inspired by traditions of communal feasting and harvest celebrations)

New Universalist Interpretation

In New Universalism, communion is more than a symbolic meal; it is an act of unity, gratitude, and shared connection. The Parable of the Shared Harvest illustrates how, through communion, individuals come together to nourish one another—body, mind, and spirit. Just as the villagers combined their offerings to create a sustaining feast, communion in New Universalism invites followers to bring their unique selves and intentions, contributing to a community that nurtures all.

Drawing inspiration from traditions of communal meals in many faiths, New Universalist communion honors Earth-centered spirituality. The bread and water (or simple food and drink) used in the ritual symbolize the Earth's gifts, reminding followers of their duty to care for the planet and to support one another. Communion in this sense becomes an exchange of gratitude and humility, recognizing that each individual's contribution strengthens the whole. Followers partake in communion not only to receive sustenance but also to reaffirm their bond with nature and their community, honoring the Earth as both giver and sustainer.

Communion: The Tapestry of Community

Imagine a beautiful tapestry, woven with threads of different colors and textures. Each thread contributes to the overall design, but none alone can form the whole. Communion is like this tapestry. Each person brings a unique "thread" of experience, intention, and spirit, weaving it together with others to form a community. Just as the tapestry's strength and beauty come from the unity of its threads, communion creates a shared bond of support, gratitude, and connection, honoring the diversity and unity of the New Universalist community.

Practical Applications and Reflections

The Parable of the Shared Harvest and the analogy of the tapestry invite followers of New Universalism to view communion as a sacred act of unity and gratitude:

- **Approach communion as a time of giving and receiving,** understanding that it symbolizes the nourishment and support shared within the community. Like the shared harvest, communion allows followers to honor both the Earth's abundance and the generosity of one another.
- **Embrace the communal spirit of communion,** recognizing that each participant brings something unique to the ritual. This sacred sharing strengthens the bonds of the community and deepens the collective gratitude for the gifts of nature and friendship.

- **Reflect on communion as an act of unity with the Earth,** appreciating the interconnectedness of all life. Communion reminds followers to care for the environment and to be mindful stewards of the resources that sustain their community.

Reflection Questions:

- How can I view communion as an act of giving as well as receiving, celebrating the unity and nourishment of my community?
- In what ways does communion deepen my connection to the Earth, recognizing the gifts that sustain life?
- How can I bring the spirit of communion into my daily life, sharing compassion, gratitude, and support with those around me?

The Parable of the Shared Harvest and the tapestry analogy teach us that communion is a time of unity, humility, and gratitude. By partaking in this ritual, we strengthen our bond with each other, honor the Earth's abundance, and reaffirm our commitment to communal care and environmental stewardship.

Marriage Ceremonies: The Parable of the Two Trees

In a meadow, there grew two young trees—an oak and a willow—planted close enough that their branches touched. As they grew taller and stronger, they each found their own path toward the sunlight, yet their roots intertwined deep below the ground, supporting each other through storms and dry seasons. Though they were different in appearance and needs, they shared the soil, giving and receiving nourishment, their roots woven tightly together.

One day, a traveler passed through the meadow and noticed how the trees seemed to lean into each other, each offering the other shade, support, and companionship. The traveler marveled at their strength, realizing that their bond did not restrict their growth but allowed each tree to grow freely, while still remaining united. Through their connection, they formed a single, harmonious presence in the meadow, each bringing beauty and strength to the other.

(Source: Inspired by nature-based parables on partnership and unity)

New Universalist Interpretation

In New Universalism, marriage is viewed as a partnership of mutual support, respect, and growth. The Parable of the Two Trees illustrates that a strong union is not about uniformity or restriction but about finding strength in difference and honoring each partner's journey. Just as the oak and willow grew together while remaining distinct, marriage in New Universalism is a commitment to walk side by side, supporting each other's personal growth while sharing a unified path.

Marriage ceremonies in New Universalism celebrate this interwoven journey, inspired by the sacred nature of partnerships in many traditions. Drawing from Indigenous teachings on balance and Eastern philosophies of duality and harmony, New Universalist marriage ceremonies emphasize love, loyalty, and respect for individuality. Through ritual elements such as handfasting or sand blending, couples symbolically weave their lives together while honoring the unique contributions of each partner. The marriage bond is seen as both a shared spiritual journey and a commitment to individual growth, creating a foundation of love, support, and shared purpose.

Marriage: The River and the Ocean

Imagine two rivers flowing side by side, each carving its own path yet moving toward a shared destination: the ocean. Along the way, they experience different landscapes, weather different storms, and nourish different communities, but ultimately, they merge as one. In marriage, two individuals come together like these rivers, embracing each other's unique journeys while uniting in a common purpose. Marriage in New Universalism is like these rivers flowing to the ocean—an interweaving of lives, experiences, and dreams, moving toward a shared horizon of love, growth, and unity.

Practical Applications and Reflections

The Parable of the Two Trees and the river analogy invite us to view marriage as a sacred partnership grounded in respect, unity, and shared purpose:

- **Honor the individuality of each partner,** recognizing that a strong marriage allows space for personal growth. Like the two trees, a healthy union nurtures both individual strengths and shared goals, creating a foundation of respect and balance.
- **Embrace partnership as a journey of mutual support,** understanding that true strength in marriage comes from lifting each other up during times of challenge and joy. Marriage ceremonies in New Universalism celebrate this lifelong commitment to encouragement and care.
- **Nurture a spirit of shared purpose,** knowing that marriage is both a union of hearts and a commitment to a shared path. Just as the rivers merge in the ocean, partners are encouraged to create a common vision that guides their journey together.

Reflection Questions:

- How can I honor both my individuality and my commitment to my partner within the union of marriage?
- In what ways can I nurture a spirit of support and respect in my relationship, helping my partner grow while embracing our shared journey?
- What shared purpose or vision can my partner and I create to guide our life together, fostering unity and harmony?

The Parable of the Two Trees and the river analogy teach us that marriage is a partnership of love, growth, and mutual support. By embracing these principles, couples create a bond that honors both the individuality and unity of each partner, cultivating a marriage grounded in strength, balance, and shared purpose.

Consort Union Ceremonies: The Parable of the Three Sisters

In a garden tended by Indigenous farmers, there grew three plants known as the Three Sisters: corn, beans, and squash. Each plant was unique, with its own shape, growth pattern, and needs.

The corn grew tall, reaching toward the sun, while the beans climbed its stalk, and the squash spread across the ground, providing shade and moisture for the roots below.

Though each plant was different, they were always planted together. The corn provided support for the beans to climb, the beans returned essential nutrients to the soil, and the squash created a living mulch that protected the roots from weeds and drought. Together, they thrived, growing stronger and more abundant than they could on their own. The Three Sisters were a symbol of unity in diversity, teaching that true partnership allows each to give and receive, supporting one another's strengths and needs.

(Source: Inspired by the Indigenous agricultural tradition of the "Three Sisters")

New Universalist Interpretation

In New Universalism, the Consort Union is celebrated as a partnership rooted in interdependence, support, and respect for individual uniqueness. The Parable of the Three Sisters teaches that a strong union embraces differences, allowing each person to thrive while uplifting the others. Like the Three Sisters, a Consort Union in New Universalism is a chosen family bond that goes beyond traditional marriage, inviting partners to build a life that honors each person's role and contribution within the relationship.

The Consort Union, inspired by Indigenous values of balance and interdependence, holds that every relationship is unique and can be built in a way that reflects each partner's gifts. This union may include polyamorous or multi-partner commitments, recognizing that love and partnership can take many forms. Rituals such as sharing vows of support, creating symbols of unity, or planting a "Three Sisters" garden can serve as acts that symbolize the uniqueness and interconnection of a Consort Union, embracing love, respect, and mutual care as guiding principles.

Consort Union: The Mosaic of Many Colors

Imagine a mosaic, made of countless stones, each with its own color, shape, and texture. While each stone is beautiful on its own, it is when they are placed together that they create a vibrant and unified image. A Consort Union is like this mosaic, where each individual contributes a unique quality to the whole, bringing strength, beauty, and depth. This union honors each person's individuality while forming a shared bond that enriches all involved, celebrating a harmony born from diversity.

Practical Applications and Reflections

The Parable of the Three Sisters and the mosaic analogy invite us to view the Consort Union as a sacred partnership that values diversity, mutual support, and shared purpose:

- **Honor the individuality of each partner,** recognizing that a Consort Union is about embracing differences as sources of strength. Like the Three Sisters, each partner plays an essential role that supports the collective.
- **Embrace the spirit of cooperation and interdependence,** understanding that a strong union allows each person to give and receive. This balance creates a nurturing environment where each partner flourishes and contributes to the shared journey.
- **Celebrate the bond of chosen family,** recognizing that a Consort Union is rooted in commitment and care. Like the mosaic, each person's unique qualities create a beautiful, unified whole, bringing color, meaning, and purpose to the union.

Reflection Questions:

- How can I honor and celebrate the unique qualities of each partner in a Consort Union, valuing the contributions each brings?
- In what ways can I practice interdependence and cooperation, building a relationship that supports and uplifts all involved?
- How does the spirit of chosen family deepen my understanding of unity and commitment in relationships?

The Parable of the Three Sisters and the mosaic analogy teach us that a Consort Union is a partnership built on respect, diversity, and shared purpose. By embracing the principles of interdependence and unity in diversity, partners create a lasting bond that honors the beauty of chosen family, building a life grounded in love, harmony, and mutual care.

Sex and Sexuality: The Parable of the Blossoming Garden

In a peaceful valley, there was a garden renowned for its beauty and diversity. Each flower, tree, and vine in the garden had its own unique fragrance, color, and shape. The garden thrived because of its balance and variety, each plant contributing something to the whole in natural harmony and because each plant was tended with care and respect. The gardener knew that for the garden to flourish, it needed balance with each plant receiving equal care, respect, attentiveness, mindful watering, and space for each flower to grow in its own way honoring each plants individuality. Some plants grew side by side in pairs, while others formed clusters or spread across the ground. Together they formed a complex and beautiful ecosystem where all forms of life were seen as essential.

Over time, the garden became a place of healing and inspiration for all who visited. It represented both the beauty of individuality and the power of natural growth when nurtured with intention. The gardener taught visitors that, like the flowers, love and connection are strongest when they grow from a foundation of respect and understanding, allowing each to bloom freely without overshadowing the other.

(Source: Inspired by nature's diversity and interconnected growth)

New Universalist Interpretation

In New Universalism, sexuality and relationships are celebrated as sacred expressions of love, human connection, individuality, diversity, and unity. The Parable of the Blossoming Garden illustrates that, like the garden, human sexuality and relationships are most vibrant and meaningful when they are nurtured with care, intention, respect and honor for each individual's unique nature. Just as each flower grows in its own way and brings its own beauty to the garden, every individual's expression of love, identity, and sexuality contribute to the richness of the human experience. New Universalism values diverse expressions of love—whether in heterosexual, LGBTQ+, or polyamorous relationships—and affirms that each form of connection and identity contributes to the harmony of the whole.

Drawing inspiration from traditions that honor the body and spirit New Universalist views on identity and sexuality emphasis mindful choice, mutual respect, and a celebration of natural diversity. Human sexuality is viewed as sacred, drawn from sources such as Eastern teachings on tantric love, Indigenous perspectives on the sacred body, and modern views on consent and autonomy, New Universalism teaches that sexuality is a celebration of love and unity. This sacred view encourages followers to approach sexuality with reverence, openness, compassion, and as an intentional act, embracing diversity in love and connection. Every expression of sexuality that is rooted in mutual respect, care, and freedom is seen as part of a shared journey toward spiritual understanding, connection, and self-acceptance. Therefore, sexuality is not only a physical act but a spiritual exchange that deepens such connections, fosters understanding, and honors the sacredness of each person.

Sex and Sexuality: The Symphony of Instruments

Imagine a symphony orchestra, where each instrument has its own unique sound, rhythm, and expression. Some instruments play solo, while others create harmony with different instruments, each contributing to the music's depth and beauty. The symphony is most powerful when all voices are respected, each sound blending with others in unity and expression. Sexuality in New Universalism is like this symphony—a diverse array of connections and expressions, where each individual brings their unique "tone" to the whole, creating a shared resonance of love, respect, and unity.

Practical Applications and Reflections

The Parable of the Blossoming Garden and the symphony analogy encourage us to approach sexuality as a natural, sacred, and diverse expression of connection:

- **Honor sexuality as a celebration of love and unity,** respecting the individuality of each person and relationship. Like the garden, diverse expressions of love create a shared harmony, enriching the whole.
- **Embrace mutual respect, care, and consent,** recognizing that sacred sexuality is about honoring each partner's freedom and well-being. By cultivating a spirit of openness, followers foster a deeper, more meaningful connection.
- **Celebrate diversity in relationships,** affirming that all forms of love—whether heterosexual, LGBTQ+, or polyamorous—are valuable. Each brings unique beauty and depth, creating a community that honors each expression of love as sacred.

Reflection Questions:

- How can I approach sexuality as both a natural and sacred expression of connection, respecting the diversity of expressions within myself and others?
- In what ways can I nurture respect, understanding, and unity in my relationships, honoring each person's unique qualities?
- How does viewing sexuality through the lens of sacredness and respect deepen my connection to myself, my partner(s), and New Universalist values?

The Parable of the Blossoming Garden and the symphony analogy teach us that sexuality is a balanced, respectful, and mindful expression of human connection. By embracing these principles, we honor the sacredness of both individuality and unity, cultivating relationships that are rooted in love, understanding, and mutual care, celebrating the diversity that makes the world whole.

Cannabis as Sacred Rite and Medicine: The Parable of the Healing Herb

In a distant land, there was a village known for its vibrant gardens, where healers cultivated a rare and potent herb known for its soothing and transformative qualities. This herb, referred to simply as "the healing herb," was respected by all, for it held properties that could heal wounds, ease pain, and calm the restless mind. The villagers regarded the herb as a divine gift, recognizing its capacity to connect them with both the earth below and the sky above.

The healers in the village taught the people to use the herb with reverence, reminding them that it was to be used not for escape, but for connection and healing. Before using the herb, each person would set an intention, whispering a prayer of gratitude to honor the plant. This ritual kept the people mindful, ensuring they did not abuse the herb's power or forget its sacred origins.

One day, a traveler came to the village, seeking relief from his worries and ailments. The villagers taught him the ways of the healing herb, explaining how to use it respectfully, with reverence and a clear purpose. As the traveler followed their instructions, he felt not only his ailments ease but a sense of unity with the land and the spirit of the village. He left the village with a newfound appreciation, understanding that healing is both a physical and spiritual journey, made sacred by the plants that serve as our allies.

(Source: Inspired by ancient traditions of medicinal herbs and plant wisdom)

New Universalist Interpretation

In New Universalism, cannabis is honored as a healing herb, a sacred tool that offers a bridge between earthly experiences and spiritual realms. The Parable of the Healing Herb illustrates that the use of cannabis, like other sacred plants, is most profound when approached with respect and mindfulness. This herb connects us with the divine source of life, grounding us in the present while expanding our awareness.

In communal and personal rituals, New Universalists are encouraged to approach cannabis with intention, recognizing it as a gift for healing, insight, and connection. The teachings of this parable emphasize the importance of gratitude and intentional use, aligning with the belief that the herb's sacred potential is realized when it is honored for its wisdom and not exploited for casual use. This reverent approach not only elevates the act of consuming cannabis but also deepens the user's connection with themselves, the community, and the natural world.

Cannabis: The Compass of Connection

Consider a compass, which guides travelers along their journey by helping them find their direction. In New Universalism, cannabis is like a compass—a sacred tool that helps individuals realign with themselves, their purpose, and the divine. When used with clarity of mind and a reverence for its power, cannabis serves as a guide for personal exploration, healing, and spiritual insight, directing the user toward greater self-awareness and connection with the cosmos.

Practical Applications and Reflections

The Parable of the Healing Herb and the compass analogy encourage New Universalists to approach cannabis as both a tool for healing and a rite of sacred connection:

- **Honor cannabis as a sacred ally,** recognizing its power to elevate mind, body, and spirit. Like the healing herb, cannabis offers its gifts when used with intention and respect, aligning users with their deepest selves.

- **Embrace the role of mindfulness and intention,** understanding that sacred plants are most powerful when used to support conscious reflection, healing, and connection. Before each use, followers are encouraged to set intentions, creating a mindful environment for the experience.
- **Respect cannabis as a bridge to spiritual insight,** viewing it not only as a physical remedy but as a guide for inner exploration. Like the compass, cannabis can lead individuals on a journey toward clarity, self-acceptance, and divine unity.

Reflection Questions:

- How can I approach cannabis as a sacred ally in my personal practice, respecting its power and purpose?
- In what ways does setting intentions and practicing mindfulness deepen my connection to the plant's healing and spiritual benefits?
- How does viewing cannabis as a sacred tool shift my perspective on its use, helping me align with my values and the teachings of New Universalism?

The Parable of the Healing Herb and the compass analogy teach us that cannabis, when used with respect and intention, is both a sacred rite and a medicine. By treating this plant as a divine gift and ally, we foster a deeper connection to themselves, the earth, and the cosmos, honoring the transformative power of cannabis as a path to spiritual insight, unity, and healing.

Last Rites: The Parable of the Butterfly's Journey

Once, there was a caterpillar that spent its days on the leaves of a tree, feeling content in its world. It crawled slowly, savoring the sunlight and the taste of green leaves, unaware of what lay ahead. One day, an instinct arose from deep within, guiding the caterpillar to create a cocoon around itself. Unsure of what would come next, the caterpillar trusted the process, surrendering to the darkness of the cocoon.

In time, the cocoon opened, and the caterpillar emerged transformed—a butterfly with wings of vibrant colors. It soared into the sky, seeing the world from new heights. What once seemed like an end was in fact a new beginning, as the caterpillar-turned-butterfly continued its journey in an entirely different form, connected to the earth below but lifted toward the heavens.

(Source: Inspired by nature's life cycles and transformation)

New Universalist Interpretation

In New Universalism, Last Rites are a sacred ritual that honors the soul's passage from one state of being to another. The Parable of the Butterfly's Journey illustrates the process of transformation, showing that death is not an end but a transition into a new phase of existence. Just as the caterpillar surrenders to the cocoon, followers are encouraged to view death as a natural and sacred transformation, one that continues the soul's journey beyond the physical.

Inspired by diverse traditions—such as the Buddhist belief in reincarnation, the Indigenous reverence for ancestral spirits, and earth-based rites acknowledging cycles—New Universalist Last Rites embrace the continuity of the soul. Through acts of anointing, prayer, and meditative reflection, the Last Rites offer comfort and peace, helping both the individual and their loved ones accept the transition. These rites honor the life that has been lived, the legacy that will remain, and the journey of the spirit toward the "starry heavens," as referenced in New Universalist teachings.

Last Rites: The Journey of the River to the Ocean

Imagine a river flowing through valleys, forests, and plains, giving life to all it touches. As it reaches the end of its path, it merges into the vast ocean, becoming part of something greater yet retaining its essence. Last Rites in New Universalism are like this journey of the river. Death represents a merging, where the individual soul joins a collective spirit while still holding the experiences, wisdom, and love gathered along the way. The river is not lost; it has simply taken on a new form within the boundless ocean.

Practical Applications and Reflections

The Parable of the Butterfly's Journey and the river analogy encourage us to view Last Rites as a sacred honoring of life's journey and a peaceful transition:

- **Approach Last Rites with reverence,** recognizing the sanctity of death as part of the cycle of life. Just as the caterpillar transforms, the individual soul continues its journey in a new way, embraced by the greater whole.
- **Embrace Last Rites as an act of connection,** offering closure and comfort to those who remain. These rites create a bridge between life and death, allowing loved ones to express gratitude, love, and peace.
- **Honor the continuity of the soul,** knowing that each individual's spirit remains connected to those they loved and the community they served. Like the river joining the ocean, the soul becomes part of a larger collective, carrying forward the essence of life's experiences and lessons.

Reflection Questions:

- How can I view Last Rites as a way to honor the sacredness of life's journey, embracing the process of transformation?
- In what ways can I offer comfort and closure to loved ones through rituals that recognize the continuity of the soul?
- How does the concept of merging with a collective spirit, like the river to the ocean, deepen my understanding of life, death, and unity?

The Parable of the Butterfly's Journey and the river analogy teach us that Last Rites are a sacred transition, honoring both the uniqueness of the individual and the continuity of the soul. By embracing these rites, followers offer peace and reverence, recognizing that life's journey is part of a larger cycle, where each spirit remains forever connected to the whole.

Funeral & Memorial Services: The Parable of the Garden's Seeds

In a small village, there lived a gardener who tended to a beautiful garden filled with flowers, herbs, and fruit trees. Over the years, the gardener shared seeds from the garden with others in the village. These seeds, carefully chosen and lovingly planted, grew into plants that nourished and inspired the community, providing beauty, food, and medicine.

One day, the gardener passed on, leaving behind a garden that continued to thrive. The villagers gathered in the garden to remember the gardener, each one holding a small seed from the plants that had been shared with them. They spoke of how the gardener's seeds had enriched their lives and honored the memory of the gardener by planting the seeds in their own gardens.

As the years passed, the gardener's legacy grew far beyond the original plot of land. Each seed, a small symbol of care, became a part of new gardens, a living tribute to the gardener's generosity and love. Through the garden, the gardener's spirit continued to live on, touching future generations and reminding them of the beauty of a life well-lived.

(Source: Inspired by the symbolic tradition of seeds as legacies and continuance)

New Universalist Interpretation

In New Universalism, funeral and memorial services are sacred gatherings that honor the legacy of those who have passed, celebrating their life, contributions, and the enduring impact they leave behind. The Parable of the Garden's Seeds illustrates how an individual's life continues to grow and blossom in the hearts and lives of those they have touched. Just as the gardener's seeds flourished in the hands of others, the lives of the departed continue to inspire, teach, and connect the community.

New Universalist funerals draw from various traditions that honor the soul's journey and legacy, including Indigenous practices of storytelling, Buddhist reflections on impermanence, and nature-centered rituals of Earth-based spiritualities. In these services, loved ones gather to share memories, offer gratitude, and reflect on the values the departed embodied. Rituals like lighting candles, creating a memory altar, or planting a tree serve as reminders of the person's lasting presence, symbolizing their continued influence as a source of love and wisdom.

Funeral & Memorial Services: The Ripple in the Pond

Imagine a stone thrown into a still pond. The stone sinks below the surface, but the ripples it creates expand outward, touching every part of the water. Funeral and memorial services in New Universalism are like these ripples. While the physical presence of the person may no longer be with us, the influence of their life continues to expand and touch others, creating waves of love, kindness, and memory. These ripples remind us that each life has a profound effect, and the memory of that life endures, connecting past and future.

Practical Applications and Reflections

The Parable of the Garden's Seeds and the ripple analogy invite us to view funeral and memorial services as opportunities to honor, remember, and celebrate the continuing legacy of loved ones:

- **Celebrate the life and legacy of the departed,** recognizing that their impact endures within the lives they touched. Just as the gardener's seeds grew beyond their original plot, each life leaves gifts that continue to shape the world.
- **Embrace remembrance as an act of gratitude and connection,** acknowledging that the lives of those who came before us form the foundation upon which we grow. Sharing stories, memories, and rituals create a lasting tribute to their spirit.
- **Foster community healing and unity,** knowing that each funeral or memorial brings the community together in love and support. By honoring the ripples left by each life, followers create a space of compassion, shared memory, and mutual care.

Reflection Questions:

- How can I honor the memory of loved ones in a way that celebrates their contributions and enduring presence?
- In what ways does reflecting on the legacy of others inspire me to live in alignment with my own values?
- How can I carry forward the gifts, teachings, and love of those who have passed, letting their influence continue to enrich my life and community?

The Parable of the Garden's Seeds and the ripple analogy teach us that funeral and memorial services are sacred acts of remembrance, gratitude, and connection. By gathering to honor the departed, we recognize the continuing influence of each life, celebrating a legacy of love, wisdom, and shared humanity that transcends time and space.

4

World Religions and Secular Philosophy

Religious Parallels

Introduction to Universal Themes Across Religions

Throughout human history, individuals and communities across the world have sought to understand the deeper meaning of life, forming various systems of belief that capture their highest values and aspirations. While specific teachings and practices may differ, a shared thread runs through the world's major religions and philosophies: a commitment to universal principles that resonate with the core of the human experience. These traditions emphasize compassion, morality, and unity, values that transcend cultural boundaries and speak to our shared humanity.

New Universalism honors the wisdom found in these diverse faiths, believing that each contains universal truths that contribute to a greater understanding of the world and our place within it. This belief reflects a fundamental aspect of New Universalist theology, which holds that truth and spiritual meaning can be found across faiths and that each tradition provides a unique perspective on universal principles. By drawing upon these shared values, New Universalism fosters an inclusive approach to spirituality that emphasizes interfaith respect and harmony, promoting understanding among people of all backgrounds.

These universal themes are not confined to any single religious doctrine or cultural tradition. Instead, they represent humanity's ongoing pursuit of morality, compassion, and peace—aspirations that all beings seek, regardless of their spiritual path. In New Universalism, this shared pursuit serves as a foundation for spiritual growth, encouraging followers to honor the unity in diversity and to engage meaningfully with beliefs and practices from across the world.

In the following sections, we will explore some of the major values and teachings of various faiths that align closely with New Universalist principles. From the love and humility emphasized in Judeo-Christianity to the mindfulness and compassion of Buddhism, the commitment to social responsibility in Islam, and the reverence for nature in Earth-based traditions, each faith contributes insights that enrich the New Universalist worldview. By drawing on these collective teachings, New Universalism seeks to create a space where diverse beliefs can coexist in harmony, forming a cohesive expression of values that inspire compassion, unity, and ethical living.

Common Values: Judeo-Christianity

In the Judeo-Christian tradition, core teachings revolve around values that speak to the heart of human connection and moral integrity. Both Judaism and Christianity emphasize principles of love, forgiveness, and humility—values that foster compassion, community, and personal responsibility. These teachings align deeply with the principles of New Universalism, which honors love as a binding force, forgiveness as a path to inner peace and reconciliation, and humility as a foundation for true wisdom.

Love and Compassion: The Command to "Love Thy Neighbor"

One of the most profound teachings found in both Judaism and Christianity is the command to "love thy neighbor as thyself." This directive is found in the Hebrew Scriptures, specifically in Leviticus, and is later emphasized by Jesus in the New Testament as a central tenet of spiritual life. In the New Universalist perspective, this commandment transcends cultural and religious boundaries, offering a timeless reminder that love is a unifying force among all people.

New Universalism adopts this teaching as a call to embrace empathy, respect, and care for others. "Loving thy neighbor" is seen not merely as a directive toward kindness but as an invitation to recognize the interconnectedness of all beings. It encourages New Universalists to view compassion as a spiritual practice that reflects our shared humanity and to extend this compassion not only to others within their community but also to those of all backgrounds and beliefs.

Forgiveness: A Path to Healing and Inner Peace

Forgiveness holds a prominent place in Christian teachings, where Jesus advocates for mercy and grace toward others, emphasizing the power of forgiveness to heal divisions and bring peace. In the New Universalist view, forgiveness is a vital step toward personal growth and communal harmony, allowing individuals to let go of grievances and find freedom in reconciliation.

In both Judaism and Christianity, forgiveness is not just a release from past grievances but a transformative process that fosters empathy and understanding. New Universalism views forgiveness as an act of healing that uplifts both the forgiver and the forgiven. By letting go of resentment and choosing compassion, individuals foster a spirit of unity, moving beyond personal struggles to create a more harmonious community. Forgiveness is, therefore, embraced as a means of cultivating inner peace and extending compassion, reflecting the shared values of humility, patience, and kindness.

Humility: The Path to Wisdom and Spiritual Growth

Humility is another key teaching within Judeo-Christian scriptures, viewed as an essential aspect of wisdom and spiritual growth. The Hebrew Bible often praises humility, seeing it as a virtue that brings individuals closer to the divine. In Christianity, Jesus' life serves as an example of humility in service to others, placing the well-being of others before oneself and recognizing the value of every person.

For New Universalism, humility represents an openness to learning, growth, and self-reflection. It calls followers to be aware of their strengths and limitations, fostering an attitude of gratitude and respect for others. Through humility, New Universalists are encouraged to see themselves as interconnected with others, understanding that true wisdom lies not in superiority but in mutual respect and collaboration. Humility becomes a foundation for both personal and communal harmony, supporting the core New Universalist values of social responsibility, filial piety, and a dedication to reasoned inquiry.

New Universalism's Perspective on Judeo-Christian Values

By incorporating the values of love, forgiveness, and humility from Judeo-Christian teachings, New Universalism builds a bridge of mutual respect between diverse beliefs. These values are not limited to any single faith but resonate as universal principles that guide New Universalists in their pursuit of a compassionate and ethical life. Through these shared teachings, New Universalism emphasizes the importance of embracing diversity while recognizing the common threads of love, kindness, and self-awareness that unite all people.

Common Values: Buddhism

Buddhism, founded on the teachings of Siddhartha Gautama, offers a path of wisdom and compassion grounded in a deep understanding of human suffering and interconnectedness. Central to Buddhist philosophy are values that cultivate awareness, kindness, and inner peace—qualities that align closely with New Universalism's commitment to living a compassionate, mindful, and interconnected life. New Universalism respects and draws inspiration from these teachings, recognizing that the Buddhist path of compassion and mindfulness provides insight into living in harmony with oneself and the world.

Compassion: The Practice of Metta (Loving-Kindness)

One of the most essential teachings in Buddhism is the practice of metta, or loving-kindness, which encourages individuals to cultivate unconditional compassion for all beings. Metta is not only a feeling of empathy but also an active wish for the happiness and well-being of others, free from selfish desire. This practice aligns seamlessly with New Universalism's belief in compassion as a guiding principle that strengthens community bonds and fosters understanding across differences.

In New Universalism, the practice of compassion extends to all of creation, embracing the Earth and all forms of life as interconnected and deserving of care. The Buddhist practice of metta reinforces the idea that kindness is not limited by borders or personal relationships but is instead a universal expression of humanity's inherent goodness. Through compassion, New Universalists aim to honor and protect the unity of all beings, acting with empathy and responsibility in our communities and in our interactions with nature.

Mindfulness: The Path of Present Awareness

Mindfulness, the practice of observing one's thoughts, emotions, and experiences without judgment, is a cornerstone of Buddhist philosophy. In the teachings of the Buddha, mindfulness serves as a means to understand the true nature of existence, leading individuals to greater clarity, peace, and wisdom. This practice encourages a heightened awareness of the present moment, allowing practitioners to live with intention and compassion.

For New Universalism, mindfulness aligns with the value of reasoned inquiry and personal reflection. By cultivating mindfulness, followers of New Universalism become more attuned to our inner lives and the world around us, learning to respond with empathy and wisdom. This awareness enhances spiritual connection, grounding us in both our individual experiences and our shared humanity. Through mindfulness, we engage with life in a deliberate and thoughtful manner, fostering a deeper respect for ourselves, others, and the natural world.

Interconnectedness: The Web of Life

In Buddhism, the concept of interconnectedness—often illustrated through the metaphor of Indra's Net—reveals the deep connections that bind all beings together. According to this teaching, each life form is a strand in an infinite web, with every action affecting the whole. This understanding of interdependence shapes Buddhist values around kindness, humility, and compassion, encouraging practitioners to recognize the impact of their actions on the wider world.

New Universalism embraces this view of interconnectedness, seeing it as an invitation to live responsibly and ethically. By understanding that each action ripples outward, New Universalists are reminded of our duty to honor and respect all life. This perspective aligns with the New Universalist pillars of Earth Stewardship and Social Responsibility, encouraging us to engage in actions that support the well-being of others and the environment. Recognizing the web of life fosters an attitude of humility and empathy, as each individual sees themselves as part of a larger, interwoven existence.

New Universalism's Perspective on Buddhist Values

Buddhist teachings on compassion, mindfulness, and interconnectedness offer profound insights into the New Universalist path. By drawing on these principles, New Universalism emphasizes the importance of living with kindness, awareness, and a sense of unity with all beings. These values reflect a holistic approach to life, one that honors the interconnected fabric of existence and promotes a life of thoughtful action and empathy. Through Buddhist values, New Universalists find guidance on the journey toward peace, self-understanding, and harmony with the world.

Common Values: Islam

Islam, a faith grounded in submission to the divine and in fostering unity within the global community, centers its teachings on mercy, charity, and a deep commitment to social justice. These principles, outlined in the Quran and the Hadith (sayings and actions of the Prophet Muhammad), emphasize the importance of compassion, generosity, and collective responsibility. In New Universalism, these values resonate as universal calls to care for one another, to extend kindness, and to act ethically within society. The Islamic emphasis on mercy, charity, and community enriches the New Universalist commitment to embodying empathy, generosity, and social unity.

Mercy: The Compassionate Nature of the Divine

Mercy, or "Rahmah," is one of the most frequently mentioned qualities of the divine in the Quran. Both God and the Prophet Muhammad are described as merciful, setting an example for humanity to follow. Islam calls on followers to show mercy not only to friends and family but to strangers, animals, and the environment. This principle of mercy shapes the way Muslims interact with others, fostering an attitude of forgiveness, understanding, and compassion.

In New Universalism, mercy is regarded as a fundamental virtue that encourages us to approach others with kindness and grace. Embracing the Islamic view of mercy, New Universalists are reminded to extend compassion freely and unconditionally, seeing mercy as an opportunity to create peace and understanding. By cultivating mercy, individuals contribute to a compassionate world, embodying the belief that each act of kindness strengthens the fabric of community and unity.

Charity: The Sacred Duty of Zakat and Almsgiving

Charity, or "Zakat," is one of the Five Pillars of Islam and reflects a deep commitment to social responsibility. The act of giving a portion of one's wealth to those in need is seen not only as a moral duty but as an essential practice of faith. Beyond the formal obligation of Zakat, Islam encourages other forms of voluntary charity, or "Sadaqah," which can include acts of kindness, service, or even a smile. This emphasis on charity encourages Muslims to see wealth as a trust from God, one that is meant to support and uplift the entire community.

For New Universalism, the principle of charity aligns with the pillar of Social Responsibility, highlighting the importance of using one's resources to benefit others. Inspired by the Islamic commitment to Zakat, New Universalists are encouraged to give generously and to engage in acts of service that strengthen the community and foster equity. Charity, in the New Universalist view, is not only a financial offering but a gesture of solidarity, a way to ensure that everyone has the support they need to thrive. Through charity, followers of New Universalism demonstrate their commitment to an inclusive, compassionate world.

Community: The Unity of the Ummah

The concept of "Ummah" in Islam represents the global community of believers, emphasizing unity, mutual support, and shared purpose. This sense of community extends beyond religious boundaries, calling on Muslims to care for all people, regardless of faith. The Ummah provides a model of togetherness, where individuals are encouraged to support one another, to stand up for justice, and to work toward the common good. This ideal of community serves as a reminder that no one is isolated; each person's well-being is interconnected with that of others.

In New Universalism, community is a cherished value that aligns with the Islamic concept of Ummah. Recognizing that individuals are inherently interconnected, New Universalists strive to create inclusive, supportive communities where everyone is treated with respect and dignity. Inspired by the values of Ummah, New Universalists honor diversity within our communities, seeing each individual's well-being as essential to the health of the whole. Through community engagement and collective action, we create a culture of empathy, solidarity, and shared purpose.

New Universalism's Perspective on Islamic Values

Islamic teachings on mercy, charity, and community offer insights that strengthen the New Universalist commitment to compassion, social responsibility, and unity. By embracing these values, New Universalists find a shared purpose in uplifting and supporting others, creating bonds that transcend cultural or religious differences. These teachings inspire us to act with kindness, generosity, and respect, embodying the belief that a compassionate and unified world is within reach. Through the values drawn from Islam, New Universalism calls us to nurture a community rooted in empathy, justice, and shared humanity.

Common Values: Hinduism

Hinduism, one of the world's oldest spiritual traditions, offers profound insights into living a life aligned with virtue, harmony, and respect for all forms of life. Two central concepts in Hindu teachings, dharma (ethical duty) and ahimsa (non-violence), shape the way Hindus approach their relationships with others, with themselves, and with the natural world. These values echo the core beliefs of New Universalism, which emphasizes integrity, social responsibility, and Earth stewardship. By embracing the principles of dharma and ahimsa, New Universalists find guidance on the path of ethical living, service, and compassionate respect for all beings.

Dharma: The Path of Ethical Duty and Responsibility

In Hinduism, dharma represents the moral and ethical responsibilities that each individual is expected to uphold. Dharma is not a rigid set of rules but rather a dynamic principle that varies according to each person's role, relationships, and stage in life. It calls for actions rooted in righteousness, service, and respect for others, encouraging individuals to live in a way that promotes harmony within society and with the natural world. Dharma emphasizes balance and self-discipline, reminding individuals that their actions contribute to the greater good of all.

For New Universalism, dharma resonates deeply with the principles of integrity and social responsibility. Dharma teaches that ethical living is not only about personal gain but about contributing to the welfare of others. In the New Universalist perspective, living one's dharma means making choices that benefit both the community and the Earth, acting with consideration for how each decision affects the interconnected web of life. By aligning with dharma, New Universalists are inspired to live with purpose, dedication, and an unwavering commitment to justice and respect for others.

Ahimsa: The Principle of Non-Violence and Respect for All Life

Ahimsa, the principle of non-violence, is a central tenet of Hindu ethics and reflects a deep respect for all forms of life. It is the belief that one should avoid harm, whether in thought, word, or action, toward any being. Ahimsa calls for compassion and kindness, encouraging individuals to recognize the inherent worth and sanctity of each life. This principle underpins Hindu practices of vegetarianism and environmental stewardship, promoting a lifestyle that honors the Earth and its creatures.

In New Universalism, ahimsa aligns with Earth Stewardship and the commitment to kindness and respect. The principle of ahimsa calls New Universalists to act in ways that protect and nurture the natural world, recognizing that harm to one part of creation affects the whole. Through ahimsa, New Universalists are encouraged to embrace peace in all interactions and to consider the broader impact of their actions on others and on the environment. The reverence for life expressed through ahimsa reinforces the New Universalist view that compassion is not only a personal virtue but a global responsibility, one that unites all beings in a shared existence.

New Universalism's Perspective on Hindu Values

The values of dharma and ahimsa offer profound insights into living a life rooted in ethical duty and compassion for all forms of life. New Universalism embraces these teachings, seeing them as an invitation to act responsibly, to respect the interconnectedness of all beings, and to promote peace in every interaction. Through dharma, New Universalists find purpose in service and integrity, while ahimsa inspires a commitment to kindness, Earth stewardship, and non-violence. These teachings guide us in creating a world that honors both the sacredness of the individual and the unity of all creation.

Common Values: Wicca and Earth-Based Faiths

Wicca and Earth-based spiritualities, often rooted in ancient traditions, honor the cycles of nature and see the Earth as a living, sacred entity. These faiths place great value on harmony with the natural world, respect for all forms of life, and recognition of the divine presence within

Earth's cycles. For followers of these traditions, nature is both a teacher and a source of spiritual connection, with each season, animal, and element reflecting aspects of the divine. New Universalism draws inspiration from these values, embracing Earth Stewardship and the interconnectedness of all life as essential aspects of spiritual growth and collective well-being.

Reverence for the Earth: Seeing Nature as Sacred

In Wiccan and Earth-based beliefs, the Earth is not merely a resource but a sacred entity deserving of respect, protection, and gratitude. Practitioners see nature as alive with spiritual energy, where rivers, forests, and mountains are expressions of the divine. Wiccans, for example, honor the Earth's cycles through the Wheel of the Year, which marks seasonal changes with rituals celebrating life, death, rebirth, and renewal. These practices encourage followers to align with nature's rhythms and to recognize their responsibility in caring for the planet.

For New Universalism, this reverence for the Earth serves as a foundation for Earth Stewardship, which calls followers to protect and nurture the environment as a sacred responsibility. Like Wiccans, New Universalists celebrate the cycles of nature and seek to live in harmony with Earth's natural rhythms, understanding that caring for the planet is an expression of respect for life itself. Through this alignment with nature, New Universalists deepen our sense of belonging within the larger web of life, cultivating gratitude and mindfulness in their daily lives.

Interconnectedness: The Web of All Beings

One of the central teachings in Earth-centered faiths is the belief in the interconnectedness of all life forms. This understanding, often symbolized as a web or a network of connections, emphasizes that every action impacts the whole. In Wicca, the concept of interconnectedness is reflected in the Threefold Law, which suggests that whatever energy one puts into the world—positive or negative—will return to them threefold. This principle encourages practitioners to act with intention and care, recognizing that their actions resonate beyond themselves.

New Universalism embraces this view of interconnectedness, recognizing that humanity is not separate from nature but a part of it. This understanding inspires New Universalists to practice kindness, integrity, and responsibility, knowing that these qualities impact the broader community and environment. By seeing all beings as connected, New Universalists are called to respect and honor the diversity of life, acting in ways that contribute to collective harmony. The web of interconnectedness aligns with the New Universalist belief in unity and social responsibility, reminding us that each action contributes to the well-being of the whole.

Rituals Honoring Seasonal Cycles and Earth's Rhythms

Earth-based traditions use rituals to celebrate the seasonal cycles and natural rhythms, seeing these as opportunities to renew spiritual connection and honor the Earth. Wiccans, for example, mark the solstices, equinoxes, and other festivals on the Wheel of the Year, each ritual inviting reflection, gratitude, and celebration of life's cyclical nature. These observances highlight the themes of growth, transformation, and rest, reminding practitioners of the importance of balance and acceptance in their lives.

In New Universalism, we also recognize the spiritual significance of the Earth's rhythms. Through practices aligned with the Wheel of the Year and lunar cycles, New Universalists observe the seasonal festivals as times to reflect, reconnect with nature, and practice gratitude. Rituals celebrating nature's cycles serve as reminders of life's constant renewal, offering moments of grounding and renewal. By honoring these natural transitions, New Universalists cultivate awareness of our place within the larger cycle of existence, fostering a sense of peace and resilience.

New Universalism's Perspective on Earth-Based Values

The values of reverence for nature, interconnectedness, and seasonal celebration found in Wiccan and Earth-based faiths deepen the New Universalist commitment to Earth Stewardship and unity. By embracing these teachings, New Universalists are reminded of our sacred responsibility to care for the Earth and to respect the bonds that connect all beings. These practices foster a sense of belonging and purpose, encouraging us to act with reverence, gratitude, and mindfulness. Through the wisdom of Earth-based faiths, New Universalism celebrates life's sacredness and our shared journey within the intricate web of existence.

Common Values: Sikhism

Sikhism, a spiritual tradition founded by Guru Nanak in the 15th century, centers on the values of equality, justice, and service. Sikhs believe in the oneness of all humanity and that each person has a duty to support the well-being of others, regardless of race, religion, or social status. These core values—rooted in equality, justice, and selfless service—align closely with New Universalism's commitment to social responsibility, inclusivity, and community unity. New Universalism draws inspiration from Sikh teachings, recognizing these values as essential to creating a world that honors the dignity and interconnectedness of all beings.

Equality: Recognizing the Oneness of Humanity

One of the fundamental teachings of Sikhism is the belief in the equality of all people. Guru Nanak emphasized that there is no distinction between individuals based on caste, gender, or background; all are equal in the eyes of the divine. This principle of equality is visible in Sikh practices such as the common use of surnames ("Singh" for men and "Kaur" for women) to remove caste distinctions, and in the design of the Gurdwara (Sikh temple), where people of all backgrounds are welcomed without question.

In New Universalism, this emphasis on equality aligns with the belief that each individual holds inherent worth and should be treated with respect and dignity. Recognizing the oneness of humanity encourages New Universalists to embrace inclusivity, fostering a community that celebrates diversity while upholding a shared commitment to peace and justice. Inspired by Sikh teachings, New Universalism rejects any forms of discrimination, seeing all people as equal partners in the journey of spiritual growth and social unity.

Justice: The Duty to Uphold Fairness and Integrity

Sikhism teaches that each person has a responsibility to stand up for justice, defending the rights of the oppressed and promoting fairness in society. The Sikh Gurus, especially Guru Gobind Singh, emphasized the importance of standing against injustice, encouraging followers to live with courage, integrity, and moral strength. This commitment to justice extends beyond personal conduct to encompass active engagement in societal issues, challenging inequality and seeking truth.

For New Universalism, the Sikh emphasis on justice resonates with the principles of social responsibility and integrity. We are encouraged to take an active role in addressing injustice, both within our communities and in the world at large. Inspired by the Sikh example, New Universalists view justice not as an abstract concept but as a call to action, one that requires individuals to advocate for fairness, equity, and the well-being of all. Upholding justice becomes an expression of compassion and empathy, reflecting New Universalism's dedication to ethical living and community harmony.

Service: The Practice of Seva and Selflessness

Seva, or selfless service, is a cornerstone of Sikh practice, encouraging followers to dedicate their time, resources, and energy to help others. This principle is demonstrated in the tradition of "Langar," the communal meal offered in every Gurdwara, where people of all backgrounds are invited to share food together, emphasizing unity and equality. The practice of Seva reminds Sikhs to live with humility and compassion, seeing service as a spiritual practice that brings people closer to the divine and to one another.

New Universalism draws upon the spirit of Seva as a model for community service and kindness. By adopting the practice of selfless service, New Universalists are encouraged to contribute to our communities, not out of obligation but as an act of love and solidarity. Service is viewed as a sacred act, one that allows us to strengthen communal bonds, support those in need, and live in alignment with the values of humility and generosity. Through Seva, New Universalists find a path to both personal growth and societal contribution, honoring the interconnectedness of all beings and the shared journey of spiritual progress.

New Universalism's Perspective on Sikh Values

The Sikh values of equality, justice, and service offer profound guidance for New Universalists, illuminating a path of integrity, inclusivity, and community care. By embracing these teachings, New Universalism affirms its commitment to a world built on respect, fairness, and compassion. Inspired by Sikhism, we seek to honor the divine presence in every person, viewing acts of justice and service as expressions of unity and shared humanity. Through these values, New Universalism promotes a way of life that celebrates diversity, uplifts the vulnerable, and strengthens the bonds that connect all people.

Common Values: Shamanistic Traditions

Shamanistic traditions, often rooted in indigenous spiritual practices across the world, hold profound wisdom that has been passed down through generations. Central to these practices are values of reverence for the Earth, respect for ancestors, and balance with the natural world. Shamanism views all elements of creation as interconnected, with each person holding a unique place within a vast web of life. These values align with New Universalism's dedication to Earth Stewardship, honoring ancestral wisdom, and maintaining harmony in the natural world.

Respect for the Earth: Honoring the Sacredness of Nature

Shamanistic traditions are deeply connected to the land, seeing the Earth as a sacred being that sustains and nurtures all life. Practitioners regard rivers, mountains, plants, and animals as holding spiritual significance, believing that every aspect of nature embodies a unique spirit and deserves reverence. This respect for the Earth is expressed in rituals, offerings, and practices that honor nature's cycles and acknowledge humanity's dependence on the environment.

For New Universalism, this respect for the Earth forms the foundation of Earth Stewardship. Inspired by shamanistic views, New Universalists recognize the Earth as a sacred gift, one that demands care, respect, and gratitude. In alignment with shamanistic teachings, New Universalism encourages practices that protect, nurture, and honor the environment, viewing these acts as expressions of spiritual devotion and ethical duty. We are encouraged to live in a way that supports the health of the planet, cultivating an awareness of the Earth's inherent value and the interconnectedness of all beings.

Reverence for Ancestors: Honoring Past Wisdom and Lineage

In shamanistic traditions, ancestors are regarded as wise guides and protectors who continue to influence the living world. Practitioners often communicate with ancestors through rituals, prayers, and offerings, seeking guidance and wisdom from those who came before. This reverence for ancestors reflects a deep respect for the continuity of life, recognizing that each generation is shaped by the sacrifices and teachings of those who preceded it.

New Universalism draws on this ancestral respect, honoring the wisdom and legacies of previous generations. Reverence for ancestors is seen not only as a form of filial piety but also as a way to draw strength and insight from the past. We are encouraged to reflect on the contributions of our forebears, recognizing that our lives are part of a larger lineage of human experience. By honoring the wisdom and traditions passed down through generations, New Universalists foster a sense of continuity and gratitude, viewing our lives as part of a sacred chain that connects past, present, and future.

Balance with the Natural World: Living in Harmony with All Beings

A core principle in shamanistic practice is the need to live in balance with nature and all living beings. Shamanistic traditions teach that imbalance—whether through environmental exploitation, social discord, or spiritual neglect—leads to suffering and disharmony. Rituals and practices in shamanism are designed to restore this balance, whether by healing individuals, strengthening communities, or reconciling relationships with nature. This commitment to balance serves as a reminder that human well-being is deeply connected to the health of the broader ecosystem.

New Universalism embraces this commitment to balance as a call to live responsibly and thoughtfully. Inspired by shamanistic principles, New Universalists seek to create harmony in our relationships with the Earth, other people, and ourselves. We are encouraged to recognize the impact of our choices, understanding that true well-being arises from living in alignment with nature's rhythms and respecting the delicate interdependence of all life. This dedication to balance supports the New Universalist values of Earth Stewardship, social responsibility, and unity, inviting us to act as guardians of harmony within both the natural and spiritual realms.

New Universalism's Perspective on Shamanistic Values

The shamanistic values of respect for the Earth, reverence for ancestors, and balance with nature offer essential guidance for New Universalists, enriching our understanding of interconnectedness and harmony. By embracing these principles, New Universalism honors a holistic view of life that respects both the visible and invisible bonds that connect all beings. These teachings inspire us to approach the Earth with reverence, to acknowledge the wisdom of past generations, and to live in a way that preserves the balance and beauty of the natural world. Through these values, New Universalism fosters a spirituality that is deeply rooted in respect, gratitude, and a sacred duty to all forms of life.

Universal Pursuit of Compassion Unity and Morality

Across the breadth of human belief and tradition, a common pursuit emerges: the desire to live a life of compassion, unity, and moral integrity. From the teachings of the world's major religions to the timeless wisdom of indigenous and shamanistic practices, these values stand as universal truths that speak to the shared journey of all humanity. In New Universalism, this shared pursuit forms a foundation upon which all people, regardless of background, can connect, learn, and grow together.

Compassion: The Core of Ethical Living

Compassion is a recurring theme within all spiritual and philosophical traditions, encouraging individuals to extend kindness, empathy, and care to all beings. In Christianity, followers are called to "love thy neighbor"; in Buddhism, practitioners cultivate metta, or loving-kindness, toward all. Islam enshrines mercy and compassion as divine qualities, while Hinduism's principle of ahimsa teaches non-violence toward all forms of life. Indigenous and Earth-based traditions also stress the importance of caring for the land and all its inhabitants, seeing compassion as a guiding force that nurtures harmony within communities and ecosystems alike.

New Universalism embraces compassion as a central pillar, believing that the active practice of kindness transforms both individuals and society. Compassion becomes an ethical foundation, fostering understanding across diverse perspectives and honoring the dignity of all beings. For New Universalists, compassion is not only an act of personal virtue but a communal practice that brings people together, creating bonds of trust, empathy, and mutual respect.

Unity: Embracing the Interconnectedness of All Life

The recognition of unity—the interconnectedness of all life—is a universal truth that appears in teachings across various cultures and faiths. Buddhism's concept of interconnectedness, as illustrated by Indra's Net, describes how every being is intricately connected, each action affecting the whole. In Sikhism, the ideal of Ummah, or community, unites all people under a shared purpose. Shamanistic traditions and Earth-based faiths teach that humans are part of an interwoven web of life, connected to nature and bound by a collective responsibility to preserve balance and harmony.

For New Universalism, this understanding of unity inspires a way of life that values inclusivity, cooperation, and reverence for the Earth. We are encouraged to see ourselves as part of a vast, interconnected community, where each individual's well-being is tied to the welfare of others. This awareness of unity guides New Universalists to act with integrity, supporting initiatives that promote environmental stewardship, social justice, and a sense of shared purpose. Unity thus becomes both a spiritual truth and an ethical directive, reminding us to cultivate harmony within ourselves and with the world.

Morality: A Shared Compass for Justice and Integrity

Morality, the commitment to live with honesty, justice, and respect, is a guiding principle within every faith and philosophy. In Hinduism, the concept of dharma emphasizes ethical duty and responsibility, encouraging individuals to act in ways that honor both self and community. Judaism and Christianity stress the importance of moral integrity, teaching followers to seek justice and treat others with fairness. Islam's principles of charity and justice reflect a commitment to uphold equity and truth, while Confucian teachings on filial piety emphasize the respect and care owed to family, elders, and society.

New Universalism draws from these moral teachings to create a framework for ethical living. By integrating values of honesty, justice, and respect, we are encouraged to pursue a life of integrity that honors the dignity and rights of all people. In New Universalism, morality extends beyond individual actions, representing a collective responsibility to uphold principles of fairness and equity within society. This shared moral compass supports New Universalists in our pursuit of a just and compassionate world, where each person contributes to the greater good.

New Universalism's Embrace of Universal Values

The pursuit of compassion, unity, and morality binds humanity in a common quest for understanding, peace, and well-being. New Universalism honors these values as foundational truths that resonate across diverse faiths, seeing them as guideposts for creating a world where people from all backgrounds can come together in mutual respect. By drawing on these universal values, New Universalism fosters an inclusive spirituality that embraces the richness of human diversity while upholding the belief in a shared ethical path.

In a world often divided by cultural and ideological differences, New Universalism offers a unifying vision rooted in the timeless principles of compassion, interconnectedness, and moral integrity. Through these values, we find inspiration to live with empathy, to seek justice, and to honor the sacredness of all life. In honoring these universal truths, New Universalism calls each person to contribute to a more harmonious and equitable world, one that reflects the deepest aspirations of humanity.

Secular and Philosophical Wisdom

Introduction to Secular Ethics and Philosophy

Throughout human history, secular philosophy and ethical frameworks have provided guidance for living a life of integrity, purpose, and compassion. From the ancient teachings of Aristotle to contemporary frameworks on human rights and environmental ethics, these secular traditions explore the same timeless questions as religious and spiritual beliefs. What does it mean to live a good life? How do we contribute to the well-being of others? What is our responsibility to the planet? These inquiries, shared across secular and spiritual domains, reflect the universal pursuit of truth and the aspiration to create a just, harmonious world.

In New Universalism, reason is a sacred path alongside spiritual insight, offering a balanced approach to understanding ethical living. We honor these philosophical traditions not as separate or opposing realms but as complementary teachings that deepen our understanding of humanity, morality, and social responsibility. By engaging with secular philosophies, New Universalism embraces a broader, more inclusive perspective that values the wisdom of rational inquiry and encourages an open, thoughtful approach to life's questions. The teachings found in secular ethics remind us that universal values like compassion, integrity, and justice are not bound to any one faith; they are principles that resonate within every heart, echoing a shared vision of the good.

Through secular philosophy, New Universalism finds a language of ethics that encourages self-reflection, civic responsibility, and a deep commitment to collective well-being. This alignment with secular and philosophical ethics supports our theology by emphasizing that truth and meaning are not only spiritual revelations but also insights born from the human experience. By recognizing this harmony, New Universalism affirms its dedication to rationality, inclusivity, and a commitment to universal truth.

Aristotle's Ethics & New Universalism

Aristotle, the ancient Greek philosopher, introduced a framework for ethical living known as virtue ethics. At the core of Aristotle's philosophy is the concept of *eudaimonia*, often translated as "the good life" or "human flourishing." Aristotle taught that a meaningful, fulfilling life is achieved through the practice of virtues—qualities such as courage, temperance, generosity, and integrity. These virtues are cultivated through deliberate action, habit, and self-reflection, shaping one's character over time. For Aristotle, virtue lies in the balance between extremes; courage, for instance, is the midpoint between recklessness and cowardice.

In New Universalism, this practice of cultivating virtues resonates with our commitment to living with integrity and compassion. Aristotle's belief that virtues must be practiced aligns with the New Universalist view that values are not simply ideals but active, lived principles. We are encouraged to see ethical living as a daily practice, where each choice, however small, contributes to personal growth and social harmony. In the spirit of Aristotle's philosophy, New Universalism regards virtues as essential elements of a meaningful life, calling on us to embody qualities that uplift ourselves and others.

Living with Courage and Integrity

Aristotle emphasized that courage and integrity are foundational virtues, guiding individuals in the face of challenges and adversity. Courage is not fearlessness, but the strength to act according to one's values despite fear or uncertainty. Integrity, similarly, requires honesty and consistency between one's actions and beliefs. For New Universalists, courage and integrity are seen as essential for pursuing truth, standing up for justice, and acting with authenticity. By cultivating these virtues, we contribute to a compassionate, principled world where individuals are empowered to act ethically even in difficult situations.

The Balance of Virtues: The Middle Way

A key aspect of Aristotle's ethics is the idea of balance, or finding the "golden mean" between two extremes. This balance reflects New Universalism's emphasis on harmony—both within the individual and within the broader community. Practicing moderation, or temperance, encourages individuals to find fulfillment without excess or deprivation, whether in material possessions, relationships, or personal ambition. In New Universalism, this balance is not a restriction but a path to wholeness, inviting us to experience life fully and meaningfully while remaining mindful of our impact on others and the environment.

Generosity and Responsibility to Others

Aristotle regarded generosity as a virtue that enhances both the giver and the community. Generosity, in his view, requires thoughtful giving, where one considers the needs of others while respecting one's own limits. For New Universalism, generosity is central to social responsibility and communal care. Inspired by Aristotle's teachings, we are encouraged to give with compassion and mindfulness, recognizing that generosity builds trust, fosters empathy, and strengthens the bonds of community. This approach aligns with New Universalism's belief that each person has a duty to contribute to the common good, creating a more compassionate and connected world.

New Universalism's Perspective on Aristotle's Ethics

Aristotle's virtue ethics offers a timeless guide to ethical living, emphasizing that a fulfilling life is achieved through the cultivation of virtues that benefit oneself and others. In New Universalism, these teachings are honored as a pathway to moral and spiritual growth, where each virtue supports the journey toward a just and compassionate world. By embodying values such as courage, integrity, and generosity, New Universalists find a framework for ethical living that transcends religious boundaries and speaks to the shared human desire for goodness, meaning, and connection.

Confucianism & New Universalism

Confucianism, a philosophical system founded by the Chinese sage Confucius, centers on the importance of ethical relationships, respect, and harmonious social order. Confucian values emphasize that a just and compassionate society begins with integrity and respect within the family unit, which then extends to the larger community. At the heart of Confucian thought is the concept of *filial piety*, or respect for one's parents and elders, as well as the importance of self-cultivation and moral integrity. In New Universalism, these values reflect our commitment to social harmony, family bonds, and responsible leadership.

Filial Piety: The Foundation of Respectful Relationships

Confucianism teaches that filial piety, or *xiao*, is the foundation of all ethical relationships. This principle calls for reverence, loyalty, and care for one's parents and ancestors, recognizing that honoring family is central to one's moral and social responsibilities. For Confucius, filial piety was not simply about obedience but about fostering mutual respect, support, and understanding between generations. In Confucian thought, respect for family extends outward, fostering empathy and loyalty within the community and cultivating a society rooted in compassion and unity.

In New Universalism, filial piety is also a reciprocal relationship that reflects mutual responsibility, respect, and care. Honoring one's parents, elders, and ancestors is encouraged, as is the reciprocal duty of elders to respect and nurture younger generations. This dynamic of mutual respect aligns with New Universalism's belief in collective well-being and personal integrity. Filial piety in New Universalism extends beyond the family, embodying a respect for community leaders, mentors, and those who serve others, reinforcing the ideal that compassion begins at home and grows outward into the world.

Harmony and Ethical Behavior in Society

A fundamental goal in Confucian philosophy is the creation of a harmonious society, achieved through personal responsibility, ethical behavior, and respect for others. Confucius emphasized that a well-ordered society depends on the moral character of each individual. By cultivating virtues like honesty, humility, and kindness, individuals contribute to a broader culture of respect and cooperation. In Confucian thought, leaders are held to high ethical standards, as they are responsible for setting an example of integrity and fairness for those they serve.

New Universalism resonates with this ideal of social harmony, emphasizing the value of ethical living within a larger community. Inspired by Confucian teachings, New Universalists are encouraged to develop qualities that contribute to peaceful, supportive environments. This practice aligns with the New Universalist belief in social responsibility, encouraging us to live with compassion, fairness, and integrity. By fostering harmony within communities, we help create a world grounded in mutual respect and ethical responsibility.

Respect for Elders and Personal Integrity

Confucianism places a strong emphasis on respect for elders, viewing them as bearers of wisdom and experience. This respect fosters continuity, as each generation learns from the insights and values of those who came before. Confucius taught that elders have an obligation to guide the younger generations with kindness, patience, and understanding. In turn, younger individuals are encouraged to honor their elders, learning from their wisdom while carrying forward values that promote well-being and unity.

For New Universalism, respect for elders is an expression of filial piety and social responsibility. The reciprocal relationship between elders and younger generations reinforces the belief in interconnectedness, where each person contributes to the well-being of others. Elders serve as mentors, sharing wisdom and guidance, while younger generations bring new perspectives and energy to the community. This mutual respect supports the New Universalist ideals of inclusivity and integrity, fostering a sense of belonging and honoring the unique gifts each person brings.

New Universalism's Perspective on Confucian Values

The Confucian principles of filial piety, harmony, and respect offer profound insights into building relationships and communities rooted in compassion and respect. In New Universalism, these teachings inspire us to embrace both family and society with care and integrity, nurturing a world where individuals feel valued, supported, and connected. By honoring these values, New Universalism encourages a way of life that upholds the dignity of all, reinforcing the belief that unity and compassion are essential to a just and harmonious society.

Existentialism & New Universalism

Existentialism, a philosophical movement that emerged in the 19th and 20th centuries, centers on themes of individual freedom, responsibility, and the search for meaning. Thinkers like Søren Kierkegaard, Jean-Paul Sartre, and Simone de Beauvoir emphasized the importance of personal choice, authenticity, and self-awareness. Existentialism teaches that each person has the freedom to shape their own path, but with this freedom comes the responsibility to live with integrity and purpose. In New Universalism, this call to embrace both freedom and responsibility aligns with the commitment to reasoned inquiry, self-reflection, and ethical action.

Freedom and the Responsibility of Choice

Existentialism teaches that individuals are "condemned to be free," as Sartre famously put it, meaning that each person is inherently responsible for the choices they make. This freedom is empowering but also demanding, as it requires individuals to define their own values, purpose, and identity without relying on societal expectations or external beliefs. In this framework, personal responsibility is seen as essential to authenticity—living in a way that genuinely reflects one's values and intentions.

In New Universalism, the freedom to choose is celebrated as a divine gift that enables each person to explore truth, meaning, and personal growth. However, this freedom is balanced by a call to act responsibly, recognizing that choices have consequences not only for oneself but also for others and the natural world. Inspired by existentialist teachings, New Universalism encourages us to make mindful decisions that honor our values, respect others, and contribute positively to society. This balance between freedom and responsibility reflects New Universalism's belief in ethical living and reasoned spiritual exploration.

Authenticity: Living in Alignment with One's Values

For existentialists, authenticity is the pursuit of living in alignment with one's true self, free from the pressures of conformity or societal expectations. Kierkegaard described this as "becoming a self," or understanding one's unique identity and purpose. Authenticity requires individuals to confront life's uncertainties and to make choices that genuinely reflect their inner convictions. This practice of self-examination and personal alignment forms the basis of a meaningful life.

New Universalism resonates with this existentialist focus on authenticity, encouraging us to live with honesty and integrity. Authenticity in New Universalism involves exploring one's beliefs, questioning assumptions, and embracing self-discovery. We are encouraged to seek our own path to truth, recognizing that spirituality is a personal journey. By fostering authenticity, New Universalism supports a life of purpose and integrity, where individuals feel empowered to express their values, contribute to the greater good, and live in harmony with their true selves.

The Search for Meaning: Creating Purpose in Life

Existentialism teaches that life's meaning is not predetermined; rather, each person must create their own purpose. Existential thinkers argue that meaning arises from one's experiences, choices, and relationships, emphasizing that a fulfilling life is crafted through engagement and intentionality. This search for meaning encourages self-awareness, resilience, and an appreciation for life's moments, even amidst uncertainty or hardship.

New Universalism aligns with this perspective, viewing the search for meaning as a fundamental aspect of spiritual growth. We are encouraged to reflect on what brings us fulfillment, to cultivate connections with others, and to engage in practices that support both personal and communal well-being. By finding purpose within ourselves and our communities, New Universalists live in a way that honors both individuality and interconnection. This active search for meaning reflects New Universalism's commitment to a life of mindful inquiry and compassionate engagement, where each person contributes to a shared vision of goodness.

New Universalism's Perspective on Existentialist Values

The existentialist values of freedom, authenticity, and the search for meaning offer a profound framework for understanding personal responsibility and purposeful living. In New Universalism, these teachings inspire us to embrace our individuality while acting with empathy and respect for others. By honoring both freedom and responsibility, New Universalists are called to live with intention, cultivating a life that is both meaningful and mindful. In alignment with existentialist thought, New Universalism fosters a spirituality that values personal growth, self-discovery, and a commitment to creating a compassionate and interconnected world.

Phenomenology & New Universalism

Phenomenology, a philosophical approach that emphasizes the lived experience of individuals within their environments, offers a profound framework for understanding the interconnectedness of mind, body, and world. Originally developed by philosophers such as Edmund Husserl and Maurice Merleau-Ponty, phenomenology has since evolved through feminist and New Materialist perspectives, enriching its focus on the embodied and relational aspects of human existence. For New Universalism, phenomenology aligns with a theology that values embodied experience, social responsibility, and deep respect for the material world. It invites us to approach life with an open heart and mind, fostering awareness, compassion, and connection with all beings.

Ahmed's Feminist Phenomenology: Centering Marginalized Experiences

Sara Ahmed's feminist phenomenology explores how lived experiences, particularly those of marginalized individuals, shape perceptions and interactions with the world. Ahmed argues that bodies experience the world differently based on their identities and societal positioning, pointing to how structural inequalities affect individual experiences of space, safety, and inclusion. By centering marginalized experiences, Ahmed's work highlights the importance of recognizing and respecting diverse perspectives, fostering empathy, and challenging systems of oppression.

In New Universalism, this attention to diverse experiences aligns with the values of inclusivity, social justice, and mutual respect. Ahmed's approach inspires us to recognize the unique experiences of others, honoring their perspectives and seeking to understand the contexts that shape them. By embracing feminist phenomenology, New Universalists commit to creating inclusive spaces where individuals of all backgrounds feel valued and respected. This alignment with Ahmed's work encourages us to engage in self-reflection, to confront biases, and to support initiatives that promote equity and inclusivity within their communities.

New Materialist Phenomenology: Embracing the Vitality of the Material World

New Materialist phenomenology, influenced by thinkers like Karen Barad and Jane Bennett, expands phenomenology's focus on human consciousness to include the material world's active role in shaping experience. This perspective challenges the traditional distinction between subjects and objects, viewing matter as vibrant and alive, with its own agency and influence. New Materialists argue that humans are in constant interaction with the world around them, interconnected through a web of relationships that includes not only people but also animals, plants, and other material entities.

This understanding resonates deeply with New Universalism's commitment to Earth Stewardship and interconnectedness. By recognizing the vitality of the material world, New Universalists are called to approach nature not as a passive resource but as a dynamic partner in spiritual and ethical life. Inspired by New Materialist phenomenology, we are encouraged to foster relationships with the Earth that are reciprocal and respectful, recognizing that all beings are interconnected through shared spaces, resources, and experiences. This perspective supports the New Universalist view that the natural world holds sacred value, inviting us to practice mindfulness, conservation, and a deep reverence for the planet.

Embodiment, Awareness, and Social Responsibility

Phenomenology as a whole places a strong emphasis on embodiment—the experience of being in a body and moving through the world with awareness and purpose. This focus on embodiment encourages individuals to recognize the significance of their actions and interactions, fostering a sense of responsibility for how they engage with others and the environment. For New Universalists, this embodied awareness aligns with values of intentionality and mindfulness, encouraging us to live with purpose, compassion, and integrity.

Embracing phenomenology's insights, New Universalists are encouraged to remain aware of our interconnectedness with others and the world. This awareness fosters social responsibility, as we recognize that each action affects not only our immediate environment but also the broader community. By engaging with phenomenological principles, New Universalists cultivate a way of life that honors the dignity of all people, respects the Earth's vitality, and values the experience of being fully present in each moment.

New Universalism's Perspective on Phenomenological Values

The values of embodied experience, inclusivity, and material connection offered by phenomenology and its feminist and New Materialist branches provide a framework that complements New Universalist principles. By embracing these philosophies, New Universalism encourages us to honor the sacredness of all beings, to act with mindfulness, and to create a world rooted in empathy and respect. Through phenomenology's lens, we find a path to live with greater awareness, compassion, and ethical responsibility, reflecting the belief that all beings share a common, vibrant world deserving of care and reverence.

Modern Human Rights Frameworks & New Universalism

Modern human rights frameworks provide a foundational guide for respecting and upholding the inherent dignity and equality of every individual. Documents like the Universal Declaration of Human Rights (UDHR), adopted by the United Nations in 1948, and subsequent human rights charters emphasize universal principles of equality, freedom, justice, and protection from discrimination. These frameworks serve as a moral compass, guiding nations and societies toward a vision of fairness and respect for all, regardless of nationality, religion, race, gender, or socioeconomic status. In New Universalism, these principles resonate deeply with our commitment to social responsibility, inclusivity, and the belief that every person holds intrinsic worth.

Equality: Recognizing the Inherent Dignity of Every Person

One of the core principles of modern human rights is the recognition of equal dignity and rights for all individuals. The UDHR begins with the statement that "all human beings are born free and equal in dignity and rights," a declaration that acknowledges the fundamental worth of each person. This principle of equality transcends cultural, religious, and political boundaries, calling for a world where every individual is valued and treated fairly.

In New Universalism, this respect for human dignity is foundational. Inspired by human rights ideals, New Universalists are encouraged to honor the inherent worth of all people, embracing diversity and fostering inclusivity within our communities. This commitment to equality aligns with New Universalism's theology of interconnectedness, where the well-being of each individual contributes to the collective good. By promoting equality, we create a compassionate environment that welcomes all people, reinforcing the belief that every life is sacred and deserving of respect.

Justice and Protection Against Discrimination

Modern human rights frameworks emphasize the importance of justice and protection from discrimination, ensuring that individuals are free from unfair treatment based on race, gender, religion, or other identifiers. This commitment to justice calls for both legal protections and a cultural respect for diversity, encouraging societies to address and dismantle systems of inequality. Human rights frameworks advocate for a world where individuals have access to equal opportunities and are protected from harm.

For New Universalism, justice is seen as an expression of compassion and respect for the interconnected web of humanity. Inspired by the principles of human rights, we are encouraged to take an active role in creating just societies, standing against discrimination and advocating for the marginalized. This commitment to justice aligns with New Universalism's emphasis on social responsibility, where each person is called to contribute to the well-being of others. By supporting initiatives that promote fairness and equity, New Universalists honor the values of integrity, empathy, and the belief that justice is essential to a harmonious world.

Freedom and the Right to Individual Beliefs

Human rights frameworks also protect the freedom of thought, conscience, and religion, acknowledging that each person has the right to explore and express their beliefs without fear of persecution. This freedom supports the diversity of human experience, recognizing that individuals must be free to seek truth, pursue knowledge, and live according to their values. In essence, the right to individual belief promotes a culture of tolerance and respect, where differences are seen as a source of enrichment rather than division.

New Universalism resonates deeply with this principle, as it holds that truth can be found across diverse faiths, philosophies, and personal experiences. We are encouraged to honor our own spiritual journey while respecting the unique paths of others. This respect for freedom aligns with New Universalism's theology of reasoned inquiry, where open-minded exploration is valued, and individuals are free to seek meaning in ways that feel authentic to them. By upholding the right to individual belief, New Universalists foster a community of respect, inclusivity, and shared understanding.

New Universalism's Perspective on Human Rights Values

The principles of equality, justice, and freedom found in modern human rights frameworks offer a universal language of compassion and respect, inspiring a vision of society that values each person's dignity. In New Universalism, these ideals serve as a guide for building communities grounded in fairness, empathy, and ethical responsibility. By embracing human rights principles, New Universalists contribute to a world where compassion and respect are extended to all, reinforcing the belief that humanity's shared values are a source of unity, growth, and peace.

Environmental Ethics and Sustainable Development in New Universalism

Environmental ethics and sustainable development represent a growing area of secular thought that seeks to define humanity's responsibility to protect and preserve the planet. As climate change, pollution, and resource depletion impact ecosystems and communities worldwide, environmental philosophy advocates for a shift in thinking—one that views the Earth not as a resource to be exploited, but as a complex, interconnected system deserving of respect and care. In New Universalism, the principles of environmental ethics resonate deeply with the commitment to Earth Stewardship, underscoring the belief that the health of the planet and the well-being of humanity are inseparable.

Respecting the Earth: Acknowledging Our Shared Home

Environmental ethics emphasizes the importance of respecting the Earth as a living, interconnected ecosystem. Thinkers like Aldo Leopold, a pioneering figure in environmental philosophy, proposed a "land ethic" in which humans view themselves as members of the Earth's community rather than as conquerors. This perspective promotes an ethical relationship with the natural world, encouraging people to act as responsible caretakers who protect and preserve their shared home.

In New Universalism, this respect for the Earth is seen as a sacred duty, a commitment to honor the planet's diversity and complexity. Inspired by environmental ethics, we are called to adopt practices that demonstrate care, such as reducing waste, conserving resources, and supporting sustainable initiatives. By fostering respect for the Earth, New Universalists recognize the sacredness of all life and acknowledge that humanity's future depends on preserving the planet's natural balance. This respect aligns with New Universalism's emphasis on humility and interconnectedness, encouraging us to see ourselves as stewards rather than owners of the Earth.

Preserving Natural Resources for Future Generations

Sustainable development is a framework that advocates for meeting the needs of the present without compromising the ability of future generations to meet their own needs. It promotes mindful consumption, conservation, and the use of renewable resources to ensure that the environment remains healthy and viable. Sustainable development also emphasizes social equity, recognizing that environmental issues often disproportionately affect vulnerable communities and future generations.

For New Universalism, this emphasis on sustainable practices is an extension of Earth Stewardship, aligning with the values of justice, compassion, and social responsibility. We are encouraged to adopt lifestyles that reduce environmental impact, recognizing that true sustainability requires both individual action and collective commitment. This principle of preserving resources for future generations resonates with the New Universalist teaching of respecting life's continuity, where each generation carries a responsibility to protect and nurture the world for those who will come after. In this way, sustainable development becomes a spiritual and ethical practice, honoring the Earth's resources and ensuring a legacy of care and mindfulness.

Mindful Consumption and Environmental Responsibility

Environmental ethics also advocates for mindful consumption—using only what is necessary and making choices that minimize harm to the environment. This principle, grounded in the concept of reducing one's ecological footprint, encourages individuals to consider the impact of their actions on the planet. By practicing mindful consumption, people contribute to a culture of sustainability that values simplicity, resourcefulness, and awareness.

In New Universalism, mindful consumption is a form of spiritual discipline, reminding followers to live with intention and respect for the Earth. Inspired by secular environmental teachings, New Universalists are called to examine our habits and choices, seeking ways to live in harmony with the natural world. This approach encourages not only individual reflection but also community efforts to promote sustainable practices. By practicing mindful consumption, we embody the values of simplicity and integrity, fostering a lifestyle that nurtures both personal growth and planetary health.

New Universalism's Perspective on Environmental Ethics

The principles of environmental ethics and sustainable development offer a framework for living in harmony with the Earth, inspiring a way of life that respects the planet's limits and treasures its resources. In New Universalism, these teachings are embraced as expressions of Earth Stewardship, guiding us to act as caretakers who preserve the beauty and vitality of the natural world. By honoring the values of respect, preservation, and mindful consumption, New Universalists affirm our commitment to a compassionate, sustainable future. This dedication to environmental ethics reflects the belief that caring for the Earth is a sacred duty, a path to both personal and collective well-being.

Parallels Between Secular Philosophies and New Universalism's Pillars

In New Universalism, the pillars of Earth Stewardship, Social Responsibility, Filial Piety, and Reasoned Inquiry form a framework for living a life that honors both the self and the collective good. Each pillar reflects universal truths that resonate across spiritual and secular philosophies, highlighting the shared values and aspirations of humanity. By drawing on secular wisdom, New Universalism strengthens its commitment to inclusivity, integrity, and ethical living, embracing teachings that transcend religious boundaries to reflect a broader pursuit of meaning, justice, and compassion.

Earth Stewardship: Honoring the Planet and Interconnectedness

The principles of Earth Stewardship find strong parallels in environmental ethics and New Materialist philosophy, which advocate for a respectful, mindful relationship with the natural world. Both perspectives view the Earth as a living entity, deserving of care and reverence. Environmental philosophers emphasize the importance of sustainability, mindful consumption, and the protection of ecosystems, while New Materialist thought encourages recognition of the Earth's agency and vitality.

For New Universalism, Earth Stewardship is a sacred duty, calling us to protect the planet and live in harmony with nature. Inspired by secular philosophies, this pillar underscores that each action affects the larger whole, encouraging us to act as guardians of the environment. By embracing the interconnectedness of all life, New Universalists practice reverence for the Earth, understanding that true stewardship involves respect, conservation, and a commitment to sustainable practices that honor future generations.

Social Responsibility: Fostering Compassion and Justice

Social Responsibility, a core pillar of New Universalism, aligns closely with secular philosophies that emphasize empathy, justice, and service to others. Aristotle's ethics promote the cultivation of virtues such as generosity and fairness, while modern human rights frameworks advocate for equality and protection from discrimination. Existentialism also contributes to this pillar, encouraging individuals to take responsibility for their actions, live authentically, and contribute to the well-being of their communities.

New Universalism embraces these values, encouraging followers to act with compassion, fairness, and a commitment to the common good. Social Responsibility within New Universalism calls for active engagement in addressing social inequalities, advocating for justice, and creating inclusive spaces where every individual feels valued. This commitment is a manifestation of the belief that a compassionate society requires each person to contribute to the welfare of others, fostering unity and respect across communities.

Filial Piety: Respecting Family, Community, and Tradition

The value of Filial Piety, deeply rooted in Confucian philosophy, emphasizes respect, gratitude, and responsibility toward family and community. In Confucian thought, filial piety extends beyond family relationships, encompassing respect for elders, mentors, and societal leaders. This respect reinforces social harmony and ethical behavior, highlighting the importance of honoring one's roots and recognizing the wisdom of previous generations.

For New Universalism, Filial Piety is a reciprocal value that encompasses both respect for elders and the responsibility of elders to guide younger generations with kindness and support. This pillar reflects the belief in honoring those who came before us while creating a nurturing environment for future generations. Inspired by Confucianism and phenomenology, New Universalism encourages us to respect tradition while fostering inclusivity, creating a community that values each member's unique contributions and experiences.

Reasoned Inquiry: The Pursuit of Truth and Personal Integrity

Reasoned Inquiry, a foundational pillar of New Universalism, aligns with philosophical traditions that prioritize critical thinking, self-reflection, and the pursuit of knowledge. From Aristotle's emphasis on virtue and ethical discernment to existentialism's call for authenticity, secular philosophies affirm the importance of questioning, exploring, and understanding one's beliefs. Reasoned Inquiry supports New Universalism's commitment to rational, open-minded exploration, where we are encouraged to seek truth through reflection, study, and engagement with diverse perspectives.

This pillar emphasizes that faith and reason are not opposing forces but complementary paths to understanding. For New Universalists, reasoned inquiry enriches spiritual growth, fostering a deep, thoughtful approach to beliefs and values. By encouraging us to embrace both spiritual insight and rational understanding, New Universalism creates a framework where faith is grounded in integrity, curiosity, and an openness to learn from all traditions, philosophies, and sciences.

The Universalist Vision: Uniting Secular and Spiritual Wisdom

Through these shared values, New Universalism bridges secular and spiritual insights, honoring both as sources of ethical guidance and inspiration. By embracing the lessons of Earth Stewardship, Social Responsibility, Filial Piety, and Reasoned Inquiry, New Universalism fosters a way of life that values compassion, integrity, and respect for all beings. These pillars affirm that the pursuit of truth and the practice of ethical living are universal human endeavors, connecting people across backgrounds, beliefs, and experiences.

In uniting secular and spiritual wisdom, New Universalism invites us to cultivate a life of meaning and connection, where personal growth is intertwined with collective well-being. This synthesis of values reflects the heart of New Universalism's theology, a call to live with purpose, kindness, and an enduring commitment to the world we share.

The Value of Scientific Understanding

Science and Spirituality: A Harmonious Relationship

In New Universalism, science and spirituality are seen as complementary pathways that together lead to a fuller understanding of life, the universe, and our role within it. Rather than existing in opposition, scientific inquiry and spiritual understanding serve as reciprocal tools for exploring universal truths. While science offers insights into the mechanics of existence—the processes that shape stars, the origins of life, and the interconnectedness of ecosystems—spirituality addresses the deeper meanings and ethical responsibilities that arise from this understanding. Together, they form a holistic framework that aligns with New Universalism's commitment to reason, humility, and respect for all life.

At its heart, New Universalism embraces a worldview that values both rational exploration and spiritual reverence. This harmonious relationship is rooted in a theology that honors reasoned inquiry, seeing it as a means to deepen faith rather than challenge it. For New Universalists, scientific knowledge offers a window into the marvels of creation, from the vastness of galaxies to the intricacies of a single leaf. By engaging with science, we are called to a deeper reverence for the Earth and the universe, recognizing the sacredness inherent in all forms of life and matter.

This perspective also aligns with New Universalism's belief in interconnectedness. Science reveals the intricate networks that bind all beings together, from the atoms that compose each living thing to the ecosystems that sustain them. Understanding these connections reinforces the spiritual truth that each part of creation is interdependent, inspiring us to embrace compassion, humility, and a commitment to ethical action. By acknowledging that scientific understanding can elevate spiritual insight, New Universalism invites a worldview that is expansive, respectful, and committed to lifelong learning.

Scientific Principles Aligned with Spiritual Wisdom

Science and spirituality together form a holistic understanding of existence, with scientific discoveries shedding light on principles that resonate deeply with the teachings of New Universalism. This alignment offers us both inspiration and guidance, reinforcing the interconnectedness of life, the humility inherent in cosmic origins, the wisdom of psychological insights, and the responsibility to care for the Earth. These principles strengthen New Universalism's commitment to reasoned spiritual inquiry, ethical living, and compassion for all beings.

Interconnectedness in Nature: Ecological Systems and the Web of Life

Ecology reveals that life operates within an intricate web of relationships, where each organism and environment is connected through energy flows, nutrient cycles, and mutual dependencies. This interconnectedness is reflected in scientific theories like the Gaia Hypothesis, proposed by James Lovelock, which suggests that the Earth functions as a self-regulating organism, with living and non-living components working together to sustain conditions for life. By viewing the Earth as a unified system, this theory encourages us to see that the health of one part affects the health of the whole.

Research on ecosystems demonstrates that when a species is removed or its habitat is damaged, it disrupts the balance of the entire system, leading to consequences that reverberate across the food chain. Examples such as the reintroduction of wolves into Yellowstone National Park show how interconnected ecosystems are; when wolves were reintroduced, the entire ecosystem stabilized, with effects seen from vegetation growth to animal populations across the region.

For New Universalists, these ecological insights support the spiritual concept of interconnectedness. We are encouraged to see ourselves as integral parts of this web, not only co-existing with but also responsible for nurturing and preserving other forms of life. This recognition of mutual dependence is foundational to the principle of Earth Stewardship, guiding us to respect and protect the natural world.

Cosmic Evolution and Human Origins: Embracing Humility and Curiosity

Cosmic evolution—the scientific study of the universe's development from the Big Bang to the present—provides a narrative that invites awe and humility. The Big Bang Theory, widely accepted among scientists, posits that the universe began roughly 13.8 billion years ago as an incredibly dense point that rapidly expanded. This expansion allowed galaxies, stars, planets, and eventually life to form. Stars, through nuclear fusion, created the elements that form everything, from the iron in our blood to the oxygen we breathe, establishing that we are all, in a literal sense, "star-stuff."

The theory of evolution, first put forward by Charles Darwin and continuously refined by scientists, explains how life on Earth has diversified over billions of years through natural selection. This perspective underscores our shared origins with all life, tracing humanity's lineage back to early single-celled organisms that thrived in Earth's primordial waters. Such discoveries speak to the remarkable journey of life, connecting each being to a common ancestry and highlighting the uniqueness of human consciousness within the vast evolutionary tapestry.

In New Universalism, these scientific perspectives encourage humility and curiosity. We are reminded of our place within the universe's vast timeline, cultivating an appreciation for the miracle of life that transcends species and individual differences. This understanding fosters compassion and respect for all beings, grounding the principle of Filial Piety in a cosmic kinship. By embracing these scientific theories, New Universalists honor both the mystery and reality of existence, recognizing that all forms of life share a sacred heritage.

Psychology and Human Experience: Insights into Compassion, Resilience, and Well-Being

Psychology offers insights into the human mind and emotions, reinforcing spiritual values of compassion, resilience, and self-awareness. Carl Jung, an influential figure in psychology, explored concepts like the collective unconscious—a shared reservoir of human experiences and archetypes that transcends individual cultures. Jung was inspired by both Western and Eastern spiritual traditions, which he integrated into his understanding of personal growth. His idea of "individuation," or the journey toward self-fulfillment, resonates with New Universalism's commitment to personal and spiritual growth, encouraging us to explore our unique path within the shared human experience.

Viktor Frankl's Logotherapy, developed after his experience in concentration camps, focuses on finding meaning as a central motivator in life. Frankl emphasized that purpose can be found within oneself or in service to others and that even suffering can hold meaning. This resonates with New Universalist beliefs that each person has a purpose, and through compassion and resilience, we contribute to the well-being of others and the larger community.

Incorporating these insights, New Universalists are encouraged to cultivate practices that support both personal and communal well-being. By fostering a mindset of self-reflection, empathy, and meaningful engagement, we nurture a life rooted in compassion and responsibility. The alignment of psychological principles with spiritual values reinforces the New Universalist understanding that mental and emotional well-being are fundamental to a balanced, spiritually enriched life.

Environmental Responsibility: Science-Backed Insights for Earth Stewardship

Environmental science highlights the pressing need to address climate change, biodiversity loss, and pollution—issues directly affecting ecosystems and human societies worldwide. The theory of climate change, supported by a consensus among scientists, shows that human activities like burning fossil fuels release greenhouse gases, trapping heat in the atmosphere and altering global climates. This disruption threatens not only polar ice caps and weather patterns but also vulnerable species and ecosystems.

Biodiversity studies emphasize the importance of preserving the variety of species on Earth, as each contributes to ecological resilience. Research has shown that the loss of even a single species can destabilize entire ecosystems, illustrating the delicate balance of life. Conservation biology advocates for protecting habitats, reducing pollution, and restoring damaged ecosystems as essential practices to safeguard biodiversity.

New Universalism's Earth Stewardship calls us to take active roles in these scientific imperatives, promoting sustainable practices, conservation efforts, and mindful consumption. By respecting and protecting the natural world, New Universalists embody the belief that caring for the Earth is a sacred duty, a commitment that serves both present and future generations. Environmental science thus provides a rational foundation for ethical and spiritual principles, reinforcing New Universalist values with practical applications.

Traditional and Naturopathic Medicine: Integrating Science and Spiritual Healing

In recent years, science has increasingly validated traditional and naturopathic medicinal practices, recognizing the therapeutic benefits of herbs, holistic care, and alternative treatments. For instance, cannabis, recognized in both medical research and New Universalist theology, offers medicinal properties that support mental and physical well-being, from reducing pain to alleviating anxiety. Other plant-based treatments, like echinacea for immunity and ginger for digestion, have been scientifically studied for their efficacy, reinforcing the healing wisdom of natural medicine.

Traditional healing practices often emphasize a holistic approach, considering not only physical symptoms but also emotional and spiritual factors. Practices like acupuncture, herbal medicine, and aromatherapy have gained scientific recognition for their therapeutic effects. For New Universalists, these natural remedies represent the sacred gifts of the Earth, resources to be used with respect, gratitude, and care.

By integrating science-backed traditional medicine with spiritual practice, New Universalism encourages a view of health that respects the body's connection to nature and spirit. This approach supports a balanced, holistic understanding of wellness, one that aligns with Earth Stewardship and honors the wisdom of ancient healing practices alongside modern scientific knowledge.

Scientific Principles as a Foundation for Spiritual Growth

The scientific insights explored here—from the interconnectedness of ecosystems to the mysteries of cosmic evolution—offer a profound foundation for both personal and communal growth. By embracing these principles, New Universalists find pathways to greater humility, compassion, and respect for all life. Science and spirituality together encourage us to engage with the world from a place of wonder, responsibility, and reverence, affirming the belief that knowledge and faith are mutually enriching.

In honoring these scientific perspectives, New Universalists are called to live ethically, to cherish the Earth, and to see our own lives as integral parts of the cosmic whole. This commitment to integrating scientific understanding with spiritual growth reflects the essence of New Universalism, a faith rooted in both reason and reverence.

Science as a Guide for Responsible Living

New Universalism values scientific understanding not only as a source of knowledge but as a guide for ethical and responsible living. By providing insights into the interconnectedness of ecosystems, the impact of human behavior on climate, and the physical and mental well-being of individuals and communities, science helps New Universalists make choices that align with the values of compassion, stewardship, and respect for all life.

Living responsibly, according to New Universalist theology, involves honoring both the rational insights science provides and the ethical imperatives those insights inspire. Whether choosing sustainable practices, advocating for social justice, or prioritizing mental health, New Universalists are encouraged to use scientific understanding as a framework for making informed, compassionate decisions that contribute to the greater good.

Personal Responsibility and Informed Decision-Making

Science offers tools to make decisions that promote well-being, from nutrition and exercise to mental health care. For instance, research in nutrition science has shown that plant-based diets reduce environmental impact and support personal health, aligning with the New Universalist value of Earth Stewardship. Mental health studies encourage mindfulness and self-care, practices that promote well-being while fostering resilience and compassion—qualities that lie at the heart of New Universalist teachings.

We are encouraged to incorporate scientific insights into our daily lives as acts of responsibility and self-care. By choosing mindful practices, such as reducing consumption of single-use plastics, managing stress through mindfulness, or making dietary choices that support health and environmental sustainability, New Universalists honor the interconnectedness of mind, body, and the environment. This approach emphasizes that responsible living is not just a personal endeavor but a practice that upholds the well-being of the broader community and planet.

Social Responsibility: Science as a Tool for Justice and Equity

Science can be a powerful tool for advancing social responsibility, supporting New Universalism's commitment to justice, equity, and community welfare. Public health research, for example, has demonstrated the benefits of equitable healthcare access, revealing that communities thrive when all individuals have the resources they need to lead healthy, fulfilling lives. Environmental science underscores the importance of addressing pollution and resource scarcity, issues that often disproportionately impact marginalized communities.

New Universalists are encouraged to use scientific knowledge as a guide for promoting social justice, advocating for policies that reduce inequalities and protect vulnerable populations. By supporting initiatives like accessible healthcare, environmental justice, and community education, we fulfill the New Universalist ideal of social responsibility, fostering a society where all individuals are valued and supported. Science, in this sense, acts as both a guide and a catalyst for creating a more just and compassionate world.

Environmental Ethics and Earth Stewardship

Science reinforces the ethical duty to care for the planet, aligning with New Universalism's Earth Stewardship principle. Climate science, for instance, has shown that human activities, such as deforestation, carbon emissions, and plastic pollution, have long-lasting effects on the Earth's ecosystems. Research in sustainable agriculture and conservation biology provides practical solutions for preserving biodiversity, reducing waste, and mitigating climate impact.

For New Universalists, acting on these scientific findings is an expression of faith and stewardship. We are encouraged to reduce our carbon footprint, support conservation efforts, and adopt sustainable practices that honor the Earth as a sacred, living system. By integrating scientific knowledge into our spiritual practice, New Universalists transform Earth Stewardship from an abstract principle into an active, ethical commitment, supporting a healthy planet for generations to come.

Holistic Worldview: Integrating Science with Spiritual Reverence

In New Universalism, science is not separate from spirituality but an essential part of a holistic worldview that values both rational understanding and spiritual reverence. By honoring scientific discoveries, New Universalists celebrate the mysteries of life and the cosmos, recognizing that each new insight deepens the sense of wonder and respect for creation. This approach encourages us to engage in lifelong learning, viewing science as a means to expand our understanding of the universe and our place within it.

Through this holistic perspective, New Universalists are called to live with intentionality and respect, embracing the dynamic relationship between knowledge and spirituality. By integrating science with faith, New Universalists cultivate a worldview that is both practical and profound, one that empowers them to live with integrity, compassion, and a deep connection to all life.

Encouraging Curiosity and Lifelong Learning

Curiosity, the desire to explore and understand, is a quality that unites the pursuits of science and spirituality. In New Universalism, curiosity is celebrated as a path to personal growth, spiritual discovery, and a fuller appreciation of the world's mysteries. Through a commitment to lifelong learning, we are encouraged to continually expand our knowledge, deepen our understanding, and cultivate an open-minded approach to life. This pursuit reflects New Universalism's belief that both the heart and mind are essential tools in the journey toward truth.

Curiosity as a Bridge Between Science and Spirituality

Curiosity connects the realms of science and spirituality, each of which seeks to answer fundamental questions about existence, purpose, and the nature of life. In science, curiosity drives exploration, leading to discoveries that reveal the intricate workings of the universe—from the vastness of galaxies to the microscopic complexity of cells. In spirituality, curiosity encourages introspection, inviting individuals to examine their beliefs, seek deeper meaning, and consider their connection to all life.

In New Universalism, this interplay between science and spirituality reinforces the belief that each journey of inquiry, whether inward or outward, is valuable. By nurturing curiosity, we embrace both scientific and spiritual paths to knowledge, finding in each a source of wonder, humility, and insight. Through curiosity, New Universalists cultivate an openness to diverse perspectives, fostering respect for other faiths, cultures, and ways of knowing.

Lifelong Learning as a Path to Growth and Humility

Lifelong learning is an invitation to see each day as an opportunity for growth and discovery. New Universalism upholds that true understanding comes not from rigid certainty but from a willingness to remain open and teachable. This commitment to learning encourages us to pursue knowledge across many fields—from environmental science to philosophy, from history to mindfulness practices—recognizing that each offers a unique window into human experience and universal truths.

By engaging in lifelong learning, New Universalists cultivate humility, understanding that knowledge is always evolving. In science, this is seen in the ever-expanding scope of discovery, as new findings reshape what we know about health, ecology, and the cosmos. In spirituality, it is the acknowledgment that life's mysteries are vast and that each person's journey adds to the richness of collective wisdom. Through lifelong learning, we affirm that wisdom is not a destination but an ongoing process, one that requires openness, patience, and curiosity.

Science and Spirituality as Companions in the Quest for Knowledge

New Universalism teaches that science and spirituality are not separate realms but companions in the quest for knowledge. Scientific insights into the natural world inspire spiritual reverence, while spiritual values guide the ethical application of scientific discoveries. This complementary relationship encourages us to view science not merely as a collection of facts but as a source of inspiration, inviting us to marvel at the universe and see our place within it.

we are encouraged to view each new discovery as an opportunity to deepen our understanding of interconnectedness, compassion, and responsibility. Whether exploring the life cycles of plants or the vast expanse of space, we find in each scientific insight a reminder of our connection to all existence. This approach to learning fosters a holistic understanding that integrates knowledge with ethical action, reinforcing New Universalism's call to live with integrity, reverence, and respect for all life.

The Pursuit of Knowledge as a Spiritual Practice

In New Universalism, the pursuit of knowledge is seen as a spiritual practice in its own right, one that fosters self-discovery, resilience, and purpose. By continually seeking knowledge, we engage in a process that strengthens our awareness of the world, ourselves, and our spiritual beliefs. Curiosity and learning, therefore, are not merely intellectual pursuits but pathways to inner growth, encouraging us to embrace the unknown with both courage and humility.

This commitment to learning extends beyond personal growth, nurturing a community of seekers who value dialogue, empathy, and shared discovery. Through reading, reflecting, and engaging with diverse perspectives, New Universalists build a community founded on mutual respect and a shared dedication to truth. By honoring curiosity and lifelong learning, we fulfill New Universalism's vision of a faith that is open, inclusive, and ever-evolving.

Ethics and Social Responsibility

5

Living with Integrity and Purpose

Social Responsibility in New Universalism

Social responsibility in New Universalism is regarded as a sacred obligation, a commitment to live ethically and contribute positively to the well-being of others and the planet. It stems from the belief that each individual is inherently interconnected with all life, sharing in the joys and challenges that shape our global community. Within this framework, social responsibility is not merely an option but a duty—one that aligns with the principles of Earth Stewardship, Filial Piety, and compassion, which form the foundation of New Universalist ethics.

Social responsibility in New Universalism extends to every corner of life, guiding us to act with integrity, empathy, and respect for both human and environmental communities. It calls each person to consider our impact, to cultivate relationships founded on mutual respect, and to uphold justice and fairness in all actions. This commitment is understood as both a personal and communal journey, where individual choices contribute to the broader harmony of society and the planet.

New Universalism views individuals as integral parts of the global ecosystem, emphasizing that our responsibilities extend beyond our immediate circles to encompass all beings, human and non-human. Every action, from supporting environmental sustainability to showing kindness in personal relationships, is seen as a thread in the vast tapestry of life. This understanding leads us to see each person as part of an extended family—a kinship that fosters empathy, unity, and a desire to protect and nurture life.

In embodying social responsibility, New Universalists honor the teaching that every being has intrinsic value and that each action has the power to uplift or harm the collective. This principle invites us to lead lives of purpose and service, reflecting New Universalism's call to approach every moment, interaction, and decision with intentionality, mindfulness, and compassion.

Personal Responsibility and Accountability

Personal responsibility is a central aspect of social responsibility in New Universalism, where each individual is called to act with integrity, mindfulness, and a commitment to positive impact. Living in alignment with this value means consistently reflecting on one's actions, assessing how they affect both self and others, and choosing to cultivate behaviors that support growth, respect, and unity. By embracing personal responsibility, we embody New Universalism's dedication to ethical living, guided by self-awareness and accountability.

In New Universalist practice, personal integrity is seen as the foundation upon which all other ethical commitments rest. We are encouraged to engage in regular self-reflection—examining our choices, intentions, and motivations honestly. Through this process, we cultivate humility and transparency, acknowledging both our strengths and areas for growth. This ongoing self-assessment is not about self-criticism but about nurturing a life that aligns with values such as compassion, fairness, and respect for all beings.

Accountability is viewed as a commitment to take ownership of one's words and deeds. We are reminded that every action, whether small or large, ripples outward, influencing relationships, communities, and the environment. By holding ourselves accountable, New Universalists develop a heightened awareness of the impact of our actions on others, striving to make choices that honor the dignity and well-being of all.

New Universalism encourages us to use this commitment to accountability as a guiding light, especially in situations of conflict or challenge. When mistakes are made, personal responsibility involves acknowledging harm and seeking to make amends, embodying both humility and empathy. By practicing accountability, we deepen our relationships and foster trust, reflecting New Universalism's vision of a world grounded in understanding and respect.

Through this personal commitment to responsibility, each individual contributes to the broader New Universalist vision of a compassionate and interconnected world. By holding ourselves to high standards of integrity and accountability, we build a foundation of trust and mutual respect within our communities, fostering a shared sense of purpose that uplifts everyone.

Practical Self-Reflection as a Spiritual Practice

Self-reflection is a foundational practice in New Universalism that enables us to examine our actions and intentions with clarity and honesty. To embody this principle, New Universalists are encouraged to set aside regular times for reflection—perhaps weekly or monthly—to examine the ways our choices align with our values and commitments. Through journaling, meditation, or contemplative prayer, we can explore questions such as:

- *In what ways do my actions serve the well-being of others and the planet?*
- *Are my choices guided by compassion, respect, and humility?*
- *How am I living out the values of Earth Stewardship, Filial Piety, and social responsibility?*

By engaging in this regular self-reflection, we deepen our understanding of personal growth areas, cultivate greater self-awareness, and strengthen our connection to New Universalist values.

Embracing Honesty and Transparency in Daily Interactions

Personal responsibility also means practicing honesty and transparency in interactions with others. New Universalists are encouraged to communicate openly, avoiding actions or words that may harm others or cause confusion. This practice calls for clarity and sincerity in relationships, fostering a foundation of trust and mutual respect within families, friendships, and communities.

Practical steps for embodying honesty include:

- *Communicating intentions clearly and authentically*: Whether in personal relationships, workplace settings, or community engagements, New Universalists are encouraged to express ourselves honestly, even when faced with disagreement or challenge.
- *Acknowledging one's own limitations*: Recognizing that everyone has areas of growth fosters humility and encourages constructive feedback and learning.
- *Listening actively and empathetically*: By approaching conversations with an open heart and a willingness to understand others' perspectives, we build relationships founded on respect and compassion.

These practices not only strengthen personal integrity but also help create a compassionate environment in which all voices are heard and valued.

Taking Ownership of Actions and Their Impact

In New Universalism, accountability is a sacred commitment to understanding and honoring the impact of one's actions. This responsibility involves recognizing how one's behavior influences others and taking active steps to align with the core values of respect, compassion, and steward-ship. To foster a meaningful sense of accountability, we can adopt practical practices such as:

- *Acknowledging mistakes openly and making amends*: Mistakes are opportunities for growth. In the spirit of humility, New Universalists are encouraged to acknowledge errors, apologize when harm is caused, and take steps to make reparations if necessary.
- *Considering the ripple effects of actions*: Before making decisions, we can reflect on the wider impact of our choices, asking how our actions contribute to or detract from harmony within our community and environment.
- *Setting personal goals aligned with New Universalist values*: Whether through volunteering, advocating for social justice, or practicing sustainable living, setting specific, achievable goals helps us stay accountable to the broader principles of New Universalism.

Accountability is not about self-criticism but about embracing the responsibility to live intentionally, cultivating a life that reflects a commitment to personal integrity, relational harmony, and community well-being.

Cultivating a Spirit of Service and Empathy

Personal responsibility in New Universalism also involves recognizing that one's actions affect not only oneself but the larger web of connections within family, community, and environment. New Universalists are called to approach others with empathy, generosity, and a willingness to serve, reflecting the belief that each individual's well-being is interconnected. We can embody this value by:

- *Offering support to those in need*: This may involve volunteering, providing emotional support, or engaging in charitable acts. By dedicating time and resources to help others, we fulfill the New Universalist call to compassion and social responsibility.
- *Respecting diversity and learning from others*: Recognizing and appreciating the perspectives, cultures, and experiences of others fosters empathy and humility.

- *Practicing forgiveness*: In moments of conflict or disagreement, we are encouraged to approach situations with understanding and forgiveness, viewing mistakes as part of the shared human experience.

By living with empathy and a commitment to service, New Universalists honor the value of interconnectedness, strengthening the bonds that unite families, communities, and the global family.

Personal Responsibility as a Path to Inner and Outer Peace

The practice of personal responsibility ultimately leads us toward a state of inner peace, built on a foundation of self-awareness, integrity, and ethical action. In New Universalism, this inner peace is viewed not as an isolated state but as a wellspring of strength that supports positive relationships and responsible living. When we engage with our values mindfully, we foster harmony both within ourselves and in the world around us.

By taking responsibility for our actions and approaching life with integrity and accountability, New Universalists build a life that contributes to global harmony. Through practices of reflection, honesty, ownership, service, and empathy, each person strengthens our spiritual journey and contributes to the collective purpose of New Universalism: a world built on understanding, compassion, and reverence for all life.

Responsibility to the Global Community

In New Universalism, responsibility to the global community is a reflection of the faith's deep commitment to interconnectedness and respect for all life. We are called to recognize that each person's well-being is interwoven with the lives of others across the world, transcending borders, cultures, and backgrounds. This sense of global responsibility is not just an ideal; it is a practical, lived commitment to foster justice, empathy, and support for those in need. By embracing this responsibility, New Universalists contribute to the global tapestry of compassion, integrity, and shared purpose.

Interdependence in a Connected World

New Universalism teaches that all life is interdependent, a truth reflected in the faith's emphasis on Earth Stewardship, Filial Piety, and social responsibility. In a world where people are more connected than ever, we are encouraged to remain aware of global challenges and to see ourselves as active participants in creating solutions. This commitment to the global community is not merely a reaction to crises; it is a proactive stance that reflects the New Universalist vision of a world in which each person contributes to the greater good.

We are encouraged to explore global issues such as poverty, climate change, inequality, and human rights, understanding that these challenges affect everyone and require collective action. By expanding our awareness, New Universalists deepen our empathy and develop a broader perspective, recognizing that all people share a common humanity and a shared responsibility to uphold justice and dignity for all.

Acting Locally with Global Awareness

New Universalism teaches that one's actions, no matter how small, have a ripple effect that can reach far beyond their immediate environment. We are encouraged to take part in local initiatives that address global issues, acting with an awareness that our choices can contribute to the well-being of people across the world. This approach aligns with the belief that true change often begins at the grassroots level, where individuals and communities work together to create sustainable solutions.

Practical ways to embody this value include:

- *Supporting local organizations that address global concerns*, such as environmental conservation groups, food banks, or educational programs.
- *Advocating for policies that promote social justice and environmental protection*, recognizing that policy change can benefit communities locally and globally.
- *Choosing sustainable and ethical products*, understanding that each purchase impacts global supply chains, labor practices, and environmental health.

By acting locally with a global mindset, New Universalists cultivate a sense of purpose and responsibility, knowing that our choices contribute to a broader movement for justice and compassion.

Seeing All People as Part of an Extended Family

In New Universalism, the concept of Filial Piety extends beyond family to encompass all humanity, encouraging us to view others as part of an extended family deserving of care and respect.

This principle invites us to see beyond divisions of nationality, ethnicity, religion, and culture, embracing a perspective that values the intrinsic worth of every person. When we approach the world with this mindset, we build bridges of understanding and cultivate empathy, which form the foundation of a peaceful and harmonious global community.

New Universalists are encouraged to actively practice empathy, reaching out to those from diverse backgrounds and listening to their experiences with open hearts. By participating in interfaith dialogues, cultural exchanges, or global service initiatives, we broaden our understanding of humanity's shared challenges and strengths. This approach fosters unity and respect, reflecting New Universalism's belief in the interconnectedness of all life.

Taking Action for Global Justice

New Universalism calls us to pursue justice, not only within our immediate communities but also on a global scale. This commitment to justice involves recognizing and addressing inequality, oppression, and harm wherever they exist. We are encouraged to support causes that promote human rights, fair treatment, and equitable access to resources, aligning with the New Universalist principles of compassion and integrity.

Practical actions for global justice include:

- *Educating oneself about global human rights issues*, such as the rights of indigenous peoples, gender equality, and refugee protection.
- *Supporting organizations that advocate for justice*, whether through financial contributions, volunteering, or amplifying their messages.
- *Engaging in advocacy and raising awareness within one's community*, understanding that small actions contribute to a larger movement for equality and dignity for all.

By committing to global justice, New Universalists embody the faith's call to honor the dignity of all people, upholding a vision of the world where fairness and respect are foundational values.

Cultivating Empathy and Service Beyond Borders

New Universalism encourages us to see service as a natural extension of empathy, prompting us to reach beyond borders and support people around the world. This service can take many forms, from participating in international volunteer programs to contributing to relief efforts during times of crisis. By serving others, we deepen our understanding of shared humanity and reinforce our commitment to New Universalist values.

Practical ways to engage in global service include:

- *Volunteering for or donating to global humanitarian organizations* that provide medical aid, disaster relief, and educational resources.
- *Participating in interfaith or intercultural service projects*, such as building homes, planting trees, or teaching skills in communities around the world.
- *Using digital platforms to connect with and support global causes*, recognizing the potential of technology to bring people together and amplify positive change.

Through these acts of service, we embody New Universalism's vision of a compassionate and unified world, where each person contributes to the well-being of the collective.

Embracing Shared Responsibility for a Compassionate Future

Ultimately, responsibility to the global community in New Universalism is a commitment to building a future rooted in compassion, understanding, and mutual support. By engaging with global issues, acting locally with a sense of broader responsibility, and cultivating empathy for all people, we honor the belief that true well-being is collective. This commitment aligns with the New Universalist vision of a world where people work together to nurture life, respect one another's dignity, and protect the Earth as a shared home.

Through this commitment to global responsibility, New Universalists not only live out our values but inspire others to join in the shared work of creating a just, compassionate, and interconnected world.

Charity, Service, and Honor

Charity, service, and honor are vital expressions of New Universalism's call to live with integrity, compassion, and a commitment to the well-being of others. Rooted in the principles of Earth Stewardship, Filial Piety, and Social Responsibility, these practices reflect New Universalism's belief that each person has a role in building a just and harmonious world. By engaging in acts of charity, committing to service, and approaching others with honor, we not only contribute to the good of society but also deepen our spiritual journey, embodying the values that define our faith.

The Role of Charity in Building Community

In New Universalism, charity is more than a single act of giving; it is an intentional practice of empathy and care that strengthens bonds within and beyond one's immediate community. Charity reflects the belief that all beings deserve respect, dignity, and support, especially in times of need. We are encouraged to view charity as an expression of our interconnectedness with others and as a way to actively contribute to the upliftment of all.

Practical ways to embody charity in daily life include:

- *Providing resources to those in need*, whether through donations, sharing resources, or offering support to local organizations that address issues like hunger, homelessness, and access to healthcare.
- *Engaging in small acts of kindness*, such as offering assistance to neighbors, contributing to food banks, or giving time and attention to those who may feel isolated.
- *Supporting community programs* that create lasting impacts, such as youth mentorship initiatives, elder care services, and educational programs.

Charity in New Universalism is understood as both a practical and spiritual discipline, one that fosters gratitude, humility, and compassion. By giving of ourselves, we not only help others but also deepen our own awareness of the shared human experience, learning to appreciate life's interconnectedness in meaningful ways.

Service as a Commitment to Social Responsibility

Service is seen as an essential expression of social responsibility in New Universalism, a proactive choice to dedicate time, skills, and energy to benefit others. This commitment reflects the belief that true fulfillment comes from contributing to the well-being of society and the Earth, aligning personal actions with the greater good. Service, in this view, is not simply an obligation but a path to spiritual growth, allowing us to embody the values of New Universalism in practical, impactful ways.

We are encouraged to explore a variety of service opportunities, such as:

- *Volunteering with local and global organizations* that address pressing issues like environmental conservation, social justice, education, and healthcare. By contributing our skills and time, we participate in creating positive change.
- *Mentoring others or sharing expertise*, recognizing that service can take many forms. Acts of service include everything from teaching skills, supporting career growth, or simply offering guidance and encouragement.
- *Participating in interfaith or intercultural service projects*, which foster community unity, respect for diversity, and a shared sense of purpose.

In New Universalism, service is viewed as an act of spiritual devotion, an opportunity to give freely and with intention. Through service, we deepen our understanding of interconnectedness and contribute to the collective goal of building a compassionate and just world.

Honor as a Foundation for Relationships and Community

Honor is an essential value in New Universalism, reflecting the belief that each individual is worthy of respect, empathy, and understanding. This value emphasizes the importance of recognizing and valuing the inherent worth of all beings, approaching others with humility and reverence. Honor guides us in building strong, respectful relationships within our communities, grounded in mutual trust and shared values.

To practice honor, we are encouraged to:

- *Engage in honest and respectful communication*, listening actively and valuing others' perspectives. By fostering open dialogue, we create environments of respect and inclusivity.
- *Treat others with integrity and fairness*, avoiding actions or words that may cause harm or perpetuate division. This includes recognizing the rights, needs, and dignity of every individual, whether in personal relationships, professional settings, or community interactions.
- *Celebrate diversity and cultural heritage*, understanding that each person's background enriches the community. Honor invites us to appreciate the diversity of the human experience, encouraging a spirit of unity amid difference.

Honor in New Universalism is not limited to individual interactions; it also extends to the environment, animals, and future generations. By practicing honor in every aspect of life, we fulfill New Universalism's call to approach the world with respect, empathy, and reverence.

Practical Integration of Charity, Service, and Honor in Daily Life

New Universalism teaches that the values of charity, service, and honor are not limited to isolated acts but are ways of being that can be integrated into daily life. We are encouraged to view each interaction, choice, and relationship as an opportunity to embody these values, reflecting our commitment to social responsibility and the well-being of all.

Practical ways to integrate these values include:

- *Setting aside regular time for charitable acts*, such as monthly donations, volunteering, or creating opportunities to help others in meaningful ways.
- *Reflecting on how service aligns with personal talents and skills*, seeking ways to use these abilities for the benefit of the community.
- *Approaching each person with the intention to honor their dignity*, seeing each interaction as a chance to practice respect and kindness.

Through charity, service, and honor, we bring our faith to life, creating a world that reflects our values of compassion, unity, and responsibility. These practices are not simply obligations but pathways to spiritual growth, helping us develop a deep sense of purpose, connection, and fulfillment.

Incorporating Charity and Service in Daily Life

In New Universalism, charity and service are seen as essential expressions of compassion and interconnectedness, both of which form the backbone of a meaningful, responsible life. Rooted in the belief that every individual's well-being is tied to the well-being of others, charity is practiced as a sacred act of empathy that uplifts those in need and strengthens the bonds within and beyond the immediate community. Charity and service are natural extensions of New Universalism's values, reflecting the commitment to live with compassion, generosity, and a conscious sense of social responsibility.

Charity as an Expression of Compassion and Social Responsibility

In New Universalist theology, charity arises from the deeply held belief that compassion is not only a virtue but a powerful force for transformation. Charity goes beyond occasional acts of giving; it is a continuous expression of care and empathy for those who may be struggling. When we engage in charitable acts, we affirm that everyone deserves dignity, support, and respect, especially in times of hardship. Charity, therefore, is viewed as a meaningful way to embody love and social responsibility.

We are encouraged to practice charity by embracing both small, spontaneous acts and intentional, organized efforts, such as:

- **Small Acts of Kindness**: These simple gestures can be woven into everyday life—offering assistance to a neighbor, buying food for someone in need, or giving one's time and attention to a person who feels isolated. These acts of charity strengthen community bonds and nurture a spirit of kindness and mutual support.
- **Community-Based Charity Efforts**: Participating in community initiatives, such as food drives, clothing donations, or local fundraising events, offers us an opportunity to connect with others and provide for immediate, tangible needs in our communities. By actively contributing to these efforts, we embody New Universalism's call to be proactive agents of change and support.
- **Supporting Broader Causes**: In addition to direct action, we are encouraged to support causes and organizations that align with New Universalist values. Whether by providing financial support, donating goods, or lending our skills, we can meaningfully participate in initiatives that address social, environmental, and humanitarian issues.

Each charitable act, regardless of scale, contributes to a world where compassion and mutual respect are practiced as guiding principles. By making charity an integral part of our lives, New Universalists reflect our shared commitment to social responsibility, promoting an inclusive and just society.

Tithes and Offerings as a Practice of Intentional Giving

In New Universalism, the practice of tithes and offerings is a sacred tradition rooted in the values of generosity, gratitude, and community support. We are encouraged to contribute a recommended ten percent of our income to the New Universalist Church as a way to sustain the church's mission, support its charitable programs, and ensure the continuation of its spiritual, educational, and community services. Tithing is seen as a commitment to the well-being of the community, reflecting each member's investment in the growth and integrity of New Universalism.

The practice of tithes and offerings is intended to be flexible and considerate of each individual's financial well-being, encouraging contributions that do not cause hardship. We are reminded that giving should come from a place of gratitude and intentionality, reflecting our spiritual commitment to support others without compromising our own needs. The emphasis on mindful, responsible giving ensures that each of us can contribute meaningfully without undue burden.

Beyond the practice of tithing, New Universalists are encouraged to make additional offerings, or alms, as expressions of our ongoing commitment to charity and compassion. These offerings may be directed toward:

- **Supporting Local and Global Causes**: We can direct our offerings to causes we feel personally connected to, such as relief funds for disaster-affected regions, support for educational programs, or assistance for health initiatives. This practice reflects New Universalism's global perspective, which encourages us to see ourselves as part of a wider world in need of mutual support.
- **Helping Individuals in Need**: We may choose to provide direct support to individuals facing hardship, whether through financial assistance, food, clothing, or other resources. This personal approach to charity fosters a more intimate connection with those in need, offering us a direct experience of compassion and empathy.

- **Contributing to Community Improvement**: We are also encouraged to support community development efforts, such as local housing initiatives, public park restoration, or education centers, that enhance quality of life and strengthen communal bonds.

This approach to charity through tithes and offerings allows us to engage in giving as a regular, intentional practice that supports both the New Universalist Church and the broader community. Each act of giving is viewed as a tangible expression of gratitude, recognizing the blessings one has and sharing them with others in a spirit of unity and respect.

Practical Guidance for Integrating Charity and Service in Everyday Life

For followers seeking to make charity a consistent and meaningful part of our lives, New Universalism offers practical guidance that emphasizes intentionality, empathy, and alignment with the faith's core values. By integrating charity into daily actions, we cultivate a spirit of generosity that enriches both our own lives and the lives of those around us.

Practical steps for incorporating charity into daily life include:

1. **Reflecting on Personal Values and Causes**: We are encouraged to identify causes that resonate with us on a personal level, such as environmental conservation, animal welfare, or education. By aligning our charitable efforts with our passions, we can give in ways that feel purposeful and fulfilling.

2. **Setting Goals for Giving**: Whether through financial contributions, volunteer work, or acts of service, we can set regular goals for our charitable giving. This structured approach encourages consistency and allows us to reflect on our progress, fostering a deeper commitment to living charitably.

3. **Engaging in Community Circles of Giving**: New Universalism values community-based charity, where we can come together in shared efforts to support local causes. By participating in group initiatives, we experience the collective strength of giving and develop bonds with others who share our commitment to compassion and social responsibility.

4. **Practicing Mindful and Joyful Giving**: We are encouraged to approach charity with a sense of joy and gratitude, viewing it as an opportunity rather than an obligation. Mindful giving reflects the awareness that charity benefits not only the recipient but also the giver, who grows in empathy, humility, and purpose.

Through these practices, charity and service become ongoing expressions of New Universalist values, reinforcing a way of life that honors compassion, connection, and shared responsibility. By weaving acts of charity into the fabric of daily life, we deepen our spiritual journey, embodying the values that lie at the heart of New Universalism.

Volunteer Work as a Spiritual Practice

Volunteer work holds a place of sacred importance in New Universalism. It is more than a contribution of time or skills; it is an act of spiritual devotion that embodies the faith's values of humility, empathy, and interconnectedness. When we engage in volunteer work, we step into a practice of living our beliefs, recognizing the profound impact we can make in the lives of others while cultivating our own spiritual growth. In this way, volunteer work serves as both a gift to the community and a transformative journey that deepens our connection to New Universalist principles and to the wider world.

Fostering Humility, Empathy, and Connection through Service

Volunteer work invites us to engage with others from a place of humility, offering our time and talents without expectation of personal gain or recognition. This selflessness allows individuals to see the world from perspectives beyond our own, fostering a deeper understanding of others' lives, struggles, and joys. By stepping outside of our comfort zones and immersing ourselves in the experiences of others, we cultivate humility—a quality that grounds us in the realization that every person's life is part of the shared human journey.

Empathy, another core value of New Universalism, is woven into the fabric of volunteer work. Through service, we develop the capacity to connect emotionally with those we serve, learning to see the world through their eyes and respond with genuine compassion. This empathy extends beyond individual interactions, fostering a broader sense of kinship and connection with humanity. In this way, volunteer work becomes a bridge that unites people across diverse backgrounds, beliefs, and experiences, strengthening the communal bonds that lie at the heart of New Universalism.

Volunteer work also serves as a means of building and sustaining relationships within one's immediate and extended community. Whether through environmental projects, social outreach, or community support, volunteer work offers us a way to actively engage with others, contributing to a shared sense of purpose and unity. This connection to community nurtures a feeling of belonging and reinforces the belief that each person's actions matter, fostering a sense of responsibility that extends beyond the individual self.

Volunteer Opportunities Aligned with New Universalism's Values

New Universalism encourages us to seek volunteer opportunities that resonate with its core values of Earth Stewardship, Social Responsibility, and Filial Piety. By choosing volunteer work that aligns with these principles, we can engage in meaningful acts of service that reflect our commitment to the teachings of New Universalism and contribute to the greater good.

- **Environmental Conservation**: As stewards of the Earth, we are encouraged to participate in conservation efforts that protect and restore the environment. This may include volunteering with organizations focused on habitat preservation, sustainable agriculture, reforestation, and pollution reduction. Activities such as community clean-ups, tree planting, and educational outreach allow us to take direct action in caring for the planet and promoting a sustainable future.

- **Supporting Underserved Communities**: New Universalism emphasizes compassion and social responsibility, encouraging us to support marginalized and underserved communities. Volunteer work in this area may involve working with food banks, shelters, community health clinics, or educational programs. By offering our time and resources to those in need, we embody the faith's commitment to social justice, ensuring that all individuals have access to essential resources and opportunities.

- **Assisting the Elderly and Vulnerable Populations**: In alignment with the principle of Filial Piety, New Universalism encourages us to honor and support the elderly and vulnerable members of society. Volunteer opportunities in this area include providing companionship to the elderly, assisting with caregiving, and participating in programs that support individuals facing mental health or physical challenges. Through these acts of service, we build relationships grounded in respect, compassion, and mutual care, contributing to a culture that values and upholds the dignity of every individual.

By engaging in volunteer work that aligns with New Universalist values, we are empowered to live out our faith in tangible ways. Each act of service is a reflection of our commitment to compassion, justice, and respect for the Earth and all its inhabitants.

Finding Personal Meaning and Joy in Volunteer Service

New Universalism recognizes that volunteer work is most impactful and fulfilling when it aligns with an individual's personal interests, talents, and passions. We are encouraged to explore volunteer opportunities that resonate deeply with each of us, as this personal connection fosters a sustained commitment to service and enriches the experience for both the volunteer and those we serve.

Practical guidance for finding meaningful volunteer opportunities includes:

1. **Reflecting on Personal Values and Interests**: We can begin by considering the causes and issues we feel most passionate about, such as environmental conservation, education, healthcare, or social justice. By aligning our volunteer work with these interests, we bring a genuine sense of joy and dedication to our service, making each experience more meaningful and impactful.

2. **Identifying Skills and Talents**: We are encouraged to reflect on our unique skills and talents, such as teaching, organizing, or working with our hands, and consider how these abilities can be applied in service to others. For example, an individual with a talent for gardening may find fulfillment in participating in urban agriculture projects, while someone skilled in organization may be well-suited for community event planning.

3. **Engaging with Local Organizations and Initiatives**: Many communities have local organizations, such as environmental groups, food banks, and community centers, that welcome volunteers. By participating in these local initiatives, we can establish meaningful connections within our community and make a direct impact in the lives of those around us.

4. **Exploring Interfaith and Intercultural Projects**: New Universalism values inclusivity and respect for all traditions, encouraging us to seek volunteer opportunities that bring people of different faiths and backgrounds together. Interfaith and intercultural projects foster unity, mutual understanding, and shared purpose, allowing us to experience the beauty of diversity within the context of service.

Through these practices, volunteer work becomes a journey of personal growth, spiritual enrichment, and communal unity. We find joy in the knowledge that our actions contribute to a better world, fostering a deepened sense of purpose and fulfillment in our lives.

Volunteer Work as a Path to Spiritual Growth

In New Universalism, volunteer work is not simply a way to help others; it is a path to spiritual growth, offering us an opportunity to embody our faith through action. Each act of service is a step toward greater empathy, humility, and understanding, reflecting the belief that spirituality is inseparable from a commitment to the well-being of others. By giving of ourselves, we expand our capacity for love and compassion, nurturing our own souls as we uplift those around us.

As a spiritual practice, volunteer work encourages us to live with intention, guided by New Universalism's values of kindness, respect, and social responsibility. It is a reminder that faith is not confined to personal reflection or worship but is meant to be shared through acts of generosity and care. Through volunteer work, we experience the interconnectedness of all beings, finding purpose and meaning in our contributions to the world.

Supporting Key Issues through Activism and Advocacy

Activism and advocacy are powerful extensions of social responsibility in New Universalism, encouraging us to take a proactive stance on issues that affect the well-being of individuals, communities, and the planet. By engaging in activism, we act as advocates for justice, compassion, and positive change, embodying New Universalism's core values in ways that extend beyond personal practice to influence the broader world. In this faith, activism is not merely a reaction to injustice but a deliberate, purpose-driven commitment to support causes aligned with ethical and social values, advancing the collective good.

Activism as an Extension of Social Responsibility

In New Universalist theology, social responsibility transcends individual and local actions, encouraging us to address systemic issues that impact the well-being of humanity and the environment. Activism represents a sacred commitment to the principles of justice, equity, and stewardship, uniting us with others who share similar values. When approached as an extension of one's faith, activism becomes a profound expression of compassion and courage, grounded in a desire to create a world where dignity, respect, and opportunity are accessible to all.

Activism also emphasizes the interdependent nature of society, reflecting New Universalism's belief in interconnectedness. We are encouraged to recognize that the struggles of others are, in many ways, our own; the well-being of individuals is linked to the health of communities, and the health of communities is tied to the vitality of the Earth itself. Thus, activism becomes an act of solidarity—a way of standing with others in their pursuit of justice and equality, embodying the belief that we are all part of a shared journey and a collective responsibility.

Thoughtful and Respectful Activism

New Universalism advocates for an approach to activism that is thoughtful, respectful, and rooted in integrity. The goal of activism, according to New Universalist principles, is to promote constructive, positive change without causing unnecessary harm or division. We are called to embody New Universalism's values of empathy and compassion, even when engaging with those who may hold opposing views. This approach emphasizes the importance of listening, understanding, and seeking common ground, fostering a spirit of respect and cooperation in the pursuit of shared goals.

Thoughtful activism includes:

1. **Respecting Diverse Perspectives**: While New Universalism encourages us to advocate for values aligned with justice, compassion, and stewardship, it also acknowledges the importance of respecting diverse perspectives. Engaging in activism should involve a commitment to listening to others' viewpoints, understanding the complexities of issues, and seeking solutions that respect the dignity of all people involved.

2. **Practicing Non-Violence and Kindness**: True to New Universalist principles, activism should always be conducted with kindness and non-violence. Activists are encouraged to reject methods that cause harm or sow division, choosing instead approaches that promote peace and unity. Whether through peaceful protests, educational outreach, or collaboration with like-minded organizations, we are reminded that the manner in which we advocate is as important as the cause itself.

3. **Setting Clear and Purposeful Intentions**: New Universalism teaches that activism is most effective when it is purposeful and well-planned. We are encouraged to set clear intentions

before engaging in advocacy, identifying specific goals we hope to achieve and strategies for reaching them. This intentional approach ensures that activism remains focused, effective, and aligned with New Universalist values.

Examples of Key Issues in New Universalist Activism

New Universalism identifies several key areas where activism can make a significant impact, inviting us to engage with issues that align with the faith's pillars of Earth Stewardship, Social Responsibility, and Equity. These causes are chosen not only for their ethical importance but for their alignment with the spiritual and communal values that lie at the heart of New Universalism.

- **Environmental Preservation and Climate Action**: Earth Stewardship is a core tenet of New Universalism, and environmental activism is seen as a sacred responsibility. We are encouraged to advocate for sustainable practices, support policies that protect natural resources, and participate in efforts to combat climate change. Activism in this area might include participating in conservation projects, supporting renewable energy initiatives, or raising awareness about the importance of biodiversity and ecological balance.
- **Social Justice and Human Rights**: Activism for social justice aligns with New Universalism's commitment to honoring the inherent worth and dignity of all people. We are encouraged to advocate for policies and initiatives that promote equality, fight discrimination, and protect the rights of marginalized communities. Social justice activism may involve supporting racial equality movements, working with organizations that advocate for LGBTQ+ rights, or promoting gender equality. By addressing these social issues, we work toward a society where every individual can live with freedom, respect, and opportunity.
- **Equitable Access to Resources**: New Universalism calls for a world where everyone has access to the resources necessary for a healthy, dignified life. We are encouraged to support initiatives that address poverty, healthcare access, and food security, advocating for equitable distribution of resources and opportunities. Activism in this area might include supporting policies that expand healthcare access, working with food security organizations, or promoting economic policies that reduce income inequality. This commitment to equity reflects New Universalism's belief that all individuals deserve the opportunity to thrive.

By supporting these causes, we contribute to a more just, compassionate, and sustainable world, fulfilling New Universalism's call to engage meaningfully with global and local challenges.

Engaging in Advocacy as a Path to Spiritual Growth

Activism is not only a means of supporting societal change but also a path to spiritual growth. In New Universalism, advocacy is seen as a way to deepen one's understanding of compassion, resilience, and responsibility, transforming the act of service into a journey of self-discovery and connection. Through advocacy, we experience the fulfillment of working alongside others to create positive change, fostering a sense of purpose and belonging that enriches our spiritual lives.

By engaging in activism and advocacy, we embody New Universalism's teachings in a way that is both practical and profound. We become beacons of hope and agents of change, demonstrating that a life lived with integrity, compassion, and dedication to social responsibility is a life that honors the sacred interconnectedness of all beings. In every act of activism, we reinforce New Universalism's vision of a world where justice, kindness, and respect guide the choices and actions of every individual.

Honor in Service and Social Responsibility

In New Universalism, honor is a guiding principle that shapes how individuals engage with others, contribute to our communities, and uphold the ethical values of our faith. Honor embodies a commitment to integrity, respect, and ethical behavior in all interactions, creating a foundation of trust, kindness, and dignity. By living honorably, we strengthen the bonds of community and foster an environment where mutual respect and understanding flourish.

Honor as a Commitment to Ethical Principles

Honor in New Universalism is grounded in a commitment to ethical principles that guide every thought, word, and action. To act with honor is to embody truthfulness, humility, and fairness, reflecting a deep respect for oneself, others, and the world. Honor calls us to uphold the values of New Universalism—compassion, integrity, and social responsibility—even when faced with challenges or adversity.

This commitment to honor extends to every area of life, from personal relationships to public service. Whether in family life, work, or community involvement, we are encouraged to act with honesty, kindness, and empathy, fostering an atmosphere of trust and respect. By living in alignment with our principles, we contribute to a culture of honor that uplifts both individuals and the wider community, creating a legacy of integrity that benefits all.

Honoring Diversity and Upholding Dignity

An essential aspect of honor in New Universalism is the recognition of each individual's inherent worth and dignity. This means honoring the diverse backgrounds, perspectives, and experiences of others, respecting their autonomy, and valuing their unique contributions to the community. New Universalism teaches that every individual is part of the interconnected web of life, deserving of respect, understanding, and compassion. By honoring others, we acknowledge the sacredness of all beings and cultivate a spirit of inclusivity that transcends cultural, social, and religious boundaries.

Honoring diversity requires us to approach each person with openness and humility, setting aside preconceived judgments and embracing a mindset of acceptance. In practice, this means actively listening to others, valuing their insights, and recognizing the shared humanity that unites all individuals. By fostering an inclusive environment rooted in honor, we contribute to a world where every person feels seen, valued, and respected.

Honor in Service and Community Involvement

Service and community involvement are profound expressions of honor in New Universalism, embodying the belief that true integrity lies in serving others with humility and compassion. Honor in service means approaching every act of charity, volunteer work, or advocacy with a sincere desire to uplift others, free from motives of personal recognition or gain. We are encouraged to serve with selflessness, offering our time, skills, and resources to benefit those in need and strengthen the fabric of our communities.

Honor in community involvement also involves a commitment to transparency, honesty, and accountability. Whether serving in leadership roles, participating in community initiatives, or supporting local projects, we are encouraged to act with integrity, fulfilling our responsibilities to the best of our abilities. By honoring our commitments, we build trust within our communities, contributing to a foundation of reliability and respect that fosters unity and cooperation.

Honor as a Path to Personal Growth and Spiritual Maturity

Living with honor is not only a means of serving others but also a path to personal growth and spiritual maturity. Honor requires self-reflection, mindfulness, and a willingness to learn from one's mistakes. We are encouraged to regularly assess our actions, intentions, and impact on others, seeking opportunities to grow in humility, empathy, and wisdom. By striving to live honorably, we cultivate a sense of inner peace and self-respect, deepening our connection to the values of New Universalism.

Honor also nurtures resilience, teaching us to face challenges with grace and courage. In moments of difficulty or moral ambiguity, we are reminded to rely on our inner values as a compass, choosing actions that align with our ethical principles. Through this commitment to honor, we develop the strength and clarity needed to navigate life's complexities, becoming role models of integrity and kindness for others.

Honor in the Global Context of Social Responsibility

New Universalism views honor as a bridge that connects individuals across cultures, nations, and communities, creating a global foundation of mutual respect and compassion. In the context of social responsibility, honor calls us to act as stewards of justice, equity, and dignity, advocating for a world where every individual's rights and well-being are protected. This sense of global honor encourages us to champion causes such as human rights, environmental conservation, and social equity, upholding the values of New Universalism on a broader scale.

By embracing a global perspective on honor, we recognize that our actions contribute to a shared vision of peace, unity, and respect. We are reminded that living with honor means standing up for what is right, even when faced with obstacles or opposition. In this way, honor becomes a powerful tool for creating positive change, inspiring us to work toward a world that reflects the values of kindness, integrity, and compassion.

Active Participation in Societal Issues

In New Universalism, active engagement in societal issues is viewed as a natural extension of social responsibility and an essential part of living with integrity and purpose. This active involvement is not limited to personal beliefs or actions; it encompasses a commitment to understanding and contributing to the well-being of the larger community. New Universalism calls on its members to be informed, compassionate participants in our societies, working toward the common good in ways that align with the values of empathy, integrity, and fairness.

Active engagement in social and political issues begins with the understanding that each person has a voice, and each voice has the potential to contribute to positive change. In New Universalist doctrine, this responsibility is an expression of social responsibility and reflects a commitment to the collective well-being. Through informed participation, we help shape communities where justice, equality, and respect for all are valued, helping to create a world that reflects the values of New Universalism.

Political Engagement Beyond Voting

Political and social engagement in New Universalism extends beyond voting, though voting remains an essential civic duty. Voting is an important first step, as it allows individuals to express our values in the selection of leaders and policies; however, true engagement calls for continued involvement beyond election cycles.

Engagement may involve attending town halls, participating in local boards, and supporting causes that align with New Universalist values. Advocacy and informed discussions are also essential forms of engagement. We are encouraged to voice our perspectives on important issues, engage in discussions that promote understanding, and actively listen to the needs and concerns of others. By doing so, we foster a more inclusive and informed dialogue within our communities, contributing to a social environment built on respect and shared goals.

In addition to these actions, New Universalism also values research and thoughtful analysis. We are encouraged to study issues that affect our communities and to look beyond surface-level debates, developing a comprehensive understanding of the social, economic, and environmental factors involved. By approaching political engagement with a spirit of curiosity and a commitment to understanding, we contribute to well-informed, balanced discussions that consider diverse perspectives and address the root causes of societal challenges.

Guidelines for Respectful and Constructive Engagement

Engaging in political and social matters is a profound responsibility in New Universalism, one that requires a foundation of respect, dignity, and compassion. We are encouraged to approach these arenas with a commitment to integrity and equity, recognizing that constructive engagement can bridge divides, deepen understanding, and foster lasting change. In a world where social and political discussions can become polarized, New Universalism teaches the importance of dialogue over division, urging us to seek common ground while staying true to our values.

Approaching Issues with Respect and Equity

Respect is central to New Universalist principles, calling on us to honor the inherent dignity of all people. In political and social engagement, this respect requires an open-mindedness that values diverse perspectives and acknowledges that each individual's experiences and beliefs contribute to a more comprehensive understanding of societal issues. New Universalism encourages members to approach each discussion and interaction with humility, listening before responding, and striving to understand viewpoints that differ from our own. By embracing respect, we embody a spirit of unity that values human connection over conflict, building a foundation for productive and compassionate engagement.

Equity, likewise, is a guiding principle in New Universalist social and political involvement. To approach issues equitably is to ensure that all voices are heard and valued, particularly those of marginalized or underrepresented communities. We are encouraged to recognize the diverse needs of society and to advocate for fair and just treatment of all individuals, irrespective of background, identity, or circumstance. This commitment to equity shapes how New Universalists engage with societal issues, encouraging us to champion policies and practices that promote inclusivity and support the well-being of the most vulnerable members of society.

Constructive Engagement: Listening, Researching, and Dialoguing

To engage constructively in social and political matters, we are encouraged to adopt a mindful, informed approach that values learning and growth. The foundation of constructive engagement begins with **listening**—a deliberate act of focusing on others' perspectives without judgment. Active listening fosters empathy, allowing individuals to build connections and understand the motivations, fears, and hopes that inform others' beliefs. Through this understanding, we can find common ground, even amid differing opinions, and foster conversations which are respectful and inclusive.

Researching issues thoroughly is equally important in constructive engagement. New Universalism emphasizes the value of knowledge, urging us to make informed decisions that reflect a comprehensive understanding of societal challenges. This involves examining multiple sources, questioning assumptions, and being willing to adapt one's stance as new information comes to light. By cultivating a well-rounded view of issues, we are better equipped to contribute meaningfully to discussions, offering perspectives which are both compassionate and informed.

Finally, **dialoguing** is the practice of open and respectful conversation that values both truth and kindness. In New Universalism, dialogue is seen as a way to connect, learn, and foster positive change. We are encouraged to engage in discussions that seek understanding over winning, prioritizing harmony and mutual respect. Through constructive dialogue, individuals can work collaboratively to identify solutions that honor the diverse needs of our communities, building a social fabric that reflects New Universalist values.

Guided by Integrity and Compassion

In all social and political interactions, integrity and compassion serve as guiding lights. Integrity calls on us to be truthful, consistent, and steadfast in our principles. This means engaging with honesty, acknowledging when we may lack information, and standing by our values even when it may be challenging. Compassion, on the other hand, ensures that we approach every issue with empathy and kindness, recognizing the shared humanity that unites all people. By balancing integrity with compassion, we can navigate complex social and political landscapes in ways that are true to ourselves and respectful of others.

Promoting Equity and Justice in Society

In New Universalism, promoting equity and justice is more than a social ideal; it is a spiritual and ethical mandate. These principles are woven into the very fabric of New Universalist values, guiding us to recognize and address systemic inequalities and injustices that affect individuals and communities. Equity and justice reflect a commitment to fairness, compassion, and the belief that all people deserve dignity and respect. By championing these principles, New Universalists actively contribute to a world that honors the interconnectedness of all humanity and the shared responsibility to uplift each other.

Understanding Equity and Justice

Equity and justice are distinct but interrelated concepts. **Equity** involves ensuring that every individual has fair access to opportunities and resources, accounting for the unique needs and challenges that different people may face. Unlike equality, which treats everyone the same, equity recognizes diversity and strives to provide the necessary support for all individuals to thrive. In New Universalism, equity is an expression of compassion in action, a commitment to fostering a society where all people, regardless of their background, can achieve their potential.

Justice, on the other hand, is the practice of upholding moral and legal principles that ensure fair treatment for all. Justice in New Universalism encompasses not only legal justice but also social and economic justice. It means taking action to dismantle structures that perpetuate inequality and advocating for policies that create an inclusive and supportive society. Justice calls for a proactive stance, challenging us to address not only the symptoms of inequality but also its root causes, creating lasting, systemic change.

Supporting Justice Through Inclusive Policies and Anti-Discrimination Efforts

Promoting equity and justice requires action at both the personal and community levels. New Universalists are encouraged to support inclusive policies that champion the rights and well-being of all people, regardless of race, gender, socioeconomic status, or other aspects of identity. This includes advocating for policies that ensure access to quality healthcare, education, housing, and other basic needs, recognizing that these are essential for fostering a society where everyone can flourish.

In addition to supporting inclusive policies, we are urged to participate in **anti-discrimination efforts**. This may involve actively opposing prejudiced behaviors, stereotypes, or institutional practices that perpetuate discrimination. In community settings, this could mean advocating for diversity and inclusivity initiatives, working to ensure that every person feels valued and included. New Universalism calls for us to be vigilant allies, standing against prejudice and supporting those who are marginalized or vulnerable.

Taking a Stand Against Injustice with Respect and Compassion

New Universalism teaches that taking a stand against injustice must be done with respect, compassion, and humility. We are called to be agents of change, not through hostility or division but through dialogue, understanding, and a commitment to the shared values of humanity. When addressing issues of injustice, New Universalists are encouraged to maintain a balanced approach, ensuring that our actions uplift rather than alienate. By focusing on common goals and building coalitions, we can create effective and lasting change in our communities.

Taking a stand may look different for each individual; for some, it could involve attending protests, while for others, it may mean engaging in policy advocacy or offering support to affected communities. The path to promoting justice is as diverse as the individuals who walk it. Yet, in all instances, New Universalism calls for us to act with integrity and empathy, ensuring that our actions are rooted in a genuine desire to create a fairer, more compassionate world.

Creating a Society that Values Every Individual

Ultimately, the goal of promoting equity and justice in New Universalism is to build a society where every individual is valued, respected, and supported. We are encouraged to view each person as a part of the global community, deserving of compassion and dignity. This commitment to valuing all individuals extends to every interaction, every decision, and every effort to create a more equitable world.

In this way, New Universalism calls on its members to be builders of a just society, one where barriers to opportunity are dismantled, where voices that have long been silenced are heard, and where every person has the chance to thrive. By promoting equity and justice, New Universalists contribute to a collective legacy of integrity, kindness, and unity, leaving a positive impact on future generations and honoring the shared humanity that binds all people.

Examples of Socially Responsible Political Engagement

In New Universalism, socially responsible political engagement is seen as a pathway to enact positive change, grounded in the principles of equity, compassion, and integrity. By taking an active role in social and political causes that align with the values of New Universalism, we can contribute to the common good and help shape a world that respects and uplifts all people. Engaging in political activities offers us a tangible way to put our values into action, reinforcing our commitment to social responsibility and honoring the interconnectedness of all humanity.

Environmental Policy Advocacy

Environmental stewardship is a core tenet of New Universalism, reflecting a profound respect for the Earth and a commitment to its care. We are encouraged to support policies that protect natural resources, reduce pollution, and address climate change. This may include engaging in advocacy for renewable energy initiatives, conservation programs, and policies aimed at reducing carbon emissions.

We can participate in environmental advocacy in several ways—by attending public meetings on local environmental issues, writing letters to lawmakers, or supporting organizations that champion sustainable practices. Through these actions, New Universalists embody the principle of Earth Stewardship, helping to create a sustainable future for all living beings.

Supporting Local Community Initiatives

Engaging with local community initiatives is another way for New Universalists to promote social responsibility. Local issues often offer opportunities for direct involvement, allowing us to see the immediate impact of our efforts. This might include supporting educational programs, health clinics, food banks, housing projects, and other resources that serve underserved communities. By contributing to initiatives that support local well-being, we demonstrate a commitment to the principles of compassion, equity, and service.

New Universalists are encouraged to seek out organizations or groups in our communities that align with our values and to volunteer our time, resources, or skills. Through consistent involvement in community initiatives, we help build stronger, more supportive communities and exemplify the values of New Universalism in our everyday lives.

Advocating for Social Justice and Equity

Advocating for social justice and equity is central to New Universalism's commitment to fairness and inclusion. We are encouraged to support causes that challenge systemic inequalities and promote the fair treatment of all individuals. This might involve supporting policies that address racial, economic, or gender-based disparities or advocating for workplace protections, healthcare access, and other issues that affect marginalized populations.

Social justice advocacy can take many forms, from participating in peaceful protests and signing petitions to engaging in discussions that raise awareness about social issues. New Universalists are encouraged to approach advocacy with an open mind, listening to the experiences of those directly affected by injustice, and standing as allies in the pursuit of a just and equitable society.

Balancing Engagement with Compassion and Integrity

While political engagement is essential, New Universalism emphasizes the importance of compassion and integrity in all forms of activism. We are encouraged to pursue positive change by focusing on unity rather than division, seeking solutions that honor diverse perspectives. By valuing compassion over partisanship and promoting open, respectful dialogue, New Universalists aim to bridge divides and build a more harmonious society.

Examples of this balanced approach may include engaging in conversations that seek understanding rather than winning debates, focusing on common ground, and collaborating with individuals or groups who may hold different views but share similar goals. This focus on balanced engagement allows New Universalists to participate meaningfully in social and political issues without compromising our commitment to empathy, respect, and integrity.

6

Universal Human Rights as Spiritual Mandate

Human Rights Across Faiths

Human Rights as a Core Spiritual Value

In New Universalism, human rights are recognized not just as a legal or ethical concern but as a deeply spiritual mandate. This perspective affirms that every individual is inherently deserving of dignity, respect, and compassion. Rooted in the understanding that all people are interconnected and share a common humanity, the commitment to human rights within New Universalism is grounded in the belief that each person is a manifestation of both the Earth and the divine cosmos—a "child of Earth and Starry Heaven." This sacred viewpoint is foundational to the New Universalist ethos, guiding members to honor, protect, and uphold the rights of every individual as an expression of universal respect and compassion.

The alignment of human rights with the spiritual values of New Universalism bridges individual actions and societal obligations. Values such as compassion, equity, and integrity serve as ethical guideposts, encouraging us to embody respect for the rights and dignity of others in our personal lives, as well as to advocate for justice and equality on a broader societal level. Human rights, seen through the lens of New Universalism, become a shared spiritual responsibility—an expression of both personal integrity and collective solidarity.

Human Rights as an Expression of Compassion and Equity

Human rights are inherently linked to the principle of compassion, which calls for empathy, understanding, and an active commitment to relieving the suffering of others. In New Universalism, compassion extends beyond individual acts of kindness to encompass a collective responsibility to ensure that all people have access to basic rights and freedoms, allowing them to live with dignity and purpose. Equity is equally vital, as it emphasizes that justice cannot be partial; it must be accessible to all, regardless of identity, background, or circumstance. These values, deeply embedded in the principles of New Universalism, reinforce the belief that everyone deserves to live free from oppression, discrimination, and injustice.

New Universalism's commitment to equity and compassion encourages us to act as advocates and allies for the rights of others, recognizing that upholding human rights is an essential part of creating a fair and harmonious society. Through daily interactions, we are called to respect the inherent worth of every person we encounter, fostering an inclusive community that honors diversity and celebrates shared humanity.

Human Rights as a Bridge Between Personal and Societal Responsibility

In New Universalism, human rights create a bridge between personal integrity and societal engagement. As individuals grow in self-awareness, responsibility, and respect for others, we contribute to the larger vision of a just society. Each person's commitment to human rights strengthens the collective, establishing a foundation of integrity and compassion that extends to every corner of the community. New Universalism encourages us to consider the impact of our actions on others, fostering a worldview that connects individual choices to broader social implications.

This bridge between personal and societal responsibility reflects New Universalism's understanding that spirituality is not isolated to individual practices but is lived out through relationships, communities, and global interactions. We are encouraged to take personal accountability for upholding human rights within our lives while supporting collective efforts to address issues such as poverty, inequality, and injustice. By doing so, we embody the New Universalist vision of a world where compassion, equity, and respect guide every action and relationship.

Religious Perspectives on Human Rights

Across diverse spiritual traditions, the principle of human rights is woven into the fabric of teachings that honor the sacredness and dignity of every individual. While different religions and philosophies approach human rights through distinct frameworks, the underlying values of compassion, justice, and respect for the inherent worth of each person form a universal thread. These perspectives resonate deeply with New Universalism's commitment to upholding human rights as a spiritual and ethical mandate, emphasizing that all individuals, as "children of Earth and Starry Heaven," deserve to live with freedom, dignity, and security.

Christianity: Human Dignity as a Reflection of Divine Love

In Christianity, the concept of human rights is rooted in the belief that every person is created in the image of God, known as *Imago Dei*, signifying an inherent worth and dignity that transcends social status, race, or nationality. This understanding of divine love asserts that each human being embodies a unique reflection of God's essence, deserving of respect, compassion, and equal treatment. The teachings of Jesus further reinforce this perspective by encouraging followers to embrace compassion, forgiveness, humility, and service to all, particularly the marginalized and oppressed.

The New Testament provides several foundational passages that underscore the Christian commitment to human dignity and equality. In Matthew 25:40, Jesus says, "Whatever you did for one of the least of these brothers and sisters of mine, you did for me." This profound statement highlights the Christian belief that acts of kindness, compassion, and justice toward others are inherently sacred, as they honor God by honoring His creation. Moreover, the parable of the Good Samaritan (Luke 10:25–37) presents a powerful illustration of how compassion should be extended beyond social and cultural divides, emphasizing that love for others is not limited by nationality, race, or creed.

The Role of Compassion, Forgiveness, and Service in Human Dignity

Christianity teaches that compassion, forgiveness, and service are more than virtues; they are mandates central to a life in alignment with God's love. Compassion is viewed as a reflection of divine love, urging believers to act with empathy and understanding toward others. Forgiveness, another key aspect of Christian doctrine, encourages the release of grudges and ill-will, fostering reconciliation and healing. Service to others is considered a sacred duty, exemplified by Jesus' life, particularly through His care for the poor, sick, and oppressed.

For New Universalists, these virtues resonate deeply within the doctrine of universal compassion and equality. Compassion, forgiveness, and service are seen not only as reflections of divine love but as pathways to social harmony and mutual respect. By embodying these values, New Universalists aim to honor the dignity of all individuals, recognizing that acts of kindness and compassion are ways to foster a more just and equitable society. The teachings of Jesus serve as an example for New Universalists to extend compassion without discrimination and to approach others with empathy and forgiveness, nurturing the community and healing divisions.

Justice and Social Responsibility in Christian Doctrine

Christianity places a strong emphasis on justice and social responsibility, urging believers to "seek justice, love mercy, and walk humbly with [their] God" (Micah 6:8). This call to justice aligns closely with the concept of human rights, as it emphasizes the need to protect the vulnerable, uplift the marginalized, and confront oppression. In the Gospels, Jesus actively challenges social norms that perpetuate inequality, treating women, lepers, and tax collectors with respect and compassion, in opposition to the norms of His time. His actions demonstrate a commitment to justice that transcends mere social obligation, positioning it as a divine commandment.

New Universalism draws from this Christian commitment to justice, recognizing the importance of addressing social injustices and upholding the dignity of all people. Inspired by these teachings, New Universalists are encouraged to advocate for equitable treatment of all individuals, regardless of their social or economic status. This alignment with Christian values empowers New Universalists to view human rights as not merely legal constructs but as moral imperatives that honor the intrinsic worth of every individual. In pursuing justice, New Universalists commit to creating a world where each person's freedom and well-being are protected as an expression of divine love.

Intersections with New Universalist Values

The Christian perspective on human dignity and compassion resonates deeply with New Universalism's core values of empathy, social responsibility, and inclusivity. New Universalism views human rights as a sacred mandate that aligns with spiritual truths found across diverse faiths. While Christianity teaches these values through the life and teachings of Jesus, New Universalism adopts them as universal principles, accessible to all people regardless of religious affiliation.

The New Universalist practice of honoring each individual as a "child of Earth and Starry Heaven" mirrors the Christian notion of all people being created in God's image. This perspective fosters a worldview that transcends social, racial, and religious boundaries, emphasizing that every person's life is imbued with sacred worth. By drawing upon these shared values, New Universalists are reminded that the pursuit of human rights is not only a social responsibility but a spiritual commitment to nurturing the divine spark within each person.

Practical Applications for New Universalists

Inspired by the Christian principles of compassion, justice, and service, New Universalists are encouraged to engage in practices that honor human dignity in our daily lives. Practical applications include:

- **Volunteering and Service**: Engaging in community service or charitable efforts as acts of compassion, following the example of Jesus' care for the vulnerable. This service is seen as a way to honor the divine essence within each person, strengthening the bonds of community.
- **Forgiveness and Reconciliation**: Practicing forgiveness in personal relationships to foster healing and unity, recognizing that holding onto anger or resentment can harm both the individual and the community. Reconciliation becomes a sacred act that mirrors the divine call for harmony.
- **Advocacy for Justice**: Taking a stand against social injustices, such as poverty, discrimination, and exploitation, by supporting policies and initiatives that protect human rights. This commitment to justice reflects the Christian call to "do justice" and to "love mercy," aligning with New Universalism's dedication to social equity.

Through these actions, New Universalists are invited to view our pursuit of human rights as an expression of divine love, grounded in compassion, justice, and respect for the dignity of all.

Islam: Justice, Equality, and Community Welfare

In Islam, human rights are seen as divinely ordained, arising from the foundational belief that all humans are created equal in the eyes of Allah. This perspective emphasizes the dignity, honor, and respect due to every person, regardless of race, class, or nationality. The Quran contains numerous teachings that affirm human rights, with justice, mercy, and compassion as central values. These teachings encourage Muslims to uphold justice and equity, ensuring the welfare of the entire community (*ummah*) while advocating for the protection and dignity of each individual.

The concept of *adl* (justice) is a guiding principle in Islam, emphasizing that Allah has commanded justice as a divine requirement. The Quran states, "Indeed, Allah commands you to render trusts to whom they are due and when you judge between people, judge with justice..." (Quran 4:58). This mandate for justice extends beyond legal frameworks; it is deeply interwoven with spiritual, ethical, and social aspects of life, making it a moral imperative for Muslims to stand up against oppression and inequality.

Mercy, Compassion, and Community Welfare in Islamic Teachings

The values of mercy (*rahma*) and compassion (*rahman*) are also deeply embedded within Islamic teachings, portraying Allah as "The Merciful, The Compassionate." Compassion is not only a divine quality but an ethical expectation for humanity, guiding Muslims to treat others with kindness, empathy, and respect. The concept of *zakat* (charitable giving) is one of the Five Pillars of Islam, reflecting the importance of social responsibility and the duty to uplift the less fortunate. Zakat serves as a practical expression of compassion and a reminder of each individual's duty to contribute positively to the well-being of the community.

In addition to *zakat*, Islam encourages acts of charity known as *sadaqah*, which may be given voluntarily at any time. *Sadaqah* emphasizes the moral obligation to care for others, reinforcing that compassion and generosity should extend beyond religious duty, becoming a way of life. The New Universalist value of compassion finds resonance in these teachings, which advocate for the upliftment and welfare of all individuals, particularly the poor and marginalized.

Human Rights and Equality in Islamic Law

In Islam, human rights are further enshrined through the concepts of *haqq al-nafs* (rights of the self) and *haqq al-ibad* (rights of others). These frameworks outline the individual's rights to safety, dignity, freedom, and well-being, as well as responsibilities toward others and society. Islamic law (Sharia) emphasizes the protection of five basic rights: the right to life, property, freedom of belief, family, and intellect. These rights form a comprehensive approach to safeguarding individual freedoms while upholding communal harmony.

For New Universalists, the principles embedded in these Islamic teachings—equality, social justice, and the communal obligation to protect and uplift each individual—are seen as essential foundations for a fair and just society. By honoring these principles, New Universalism embraces the ethical mandate to protect each person's intrinsic worth, advocating for human rights not only as a social construct but as a sacred trust to be preserved and respected.

Alignment with New Universalist Values

The Islamic perspective on justice, equality, and community welfare aligns closely with New Universalism's core values of social responsibility, compassion, and equity. New Universalists believe that each individual has a divine purpose and deserves to be treated with fairness, reflecting the belief that the respect for human dignity is universal across all spiritual and ethical traditions. Inspired by the Islamic principles of justice and equality, New Universalists are encouraged to engage in actions that promote fairness, including advocacy for social reform, volunteer work, and support for vulnerable populations.

Moreover, the emphasis on community welfare within Islam resonates with New Universalism's commitment to Earth Stewardship and social responsibility. By fostering a sense of interconnectedness and accountability, New Universalists are reminded that our actions impact not only our immediate surroundings but the global community. This reflection encourages a collective commitment to a world in which justice and compassion prevail, echoing Islamic ideals of communal support and moral duty.

Practical Applications for New Universalists

The teachings of Islam offer New Universalists valuable insights into how we might embody compassion, justice, and social responsibility in practical ways. Suggested applications include:

- **Charitable Giving and Service**: Inspired by *zakat* and *sadaqah*, New Universalists are encouraged to incorporate charitable giving into our lives, donating to causes that uplift the less fortunate or volunteering with organizations that promote equity. Regular acts of service deepen compassion and social responsibility within the New Universalist community.
- **Advocacy for Justice**: Following Islam's emphasis on justice (*adl*), New Universalists are encouraged to advocate for policies and actions that support equality and fairness, particularly in cases of discrimination or systemic injustice. By actively supporting justice, New Universalists fulfill the spiritual mandate to create a more equitable world.
- **Promoting Community Welfare**: Inspired by Islam's commitment to community welfare, New Universalists are reminded to engage in initiatives that benefit the collective, whether through local environmental efforts, social support programs, or educational outreach. These actions reflect the values of interconnectedness and compassion central to New Universalism.

In this way, Islamic teachings on justice, equality, and community welfare enrich New Universalism's understanding of human rights, urging believers to see each person as worthy of dignity, respect, and support. This perspective reinforces the New Universalist commitment to uphold human rights as a spiritual mandate, building a society rooted in compassion, equity, and unity.

Buddhism: Compassion, Non-violence, and Reducing Suffering

In Buddhism, compassion (*karuna*) is a core ethical principle, seen as essential for alleviating suffering not only for oneself but for all beings. This compassion is intimately connected with the Buddhist understanding of suffering (*dukkha*) as an inherent part of life, a state from which all beings seek liberation. By cultivating compassion, non-violence (*ahimsa*), and mindfulness, Buddhists strive to reduce suffering and contribute to a harmonious world. These values promote an inclusive, respectful view of human dignity and align closely with New Universalism's commitment to social responsibility and universal compassion.

The Principle of Compassion as Universal Care

Buddhism teaches that compassion is not merely an emotional response but an ethical imperative rooted in the belief that all beings are interconnected. Compassion, in the Buddhist sense, involves a willingness to empathize with the pain and struggles of others and actively seek to alleviate them. The *Metta Sutta*, or the "Loving-Kindness Sutra," encourages practitioners to "radiate boundless love towards the entire world," underscoring that compassion should be extended to all beings, not just humans. This call to universal compassion resonates deeply with New Universalism's view of human rights as extending beyond any single culture, community, or religion, affirming that each individual deserves respect, care, and freedom from suffering.

The concept of *karuna* (compassion) extends beyond alleviating physical suffering; it is also about respecting each person's dignity, supporting their well-being, and fostering empathy in all relationships. In New Universalist theology, compassion is seen as a spiritual and social responsibility, guiding members to care for others and recognize their inherent worth. Inspired by Buddhist teachings, New Universalists strive to embody compassion by supporting humanitarian causes, engaging in nonviolent actions, and promoting policies that alleviate suffering in society.

Non-violence (Ahimsa) and the Commitment to Peace

Buddhism holds *ahimsa*—the principle of non-violence—as fundamental to ethical conduct. Ahimsa encourages Buddhists to refrain from causing harm to any living being, a concept that extends from individual actions to societal systems. By practicing non-violence in thought, word, and deed, Buddhists commit to creating a peaceful world and respecting all forms of life. This non-violent ethos finds resonance in New Universalism's emphasis on peace, integrity, and Earth Stewardship, as both traditions recognize the sacredness of life and the responsibility to protect and honor it.

In practical terms, *ahimsa* in Buddhism translates to actively choosing kindness, compassion, and restraint. This includes not only physical actions but also the rejection of harmful speech, prejudice, and discriminatory practices. For New Universalists, embracing non-violence means advocating for justice and equality without causing harm. In supporting human rights, New Universalists are encouraged to act with sensitivity and to strive for peaceful solutions, whether engaging in social justice, environmental activism, or community service.

Reducing Suffering: Compassionate Action as a Spiritual Mandate

In the Buddhist tradition, reducing suffering for all beings is seen as a sacred duty. This commitment is evident in the Bodhisattva ideal—a vow to work tirelessly for the welfare of all sentient beings, often delaying one's own enlightenment to serve others. The Bodhisattva's dedication to relieving suffering aligns with New Universalism's call for proactive compassion, social responsibility, and community service. While New Universalists do not take vows in the Buddhist sense, the community does share a collective commitment to reducing suffering in the world, whether through charitable giving, volunteer work, or supporting mental health initiatives.

In New Universalist practice, alleviating suffering is seen as both a personal and communal responsibility, guiding us to extend kindness and compassion to all. By following Buddhist-inspired practices like mindful listening, intentional generosity, and service to those in need, New Universalists foster a world that seeks to lessen harm and support healing. In this way, New Universalism honors the Buddhist principle of *karuna* by integrating compassionate action as a core aspect of daily life.

Aligning with New Universalist Values

The Buddhist values of compassion, non-violence, and reducing suffering align seamlessly with New Universalist beliefs in universal human rights, social responsibility, and Earth Stewardship. Compassion, in both traditions, transcends cultural or religious boundaries, encouraging individuals to act from a place of empathy, understanding, and respect for others. New Universalism, inspired by Buddhism, invites its community members to consider how our actions impact others, prompting us to be mindful, considerate, and proactive in promoting harmony.

By incorporating these Buddhist principles, New Universalists find a balanced approach to spiritual and social responsibility. Compassion is not merely an ideal; it is an active choice to create a more caring world. Non-violence extends beyond the absence of conflict, embracing the positive cultivation of kindness and equity. And the dedication to reducing suffering reflects a commitment to practical, compassionate engagement that values the well-being of all.

Practical Applications for New Universalists

The teachings of Buddhism offer New Universalists insightful ways to embody compassion, non-violence, and care for others through mindful, ethical choices. Suggested practices include:

- **Mindfulness Meditation and Compassionate Reflection**: Inspired by Buddhist meditation practices, New Universalists can integrate mindfulness into our daily routine. Mindful breathing, compassionate reflections, or a meditation practice can deepen one's sense of empathy and prepare us to approach others with greater understanding.
- **Acts of Compassion**: Encouraged by Buddhist teachings, New Universalists are invited to perform acts of compassion regularly. Whether through volunteering, supporting marginalized groups, or offering emotional support to loved ones, these acts help embody compassion as a lived, active principle.
- **Promoting Non-violence and Conflict Resolution**: Guided by *ahimsa*, New Universalists can choose to engage in peaceful conflict resolution in personal and community settings. By promoting dialogue, compromise, and understanding, New Universalists contribute to creating a peaceful, just society.

Buddhist teachings on compassion, non-violence, and reducing suffering provide New Universalism with profound insights into human rights as a sacred mandate. In honoring these values, New Universalists strive to foster a world where compassion prevails, and each person's right to dignity, safety, and well-being is respected.

Judaism: Justice, Repairing the World, and Social Responsibility

In Judaism, the concepts of justice (*tzedek*), social responsibility, and "repairing the world" (*tikkun olam*) are central to both individual practice and communal life. These principles underscore a duty to pursue justice, kindness, and peace, extending beyond personal morality to include a commitment to the welfare of society as a whole. New Universalism deeply respects these values, drawing inspiration from Judaism's emphasis on social responsibility, the inherent dignity of all people, and the communal obligation to uplift others and promote equity.

Justice (*Tzedek*) as a Sacred Duty

In Jewish tradition, *tzedek*—or justice—is not just a legal principle but a profound moral imperative. Rooted in the Hebrew scriptures, justice is a recurring theme, guiding individuals and communities to act with integrity and fairness. One of the most well-known verses in the Torah, "Justice, justice you shall pursue" (*Deuteronomy 16:20*), underscores the importance of actively seeking justice. This phrase implies that justice is not passive but requires deliberate, ongoing action. Justice in Judaism reflects a commitment to fairness, equity, and compassion, demanding that each individual take responsibility for the well-being of others, particularly the marginalized.

New Universalism embraces this commitment to justice as a spiritual mandate, seeing it as foundational to a world that honors human rights, respects diversity, and uplifts the oppressed. Inspired by *tzedek*, New Universalists are encouraged to work towards social equity and fairness in both personal actions and communal efforts. This may include advocating for inclusive policies, addressing systemic injustices, or supporting initiatives that promote fairness and dignity for all. *Tzedek* also inspires New Universalists to engage in self-reflection, examining how personal actions and community practices impact others and contribute to a just society.

Repairing the World (*Tikkun Olam*): An Ethical and Spiritual Responsibility

The concept of *tikkun olam*, or "repairing the world," emphasizes the role of each individual in creating a more just, peaceful, and compassionate world. Traditionally, *tikkun olam* referred to a specific set of practices aimed at correcting social imbalances, but over time, it has come to represent a broad commitment to social justice, environmental care, and human rights. *Tikkun olam* calls upon each person to act as a steward of society, with an active duty to make the world better for future generations.

In New Universalism, *tikkun olam* is embraced as a model for Earth Stewardship and social responsibility, reflecting a shared commitment to leaving a positive legacy. By promoting *tikkun olam*, New Universalists are encouraged to engage in practices that uplift communities, support environmental sustainability, and champion human rights. This could include community service, participating in initiatives that address environmental challenges, or supporting organizations dedicated to social reform. *Tikkun olam* also emphasizes the power of collective action, reminding New Universalists that meaningful change often requires unity, cooperation, and shared responsibility.

Social Responsibility and the Value of Kindness

Judaism places strong emphasis on *chesed*, or loving-kindness, which extends beyond mere empathy to involve active concern for the well-being of others. In the Torah, kindness is exemplified through stories of hospitality, generosity, and compassion. The Jewish concept of *chesed* teaches that kindness is a social obligation, not only an individual virtue. This ethos of kindness and social responsibility is reflected in community practices such as the *mitzvot* (commandments), many of which focus on helping others and creating a more equitable society.

For New Universalism, *chesed* serves as an inspiration for cultivating kindness, both in personal interactions and in broader social engagement. Kindness, as a principle, is central to New Universalist theology, emphasizing that every individual has the capacity and duty to uplift others through compassion, generosity, and supportive actions. Kindness in New Universalism is not limited to interpersonal relationships but extends to activism, charity, and service, creating a more compassionate and just society.

Community and Mutual Responsibility: The Strength of Collective Action

In Jewish tradition, the concept of mutual responsibility is encapsulated in the idea that "all Israel is responsible for one another." This reflects a belief that individuals are interconnected within their communities and bear collective responsibility for one another's welfare. This sense of communal responsibility encourages individuals to look beyond personal interests, prioritizing the well-being of society as a whole. Jewish teachings encourage participation in communal life, helping those in need, and standing up for justice—values that resonate deeply with New Universalism.

New Universalism incorporates this collective approach, teaching that every person is a valuable part of the larger human family and that social responsibility extends to supporting all members of society, regardless of background, belief, or nationality. Inspired by the Jewish emphasis on communal well-being, New Universalism encourages members to foster inclusivity, empathy, and collaboration within our communities. Whether through local volunteer work, advocacy, or simple acts of support, the New Universalist approach to mutual responsibility reflects a shared commitment to collective growth, justice, and compassion.

Aligning with New Universalist Values

The Jewish values of justice, *tikkun olam*, kindness, and mutual responsibility provide New Universalism with a model for understanding human rights as more than abstract principles but as active responsibilities. Justice, in both traditions, emphasizes the importance of fairness and equity, particularly for the marginalized and vulnerable. *Tikkun olam* highlights the duty to protect and improve the world, underscoring New Universalism's call for environmental stewardship and social responsibility. And the Jewish principles of kindness and mutual responsibility reflect New Universalism's dedication to fostering a compassionate, inclusive, and supportive community.

In drawing from Judaism, New Universalists find a well-rounded foundation for ethical living that balances personal responsibility with social engagement. The commitment to justice ensures that individuals actively oppose inequality, discrimination, and injustice. The duty to repair the world calls for meaningful actions that promote sustainability, equity, and peace. And the emphasis on kindness and mutual responsibility provides guidance for building communities rooted in empathy, respect, and shared humanity.

Practical Applications for New Universalists

Judaism's teachings on justice, *tikkun olam*, and social responsibility offer New Universalists concrete ways to enact these values in our daily lives. Suggested practices include:

- **Pursuing Justice in Personal and Community Decisions**: Inspired by *tzedek*, New Universalists can seek justice by advocating for fairness in workplaces, schools, and local communities. This may include supporting policies that promote equality, defending the rights of marginalized groups, or engaging in fair practices that benefit all.
- **Embracing *Tikkun Olam* through Environmental and Social Action**: By adopting the Jewish commitment to repair the world, New Universalists can participate in activities that uplift communities, protect the environment, and support the well-being of future gen-

erations. This could involve planting trees, reducing waste, or advocating for policies that combat climate change and protect natural resources.

- **Practicing Kindness and Social Responsibility Daily**: Following the value of *chesed*, New Universalists are encouraged to practice kindness through small but meaningful acts, such as helping a neighbor, offering support to those in need, or contributing to charity. Acts of kindness help build a compassionate community and create positive change.

Judaism's values of justice, *tikkun olam*, and social responsibility resonate deeply within New Universalism, inspiring us to live with integrity, compassion, and purpose. By upholding these values, New Universalists contribute to a world where human rights are respected, communities are uplifted, and each individual is honored as part of a shared human family.

Hinduism: Dharma, Ahimsa, and the Sacredness of Life

In Hinduism, core values such as *dharma* (ethical duty), *ahimsa* (non-violence), and respect for the sacredness of all life are central to both personal and societal ethics. These principles guide adherents in living a balanced, moral life that honors the inherent dignity of all beings. In New Universalism, these values inspire a commitment to compassion, justice, and respect for individual dignity, providing a framework that supports the pursuit of universal human rights and personal integrity.

Dharma: The Foundation of Ethical Duty

Dharma in Hinduism is a multifaceted concept encompassing duty, righteousness, law, and ethical conduct. It is seen as a universal moral order, guiding individuals in making decisions that align with the welfare of society, the environment, and personal growth. Each individual's *dharma* is shaped by their unique roles and relationships, encouraging a life of integrity, kindness, and service to others. The Bhagavad Gita, one of Hinduism's central texts, illustrates *dharma* as a sacred duty, where upholding righteousness and ethical conduct serves not only personal growth but also societal harmony.

In New Universalism, *dharma* is recognized as an ethical principle that aligns with the pursuit of social responsibility, accountability, and compassion. By adopting the concept of *dharma*, New

Universalists are encouraged to reflect on how our actions affect others and to approach life with integrity, respect, and a commitment to contributing positively to our communities. This principle also reinforces the New Universalist belief that each individual has a unique purpose within the larger interconnected community and that fulfilling one's duties with honor and kindness benefits the collective whole.

Ahimsa: The Practice of Non-Violence and Compassion

Ahimsa, or non-violence, is a principle found across many Indian spiritual traditions, including Hinduism, Jainism, and Buddhism. In Hinduism, *ahimsa* emphasizes respect and kindness toward all living beings, grounded in the belief that all life is sacred and interconnected. Mahatma Gandhi famously advocated for *ahimsa* as both a personal and political philosophy, demonstrating how non-violence can serve as a powerful tool for social change. *Ahimsa* is practiced not only as a moral ideal but as an actionable way of living that respects life, reduces suffering, and promotes harmony.

New Universalism draws upon the concept of *ahimsa* to promote compassion, respect, and ethical behavior toward others and the environment. This principle informs the New Universalist commitment to Earth Stewardship and social responsibility, encouraging members to make choices that minimize harm and foster well-being for all. In everyday practice, *ahimsa* in New Universalism may include mindful consumption, compassionate interactions, and advocacy for non-violence in both personal conduct and societal issues. This practice extends beyond human interactions, embracing a holistic respect for all forms of life and emphasizing the interdependence of all beings.

Sacredness of Life: Honoring All Beings

The Hindu worldview emphasizes the inherent divinity within all forms of life, seeing each being as a manifestation of the divine. This understanding fosters a profound respect for life in all its diversity, encouraging practices that honor the sacredness of nature and the interconnectedness of all existence. The principle of the sacredness of life can be seen in various Hindu rituals, such as offering respect to rivers, trees, and animals, and the commitment to vegetarianism practiced by many Hindus as an expression of non-violence and reverence for life.

New Universalism embraces this reverence for life, recognizing the sacred in all beings and advocating for the protection of both human rights and environmental integrity. In New Universalist theology, the sacredness of life is reflected in the commitment to equity, compassion, and

Earth Stewardship. Just as Hinduism reveres nature as a manifestation of the divine, New Universalism encourages us to view all life as inherently valuable, fostering a culture of respect, care, and mindful coexistence. This respect for the sacredness of life inspires us to engage in practices that support biodiversity, reduce harm, and advocate for policies that uphold the dignity and rights of all beings.

Balancing Personal Responsibility with Social Ethics

In Hinduism, the pursuit of personal growth is inseparable from one's duty to society. By fulfilling their *dharma*, individuals contribute to the collective well-being, maintaining a balance between personal advancement and social harmony. This responsibility to the broader community is reflected in Hindu teachings on selflessness, kindness, and generosity, urging individuals to consider the needs of others and prioritize ethical conduct.

For New Universalism, this balance of personal and social ethics serves as a model for living with integrity and purpose. By upholding *dharma*—a principle of moral responsibility—New Universalists are encouraged to take accountability for our actions, contribute to societal welfare, and embody values of compassion and justice in our daily lives. In this way, New Universalism promotes a vision of ethical living that recognizes the interconnectedness of individual well-being with the health and harmony of society at large.

Aligning with New Universalist Values

The values of *dharma*, *ahimsa*, and reverence for life offer New Universalists a profound ethical foundation, providing guidance on how to live responsibly and compassionately within an interconnected world. These principles align closely with New Universalism's pillars of Social Responsibility, Earth Stewardship, and Filial Piety. The commitment to *dharma* reinforces New Universalism's focus on ethical integrity and personal accountability, while *ahimsa* inspires compassion, non-violence, and respect for all beings. Finally, the sacredness of life resonates with New Universalism's dedication to environmental preservation, social equity, and the acknowledgment of the divine in all forms of existence.

Practical Applications for New Universalists

Hinduism's teachings on *dharma*, *ahimsa*, and reverence for life offer New Universalists valuable insights into ethical conduct, social responsibility, and Earth Stewardship. Suggested practices include:

- **Practicing *Ahimsa* in Daily Interactions**: Inspired by *ahimsa*, New Universalists can cultivate non-violence in thoughts, words, and actions, fostering compassion in relationships and making choices that reduce harm to the planet and its inhabitants. This might include reducing consumption, choosing cruelty-free products, and supporting organizations that promote animal welfare.
- **Living with Purpose through *Dharma***: Embracing *dharma* as a call to act ethically, New Universalists are encouraged to approach each role in life with integrity and dedication, considering how our actions contribute to the well-being of others. This could involve mentoring others, contributing to community initiatives, or participating in projects that promote social welfare.
- **Honoring Life's Sacredness in Environmental Action**: Reflecting Hindu reverence for life, New Universalists are urged to engage in Earth Stewardship practices, such as conserving natural resources, supporting biodiversity, and advocating for policies that protect the environment. Practical steps include reducing waste, planting trees, and participating in efforts that honor and protect ecosystems.

Hinduism's values of *dharma*, *ahimsa*, and reverence for life provide New Universalists with an ethical guide that emphasizes compassion, responsibility, and respect for all beings. By integrating these values into daily life, New Universalists can contribute to a world that honors human rights, upholds environmental responsibility, and fosters unity across cultures, beliefs, and ecosystems.

Wicca and Pagan Approaches: Honoring All Life and Upholding Ethical Responsibility

In Wicca and various Pagan traditions, respect for the Earth and all its inhabitants is central to spiritual and ethical beliefs. These traditions emphasize a profound respect for life, non-violence, personal accountability, and the interconnectedness of all beings, values that align closely with New Universalism's dedication to human rights, Earth Stewardship, and social responsibility. Through rituals, practices, and ethical teachings, Wiccan and Pagan communities emphasize the importance of living harmoniously within nature and respecting the diversity of life—a principle that extends to human rights and social equality.

The Wiccan Rede and the Principle of Harm None

One of the foundational ethical statements in Wicca is the Wiccan Rede, which states, *"An it harm none, do what ye will."* This principle emphasizes that actions should be free from harm to others, promoting responsibility, mindfulness, and compassion. The Rede serves as a guiding principle for personal freedom that is balanced with respect for the well-being of others, aligning with New Universalism's call for integrity, non-violence, and social responsibility. It reflects an ethic that embraces individual freedom while underscoring the importance of ethical boundaries and empathy.

For New Universalism, the principle of "harm none" serves as an ethical guide that resonates with the commitment to universal human rights. By adopting this principle, New Universalists are encouraged to consider the consequences of our actions, taking responsibility to minimize harm and promote well-being within our communities. This emphasis on non-harm is extended beyond human interactions to include the environment and all living beings, fostering an approach that is both compassionate and conscientious.

Reverence for Nature and the Sacredness of All Life

Pagan traditions, including Wicca, honor the Earth as a living, sacred entity. The natural world is viewed as a manifestation of the divine, with each plant, animal, and human being inherently worthy of respect and care. This reverence for nature encourages practices that protect ecosystems, conserve resources, and promote biodiversity, aligning with New Universalism's focus on Earth Stewardship. In Pagan beliefs, nature is not only revered but is also a source of wisdom and guidance, teaching individuals about the cycles of life, death, and renewal.

In New Universalism, the Pagan view of the Earth as sacred provides a framework for recognizing environmental stewardship as a moral obligation. By honoring the planet, New Universalists are reminded of our duty to protect the environment, advocate for sustainability, and respect the intricate balance of ecosystems. This commitment to the Earth is reflected in practical actions, such as reducing waste, supporting conservation efforts, and advocating for policies that protect natural resources and the rights of Indigenous communities to maintain their lands and cultural practices.

Inclusivity and Respect for Diversity

Wiccan and Pagan communities are known for their inclusivity and acceptance of diverse paths, orientations, and beliefs. Many Pagan traditions emphasize the importance of celebrating diversity in all its forms, fostering an environment where individuality and personal freedom are respected. In this way, Wicca and other Pagan beliefs support the rights of individuals to live freely, aligning with New Universalism's emphasis on respect, equity, and inclusivity for all.

This acceptance of diversity is a cornerstone of New Universalism, which advocates for human rights and equality regardless of race, gender, sexual orientation, or background. Inspired by Pagan inclusivity, New Universalists are encouraged to support social equality and promote tolerance, recognizing the inherent dignity and worth of each individual. This commitment to diversity extends to supporting policies that protect the rights of marginalized communities and ensuring that everyone has access to equal opportunities, fostering a society that values all individuals.

Seasonal Cycles and the Value of Community

Wiccan and Pagan traditions honor the cyclical nature of life, often celebrated through the Wheel of the Year—a series of seasonal festivals that align with the cycles of nature. These festivals are opportunities for community gathering, reflection, and celebration of life's rhythms, fostering a sense of connection with both the Earth and each other. This recognition of life's cycles encourages an acceptance of change, growth, and renewal, teaching that every season, stage, and experience has inherent value.

For New Universalism, these seasonal celebrations serve as reminders of the interconnectedness of all life and the importance of community support. The seasonal festivals provide opportunities for communal reflection, gratitude, and unity, reinforcing the belief that the well-being of one affects the whole. In this way, New Universalists are encouraged to foster community bonds, support one another, and celebrate the diversity of experiences and perspectives within our community, reinforcing a sense of shared purpose and belonging.

Aligning with New Universalist Values

The Wiccan Rede, respect for the Earth, and Pagan inclusivity provide New Universalists with an ethical foundation that champions compassion, environmental responsibility, and social equity. By integrating these values into daily life, New Universalists are encouraged to adopt a worldview that respects all beings, promotes diversity, and fosters harmony between humanity and the Earth. In doing so, we contribute to a society that values the rights, dignity, and well-being of all individuals and honors the natural world as a sacred trust.

Practical Applications for New Universalists

Pagan values offer New Universalists practical ways to integrate respect, compassion, and inclusivity into our daily lives. Suggested practices include:

- **Embracing the Principle of Non-Harm**: By adopting the Wiccan Rede's principle of "harm none," New Universalists can practice mindfulness in interactions, making choices that reflect compassion and respect for others' well-being. This principle may also guide decisions regarding consumption, conflict resolution, and interactions within the broader community.
- **Honoring Earth's Sacredness through Environmental Action**: Inspired by Pagan reverence for the natural world, New Universalists can engage in Earth Stewardship practices, such as reducing consumption, conserving natural resources, and advocating for environmental protection. Supporting eco-friendly policies, reducing plastic use, and participating in community clean-ups can help protect the environment.
- **Promoting Diversity and Inclusivity**: Drawing from Pagan acceptance of diverse spiritual paths, New Universalists are encouraged to foster a culture of inclusivity, respecting individual differences and advocating for the rights of all people. This may include supporting equal access to resources, promoting diversity within community spaces, and creating inclusive policies.
- **Celebrating Seasonal Cycles as a Community**: By observing the seasonal festivals, New Universalists can connect with the rhythms of nature and our community, reflecting on the cycles of growth, rest, and renewal. These gatherings foster unity, gratitude, and mutual support, reinforcing the belief that all beings are interconnected within the broader cycle of life.

The ethical teachings of Wicca and Pagan traditions offer New Universalists guidance on how to live with respect, inclusivity, and environmental consciousness. Through practical applications, these values can be embodied in ways that honor the rights and dignity of all individuals, promoting harmony within society and with the natural world.

Secular Approaches: The Universal Declaration of Human Rights and Ethical Foundations for Equality

In addition to spiritual and religious perspectives, secular frameworks for human rights provide essential principles that align closely with the core values of New Universalism. Documents like the Universal Declaration of Human Rights (UDHR) reflect the belief that every individual possesses inherent dignity and worth. By grounding human rights in secular ethics, these frameworks affirm that equality, justice, and respect are fundamental rights for all individuals, regardless of background or belief. For New Universalism, these secular principles offer a bridge between diverse spiritual, religious, and cultural traditions, reinforcing the faith's commitment to universal truths.

The Universal Declaration of Human Rights: A Global Framework

Adopted by the United Nations General Assembly in 1948, the UDHR is a foundational document that articulates the inalienable rights of every individual. Written in response to the atrocities of World War II, the Declaration serves as a reminder of humanity's shared responsibility to protect dignity and justice. Articles within the UDHR address fundamental rights such as freedom of speech, equality before the law, the right to work, and protection against discrimination.

The New Universalist commitment to human rights finds resonance in the UDHR's emphasis on equality and respect. The Declaration aligns with New Universalism's belief in honoring the dignity of all people and fostering compassion, equity, and integrity within society. By upholding the values of the UDHR, New Universalists are reminded of our duty to respect and advocate for the rights of others, recognizing that these principles are part of a shared human heritage that transcends spiritual and cultural boundaries.

Humanism and Secular Ethics: Compassion and Reason as Guides

Humanism, a secular philosophy that emphasizes human welfare and ethical responsibility, aligns with New Universalism's values of reasoned inquiry and social responsibility. Humanists believe that individuals can lead fulfilling, ethical lives by relying on reason, empathy, and compassion rather than adherence to supernatural beliefs. This approach mirrors New Universalism's view that reason and compassion are complementary, guiding principles for spiritual growth and responsible living.

In New Universalism, humanist ethics provide an example of how compassion, kindness, and mutual respect can create inclusive communities. By adopting principles of humanism, New Universalists are encouraged to support efforts that promote social welfare, equality, and human rights, using reason and empathy as tools to address social challenges. This alignment underscores New Universalism's commitment to ethical living and encourages us to advocate for justice and equality in all aspects of life.

Social Contract Theory: Justice, Rights, and Collective Responsibility

Social contract theory, developed by philosophers such as John Locke, Jean-Jacques Rousseau, and Thomas Hobbes, argues that individuals consent to form societies and governments to protect their natural rights. This concept of mutual responsibility, where individuals contribute to and benefit from the collective well-being, reflects New Universalism's focus on communal values and social responsibility. The idea of a social contract emphasizes the importance of safeguarding individual rights while also promoting the common good.

For New Universalists, social contract theory provides a foundation for viewing human rights as essential to a just society. This theory supports the belief that individuals have both rights and responsibilities within our communities, emphasizing cooperation, accountability, and a commitment to fairness. New Universalists are encouraged to contribute positively to society, uphold justice, and support policies that protect human rights for all. Through this approach, we foster communities rooted in trust, shared values, and respect for diversity.

Environmental and Animal Rights: Expanding the Concept of Rights Beyond Humanity

Secular approaches to ethics have expanded to include environmental and animal rights, recognizing that human welfare is deeply interconnected with the health of the planet and the well-being of all living beings. Environmental ethics argue that humans have a moral responsibility to protect ecosystems and preserve biodiversity, while animal rights advocates emphasize that animals, as sentient beings, deserve respect and humane treatment. These perspectives align with New Universalism's commitment to Earth Stewardship, honoring the intrinsic value of all life.

New Universalists are encouraged to view environmental and animal rights as integral components of a holistic approach to human rights. By embracing the ethical principles of sustainability, conservation, and compassion for all beings, we are reminded of our duty to care for the Earth and its inhabitants. This inclusive approach reinforces the belief that human rights cannot be separated from environmental responsibility, as the well-being of individuals, communities, and the planet are interdependent.

Secular Approaches in New Universalist Practice: Practical Applications

Secular human rights frameworks and ethical philosophies offer New Universalists valuable insights for living responsibly, compassionately, and equitably. Suggested applications for integrating these secular values include:

- **Advocating for Human Rights in Local and Global Communities**: Inspired by the UDHR and humanist ethics, New Universalists are encouraged to support initiatives that promote equality, justice, and protection for vulnerable communities. This might include volunteering with human rights organizations, supporting refugee aid, or promoting policies that ensure fair treatment for all.
- **Promoting Environmental Sustainability and Animal Welfare**: Drawing on secular environmental ethics, New Universalists can engage in sustainable practices, advocate for policies that protect natural habitats, and support animal rights organizations. Actions such as reducing waste, supporting eco-friendly businesses, and choosing cruelty-free products contribute to a culture of compassion and responsibility toward all beings.
- **Engaging in Reasoned, Ethical Dialogue on Social Issues**: By following the principles of humanism and social contract theory, New Universalists are encouraged to engage in constructive discussions about social issues, promoting solutions that honor human dignity and uphold justice. This may include participating in forums, voting on human rights issues, or educating others on the importance of equality and fairness in society.
- **Practicing Personal Integrity and Accountability**: Inspired by secular ethics, New Universalists are reminded to practice integrity in personal and community relationships, honoring our commitments and treating others with respect. By embracing responsibility, empathy, and honesty, we contribute to a society that values truth and justice, upholding the foundational principles of New Universalism.

Secular philosophies on human rights, ethics, and environmental responsibility enrich the New Universalist commitment to creating a just and compassionate society. By integrating these principles into daily actions and community involvement, New Universalists embody a worldview that honors human dignity, protects the planet, and fosters harmony across diverse beliefs and traditions.

The Universality of Human Rights in Spiritual Traditions

Across the diverse landscapes of spiritual and philosophical traditions, a shared commitment to human rights emerges as a universal value. Each tradition's teachings on human dignity, justice, and compassion emphasize the sacred worth of all individuals, reflecting a deep-seated belief in the interconnectedness of humanity. Whether viewed through the lens of divinity, ethical duty, or social responsibility, human rights stand as a testament to our shared humanity. In New Universalism, these universal rights are recognized not merely as ethical guidelines but as sacred mandates essential for creating a compassionate, equitable, and just world.

Human Dignity as a Universal Principle

A core element in the teachings of every major spiritual tradition is the concept of human dignity—the inherent worth and respect due to each individual. This principle is often rooted in the belief that each person carries a divine spark, a reflection of a higher power, or simply the essence of life itself. Whether seen through the Christian perspective of being "made in the image of God," the Islamic view that every soul is precious, or the Buddhist understanding of interconnected existence, these values emphasize that dignity and respect are fundamental to all relationships.

New Universalism embraces these principles, acknowledging the sacred dignity of all people. This belief calls us to act with respect, compassion, and understanding toward others, seeing them not as separate beings but as part of an interconnected whole. In recognizing each individual's dignity, New Universalists are encouraged to embody values of empathy and kindness in all aspects of life, from interpersonal relationships to social advocacy, thus fostering a society that values human rights as an expression of our shared humanity.

Commitment to Justice and Compassion as Ethical Pillars

Across traditions, justice and compassion serve as ethical cornerstones that support human rights. Whether in the Judaic concept of *tzedek* (justice), the Islamic principle of *adl* (fairness), or the Hindu value of *dharma* (ethical duty), justice represents a commitment to equity, fairness, and accountability. Compassion, similarly, is a fundamental element in spiritual teachings worldwide, reminding individuals to act selflessly and care for the well-being of others.

In New Universalism, justice and compassion are woven into the fabric of spiritual practice. We are encouraged to not only seek personal enlightenment but to actively contribute to a fair and compassionate society. This commitment aligns with the view that human rights are not only a societal responsibility but a sacred duty. By championing social justice, supporting fair treatment, and caring for marginalized or vulnerable individuals, New Universalists bring these ethical pillars into everyday life, upholding the rights of all as a reflection of spiritual and social values.

Global Expressions of Human Rights and Cultural Practices

The concept of universal human rights finds expression in cultural practices and teachings across the globe. Indigenous cultures often emphasize community well-being and harmony with nature, which includes respect for each individual's place within the community. In many African and South American societies, principles of ubuntu and *sumak kawsay* ("the good life") reflect values of interconnectedness, mutual respect, and shared responsibility—essentially seeing one's humanity reflected in others. These teachings underscore that human rights are not merely personal privileges but collective responsibilities.

In New Universalism, these cultural expressions serve as powerful examples of a global commitment to respecting individual rights and fostering community harmony. Recognizing the global variety of ways in which human rights are upheld, New Universalists are encouraged to approach our own practices with humility, openness, and respect for diverse perspectives. By learning from these traditions, we can broaden our understanding of justice and equality, embracing human rights as a universal ideal that transcends cultural boundaries.

Human Rights as Foundational to a Compassionate Society

For New Universalism, human rights are foundational to building a compassionate society that values every individual's inherent worth. By respecting these rights, we are called to create environments where people feel safe, valued, and supported. This commitment not only strengthens interpersonal relationships but also lays the groundwork for a just and inclusive world, where diversity is celebrated, and each person's unique voice is heard.

New Universalism emphasizes that human rights are inseparable from the values of Earth Stewardship, Filial Piety, and Social Responsibility. These pillars encourage us to honor all beings, care for the Earth, and contribute to the well-being of others. By embracing these principles, New Universalists uphold a worldview that sees the pursuit of human rights as sacred, fostering both personal growth and societal harmony. This perspective strengthens the collective goal of creating a world that respects diversity and encourages shared responsibility for the welfare of all.

Practical Applications and Expressions of Human Rights in New Universalist Practice

New Universalism provides a framework for incorporating these values into everyday life, encouraging actions that respect and uphold human rights:

- **Respecting Individual Differences**: In all personal and communal interactions, New Universalists are encouraged to act with empathy, respecting diverse beliefs, identities, and backgrounds. This practice of inclusivity allows for meaningful connections and a greater appreciation of the shared human experience.
- **Supporting Social Justice Initiatives**: Whether through advocacy, volunteering, or financial support, we are encouraged to engage in efforts that promote equality and justice, such as supporting anti-discrimination policies, equal access to resources, and human rights campaigns.
- **Promoting Fairness in Community and Workplace**: Practicing fairness in daily actions, such as treating coworkers equitably, honoring others' contributions, and fostering a supportive environment, helps create inclusive spaces that reflect New Universalism's commitment to justice.
- **Engaging in Dialogues on Human Rights**: By participating in discussions on human rights issues, New Universalists can expand our understanding of global challenges and advocate for meaningful change. These dialogues promote awareness, empathy, and a shared commitment to a fair and just world.

Championing Equity and Justice

In the heart of New Universalism lies a profound commitment to equity and justice—principles that extend beyond societal constructs and resonate deeply with our spiritual calling. New Universalism upholds equity and justice as sacred duties, woven into our theology and enacted in our daily lives. These ideals reflect a broader commitment to honor every individual's inherent worth, to champion fairness in all interactions, and to dismantle barriers to justice.

As we explore the meaning of equity and justice, we find a tapestry of insights from spiritual, religious, and philosophical traditions, each emphasizing the importance of treating others with dignity and fairness. Whether expressed through the spiritual duty of compassion, the ethical call to defend the vulnerable, or the belief in universal human rights, equity and justice remain foundational to the shared human experience.

In New Universalism, championing equity and justice is not merely a passive acceptance of these values; it is an active, intentional practice. We are called to engage with these principles consistently, viewing justice as the natural extension of kindness and equity as a manifestation of respect. By embodying these principles, New Universalists strive to cultivate a society that respects diversity, fosters empathy, and promotes the well-being of all.

Equity and Justice in a Spiritual Context

In New Universalism, **equity** and **justice** are not only social imperatives but also sacred values, deeply intertwined with our spiritual mission. These principles reflect the belief that all individuals are inherently valuable, deserving of fairness, respect, and dignity. As part of our spiritual path, equity and justice go beyond societal definitions, forming an integral part of New Universalist theology and guiding us in both personal conduct and collective responsibility.

Equity as a Reflection of Compassion and Balance

Equity within a spiritual context means acknowledging that each person's needs, backgrounds, and circumstances are unique. Rather than a "one-size-fits-all" approach, equity involves creating conditions that recognize these differences and ensure everyone has a fair chance to thrive. This aligns with the New Universalist pillar of **compassion**, which calls us to see others' needs and respond with empathy, aiming to balance disparities in ways that uphold each individual's inherent worth.

In New Universalism, equity reflects a deeper understanding of **balance**—not only in how we distribute resources but also in how we honor each person's path. Earth-based traditions, such as those that emphasize the cyclical balance of nature, inspire us to see equity as the natural order of relationships. Just as ecosystems function with interdependent, balanced contributions, so should human societies create environments where all members are supported according to their needs.

Justice as a Sacred Duty

Justice in New Universalism extends beyond legal or institutional realms; it is a sacred duty grounded in a commitment to right action, moral integrity, and communal well-being. Justice calls us to act in ways that honor truth, protect the vulnerable, and prevent harm. As a faith community, New Universalism views justice as central to our expression of **social responsibility** and **filial piety**—values that guide our relationships with each other and with the world.

Justice is, in essence, a manifestation of **truth and compassion** combined. It is not merely a response to wrongdoing but a proactive stance to prevent harm, uplift the oppressed, and create structures that reinforce dignity for all. In this sense, justice becomes a continuous, active process in which we align ourselves with moral truth, advocate for ethical structures, and contribute to a society where everyone can live free from oppression.

Connection to New Universalist Values

These principles of equity and justice closely align with the core values of New Universalism:

- **Social Responsibility**: Justice and equity require us to engage actively in the welfare of our communities, ensuring that we support and protect all individuals. Social responsibility calls us to recognize injustice, challenge it, and work toward solutions that create fair opportunities and protections for everyone.
- **Filial Piety**: Traditionally understood as a reverence for family, elders, and community, filial piety in New Universalism also applies to our treatment of the broader human family. Practicing filial piety involves upholding justice and equity as expressions of love and respect, fostering bonds of trust and mutual care that extend beyond our immediate circles.

- **Reasoned Inquiry**: Justice and equity require us to examine the world critically, question social norms, and make informed decisions that reflect ethical values. Through reasoned inquiry, New Universalists are called to discern injustices, understand systemic inequalities, and work thoughtfully to create positive change.

In living out these values, New Universalists are reminded that equity and justice are not only ethical mandates but spiritual responsibilities. They form the basis of a just society where we support one another and uphold the dignity of every person. This understanding calls us to actively engage in creating balance and to work toward a fair society, not simply as members of humanity but as followers of a spiritual path that honors the shared dignity of all beings.

Guidelines for Supporting Justice in Daily Life

In New Universalism, justice is woven into the fabric of our daily lives. Living justly means choosing actions that reflect compassion, fairness, and empathy in every interaction, guided by the recognition that each individual is an essential part of our interconnected human family. The following principles offer guidance on how to embody justice daily, aligning our spiritual practice with practical actions that champion the values of integrity, equity, and kindness.

Practicing Mindful Awareness in Daily Interactions

Mindful awareness—the practice of fully observing our thoughts, emotions, and actions in the present—grounds us in compassion and clarity. In New Universalism, mindful awareness is a spiritual practice that attunes us to the sacredness of every interaction, seeing each person as a unique reflection of humanity's collective spirit. Practicing mindful awareness helps ensure that our words and actions affirm the dignity and worth of others. This awareness allows us to approach each conversation with a spirit of humility and openness, fostering a climate of mutual respect.

For example, mindful awareness in daily interactions may involve slowing down to truly listen to a friend or colleague, giving full attention to their words and feelings, or taking a moment to reflect on our responses in challenging conversations. This approach deepens empathy and discourages reactive judgments, creating space for understanding and thoughtful connection.

New Universalism encourages practitioners to make mindful awareness part of our spiritual routine, whether through brief moments of silence, meditation, or intentional breathing exercises that create stillness and clarity. When practiced consistently, this mindful approach builds a foundation of justice that honors the humanity and experience of everyone we encounter.

Standing Up Against Discrimination and Prejudice

Within New Universalism, justice extends beyond passive support to active intervention when witnessing injustice. Standing up against discrimination and prejudice is a practice rooted in courage and respect, embodying our commitment to protecting human dignity. Confronting harmful actions or words—whether in a workplace, social setting, or online—sends a message that all individuals are deserving of fair and respectful treatment.

Engaging in this practice does not always require confrontation. Instead, it involves choosing responses that counteract negativity, using our influence to challenge harmful assumptions constructively. New Universalist theology encourages us to do so with empathy, seeking dialogue over discord, and understanding over judgment. For example, addressing a prejudiced remark with questions or observations that invite reflection rather than accusation can promote greater openness and learning for everyone involved.

Justice in New Universalism is not about division but healing. By standing up to discrimination with compassion, we transform potentially negative experiences into opportunities for growth and healing. In doing so, we embody the New Universalist call to safeguard human rights and foster inclusivity, not only in word but also in action.

Engaging in "Small Acts of Justice" as Daily Practice

In New Universalism, small acts of justice are seen as powerful, consistent gestures that ripple outward, creating a cumulative effect of positive change. Small acts of justice can range from supporting a friend in need, donating to a cause, or showing patience to someone who is struggling. Even small contributions to community service, such as participating in neighborhood cleanups or offering time to support local nonprofits, reinforce the idea that justice begins with individual, accessible choices.

To emphasize this practice, New Universalism encourages acts of justice as expressions of **filial piety** and **social responsibility**, essential pillars that ground our spiritual and ethical responsibilities to others. Daily gestures, when performed with intention, align our individual lives with a universal calling toward equity and kindness. These practices reflect the understanding that everyone has the capacity to contribute to justice, regardless of material resources or social status.

Furthermore, New Universalists may create a spiritual practice around "small acts of justice," taking time at the beginning or end of the day to reflect on moments when they helped or uplifted others. This reflection reinforces the role of justice in one's spiritual journey, guiding a sustained commitment to fairness and compassion that is lived, not only believed.

Supporting Equitable Policies and Community Initiatives

Championing justice extends into the realm of societal and structural support. For New Universalists, advocating for equitable policies and engaging with community initiatives are powerful ways to practice justice on a broader scale. Engaging with these efforts reflects a proactive commitment to fostering an environment where everyone has equal access to resources, rights, and opportunities.

Equitable policies ensure that systems work fairly for all, aligning with the New Universalist ideal of **earth stewardship** and **social responsibility** by protecting people's rights to sustainable and just living conditions. Supporting policies such as environmental protections, accessible healthcare, fair wages, and educational equity demonstrates our care for the world and the well-being of all people. Voting thoughtfully, joining local or national campaigns, and educating oneself on key issues are practical ways to influence policy toward fairness.

In addition to policy support, New Universalists are encouraged to connect with local organizations that address these needs directly. Whether by participating in programs that provide housing, food security, or mental health services, or by volunteering for causes that uplift marginalized groups, community involvement reinforces our bond with humanity. To nurture this connection, New Universalists are invited to regularly assess how our skills, resources, and time can contribute to movements that promote justice and equality.

Offering Support and Solidarity to Marginalized Groups

At the heart of New Universalism lies the understanding that all individuals deserve respect and equal opportunity, regardless of race, gender, orientation, economic status, or background. Practicing justice, therefore, involves **offering support and solidarity** to those whose voices have historically been marginalized. True justice, as New Universalism teaches, is both an action and a stance of solidarity, recognizing shared human experiences while acknowledging the specific struggles of those who have faced systemic inequity.

New Universalists are encouraged to build partnerships with communities or organizations that champion marginalized voices. For example, allyship with movements focused on disability rights, gender equality, and racial justice provides a foundation for creating inclusive spaces. In doing so, we reinforce that justice requires not only empathy but active support for those who need it most.

This practice of solidarity also extends into personal interactions and intentional community building. Through simple actions—such as creating safe, inclusive spaces, showing sensitivity to the experiences of others, and being open to listening—we uphold New Universalism's principles of kindness, tolerance, and respect. In championing these values, we contribute to a world where all people are seen, valued, and empowered.

Cultivating Patience and Perseverance in the Pursuit of Justice

Justice is a long and often arduous journey. Deeply held structures of inequality and injustice can take generations to address, requiring patience, resilience, and a steadfast commitment. For New Universalists, **patience and perseverance** are essential virtues that sustain our dedication to creating a fair and compassionate world. Rooted in the understanding of nature's cycles and the transformative power of time, New Universalism teaches that true justice unfolds gradually, nurtured by consistent and patient effort.

This approach is spiritually resonant, as New Universalism views life's cycles—the ebb and flow of seasons, the growth and decay of life—as metaphors for the journey of social change. Just as the Earth transforms slowly and predictably, our efforts to enact justice may progress through incremental steps rather than immediate results. Patience allows us to remain hopeful in the face of setbacks, while perseverance empowers us to continue our work even when outcomes are uncertain.

In cultivating patience and perseverance, New Universalists are encouraged to see justice as an ongoing commitment that extends beyond individual efforts or lifetimes. This perspective allows us to contribute to a legacy of justice and kindness, knowing that our actions form part of a larger, continuous movement toward equity and compassion. By nurturing patience and perseverance, we honor the Earth's rhythm of change, anchoring ourselves in a spirit of hope that empowers others and uplifts the world.

Championing Tolerance and Kindness

Tolerance and kindness are two foundational principles in New Universalism, representing the respect and compassion that we strive to cultivate within ourselves and toward all others. These virtues invite us to honor the dignity of each individual and to act with an understanding that embraces diversity. Within New Universalism, tolerance and kindness are not passive qualities but active practices that shape our daily lives, reflecting our commitment to both **Social Responsibility** and **Filial Piety**. Championing these values helps build a compassionate, inclusive community that respects differences while celebrating shared humanity.

Tolerance: Embracing and Honoring Differences

In New Universalism, tolerance is understood as the acceptance of others' beliefs, identities, and perspectives, even when they differ from our own. Tolerance allows us to create a shared space where diversity is valued and individual freedoms are respected. This acceptance, however, does not imply mere coexistence; it is an active and engaged process of seeking to understand, to learn from, and to respect the uniqueness of each individual.

Tolerance is grounded in the New Universalist belief in **reasoned inquiry and openness**. To practice tolerance is to approach others with curiosity rather than judgment, seeking to understand their experiences and values. This practice is deeply spiritual, as it involves seeing others as reflections of the same universal truths that guide us all. Embracing this belief allows us to recognize that every individual, regardless of their background, holds a perspective that contributes to our collective wisdom.

In practice, tolerance means listening fully and openly to others, suspending preconceived notions and biases. It involves respecting different worldviews, cultural practices, and belief systems, seeing them as vital expressions of humanity's shared quest for meaning. New Universalists are encouraged to engage with people from all walks of life, recognizing that each interaction offers an opportunity to broaden our perspectives, deepen our empathy, and strengthen our sense of community. This commitment to tolerance challenges us to continuously expand our understanding, celebrating differences as sources of learning and growth.

Kindness: Cultivating Compassionate Actions and Interactions

Kindness, in New Universalism, goes beyond polite gestures; it is a profound and active expression of compassion and a reflection of our commitment to seeing others through the lens of shared humanity. Kindness requires empathy, the ability to feel with others, and the willingness to act in ways that ease suffering, uplift spirits, and foster joy. It is kindness that transforms tolerance from passive acceptance into meaningful, heartfelt connection.

In New Universalist doctrine, kindness is seen as a form of spiritual service, a way to embody the values of **Filial Piety** and **Earth Stewardship**. To be kind is to care for the well-being of others, just as we would care for family or for the Earth itself. By choosing kindness, we acknowledge that each person's experience and challenges are worthy of our respect and that our actions have the power to bring healing and harmony.

Practically, kindness can be woven into everyday actions: offering support to a friend in need, showing patience with strangers, or reaching out to those who may feel marginalized. It is the gentle words spoken in a moment of conflict, the willingness to help without expectation, and the quiet acts of generosity that often go unseen. In New Universalism, we view kindness as a guiding principle that transforms ordinary moments into sacred exchanges, creating a ripple effect of positivity and compassion.

The Role of Tolerance and Kindness in Justice Work

New Universalism holds that tolerance and kindness are essential to creating a just and equitable society. Justice, when combined with kindness, becomes not merely a pursuit of fairness but a commitment to healing and understanding. Tolerance grounds our justice work in humility, reminding us to honor diverse perspectives, while kindness adds a layer of compassion that softens even the most challenging interactions. Together, these values create an environment where justice is pursued not through division but through unity and respect.

In social and political advocacy, New Universalists are called to champion issues with kindness, recognizing that each individual is more than their views or actions. By approaching others with respect, even in moments of disagreement, we build bridges rather than barriers. This approach allows us to communicate with integrity and compassion, promoting positive change without perpetuating hostility. New Universalists are thus encouraged to approach activism as a form of service, seeking to elevate others and uplift society in ways that honor the dignity of all.

Practicing Tolerance and Kindness as Daily Spiritual Disciplines

To make tolerance and kindness meaningful parts of daily life, New Universalism emphasizes them as spiritual disciplines that require intention and consistency. Here are some practices to incorporate these values in both personal and communal settings:

1. **Daily Reflections on Tolerance and Kindness**

   Set aside time each day to reflect on moments where tolerance and kindness could be expressed more fully. Reflect on interactions from the day, considering whether you listened without judgment, responded with empathy, or acted with compassion. This daily reflection deepens awareness and helps cultivate a mindset that prioritizes these values in future interactions.

2. **Acts of Kindness as Rituals of Compassion**

   In New Universalism, small acts of kindness are viewed as rituals of compassion, each act symbolizing our commitment to our shared humanity. This can include simple gestures like offering a meal to someone in need, volunteering time to support a community project, or sending a note of encouragement to a friend. By treating these actions as sacred, we remind ourselves that kindness is an active expression of spiritual values.

3. **Engaging with Different Perspectives**

   Practicing tolerance involves actively engaging with perspectives that differ from our own. This could be as simple as reading about a belief system or attending a cultural event, with the intention of learning and appreciating a perspective that may be new to you. Approaching these experiences with curiosity and openness can deepen empathy and broaden understanding, reinforcing our commitment to universal respect.

4. **Practicing Kindness in Difficult Situations**

   True kindness is often tested in challenging moments. New Universalists are encouraged to meet difficult situations with compassion, seeking to respond with understanding rather than anger. For instance, if faced with a disagreement or conflict, practicing patience, listening with an open heart, and speaking with gentleness can help de-escalate tension and pave the way for reconciliation.

5. **Community Gatherings and Rituals that Emphasize Compassion**

   Within New Universalist communities, rituals that emphasize compassion and inclusivity are common. These gatherings can serve as opportunities to celebrate the diversity within the community, such as hosting a multi-faith dialogue, honoring various cultural practices, or creating inclusive ceremonies that welcome people from all backgrounds. Such practices build solidarity and reinforce the principles of tolerance and kindness in a communal setting.

6. **Encouraging Children and Youth to Practice Tolerance and Kindness**
Instilling these values in children and youth creates a foundation for future generations to carry forward. New Universalist education and guidance encourage young people to embrace differences, show respect to others, and act with kindness in all interactions. Storytelling, role-playing, and community service activities that focus on kindness and inclusivity can help young people develop empathy and an appreciation for diversity from an early age.

Reflection: The Transformative Power of Tolerance and Kindness

In New Universalism, tolerance and kindness are not just ethical principles; they are transformative forces that foster unity, heal divisions, and elevate the human spirit. Each act of tolerance opens the heart to understanding, bridging gaps between individuals and communities. Each act of kindness brings light into the world, reminding us that compassion is a powerful force that can transform even the smallest gesture into a meaningful connection.

By making tolerance and kindness central to our lives, we honor the shared divinity within each person, recognizing our interconnectedness with all of humanity. New Universalism teaches that these values, when practiced consistently, allow us to embody the spiritual ideals of compassion, integrity, and respect for all. They serve as pillars that support a just society, a harmonious community, and a life of purpose, where every interaction reflects the beauty of our shared existence.

Justice in Action

Justice is a principle that moves beyond words; it is demonstrated through actions that uphold dignity, protect rights, and create a fair and equitable society. Within New Universalism, justice is both a spiritual and practical mandate, urging us to take consistent, compassionate actions that benefit both individuals and the wider community. By examining diverse examples of justice across traditions, we see how New Universalism's commitment to social responsibility, compassion, and equity aligns with humanity's shared pursuit of a just world.

Seva in Sikhism: Selfless Service for the Greater Good

Seva, or selfless service, is a core concept in Sikhism that emphasizes humility, equality, and compassion. Sikhs are taught to serve others without expectation of reward, seeing each act of service as a way to honor the divine presence within all beings. A common practice is the **langar**, a community kitchen where people gather to share meals, often provided free of charge to anyone in need. The langar is a powerful example of justice in action, breaking down social barriers and promoting inclusivity by feeding people of all backgrounds.

In New Universalism, **service** and **charity** are seen as central acts of compassion, reinforcing the belief that true justice is found in actions that uplift and include. By serving others selflessly, New Universalists reflect the values of kindness, respect, and equality, seeing each act of service as an expression of our shared humanity. The practice of seva encourages us to recognize our duty to support one another and to honor the intrinsic worth of every person.

Satyagraha in Gandhian Philosophy: Nonviolent Resistance to Injustice

Mahatma Gandhi's concept of **satyagraha**, or "truth force," reflects a commitment to justice through nonviolent resistance. Satyagraha asserts that true power lies in moral integrity, courage, and the unwavering pursuit of truth, rather than in violence or domination. Gandhi used satyagraha to lead peaceful protests and inspire movements for social change, advocating for independence, human rights, and social equality. His approach teaches that justice can be pursued with compassion and that even the most entrenched systems of injustice can be transformed through peaceful means.

For New Universalism, Gandhi's example illustrates how **reasoned inquiry** and **compassionate action** can work hand in hand in the pursuit of justice. New Universalists are encouraged to approach social issues with integrity, advocating for change without harming others. By embodying principles of nonviolence and standing firm in the pursuit of equity, we uphold justice as a path to both societal transformation and spiritual growth.

Ubuntu in African Philosophy: Embracing Shared Humanity

The African philosophy of **Ubuntu** embodies the idea that "I am because we are." Ubuntu emphasizes interconnectedness, compassion, and community, teaching that one's humanity is inextricably linked to the humanity of others. This concept of justice extends beyond individual rights to encompass communal welfare, promoting solidarity and cooperation. In African communities, Ubuntu is often expressed through collective decision-making, resource-sharing, and communal support, recognizing that each person's well-being depends on the well-being of all.

Ubuntu aligns with New Universalism's vision of **Filial Piety** and **Social Responsibility**, as it encourages us to view each person as part of an extended human family. Practicing Ubuntu within New Universalism means embracing others as kin, and advocating for policies and actions that uplift and protect the community. Justice, in this sense, becomes a shared endeavor, where individuals work together to create a world rooted in respect, empathy, and unity.

Environmental Justice and the Rights of Nature

In recent decades, the concept of **environmental justice** has emerged as a movement that recognizes the importance of protecting both people and the planet. Environmental justice advocates for policies and practices that address the inequitable burden of environmental degradation on vulnerable communities, emphasizing the right to a safe and healthy environment for all. The **Rights of Nature** movement, inspired by Indigenous perspectives, extends justice to the natural world, arguing that rivers, forests, and ecosystems have intrinsic rights and deserve protection.

For New Universalism, environmental justice resonates with the value of **Earth Stewardship** and the recognition of nature's sacredness. We are encouraged to engage in advocacy, conservation efforts, and sustainable practices, viewing environmental justice as a moral obligation to protect the Earth and ensure a future for all. By championing the rights of nature, New Universalists reaffirm our commitment to a harmonious relationship with the environment, rooted in respect, responsibility, and reverence.

Charitable Giving and Almsgiving Across Traditions

Charitable giving is a common practice across numerous spiritual and philosophical traditions. In Islam, **Zakat** is an obligatory form of almsgiving, seen as a means of purifying wealth and redistributing resources to benefit the less fortunate. In Christianity, **tithing** and charitable donations are seen as acts of service and generosity, emphasizing the importance of supporting those in need. In Buddhism, **dāna** or "giving" is practiced as a means of cultivating compassion and detachment, recognizing that generosity strengthens community bonds and alleviates suffering.

Within New Universalism, the practice of **Tithes and Offerings** is encouraged as a way to support both the faith community and broader charitable efforts. We are taught that giving is a form of justice, where resources are shared to benefit others and promote equality. By contributing to causes that align with New Universalist values, we can embody the principles of justice, kindness, and humility, helping to create a society that values generosity and collective well-being.

Modern Social Movements: Championing Justice in the Contemporary World

In contemporary society, numerous social movements reflect the pursuit of justice, advocating for the rights of marginalized communities and addressing systemic inequalities. Movements like **Black Lives Matter**, **LGBTQ+ Rights**, **Women's Rights**, and **Disability Rights** represent the ongoing struggle for equity and dignity, challenging societal structures that perpetuate discrimination. These movements call for policies that protect human rights, promote inclusivity, and dismantle oppression.

For New Universalists, engaging with these movements is an extension of the commitment to **equity, compassion, and social responsibility**. We are encouraged to support initiatives that seek to uplift those who face injustice, viewing activism as a spiritual practice that fosters empathy and strengthens community bonds. By standing with marginalized communities, New Universalists affirm the belief that every individual is inherently worthy of respect, dignity, and opportunity.

Justice as a Collective and Spiritual Mandate

Justice, in New Universalism, is not an abstract ideal but a lived commitment, reflected in daily actions and community involvement. Through diverse examples, we see that the pursuit of justice transcends cultural, religious, and philosophical boundaries, uniting humanity in a shared quest for dignity, equity, and compassion. Each tradition and movement offers unique insights into justice, reminding us that this value is both universal and deeply personal.

As New Universalists, we are called to champion justice by embracing these teachings and applying them in our lives. Whether through small acts of kindness, engagement with social causes, or contributions to community welfare, each action strengthens the collective spirit of humanity. Justice, as a spiritual mandate, challenges us to live with integrity, respect, and humility, creating a world that reflects the sacredness of all life.

In New Universalism, justice is woven into the fabric of our spiritual practice, inspiring us to act with compassion and courage. By drawing on the wisdom of varied traditions and championing justice in all interactions, we honor the universal truths that connect us, striving to build a just, compassionate, and harmonious world.

Respect for Diversity

In New Universalism, diversity is not merely an aspect of human experience; it is an essential manifestation of the divine presence in our world. New Universalism holds a profound respect for diversity as a spiritual mandate, an ethical obligation, and a path to mutual understanding. In embracing this ideal, New Universalism encourages us to honor the unique qualities and perspectives that arise from different backgrounds, cultures, and beliefs, and to view each individual as a reflection of a shared humanity. Respecting diversity deepens our collective spirituality, inviting us to embrace the full spectrum of human expression, and serves as a guiding principle for fostering an inclusive, just, and compassionate world.

Respect for diversity connects us to New Universalism as we recognize that diversity reflects a universal truth: the interwoven and multifaceted nature of all life. Like the varied ecosystems that together sustain our planet, diverse human identities and perspectives contribute to the richness and resilience of the global community. This belief in the inherent value of diversity is rooted in New Universalism's foundational values of Earth Stewardship, Filial Piety, Social Responsibility, and Reasoned Inquiry. Each of these pillars underscores a commitment to honoring the Earth and humanity in all its forms, celebrating diversity as a source of wisdom, strength, and unity.

New Universalism embraces diversity as a spiritual and cultural value, examining how inclusivity enriches our community and our faith. We are encouraged to engage in practical approaches for nurturing respect, fostering inclusivity, and creating spaces where individuals of all backgrounds feel valued and seen. By celebrating diversity in our rituals and daily practices, we fulfill our commitment to a world rooted in compassion, equity, and mutual respect—core elements that align with New Universalism's vision for an interconnected and inclusive global society.

Diversity as a Spiritual and Cultural Value
In New Universalism, diversity is not merely an aspect of human society—it is a spiritual and sacred principle that reflects the very nature of existence. Just as nature thrives through ecosys-

tems composed of varied species, landscapes, and intricate connections, human diversity is a powerful, sustaining force that enriches our collective experience and deepens our understanding of universal truth. Diversity offers a living testament to the divine wisdom embedded in all of creation, embodying the principle that every person, community, and culture is a unique expression of the sacred whole.

Diversity in human culture encompasses the full spectrum of racial, ethnic, cultural, gender, and sexual identities, as well as the array of beliefs, abilities, and personal expressions that make each individual distinct. In New Universalism, this vastness is seen as a reflection of the boundless creativity and inclusivity of the divine. By recognizing and valuing this variety, New Universalism upholds the belief that each path, perspective, and way of life is a gift that contributes uniquely to our shared journey. When we embrace diversity, we honor the sacred right of every person to live as they are, without fear or judgment, recognizing that all are worthy of dignity, respect, and love.

Diversity & New Universalist Values

Central to New Universalism is the idea that diversity enriches the collective, adding depth and resilience to society much like a biodiverse ecosystem fosters greater adaptability and strength in nature. Each individual brings to the community distinct insights, traditions, and experiences that collectively deepen our shared understanding. This aligns with the New Universalist values of Social Responsibility and Filial Piety, which call us to nurture our communities with empathy, understanding, and respect for each other's inherent worth. Social Responsibility, in this context, becomes an active commitment to building spaces where everyone, regardless of identity or background, feels valued and included. Filial Piety expands beyond family and generational respect to encompass all relationships, urging us to honor the dignity, wisdom, and contributions of each person.

This view of diversity as essential to a healthy and vibrant community also reflects the principle of interconnectedness, a cornerstone of New Universalist thought. As in nature, where every organism has a role that contributes to the balance and well-being of the whole, each person's unique identity and perspective contribute to a broader harmony. By appreciating and celebrating diversity, we acknowledge that our differences are not obstacles to unity but essential threads in the tapestry of existence. This interconnectedness teaches us that when we honor and respect diversity, we are also honoring and respecting the divine source of all life.

Spiritual Depth of Embracing Diversity

New Universalism calls for a worldview that sees diversity as a divine expression to be cherished rather than merely tolerated. Every culture, tradition, and individual represents a facet of the universal truth, each offering insights that illuminate different aspects of the human journey. By embracing diversity, we approach the world with humility, recognizing that no single culture or identity holds a monopoly on wisdom or spiritual insight. This openness creates a path to greater empathy and a deeper sense of unity with all of humanity, as we begin to see ourselves in others and others within ourselves.

In this way, diversity is a spiritual teacher, guiding us toward an understanding of life that transcends our personal experiences and beliefs. When we engage with others whose lives differ from our own, we expand our spiritual capacity for compassion, patience, and understanding. By exploring diverse traditions, stories, and beliefs, we are reminded of the universal truths that connect us all, even across vast cultural, ideological, or geographical divides. New Universalism, therefore, encourages us to view every interaction, tradition, and individual as an opportunity for growth and learning, fostering a spirituality that is both inclusive and expansive.

Practical Applications of Valuing Diversity

Living in a way that honors diversity requires conscious effort and intention. New Universalism encourages us to engage actively with diverse perspectives, seeking out conversations, stories, and traditions that challenge and broaden our worldview. This commitment to inclusivity extends beyond personal interactions to community-building and social engagement, where we strive to create spaces that reflect the full spectrum of human experience. In both personal and communal settings, New Universalism calls for a respect that transcends tolerance, embracing each person's unique identity and heritage as sacred.

Respect for diversity can also be expressed through participation in cross-cultural events, learning new languages, supporting cultural initiatives, and educating ourselves on the histories and struggles of various communities. These acts of openness and engagement foster mutual respect, empathy, and a greater understanding of the challenges and joys that shape others' lives. By making diversity an integral part of our spiritual practice, we create a faith that truly mirrors the inclusivity, creativity, and resilience of the natural world.

In recognizing diversity as a spiritual and cultural value, New Universalism reaffirms its commitment to an inclusive and compassionate worldview. This dedication to diversity enriches our understanding of universal truth, reminding us that every individual, tradition, and perspective offers a vital piece of the greater whole. By honoring diversity in all its forms, we cultivate a spirituality that values the unique paths of others as essential to the shared journey of humanity, fostering a global community grounded in respect, love, and unity.

Embracing Inclusivity in Community and Society

In New Universalism, inclusivity is more than a guiding principle; it is a foundational practice essential to creating a community where each person feels valued, understood, and genuinely welcomed. Inclusivity extends beyond mere acceptance, seeking instead to actively honor and celebrate each individual's identity, heritage, and lived experiences. When we commit to inclusivity, we commit to building a faith community—and a broader society—that respects all backgrounds, identities, and beliefs as integral to the human experience.

Inclusivity reflects New Universalism's values of Social Responsibility and Filial Piety. Social Responsibility calls us to be mindful of the welfare of those around us, fostering a spirit of unity and compassion in all interactions. Filial Piety, traditionally emphasizing respect within family, is expanded in New Universalism to include all relationships, encouraging us to approach each person with reverence, respect, and openness. This practice creates a culture of genuine acceptance, ensuring that every individual—regardless of race, gender, religion, sexual orientation, or ability—feels they belong.

Practical Steps to Foster Inclusivity

Creating a culture of inclusivity begins with the commitment to engage actively with diverse perspectives. This means seeking opportunities to understand others' experiences and fostering an environment where all voices can be heard. New Universalism encourages us to adopt practical practices that make inclusivity a tangible reality in everyday life.

Actively Listen and Show Empathy

One of the most powerful ways to embrace inclusivity is by listening to others without judgment. This act of active listening allows us to understand people's stories and experiences, fostering empathy and breaking down barriers of misunderstanding. By showing a genuine interest in others' viewpoints and life journeys, we create spaces where people feel seen and respected.

Challenge Personal Assumptions

Inclusivity often begins with the willingness to question our own assumptions and prejudices. In New Universalism, self-reflection is a core practice, encouraging us to examine our beliefs and attitudes. This introspection allows us to approach others without bias, cultivating a mindset that values openness and adaptability. Regularly challenging personal assumptions fosters a more inclusive outlook and prepares us to engage meaningfully with diverse communities.

Create Welcoming Environments

Inclusivity can be practiced by ensuring that both personal and communal spaces are open and welcoming to all. This may involve small actions, such as displaying symbols of inclusivity, using language that respects everyone's identity, and being mindful of accessibility. By fostering spaces where all individuals feel physically and emotionally safe, we embody New Universalism's commitment to respect and hospitality.

Value Diverse Perspectives in Discussions

Whether in personal conversations or community gatherings, valuing diverse perspectives encourages a culture of mutual respect and understanding. New Universalism promotes dialogue that welcomes all viewpoints, seeking wisdom in different beliefs and backgrounds. Through this, we can build community dialogues that enrich our collective understanding and allow individuals to express their unique viewpoints without fear of exclusion or judgment.

Engage in Ongoing Learning

Inclusivity is a dynamic practice that evolves as we learn more about ourselves and the world around us. New Universalism encourages lifelong learning, urging us to educate ourselves about different cultures, identities, and social challenges. This continuous process of learning deepens our awareness and equips us to engage with others from a place of informed understanding and respect.

Inclusivity as a Communal and Spiritual Practice

Inclusivity, while deeply personal, is also a communal practice that strengthens the bonds within the New Universalist faith community and society at large. When practiced collectively, inclusivity becomes a reflection of our spiritual values, reinforcing the belief that every person contributes uniquely to the whole. New Universalism views inclusivity as a form of spiritual stewardship, reminding us that our community's strength lies in its diversity. By embracing inclusivity as a communal value, we foster a spiritual culture that celebrates the interconnectedness of all people, honoring each person's distinct contribution to our shared journey.

Through inclusivity, New Universalism embodies the principle that diversity within unity enhances spiritual growth. When we cultivate inclusive communities, we honor the divine presence in each person, affirming that every life is inherently valuable and worthy of love. This commitment transforms inclusivity from a moral obligation into a sacred practice, deepening our connection with one another and grounding our community in a spirit of universal belonging.

Respect for Different Identities and Beliefs

Respect is a cornerstone of New Universalism, guiding our interactions with one another and shaping our approach to diversity. New Universalism recognizes that each individual holds a unique identity, shaped by their beliefs, culture, experiences, and values. When we respect others' identities and beliefs, we affirm the inherent dignity of every person, fostering a community grounded in mutual understanding and compassion. By honoring diverse worldviews, we cultivate an inclusive space where each person feels their journey and spirituality are valued.

In New Universalism, respect for diversity extends beyond mere acceptance. It requires active engagement and curiosity about others' perspectives, encouraging us to learn from one another in a spirit of humility and openness. This respect is rooted in our theological commitment to Reasoned Inquiry, which calls us to explore truth across traditions and to hold space for varying expressions of the divine. Embracing this diversity broadens our understanding of universal truths, enhancing both individual and communal spiritual growth.

Respect- A Pathway to Unity

New Universalism's commitment to respect is also a pathway to unity. By respecting diverse identities and beliefs, we acknowledge the shared values that bind us together, even in the midst of difference. New Universalism teaches that each faith tradition, philosophy, and cultural practice carries pieces of universal wisdom that reflect humanity's collective pursuit of truth, morality, and meaning. When we honor these diverse perspectives, we strengthen our connection to the broader human community, transcending boundaries of race, religion, and culture.

Honor Others' Right to Hold Different Beliefs

Respecting others' beliefs does not require agreement but does involve recognizing each individual's right to their perspective. In New Universalism, we refrain from judgment or attempts to convert others. Instead, we approach diverse beliefs as an opportunity to expand our understanding, recognizing that every faith and philosophy has something to teach us. By valuing others' spiritual paths, we cultivate an environment where everyone feels free to explore their beliefs without fear of discrimination.

Approach Differences with Humility

Humility is a vital component of respect, reminding us that we do not hold a monopoly on truth. In New Universalism, humility means acknowledging that our understanding of the divine and the universe is always growing. By approaching differences with humility, we remain open to learning from others, recognizing that diverse perspectives can enrich our own spiritual journey. This practice of humility allows us to see others' beliefs as complements rather than contradictions to our own.

Practice Empathy and Curiosity

Empathy and curiosity help us approach others with a genuine desire to understand. In New Universalism, we are encouraged to listen deeply, seeking to understand the lived experiences and beliefs of others. This empathetic approach builds bridges of understanding, allowing us to see the common humanity that underlies diverse identities. Curiosity, when paired with respect, allows us to engage with others' beliefs thoughtfully, fostering dialogue that brings us closer to one another.

Celebrate Common Ground and Unique Differences

Respect for diversity is both an acknowledgment of our shared values and an appreciation for our differences. New Universalism calls us to celebrate commonalities, such as compassion, kindness, and justice, while honoring the unique expressions of these values in each tradition. By finding common ground, we build unity; by celebrating differences, we enrich our spiritual understanding. This dual focus helps us embrace diversity in its fullness, viewing it as a divine expression of life's complexity and beauty.

Respect in Practice: Building Inclusive Spaces

Respecting diversity is not solely a personal endeavor but a communal practice that shapes the ethos of New Universalist spaces. In New Universalism, building inclusive spaces means creating environments where all identities and beliefs are honored, allowing each individual to feel truly valued. This practice involves intentional acts that signal respect, from including varied perspectives in community discussions to recognizing and celebrating important cultural and religious holidays from different traditions.

New Universalism encourages us to model respect through active participation in interfaith and intercultural dialogues, working together with other communities to foster mutual understanding. This engagement is grounded in our commitment to Social Responsibility, reminding us that respect for diversity enhances the well-being of all. By promoting respect within and beyond our community, New Universalism seeks to create a society where everyone's identity and beliefs are treated with dignity and reverence.

Ultimately, respect is a bridge that connects us to the vast array of human experiences. In New Universalism, respect for diversity is more than a value; it is a sacred practice that nurtures unity, compassion, and growth. When we honor the unique contributions of each identity and belief, we move closer to a world that reflects the beauty of collective human wisdom, embodying New Universalism's vision of a just, inclusive, and spiritually enriched global community.

Celebrating Diversity Through Ritual and Practice

In New Universalism, we honor diversity not only in our beliefs but in our practices, embracing various ways to celebrate the unique cultures, traditions, and perspectives that enrich our lives. Celebrating diversity through ritual is an active expression of our commitment to inclusivity, fostering a sense of unity and belonging within the New Universalist community. Through personal and communal practices, we recognize that diversity is a divine gift, reflecting the vast creativity and beauty inherent in humanity.

Rituals and celebrations hold a special place in New Universalism as powerful acts that connect us with others and with the sacred. By incorporating global traditions, honoring international observances, and learning from various cultural practices, we cultivate a living expression of respect that reaches beyond mere acceptance to a deep reverence for the wide spectrum of human experience.

Honoring Global Festivals and Cultural Celebrations

A meaningful way to celebrate diversity is through the observance of global festivals and cultural holidays. In New Universalism, we acknowledge that each culture has unique days of significance that connect communities with their heritage, history, and spiritual beliefs. Recognizing and celebrating these festivals within New Universalist gatherings allows us to share in the beauty of various traditions while fostering unity and mutual understanding.

Examples of diverse festivals we may honor include Diwali (the Hindu festival of lights symbolizing the victory of light over darkness), Eid al-Fitr (a Muslim festival celebrating compassion and gratitude), and Indigenous Pow Wows or cultural days that honor connection to the land. Each celebration becomes a window into the values, joys, and expressions of the community from which it arises. By acknowledging these festivals within our own community, we deepen our appreciation of shared human experiences, such as joy, gratitude, and reverence for the sacred.

Integrating Diversity into Personal Rituals

New Universalism also encourages individuals to explore and incorporate elements from various spiritual traditions in their personal practices. By drawing from other traditions with respect, we gain insights into diverse ways of connecting with the sacred. For example, one might practice mindfulness meditation drawn from Buddhism, connect with nature through Indigenous practices, or use mantras from Eastern traditions as a way of centering. In each case, these practices are not adopted superficially but are integrated with intentionality, honoring the tradition's origins and significance.

Personal rituals can also involve creating a "diversity altar" that reflects various spiritual or cultural symbols, reminding individuals of humanity's interconnectedness. Such an altar might include representations of sacred texts, symbols of compassion and peace from various cultures, and natural elements that signify life's universal beauty. These personal rituals invite us to reflect on our relationship with the broader world, fostering a deeper connection to the diverse ways in which people seek meaning.

Community Rituals That Celebrate Inclusivity

Communal rituals are a powerful way to collectively honor diversity within the New Universalist community. These shared practices can include multi-faith prayer circles, storytelling gatherings, and shared meals where traditional foods from different cultures are enjoyed and celebrated. Multi-faith prayer circles allow participants to offer prayers from their individual traditions, fostering an atmosphere of unity through shared spiritual intent. Storytelling gatherings provide space for individuals to share their heritage and beliefs, deepening the community's appreciation of each member's unique background.

Shared meals are another way to celebrate diversity, as food often carries deep cultural and spiritual significance. Organizing potlucks where participants bring dishes from their cultures allows members to experience each other's traditions in a tangible and enjoyable way. These gatherings not only build community bonds but also remind us of the sacredness of hospitality and the joy of sharing in each other's experiences.

Celebrating International Days of Diversity and Inclusion

New Universalism encourages its members to recognize international observances that promote inclusivity, equality, and cultural appreciation. Days such as World Day for Cultural Diversity (May 21), International Day of Tolerance (November 16), and Human Rights Day (December 10) provide opportunities to reaffirm our commitment to universal values that transcend cultural and national boundaries. Observing these days within the community can involve organized events, workshops, and discussions, which reinforce our dedication to justice, empathy, and understanding.

By engaging with these international observances, we align ourselves with a global movement toward inclusivity and respect. These observances serve as a reminder that New Universalism is part of a larger, interconnected community dedicated to peace and dignity for all. Incorporating these dates into our community calendar honors the significance of diversity as a fundamental principle that unites rather than divides.

Making Inclusivity a Daily Practice

In New Universalism, celebrating diversity is not limited to special occasions or designated festivals; it is an ongoing commitment that we carry into our daily lives. Inclusivity becomes a way of living, guiding our actions, interactions, and thoughts. Daily practices, such as actively listening to others, challenging our own biases, and making an effort to learn about cultures and perspectives different from our own, embody the New Universalist spirit of respect.

Simple gestures like welcoming newcomers warmly, practicing empathy in conversations, and recognizing each person's inherent worth contribute to an environment where everyone feels valued. These small acts of kindness and inclusion transform our communities into spaces of belonging, where diversity is not only accepted but embraced.

Diversity as a Source of Collective Growth

At its core, celebrating diversity in New Universalism is a celebration of humanity's shared journey. Through diverse perspectives, traditions, and practices, we gain a deeper understanding of universal truths, finding inspiration, guidance, and strength in each other's unique experiences. This diversity enriches our community, making it vibrant and reflective of life's vastness.

In embracing diversity through ritual and practice, New Universalism strives to model a world where differences are celebrated as gifts that bring us closer together. By honoring each person's distinct path while uniting around shared values, we create a community where compassion, respect, and joy flourish—a community that reflects the beauty of life's many facets and invites each of us to grow, learn, and be enriched by the presence of others.

Earth Stewardship

7

The Sacred Duty to Protect and Heal the Earth

Earth Stewardship as a Sacred Duty

In New Universalism, Earth Stewardship is one of the highest expressions of our faith, binding us in both spiritual responsibility and ethical accountability to protect and honor the planet we call home. To engage in Earth Stewardship is to recognize the sacredness of all life and the divine threads that connect us to every being, every ecosystem, and every element of the natural world. This practice embodies our belief that Earth itself is a living entity—worthy not only of respect but of deep reverence. To steward the Earth is to see ourselves as caretakers of a sacred trust, guardians of a planetary heritage that is as ancient as it is intricate.

Our faith teaches that the Earth, like humanity, possesses a divine essence and a unique voice. To neglect or harm the Earth is to sever our connection with this essence, and to uphold it is to honor the sacred in tangible, life-sustaining ways. Through Earth Stewardship, we live out our commitment to a life that is ecologically balanced, spiritually conscious, and attuned to the profound interdependence of all things. In embracing this duty, we acknowledge that the world we inhabit is not ours to dominate or exploit but a living community to which we belong, requiring our humility, wisdom, and active care.

Spiritual Foundations of Earth Stewardship

The principles of Earth Stewardship are rooted in the spiritual heart of New Universalism, reflecting teachings drawn from Indigenous wisdom, Neo-Paganism, and insights from Earth-centered traditions across the world. These traditions teach that the Earth is sacred ground, that the soil, waters, skies, and creatures are not mere resources but our kin in the journey of life. Indigenous traditions remind us that all life flows from a shared source and that every being, human and non-human, has a unique role in maintaining the delicate balance of the natural world. This interconnected view resonates deeply with New Universalism, calling us to revere and protect the Earth as a sacred act.

In Neo-Paganism, the cycles of the seasons, the rhythm of the moon, and the ever-renewing forces of nature are celebrated as expressions of the divine. This perspective teaches us that to live in harmony with nature is to align our lives with the universal patterns of growth, decay, renewal, and transformation. Earth Stewardship, then, becomes a form of spiritual practice that reconnects us to these rhythms, reminding us of the cyclical nature of existence and of our place within this eternal circle of life.

For New Universalists, these teachings translate into a call to action—a recognition that to live responsibly is to live reverently, with a profound awareness of the effects our choices have on the world around us. In honoring this duty, we strive to balance our human needs with the needs of the natural world, cultivating a relationship with the Earth that is marked by gratitude, humility, and respect. This commitment invites us to look at every aspect of our lives—our consumption, our waste, our energy use, and our impact on ecosystems—as opportunities to live out our faith in practical and meaningful ways.

Earth Stewardship in New Universalism also draws from scientific insights, which serve as modern revelations of the complex interconnections that sustain life on Earth. Through scientific understanding, we come to appreciate the intricate webs that connect species, ecosystems, and climate systems, and we recognize our role within these networks. This knowledge reinforces our belief that humanity is not separate from nature but part of a larger whole, a vast community of beings whose well-being is intertwined. Our stewardship, therefore, is a call not only to protect nature but to actively participate in the restoration and healing of the planet, recognizing that the health of the Earth and the health of humanity are inseparable.

In New Universalism, Earth Stewardship is thus a form of devotion, a way of expressing our love for life itself. It is a practice that brings us closer to the divine by reminding us of the beauty, resilience, and sanctity of the natural world. As we tend to the Earth, we engage in a spiritual relationship that affirms our place within the web of life and honors our responsibility to those who will come after us. Earth Stewardship is our promise to the future, a vow to safeguard the planet not only for our own sake but for all beings, human and non-human, who share this Earth and for those yet to come.

Core Principles of Ethical and Sustainable Living

In New Universalism, Earth Stewardship is woven into the fabric of our daily lives through principles that guide our relationship with the natural world. These core principles—Interconnectedness, Responsibility and Accountability, and Balance and Moderation—are central to our ethical and sustainable living practices, grounding us in values that honor life's interdependence and promote harmony between human existence and the ecological systems we inhabit. These principles are foundational to our ethical and sustainable way of life, and they provide a spiritual framework that encourages mindful choices, personal growth, and the collective good. Through these principles, New Universalists cultivate a relationship with the Earth that reflects reverence, compassion, and shared purpose. By following these principles, we affirm our commitment to living in ways that respect the Earth's capacity to support all beings now and in the future.

Interconnectedness

The principle of interconnectedness is a profound recognition that all life forms are woven into the fabric of the natural world, where each being and element has a purpose and role that contributes to the greater whole. In New Universalism, interconnectedness is more than a concept; it is a way of being that underscores the unity between humanity, Earth, and the cosmos. This principle reminds us that each action we take impacts the environment, animals, ecosystems, and future generations. Just as a forest thrives through the mutual support of its diverse species, our lives are enriched by recognizing and honoring this unity.

Practical Applications:

Mindful Consumption

In practicing mindful consumption, New Universalists recognize that every choice we make about what we consume has a ripple effect that touches the lives of people, animals, and ecosystems. When we choose sustainably sourced and ethically produced goods, we honor the web of life from which these products originate. This may mean choosing local and organic produce, which not only nourishes our bodies but also reduces environmental impact by minimizing transportation needs and harmful agricultural practices. Each choice becomes an act of reverence, acknowledging the interconnectedness between our lives and the natural world. Through such mindful practices, we are reminded that Earth's resources are a gift, and our respect for this gift reinforces our unity with all life.

Reducing Waste

The practice of waste reduction is a form of humility and gratitude. By composting food scraps, recycling responsibly, and minimizing single-use plastics, we demonstrate our respect for the planet's resources and ecosystems. Each item we discard enters into a larger cycle of decomposition and renewal, a process that mirrors the cycles in our spiritual lives. When we reduce waste, we contribute to a cleaner environment, lessen the burden on landfills, and protect wildlife habitats. In New Universalism, minimizing waste is a testament to our interconnectedness with the Earth, a daily reflection of our doctrine that what affects one affects all. As such, waste reduction becomes not merely a practical step, but a spiritual practice of honoring Earth's natural balance.

Community Engagement

Active participation in community-based environmental initiatives, such as tree planting, water clean-ups, or conservation projects, embodies interconnectedness in a tangible way. These communal efforts are expressions of solidarity and collective responsibility, where our combined actions reflect a shared commitment to Earth Stewardship. When we engage in these activities, we foster deeper bonds with others who share our values, enhancing our sense of belonging and unity. Community engagement in environmental care is both an expression of compassion and a recognition that, together, we have a more significant impact on the world around us. Through these acts, we learn that interconnectedness is not just an idea; it is a lived experience that deepens our spiritual connection to both humanity and the Earth.

In recognizing interconnectedness, New Universalists view every life form as sacred, reflecting the Divine's wisdom in nature. By cultivating respect for all beings, we deepen our spirituality, connecting our well-being to that of the Earth. Interconnectedness guides us to live harmoniously, realizing that our actions contribute to a larger purpose, reinforcing the New Universalist principle of unity within diversity.

Responsibility and Accountability

Responsibility and accountability in Earth Stewardship emphasize the necessity of owning our impact on the environment. In New Universalism, we are taught that responsibility is both personal and collective, requiring that we act with awareness, integrity, and a sense of duty. Accountability means not only being honest with ourselves about our environmental footprint but also holding institutions, businesses, and governments accountable for their actions that affect the Earth. This principle challenges us to step beyond convenience and make deliberate choices that respect ecological systems.

Practical Applications:
Eco-Friendly Transportation

Opting for eco-friendly transportation—such as walking, cycling, or using public transport—extends our sense of responsibility to each step we take and every mile we travel. This choice reduces carbon emissions and promotes cleaner air, helping to preserve the health of communities and ecosystems. Within New Universalism, traveling responsibly is an acknowledgment of our impact on the climate and environment. It is an embodiment of accountability, a reminder that our everyday decisions shape the world we inhabit. Each conscious choice to reduce pollution reflects our responsibility to the planet and our fellow beings, reinforcing the principle that caring for the Earth begins with individual actions.

Conscious Purchasing

In New Universalism, the decision to purchase goods mindfully is a reflection of our values, as we consider the origins, impacts, and long-term effects of our choices. Conscious purchasing involves choosing products with a minimal environmental footprint, supporting companies that prioritize ethical labor practices, and favoring items that are durable or can be repurposed. For instance, buying from local artisans or second-hand stores not only reduces waste but also supports sustainable economic practices. Each purchase we make thus becomes a deliberate statement of accountability and respect for the interconnected systems that produce, transport, and deliver goods. This mindful approach to purchasing reinforces our doctrine of Earth Stewardship, showing that even small actions reflect our greater commitment to a sustainable world.

Supporting Ethical Policies

Engagement with environmental policies and advocacy is an extension of our spiritual commitment to justice and accountability. Supporting legislation that protects wildlife, promotes renewable energy, or upholds environmental protections amplifies our voice within the wider community. In New Universalism, advocating for policies that protect Earth's ecosystems reflects our collective responsibility to ensure a safe and sustainable future. By voting for eco-conscious candidates, supporting environmental organizations, and joining in community discussions, we take responsibility not only for our actions but for the policies that shape the future of our world. This aspect of responsibility reinforces the New Universalist principle that each of us, as stewards of the Earth, has a role in shaping a just and sustainable society.

Responsibility in New Universalism is a sacred duty, a form of reverence that acknowledges our power to affect the environment positively or negatively. Taking responsibility aligns with our doctrine of social responsibility, as every conscious action reflects our commitment to the collective welfare. Through accountability, we foster an ethical culture that respects the interconnected web of life, reinforcing the spiritual and moral necessity to care for our shared home.

Balance and Moderation

Balance and moderation are central to New Universalist philosophy, reminding us that sustainability arises from a mindful balance between human needs and ecological health. Moderation teaches us that life's true abundance comes not from accumulation but from aligning our lifestyle with nature's cycles. Just as nature has times of growth, dormancy, and renewal, we are encouraged to live within limits, avoid excess, and cultivate gratitude for the resources we have. Moderation reflects our respect for Earth's finite resources, fostering a relationship of care and appreciation.

Practical Applications:

Mindful Energy Use

Practicing mindful energy use—turning off unnecessary lights, using energy-efficient appliances, and prioritizing natural lighting—demonstrates an awareness of our dependence on Earth's resources and our commitment to using them respectfully. Every kilowatt saved is a gesture of gratitude for the energy the planet provides, and our moderation becomes a reflection of our spiritual respect for Earth's finite resources. Through this practice, we align ourselves with the cycles of nature, recognizing that just as plants and animals thrive within limits, we too must learn to live within sustainable bounds. Mindful energy use connects us to the rhythms of nature, reinforcing our commitment to balance in all aspects of life.

Sustainable Eating Habits

Embracing sustainable eating habits—such as reducing food waste, choosing seasonal and local produce, and incorporating more plant-based options—demonstrates our respect for the Earth's ability to nourish us. In New Universalism, food is seen as a sacred gift from the Earth, and we honor this gift by consuming mindfully and minimizing our ecological footprint. Seasonal and local foods align our diets with the natural cycles, connecting us more deeply to the rhythms of the land and reducing the resources required for transport and storage. In addition, embracing plant-based foods can reduce environmental strain on resources. Each meal prepared with intention becomes an expression of gratitude and reverence, transforming everyday sustenance into a meaningful practice of balance and moderation.

A Minimalist Approach

In New Universalism, a minimalist lifestyle is viewed as an intentional way of honoring life's essentials and avoiding excessive consumption. Minimalism is not about deprivation but about focusing on what truly matters—connection, experience, and purpose. By prioritizing quality over quantity, reducing material possessions, and choosing simplicity, we reflect a life in balance with Earth's resources. Each item we choose to keep becomes a reminder of our commitment to sustainability, as we intentionally reduce waste and consumption. This practice encourages us to find joy not in accumulation but in the richness of mindful living, aligning our lives with the planet's natural rhythms. Minimalism is an active expression of Earth Stewardship, as we choose harmony with nature over the pursuit of excess.

Balance and moderation are spiritual disciplines in New Universalism, grounding us in a life of simplicity and reverence. By embodying these values, we honor the rhythms of nature, recognizing that overconsumption disrupts ecological harmony. Living in balance mirrors the cyclical nature of the universe, reinforcing the New Universalist commitment to sustainable living and harmony with the Earth's cycles.

Ethical Imperatives for Protecting the Earth

In New Universalism, our commitment to Earth Stewardship is not merely an aspiration; it is an ethical mandate, rooted in the understanding that all beings and ecosystems have intrinsic value and that future generations depend on the actions we take today. The ethical imperatives for Earth Stewardship call for mindful conservation, a deep respect for biodiversity, and a commitment to safeguarding resources for those who will come after us. These principles are woven into our spiritual lives as expressions of reverence, compassion, and responsibility, creating a shared framework through which New Universalists honor our interconnected existence on Earth.

Conserving Natural Habitats
Guardianship of Habitats

Conserving natural habitats is one of our most direct ways of showing respect for the Earth's diversity and beauty. From forests to oceans, each habitat serves as a sanctuary for countless species and as a vital component of Earth's ecological balance. In New Universalism, we see these habitats as sacred spaces that must be preserved to maintain harmony within the global ecosystem. This guardianship entails protecting areas from deforestation, pollution, and unsustainable development practices, thus ensuring that these spaces can continue to support diverse life forms. By participating in conservation efforts—whether through advocacy, volunteer work, or supporting preservation organizations—New Universalists act as stewards of these vital ecosystems, embodying a spiritual commitment to safeguard the natural world.

Spiritual Connection to Place

Honoring natural habitats also reflects a reverence for specific landscapes and ecosystems, which are often woven into the spiritual practices of Indigenous and Earth-based traditions. Many sacred places—mountains, rivers, forests—hold historical, cultural, and spiritual significance for the communities that dwell around them. In New Universalism, respecting these sites means acknowledging the intergenerational relationships between people and land, recognizing that the sanctity of place contributes to spiritual well-being. Through rituals, meditations, and seasonal celebrations, New Universalists strengthen our connection to the natural world, renewing our resolve to protect these sacred spaces.

Respecting Biodiversity
A Celebration of Life's Diversity

Respect for biodiversity goes beyond admiration for the variety of life on Earth—it is an ethical imperative that acknowledges each species' unique role within the ecosystem. Each plant, animal, and microorganism contribute to the balance of life, sustaining cycles that support not only their survival but our own. New Universalism teaches that by respecting biodiversity, we honor the wisdom of nature's design, where each element has purpose and place. From protecting endangered species to supporting habitats that sustain pollinators and other vital organisms, New Universalists are called to actively engage in the preservation of biodiversity as a sacred duty, promoting the understanding that all life is interwoven and essential.

Practices for Biodiversity Preservation

Practically, respecting biodiversity may involve choosing organic foods, supporting sustainable agriculture, or participating in habitat restoration projects. By making conscious choices that align with ecological harmony, we can mitigate the damage caused by monoculture farming, deforestation, and industrial practices. For New Universalists, these choices are expressions of compassion and respect, illustrating that humanity's needs do not supersede the needs of other species. Additionally, biodiversity gardens and pollinator habitats can be incorporated into personal and communal spaces, serving as physical reminders of our commitment to sustain and celebrate life's diversity.

Preserving Resources for Future Generations
Legacy of Earth Stewardship

Preserving resources for future generations requires New Universalists to live with intention, practicing sustainability as a form of love and duty toward those who will inherit the Earth. This principle is rooted in our understanding that each generation is part of an unbroken lineage, with a responsibility to pass on a world that can sustain future life. New Universalism teaches that we are custodians of Earth's abundance—not owners entitled to exploit it. Through moderate consumption, resource conservation, and waste reduction, we contribute to an enduring legacy of sustainability, ensuring that future generations may also experience Earth's beauty and bounty.

Sustainable Practices for Longevity

In practice, preserving resources can take the form of using water efficiently, supporting renewable energy, and reducing our carbon footprint. Engaging in sustainable practices, such as solar energy adoption, water conservation techniques, and waste reduction, are all ways New Universalists embody Earth Stewardship. Additionally, supporting policies and technologies that aim to reduce environmental harm, such as carbon-neutral initiatives or conservation legislation, reflects a broader commitment to the Earth's longevity. By integrating these practices into daily life, we align our actions with the principle of sustainability, honoring our shared responsibility for the future.

Embodying Earth Stewardship in Community Life

Promoting Collective Responsibility

New Universalism emphasizes that Earth Stewardship is both a personal and communal responsibility. While individual actions matter, the larger impact lies in community-driven efforts and cultural shifts toward sustainability. By fostering an environment where community members work together to reduce waste, support sustainable agriculture, and promote green initiatives, New Universalist communities can lead by example, encouraging wider societal change. Through community gardens, recycling programs, conservation education, and organized cleanups, members enact the core values of respect, accountability, and interconnectedness, demonstrating that Earth Stewardship is a shared and vital commitment.

Educating and Inspiring Future Generations

A key component of Earth Stewardship is the active engagement in educating younger generations about sustainability and environmental ethics. Within New Universalism, imparting these values is seen as a sacred duty, cultivating an ethic of care and respect for the Earth from an early age. Community-based environmental education, nature workshops, and eco-activist mentorship programs are all pathways for fostering a deep and enduring commitment to Earth Stewardship in future generations. By inspiring young people to value and protect the natural world, New Universalists contribute to a cycle of awareness, compassion, and action that will persist long into the future.

Environmental Wisdom Indigenous & Pagan Traditions

Introduction to Earth-Based Spiritual Wisdom

In New Universalism, Earth Stewardship is not merely an ethical commitment but a profound spiritual mandate, rooted in reverence for the Earth as a sacred entity deserving of respect, care, and reciprocity. This perspective draws deeply on the wisdom of Indigenous and Neo-Pagan traditions, whose practices and beliefs emphasize an interconnected relationship with nature and a balanced approach to living on Earth. For countless generations, these traditions have cultivated an understanding that humanity and nature are bound in a relationship of mutual dependence and respect, a vision that aligns closely with New Universalism's theological commitment to protecting and healing our planet.

In Indigenous cultures across the globe, the Earth is often regarded not as a resource but as a living, breathing being—a mother who provides for her children and demands respect and gratitude in return. From North American Native cultures viewing the land as Mother Earth to Aboriginal Australian teachings about the Dreamtime, where ancestral spirits shaped the land and left it in the care of humanity, the common thread in Indigenous teachings is a relationship rooted in respect and reciprocity. This concept profoundly influences New Universalism, framing our approach to Earth Stewardship not merely as environmental responsibility but as a sacred trust. The Earth is seen as a partner in a spiritual exchange, deserving of protection and reverence in both communal and individual practices.

Neo-Pagan traditions also bring forward a powerful view of the Earth as sacred. Through the celebration of nature's cycles, elements, and energies, Neo-Pagan beliefs encourage an ongoing, harmonious relationship with the environment. The Wheel of the Year, which marks seasonal changes through festivals like the Winter Solstice and Summer Solstice, reminds us of life's cyclical nature and the importance of living in balance with Earth's rhythms. Such observances align with New Universalism's vision of honoring seasonal cycles and embodying gratitude and humility toward the Earth and all its creatures.

These teachings from Indigenous and Neo-Pagan traditions offer timeless wisdom, grounding New Universalism's Earth Stewardship doctrine in a lived spirituality that values interconnectedness, respect for natural cycles, and a commitment to caring for the Earth. Incorporating this spiritual heritage into New Universalist theology deepens our understanding of environmental ethics and strengthens our dedication to living sustainably. By drawing from these ancient, Earth-centered perspectives, New Universalism upholds the principle that true stewardship of the Earth is inseparable from our spiritual practice, cultivating a life in harmony with the planet and all its beings.

Through the following exploration of specific teachings—such as reciprocity, respect, reverence for nature, and commitment to future generations—New Universalism offers a path that encourages each of us to embody Earth Stewardship in practical, respectful ways, honoring both the spirit of these traditions and the ongoing responsibility we hold to preserve our world.

Lessons from Indigenous Traditions

The belief that Earth is a sentient, sacred being forms the heart of many Indigenous traditions which emphasize the relationship between humans and the Earth as one of profound respect, interdependence, and reverence. Earth is seen as a provider and a sacred entity, teaching us about sustainability, harmony, and the need to preserve our shared home for future generations. These teachings remind us that the Earth is not merely a resource to be used but a living, conscious entity deserving of care and respect. Through the lens of Indigenous wisdom, New Universalism honors these perspectives, recognizing the deep wisdom in Indigenous traditions and incorporating their foundational values of Earth reverence and stewardship into our theology and daily practices. These lessons have enduring significance, reminding us of our role not as owners or consumers, but as guardians and kin. To respect the Earth as a living entity calls us into relationship with it—one grounded in reciprocity, humility, and reverence. For New Universalists, this understanding opens pathways to deeper alignment with Earth-based principles, offering spiritual practices and teachings that foster a connection with nature rooted in mutual respect and compassion.

Respect for the Earth as a Living Being

Across numerous Indigenous traditions, Earth is revered as a being that embodies life and consciousness. Far from seeing the natural world as a mere resource, many Indigenous cultures approach the Earth as a mother, a guide, and a powerful, interconnected entity. This relationship with Earth inspires practices of care, protection, and reverence, viewing the planet as the foundation of all life and deserving of respect in return. In New Universalism, such practices and beliefs resonate with our commitment to Earth stewardship, urging us to recognize Earth's inherent value and respond with humility and responsibility.

In Anishinaabe (Ojibwe) culture, for instance, the Earth is considered "Aki," a living, breathing force that carries wisdom and sustains life. The Anishinaabe honor Aki by offering tobacco as a gift before gathering any plants, herbs, or medicines, acknowledging the sacrifice of the plant for human use and ensuring a balanced, respectful relationship with nature. This act of offering creates a space of humility and gratitude, underscoring that taking from the Earth is a sacred exchange rather than an entitlement. Within New Universalism, such practices can inspire our own relationship with Earth to be one of conscious respect, approaching every act of consumption with mindfulness and gratitude.

The Haudenosaunee (Iroquois Confederacy) also exemplify respect for Earth as a living being. In their tradition, the Thanksgiving Address, or "The Words That Come Before All Else," is recited before any major gathering or ceremony.

"We have been given the duty to live in balance and harmony with each other and all living things. So now, we bring our minds together as one as we give greetings and thanks to each other as people. Now our minds are one. We are all thankful to our Mother, the Earth, for she gives us all that we need for life.

We return thanks to our mother, the earth, which sustains us. We return thanks to the rivers and streams, which supply us with water. We return thanks to all herbs, which furnish medicines for the cure of our diseases. We return thanks to the moon and stars, which have given to us their light when the sun was gone."   (ref. Appendix: Haudenosaunee Thanksgiving Address)

This address expresses gratitude to the natural world, from the waters and the plants to the animals and the four winds, recognizing each as a conscious being that plays a role in the interconnected web of life. Through this tradition, the Haudenosaunee affirm a worldview in which all parts of nature are honored and respected. For New Universalists, this Address can serve as an inspiration to approach life with gratitude for the natural world, cultivating an attitude that values and reveres all beings in the ecological system.

Indigenous Australian traditions, particularly those of the Yolngu and the Arrernte peoples, also reflect this deep respect for Earth as a living entity. Many of these cultures have a concept of "Country" that refers not just to land but to a complex network of relationships among the land, plants, animals, humans, and ancestral spirits. To the Yolngu, Country is alive and holds knowledge, history, and a spiritual essence. This worldview calls people into a relationship of care and responsibility, as harming the land would disrupt this network and offend ancestral spirits. The Yolngu practice of songlines—a sacred form of song and storytelling that maps the land and its sacred sites—preserves and honors this relationship, reminding people of their duty to respect and protect Country. For New Universalism, this concept offers a vision of Earth not only as our home but as a repository of spiritual wisdom and lineage, encouraging us to protect and honor it as we would a sacred inheritance.

The Andean Indigenous peoples, including the Quechua and Aymara, embody a similar reverence through their relationship with Pachamama, or "Mother Earth." Pachamama is considered the giver of life, food, and shelter, and is honored through ceremonies and offerings that seek to maintain harmony between human communities and the natural world. The Q'ero people of Peru, for instance, perform "Despacho" ceremonies, in which they offer gifts to Pachamama—often including grains, flowers, shells, and coca leaves—to express gratitude and ensure balance in their relationship with the land. This practice encourages a mindset of reciprocity and fosters a deep respect for the gifts of the Earth. New Universalists can draw from this practice by incorporating similar acts of gratitude and reciprocity into daily life, recognizing that a relationship with Earth requires ongoing mindfulness and intentionality.

In each of these traditions, the concept of Earth as a living being calls individuals to act in ways that honor and protect the natural world. For New Universalists, these practices provide a spiritual model of respect, stewardship, and gratitude. The reverence Indigenous cultures demonstrate through offerings, ceremonies, and rituals of gratitude echoes New Universalist principles of Earth stewardship and interconnectedness. As we adopt and adapt these practices, it is essential to remember and respect their origins, acknowledging the teachings of the cultures from which they come.

By embracing these principles, New Universalists are reminded that every interaction with nature—whether it be gathering resources, altering landscapes, or consuming Earth's gifts—should be approached with humility, reverence, and a sense of responsibility to sustain and protect our shared, living planet.

Reciprocity and Gratitude

Reciprocity and gratitude are foundational values in many Indigenous traditions, emphasizing the understanding that humans are not separate from, but part of, an interconnected web of life. In this view, nature provides abundantly for human needs, and it is the responsibility of people to give back to the Earth as an expression of gratitude and respect. For New Universalism, these values echo the principles of Earth Stewardship and interconnectedness, underscoring the need to balance what we take from the Earth with what we give in return.

Among the Lakota and other Plains Indigenous tribes, the value of reciprocity is embodied in the practice of "Wopila," which is a ceremony of thanksgiving. After hunting or harvesting, participants offer prayers, songs, and sometimes material gifts to express their gratitude to the animal or plant for its sacrifice. The Lakota view this act as a reciprocal exchange, recognizing that each gift from the Earth entails a responsibility to honor and sustain the giver. This practice calls New Universalists to reflect on the sacred exchange involved in every resource we use, whether it be food, water, or material goods, and to seek ways to repay these gifts through acts of conservation, sustainable living, and intentional gratitude.

The Māori of New Zealand embody reciprocity and gratitude through the concept of "kaitiakitanga," or guardianship. This term signifies the responsibility humans hold as caretakers of nature, a duty owed not only to the land but also to future generations. The Māori belief that the Earth is a sacred ancestor, Papatuanuku (Earth Mother), strengthens this duty, as the relationship with Earth is seen as familial. Offerings, songs, and dances are performed to honor this bond and to express appreciation for the natural world. Kaitiakitanga inspires New Universalists to see

Earth stewardship as a continuous relationship that demands both gratitude for present resources and a commitment to preserving them for those yet to come.

The Potawatomi people of North America, particularly as described by Dr. Robin Wall Kimmerer, a botanist and member of the Potawatomi Nation, emphasize the "Honorable Harvest." This principle teaches that when taking from nature, one should do so respectfully, only take what is needed, and give back to the land. Dr. Kimmerer's articulation of the Honorable Harvest includes practices such as asking permission before harvesting, never taking the first plant seen, and leaving something in return, like tobacco or an offering of water. These practices invite New Universalists to consider every act of consumption as an opportunity to cultivate gratitude and restraint, recognizing that the Earth's resources are finite and that we must honor them by avoiding waste and overuse.

In Andean Indigenous traditions, the principle of "Ayni" underscores the importance of reciprocity not only with other people but with the land itself. Ayni can be understood as a spiritual principle of mutual aid that governs relationships among people, as well as between humans and the natural world. For example, during planting and harvesting seasons, the Aymara and Quechua communities practice ayni by working each other's fields collectively, then sharing the harvest in a communal meal to honor the Earth's bounty. Similarly, before drawing water from rivers or springs, an offering may be given to Pachamama (Mother Earth) as a way to acknowledge her role in sustaining life. This principle of ayni invites New Universalists to recognize that our relationship with Earth is a mutual one, where the gifts we receive require acts of gratitude and care in return.

Across these traditions, gratitude is not merely an internal feeling but is expressed through action and ritual. This approach encourages New Universalists to embody gratitude in tangible ways, such as leaving offerings for the land, conserving resources, or supporting sustainable initiatives. For instance, when celebrating a harvest or a meal, New Universalists might include a moment of reflection or a symbolic gesture, such as setting aside a portion of the meal to acknowledge the Earth's gifts, honoring the spirit of reciprocity.

Reciprocity and gratitude are pathways to deepen our connection with nature, reminding us that we are active participants in the ecosystems that sustain us. By embracing these values, New Universalists are called to live in balance with the Earth, consciously choosing actions that honor the natural world and acknowledge our dependence on it. When gratitude is expressed through reciprocal actions—whether through acts of conservation, environmental advocacy, or daily rituals of thanks—it cultivates a spirit of respect, humility, and interconnectedness that reflects the core values of New Universalism.

Long-Term Vision

A deep commitment to long-term vision is central to many Indigenous traditions, encapsulating the understanding that each generation bears responsibility not only for the present but also for the future. This perspective invites individuals to consider the impact of their actions beyond their immediate needs, honoring the lives and well-being of those yet to come. New Universalism embraces this principle, emphasizing the spiritual and ethical duty of cultivating sustainability, respect, and foresight for the benefit of future generations.

One of the most prominent teachings on long-term vision is the Haudenosaunee (Iroquois) concept of the "Seventh Generation Principle." This philosophy suggests that decisions made today should take into account their effects on the next seven generations, an outlook rooted in both respect for life and responsibility toward future inheritors of the Earth. The Seventh Generation Principle reflects a worldview that regards the Earth as a sacred trust, reminding New Universalists that every choice—whether in personal consumption, environmental policy, or community planning—carries a ripple effect that extends far beyond the present. By adopting this principle, we are encouraged to reflect carefully on the long-term consequences of our actions, prioritizing sustainability and stewardship.

In the Hopi tradition, teachings emphasize the importance of foresight and "staying in harmony" with natural cycles as a way to ensure the survival and health of both people and ecosystems. The Hopi prophecies, which caution against environmental degradation and overexploitation, serve as a reminder of the dangers of shortsightedness. This wisdom invites New Universalists to embrace a lifestyle that aligns with the natural rhythms of the Earth and to practice moderation and restraint as essential aspects of Earth Stewardship. In doing so, we are encouraged to view Earth's resources not as expendable commodities but as precious gifts to be used wisely, with future generations in mind.

Similarly, the Australian Aboriginal concept of "Dreaming" holds that ancestral knowledge and stories provide a map for living in harmony with the land over the long term. Dreaming stories convey principles of land care, resource use, and respect for biodiversity, all of which are passed down through generations to preserve environmental balance. This wisdom promotes a profound sense of responsibility toward the land and all its life forms, inspiring us to honor ancestral teachings and practices that prioritize conservation, biodiversity, and ecological wisdom.

The Māori people of New Zealand hold to the concept of "whakapapa," which refers to genealogical connections between humans, animals, plants, and the land. Whakapapa emphasizes that each individual exists within a vast web of relations that spans generations. This understanding instills a sense of accountability, as each generation is seen as a caretaker with obligations to protect and sustain the world for their descendants. For New Universalists, whakapapa serves as a powerful reminder that actions today are part of a continuum that shapes future realities, encouraging an ethical approach to stewardship that honors the interconnectedness of all life.

In Andean cultures, the Aymara and Quechua people hold a worldview known as "sumaq kawsay," or "good living." Sumaq kawsay promotes a balanced, harmonious life in which individuals prioritize collective well-being and ecological health over material accumulation. Central to this philosophy is the idea that people should strive to live within the natural limits of their environment, preserving resources and ensuring that the needs of future generations can be met. This long-term outlook fosters a deep sense of duty to protect the land, water, and ecosystems essential for a flourishing future. New Universalists draw inspiration from sumaq kawsay, adopting principles of sustainable living, minimalism, and community-mindedness.

Long-term vision challenges New Universalists to think beyond immediate desires and conveniences, fostering a sense of duty to the future. Practical applications of this principle can include reducing waste, supporting renewable energy sources, conserving water, and choosing sustainable products. In daily life, long-term vision can manifest through small yet impactful decisions, such as planting trees, supporting ecological conservation projects, and advocating for policies that protect biodiversity and reduce pollution.

By embracing a long-term vision, we are called to become guardians of the Earth who make conscious choices for the well-being of those who will inherit the planet. This commitment to future generations, drawn from Indigenous wisdom, reinforces New Universalism's dedication to a world where respect for life, balance, and sustainability are guiding principles. Through mindful actions, we contribute to a legacy that reflects care, respect, and a profound sense of interconnectedness with all beings, now and in the future.

Environmental Teachings from Neo-Pagan Traditions

Neo-Pagan traditions embrace the Earth as a sacred entity, intertwining their spiritual practices with the natural world's rhythms, elements, and life forms. This approach to spirituality emphasizes harmony with the Earth, seeing each seasonal shift, element, and landscape as a manifestation of divine energy. New Universalism draws inspiration from Neo-Pagan teachings in its commitment to Earth Stewardship, honoring the Earth's vitality, and recognizing our interconnectedness with all forms of life. Through practices that reverently engage with the cycles of nature, the elements, and intentional acts of Earth healing, Neo-Paganism offers profound insights into living sustainably and in awe of the natural world.

Reverence for Natural Cycles

One of the core tenets of Neo-Paganism is a deep reverence for the Earth's natural cycles, a perspective embodied through the Wheel of the Year. The Wheel of the Year is a calendar of eight seasonal festivals (or "Sabbats") that celebrate key transitions within the natural world: solstices, equinoxes, and cross-quarter days between them. By observing these celebrations, Neo-Pagan practitioners honor the ebb and flow of life, the dynamic interplay of birth, growth, harvest, and rest. These observances encourage a deep respect for nature's rhythms and reinforce the importance of living in harmony with these cycles. New Universalism, in aligning with this reverence for natural cycles, embraces these teachings to encourage sustainable practices and reflection on the cyclical nature of life.

In celebrating the cycles of nature, Neo-Paganism instills a mindful relationship with the Earth's seasons, an approach that encourages individuals to harmonize their lives with natural changes. For example, during the Winter Solstice—a time of the longest night and the return of light—Neo-Pagan traditions focus on themes of introspection, resilience, and hope. This seasonal observance serves as a reminder of nature's capacity for renewal and resilience, and it invites individuals to reflect on their own journeys of transformation and hope. The Spring Equinox, another pivotal point on the Wheel of the Year, emphasizes balance, renewal, and growth. It is a time for planting seeds, both literally and figuratively, symbolizing the renewal of life and the potential for personal and spiritual growth. Through such observances, New Universalism encourages us to see our lives as part of an interconnected, ongoing cycle, inspiring a sense of patience and resilience.

The Neo-Pagan reverence for natural cycles also imparts lessons in sustainable living. By honoring the phases of growth, harvest, and rest within nature, these traditions encourage living in balance with what the Earth provides. We are reminded to consume mindfully, honor periods of rest, and respect the limitations of natural resources. This perspective aligns with New Universalism's call for ecological mindfulness and conservation, urging us to adopt seasonal practices such as eating local and seasonal foods, conserving energy, and supporting biodiversity.

The observance of seasonal rhythms in Neo-Paganism reinforces the idea that life flows in a circle, reminding practitioners of life's continuity and interconnectedness. Each cycle within the Wheel of the Year becomes an opportunity to cultivate gratitude for nature's gifts, to reflect on personal growth, and to recommit to the Earth's well-being. By embracing this cyclical view, New Universalists are encouraged to approach life with an awareness of both life's fragility and resilience, fostering a practice of care and respect for all living things.

Neo-Pagan reverence for natural cycles invites New Universalists to recognize and celebrate life's natural rhythms, fostering a spirituality that is grounded in the Earth. Through alignment with these seasonal patterns, we are reminded of our role as custodians of the Earth, committed to honoring the planet's ongoing vitality and beauty.

Honoring Elements and Nature Spirits

In Neo-Pagan traditions, the elements—Earth, Water, Fire, and Air—are revered as sacred forces that shape life and reflect the divine presence within nature. Each element is seen as embodying unique qualities, energies, and wisdom that contribute to the balance and vitality of the natural world. Alongside these elements, many Neo-Pagan traditions honor nature spirits or deities believed to dwell within landscapes, plants, animals, and other natural forms. This perspective inspires a deep respect for the environment, fostering a mindful and reverent relationship with all aspects of the Earth. In New Universalism, honoring these elemental forces and recognizing the life spirit within all aspects of nature encourages both practical and spiritual stewardship, nurturing a connection to Earth that is both intentional and sacred.

The Sacred Qualities of the Elements

Neo-Paganism teaches that each element holds its own symbolic and spiritual significance. For instance:

- **Earth** represents stability, abundance, and the grounding force that sustains all life. It symbolizes physicality, endurance, and the nurturing power of the land.
- **Water** embodies emotions, intuition, and adaptability, representing the flow of life, purification, and the interconnectedness of all beings.
- **Fire** is associated with transformation, passion, and vitality, representing the creative force that inspires growth and change.
- **Air** signifies intellect, communication, and freedom, representing the breath of life, knowledge, and connection.

This reverence for the elements aligns with New Universalism's commitment to living in harmony with the Earth. Each element calls us to recognize and honor the roles they play in our lives: Earth as our foundation, Water as our sustainer, Fire as our energy, and Air as our life force. This holistic understanding encourages us to treat each element with respect, practicing mindful resource use, conserving water, reducing pollution, and safeguarding natural landscapes. In revering these elements, New Universalists are reminded of our dependence on nature's gifts and our duty to protect these gifts for future generations.

Respecting Nature Spirits

In addition to the elements, Neo-Pagan traditions honor the presence of spirits or energies within natural features, from trees and rivers to mountains and fields. These spirits are seen as guardians of the land, deserving respect and reverence. Neo-Pagans may leave offerings, say prayers, or perform rituals to acknowledge and honor these spirits, fostering a sense of reciprocity and gratitude for the Earth's abundant resources. This practice serves as a reminder that all aspects of nature are interconnected, each with its own role and intrinsic worth.

For New Universalists, honoring the spirit within nature is a way to foster mindfulness and respect for the environment. Recognizing that landscapes, plants, and animals hold a sacred presence, New Universalism encourages us to approach nature with humility and care. This belief can be expressed in small acts of reverence, such as speaking words of gratitude before harvesting plants, cleaning up natural areas, or offering food or water to wildlife. Each of these acts affirms a commitment to reciprocity, recognizing that the Earth sustains us and that we have a duty to sustain it in return.

Integrating Elemental Reverence and Nature Spirits into New Universalist Practice

In New Universalism, the reverence for elements and nature spirits inspires rituals and daily practices that honor the sacredness of the Earth. For example, personal altars may incorporate representations of the elements—a small bowl of water, a candle for fire, a plant or stone for earth, and an incense stick for air. This practice allows practitioners to honor each element as part of their daily routine, fostering a deeper awareness of nature's presence in their lives.

Community ceremonies may also incorporate elemental invocations, where each direction is called upon to invoke the strength and wisdom of Earth, Water, Fire, and Air. These rituals create a sacred space that acknowledges the Earth's dynamic energies, encouraging participants to feel their connection to the natural world and the life force that flows through all beings.

Honoring elements and nature spirits within New Universalism reinforces the commitment to Earth Stewardship by encouraging a respectful and mindful interaction with the environment. By acknowledging the sacred qualities of the elements and the spirits within nature, New Universalists are invited to see the Earth not as a resource to be exploited but as a living, breathing entity deserving of care and reverence. This perspective instills a sense of sacred responsibility, reminding us that by honoring the Earth, we honor the interconnected spirit of all life.

Rituals for Earth Healing

Neo-Pagan traditions place a profound emphasis on rituals designed to heal, honor, and connect with the Earth. These practices stem from a belief in the interconnectedness of all life and the understanding that humanity's well-being is intricately tied to the health of the natural world. Through Earth-healing rituals, Neo-Pagans actively seek to restore balance, offer gratitude, and set intentions for the renewal of nature. In New Universalism, adopting Earth-healing rituals serves as a meaningful way to practice Earth Stewardship, affirming a sacred duty to protect, nurture, and rejuvenate the planet we share.

Tree Planting as a Symbol of Renewal

Planting trees has long been a cherished ritual in both Neo-Pagan and Indigenous traditions, symbolizing a commitment to life, renewal, and the continuity of nature. Trees are seen as guardians of the Earth, providing shelter, oxygen, and habitats for countless species. Neo-Pagans may perform tree-planting ceremonies with specific intentions, such as promoting community health, combatting climate change, or honoring a loved one.

In New Universalism, tree-planting ceremonies offer a powerful opportunity to engage in Earth-healing practices that support environmental balance. Individuals or groups may gather for a ceremony where each participant offers a blessing, places a handful of soil at the tree's base, or says a prayer for its growth and protection. The act of planting a tree is also symbolic of long-term vision and responsibility, as each tree will contribute to the health of future generations. Through these ceremonies, New Universalists connect with the Earth in a tangible way, leaving a living legacy of stewardship and hope.

Offerings to Bodies of Water

Water has deep spiritual significance in many Earth-centered traditions and is revered as a life-giving, purifying element. Neo-Pagans often honor bodies of water—such as rivers, lakes, and oceans—through rituals and offerings intended to express gratitude and renew the connection between humanity and water. Offerings may include flowers, natural objects, or prayers spoken with reverence, asking for the health and restoration of the waters.

For New Universalists, water offerings can be a way to acknowledge the crucial role that water plays in sustaining life. Rituals around water may include lighting a candle near a river or lake, collecting litter along the shoreline as an act of reciprocity, or performing a silent meditation by the water's edge. In these moments, we focus on the beauty and necessity of water, expressing a commitment to its conservation and protection. Such ceremonies inspire reverence for natural resources, instilling a mindful awareness of water's sacredness and the human responsibility to prevent its pollution and depletion.

Blessings for Soil Health

Soil is often referred to as the "skin of the Earth," and its health is critical for sustaining plant life, biodiversity, and food security. In Neo-Pagan traditions, the soil is honored as a living entity that holds memories of past generations and provides for future ones. Some rituals involve sprinkling seeds, herbs, or compost on the soil to symbolize gratitude, renewal, and commitment to nurturing the Earth's fertility.

New Universalists may adopt soil-blessing ceremonies, gathering to offer words of gratitude, placing compost or natural fertilizer on the ground, or planting seeds as an act of healing. These rituals encourage participants to recognize soil's central role in sustaining life and to acknowledge our dependence on it for food, shelter, and well-being. By honoring the soil through ceremony, New Universalists cultivate an awareness of our responsibility to care for and preserve this essential resource. This mindfulness can lead to practical actions, such as supporting organic agriculture, reducing pesticide use, and practicing sustainable gardening methods.

Seasonal Rituals of Renewal and Healing

In Neo-Paganism, the seasonal festivals—such as those celebrated in the Wheel of the Year—often include rituals that honor Earth's cycles of growth, harvest, death, and rebirth. These ceremonies serve as reminders of nature's resilience, teaching participants to respect and protect its rhythms. Seasonal rituals may include activities such as scattering wildflower seeds in the spring, harvesting crops with gratitude in the fall, or lighting bonfires to symbolize the return of light and warmth.

For New Universalists, celebrating the changing seasons with Earth-healing rituals can foster a deeper sense of connection to nature's cycles. During spring, we may scatter seeds in meadows or gardens, symbolizing new beginnings and growth. In autumn, we may hold a harvest ritual, where the community gathers to express gratitude for the Earth's abundance. In winter, we may light candles and offer prayers for the Earth's renewal, honoring the quiet restfulness of the season. These seasonal ceremonies nurture a respect for nature's cyclical patterns, encouraging a relationship with the Earth that is both reverent and regenerative.

Creating a Collective Consciousness of Healing

Ultimately, Earth-healing rituals in New Universalism are more than symbolic gestures; they are acts that cultivate a collective consciousness of respect, responsibility, and reverence for the Earth. By gathering together to plant trees, bless water, honor soil, or celebrate seasonal cycles, New Universalists are reminded of our role as stewards of the planet. These rituals reinforce a commitment to ecological care and inspire daily actions that promote environmental health, from reducing waste and conserving water to supporting conservation initiatives.

Through Earth-healing rituals, New Universalism teaches that the relationship with the Earth is reciprocal: by giving back to nature through acts of healing, we receive the blessings of a healthier planet, a deeper spiritual connection, and a strengthened community. In honoring the Earth as a living entity, New Universalists uphold our sacred duty to protect and heal, embodying the values of Earth Stewardship in a way that is both meaningful and transformative.

Integrating Indigenous and Neo-Pagan Wisdom into Modern Life

Drawing inspiration from Indigenous and Neo-Pagan traditions offers New Universalists a meaningful pathway to honor the Earth and embrace a life centered on interconnectedness, gratitude, and sustainability. The integration of these time-honored practices can transform everyday actions into acts of reverence and stewardship, fostering a deeper bond with the natural world; however, it is essential to approach these practices with respect, cultural awareness, and an understanding of their origins. By honoring the teachings of Indigenous and Neo-Pagan traditions, we can create a balanced approach that respects tradition while adapting it to meet the needs of the present.

Practicing Daily Gratitude

One of the simplest yet most profound practices to adopt is the regular expression of gratitude for the Earth's gifts. In many Indigenous cultures, gratitude is woven into every aspect of life. Gratitude is often given for the sun's warmth, the trees' shelter, the water's nourishment, and the food that sustains life. This practice shifts one's mindset from seeing nature as a resource to seeing it as a living partner.

Incorporating daily gratitude into modern life can be as simple as taking a moment before meals to acknowledge the journey of each ingredient, from soil to table, and to thank the Earth for its sustenance. For those in New Universalism, gratitude can become a spiritual practice that aligns with the value of Earth Stewardship, nurturing a continual awareness of one's interdependence with the natural world. we may choose to start or end each day with a few words of thanks, fostering a routine that deepens appreciation for life's interconnected web.

Honoring Natural Cycles and Seasons

Neo-Pagan traditions teach that life's natural rhythms are inherently sacred and worth honoring. Observing the cycles of the moon, marking the equinoxes and solstices, and celebrating seasonal changes are ways to maintain a connection with nature's flow. These observances serve as reminders that each season brings unique opportunities for growth, reflection, and renewal, echoing life's broader patterns.

In New Universalism, honoring these natural cycles can be as simple as taking a mindful walk in nature observing the subtle shifts in the landscape with each season. We might create a seasonal altar in our homes, incorporating elements from nature that reflect the current time of year—such as flowers in spring, leaves in autumn, or evergreen branches in winter. By integrating these practices, we not only deepen our awareness of nature's cycles but also cultivate a rhythm in our own lives that respects both rest and renewal, work and contemplation.

Engaging in Conservation and Eco-Conscious Living

One of the most practical ways to honor Earth-centered wisdom is by committing to conservation and eco-conscious choices. Indigenous and Neo-Pagan traditions often emphasize the importance of taking only what is needed, using resources mindfully, and giving back to the land. These principles are directly applicable in modern contexts, where environmental conservation has become increasingly urgent.

For New Universalists, engaging in conservation efforts can take many forms—reducing waste, choosing sustainable products, supporting local farmers, or volunteering with environmental organizations. We may also participate in community clean-up efforts, tree-planting projects, or conservation initiatives as a way to put these principles into action. By embedding these eco-conscious practices into daily life, New Universalists fulfill our commitment to Earth Stewardship and embody a life of respect, compassion, and responsibility toward the planet.

Participating in Rituals and Ceremonies Mindfully

Engaging in Earth-honoring rituals is another meaningful way to integrate the wisdom of Indigenous and Neo-Pagan traditions; however, it is vital to approach these rituals with sensitivity to their cultural origins, ensuring they are practiced with respect rather than appropriation. For New Universalists, this may mean adapting rituals in ways that honor their essence without imitating practices specific to cultures to which we do not belong.

One respectful approach is to create personal, or family rituals inspired by Earth-centered values, such as setting intentions for each season, giving offerings of water or seeds, or spending time in quiet reflection outdoors. These rituals do not need to replicate Indigenous or Neo-Pagan customs precisely but can embody the spirit of reverence for nature. By doing so, we foster a spiritual connection with the Earth that is both authentic and culturally respectful.

Acknowledging the Origins and Cultural Context

Respecting the origins of these teachings is fundamental. Many of the practices inspired by Indigenous wisdom carry a history of spiritual depth and cultural significance that should not be overlooked. New Universalism encourages us to educate ourselves about the cultures from which these traditions arise, ensuring that practices are not appropriated but honored. This could involve reading about Indigenous perspectives, learning from leaders within those communities, and supporting Indigenous environmental initiatives.

Neo-Pagan traditions, which often draw upon a blend of ancient European and Earth-centered spiritual beliefs, also provide rich teachings on interconnectedness and reverence for nature. When adopting these practices, it is essential to honor the intentions behind them, recognizing that they are not merely symbolic but carry the legacy of peoples who have long celebrated the Earth's sacredness. By practicing in this way, New Universalists demonstrate humility, gratitude, and respect for diverse cultural legacies, embodying a truly inclusive and reverent approach.

Integrating Earth Wisdom as a Daily Compass

Incorporating Indigenous and Neo-Pagan wisdom into modern life need not be limited to ceremonial observances; it can become a daily compass guiding one's values and actions. By aligning with Earth-centered principles, New Universalists embrace a worldview that respects life in all its forms, fosters resilience through reciprocity, and acknowledges humanity's place within the natural order. From everyday choices, such as sustainable living and eco-conscious consumption, to practices of gratitude and celebration, the values drawn from these traditions offer enduring guidance.

By embracing Earth-centered practices with mindfulness and respect, New Universalists cultivate a spirituality that bridges ancient wisdom with modern responsibility. This integration of Earth wisdom not only fosters environmental stewardship but also deepens our spiritual journey, aligning New Universalist values with the rhythms and sacredness of the living Earth. Through this path, New Universalism honors both the timeless beauty of nature and the rich cultural traditions that have long safeguarded its truths.

Living Sustainably

Reducing One's Ecological Footprint

In the practice of Earth Stewardship, New Universalism recognizes the essential responsibility to live with an awareness of our ecological footprint—the measure of how much each individual's lifestyle impacts the Earth's resources and ecosystems. This concept serves as a lens through which we examine our habits, consumption, and overall effect on the planet. In New Universalist theology, reducing our ecological footprint is not only an environmental action; it is a deeply spiritual endeavor, a commitment to respect, moderation, and responsibility that honors the sacred bond we share with Earth.

Reducing one's ecological footprint is about making conscious choices that minimize harm to the environment, preserving its richness for current and future generations. This value connects to the universal principle of moderation, a virtue shared by numerous spiritual traditions as a path to balance and inner harmony. Moderation in this context means embracing simplicity, prioritizing what we truly need over excess, and letting go of the habitual consumption patterns that harm our planet's ecosystems.

New Universalist theology calls on us to embrace this moderation as a form of reverence. When we reduce our ecological footprint, we make space for the Earth to renew itself and provide for all living beings, both now and for future generations. This approach is consistent with Indigenous principles of care for the "Seventh Generation" and the Neo-Pagan emphasis on respecting the cycles of life—principles that remind us to act as caretakers rather than exploiters.

This commitment also resonates with New Universalism's emphasis on personal and communal responsibility. By being mindful of our ecological footprint, we recognize that our actions have tangible effects on the world around us, impacting the air, water, and soil, as well as all forms of life that depend on these shared resources. Living sustainably through small, mindful actions helps protect the delicate balance of ecosystems, reduce pollution, and conserve resources for future generations.

Reducing one's footprint becomes a form of spiritual practice that aligns with our values of humility, gratitude, and interconnectedness. It encourages a continuous awareness of how we can each act as stewards of the Earth, moving through life with the intention of leaving as little impact as possible. This intentional moderation fosters gratitude for what we have and respects the limitations of the planet, reminding us that every choice is a sacred interaction with the Earth.

In New Universalism, to reduce one's ecological footprint is to live in harmony with the natural world, honoring the spiritual duty of Earth Stewardship through daily choices that reflect respect, reverence, and responsibility.

Practical Steps for Sustainable Living:

Conservation and Energy Efficiency

In New Universalism, energy conservation and efficiency are seen as vital ways to embody Earth Stewardship and respect the delicate balance of nature. By reducing energy consumption and conserving resources, we honor the interconnectedness of all life, recognizing that our use of energy and resources has a direct impact on the Earth's ecosystems. This practice of conservation is not simply an environmental choice; it's a spiritual commitment to live thoughtfully, honoring the natural world by minimizing harm and preserving resources for the well-being of all.

Energy Efficiency and Conservation at Home

Simple steps in daily life can significantly reduce our energy consumption. For example, by using energy-efficient appliances and lighting, adjusting thermostats to avoid excessive heating and cooling, and turning off lights and electronics when not in use, we reduce our energy footprint. Small actions like unplugging devices and choosing energy-saving settings on appliances demonstrate mindfulness toward Earth's resources, reflecting a respect for the natural world and an acknowledgment of the impact of our daily habits.

Furthermore, choosing renewable energy sources where possible, such as solar or wind power, allows us to tap into energy that replenishes naturally, lessening reliance on fossil fuels. For many

New Universalists, investing in renewable energy, whether by installing solar panels or supporting community energy programs, becomes a way to actively participate in Earth's cyclical renewal and express gratitude for the gifts of nature.

Water Conservation

Water, the source of life, is one of our most sacred resources. Conservation practices such as limiting shower times, using low-flow fixtures, and repairing leaks reflect our reverence for water and the ecosystems it nourishes. Watering plants in the early morning or late evening conserves moisture, aligning our habits with nature's rhythms, while rainwater collection can support gardening needs without draining community resources.

Practicing water conservation is also a reminder of the interdependence of life. From the water that sustains our bodies to the rivers that nourish forests and wetlands, every drop connects us to the Earth's larger cycles. By being mindful of our water use, we recognize water as a sacred gift, shared among all living beings and vital to Earth's continued vitality.

Transportation Choices

In New Universalism, thoughtful transportation choices serve as another expression of our commitment to conservation. Walking, cycling, carpooling, or using public transportation reduces emissions, conserves fuel, and contributes to cleaner air and healthier communities. For those who drive, maintaining vehicles regularly to maximize fuel efficiency and opting for fuel-efficient vehicles are ways to make daily transportation choices that align with our values of responsibility and sustainability.

Embracing Minimalism in Energy Use

Living with energy consciousness promotes a lifestyle rooted in simplicity and respect for the Earth. Reducing consumption encourages us to reflect on our true needs, avoiding wasteful habits and cultivating gratitude for the resources we use. Embracing minimalism in energy consumption invites us to prioritize what is essential and let go of excess. This mindset allows us to live in harmony with Earth's rhythms, respecting its limits while fostering a sense of contentment that arises from mindful, sustainable living.

In each of these practices, conservation becomes a daily act of reverence, a way to live our spiritual commitment to Earth Stewardship. Through careful attention to energy and resource use, we cultivate a lifestyle that is responsible, respectful, and regenerative, embodying New Universalism's values in every interaction with the planet.

Mindful Consumption

In New Universalism, mindful consumption is seen as a reflection of gratitude, respect, and intentionality in our relationship with the Earth. Every choice we make about what to purchase, use, and consume impacts the environment, the economy, and our communities. Mindful consumption encourages us to consider the full cycle of our purchases—the resources needed to create them, the people involved in production, and their ultimate impact on the Earth. By aligning our consumption with these values, we make decisions that support ecological balance, fair labor practices, and resource conservation.

Thoughtful Purchasing: Choosing Quality over Quantity

Mindful consumption begins with the principle of quality over quantity. Instead of seeking more possessions, New Universalism encourages us to invest in well-made, durable items that align with our values. By choosing quality products, we reduce the need to replace items frequently, lessening waste and conserving resources. Each purchase becomes an intentional act, reflecting our desire to minimize environmental impact and live more simply. This approach fosters gratitude for the things we own, encouraging us to value each item and the resources used to create it.

For example, investing in well-crafted clothing or sturdy household items supports sustainable consumption and reduces the demand for quick, disposable products. This also aligns with environmental values by reducing landfill waste and energy consumption associated with mass production. Such choices invite us to take a slower, more reflective approach to consumption, grounded in an appreciation for well-made items and the hands that crafted them.

Supporting Ethical and Sustainable Brands

In New Universalism, choosing to support companies and brands committed to ethical practices reflects our dedication to social responsibility and respect for Earth's resources. Ethical companies prioritize fair wages, safe working conditions, and environmentally friendly production methods. Supporting these brands promotes a just economy that values the well-being of people and the planet, aligning our economic choices with New Universalist values of compassion and fairness.

When possible, we can seek out certifications like Fair Trade, Organic, or B-Corporation status, which indicate commitments to sustainability and ethical labor practices. By choosing products that honor the dignity of workers and reduce environmental harm, we participate in a cycle of respect and equity. Our purchases become a form of advocacy, supporting practices that align with our values and discouraging those that exploit or degrade.

Reducing Impulse Purchases and Practicing Minimalism

Practicing minimalism and reducing impulse buying are central to mindful consumption. In a culture that encourages constant acquisition, New Universalism invites us to pause and reflect before making purchases. By asking questions such as, "Do I truly need this?" and "How will this impact the environment?" we foster a deeper awareness of our consumption habits. This reflection helps us to distinguish between needs and wants, encouraging us to find contentment in simplicity.

This mindful approach reduces clutter, conserves resources, and allows us to focus on what truly brings meaning and joy. Minimalism is a powerful practice for living in alignment with Earth Stewardship, reducing unnecessary strain on the Earth's resources, and finding satisfaction in experiences, relationships, and personal growth rather than material possessions.

Embracing Secondhand and Recycled Options

Buying secondhand or recycled products extends the life cycle of items, keeping them out of landfills and reducing the demand for new resources. By choosing pre-owned clothing, furniture, or electronics, we participate in a circular economy that values reuse over disposal. This practice aligns with New Universalism's principle of resource conservation and is a tangible way to reduce our ecological footprint.

Incorporating secondhand shopping as a regular habit invites creativity and allows us to find unique, high-quality items that might otherwise be discarded. It also serves as a reminder of the abundance that already exists around us, encouraging gratitude for resources already in circulation. When possible, participating in local exchanges, thrift stores, or online marketplaces can foster a community-focused approach to consumption, where goods are shared and reused in ways that benefit both individuals and the Earth.

Supporting Local Artisans and Producers

When we support local artisans, farmers, and producers, we invest in our communities and reduce the environmental cost of transporting goods over long distances. By purchasing locally made products, we contribute to local economies, foster meaningful connections within our communities, and reduce carbon emissions associated with large-scale shipping.

Purchasing local, handcrafted goods reduces reliance on mass-produced items, supports small businesses, and contributes to a more sustainable, community-centered economy. In food choices, supporting farmers' markets or Community Supported Agriculture (CSA) programs provides access to fresh, seasonal produce while minimizing the environmental impact of large-scale agriculture and transportation.

Celebrating Mindful Consumption as a Sacred Act

Mindful consumption is, ultimately, an act of reverence and gratitude. By thoughtfully choosing what we bring into our lives, we honor the Earth's resources, respect the hands that made each item, and reduce waste. This practice aligns with New Universalism's call for intentional, ecologically responsible living, turning each choice into a sacred moment that affirms our commitment to a balanced, sustainable world. Through mindful consumption, we cultivate a lifestyle of care, simplicity, and purpose, living fully in alignment with our spiritual values.

Recycling and Waste Reduction

In New Universalism, recycling and waste reduction are expressions of our respect for Earth's resources and our commitment to leaving a lighter footprint on the planet. These practices go beyond mere convenience, reflecting a deep, intentional choice to honor the interconnected web of life by conserving resources, minimizing pollution, and contributing to a more sustainable future. Recycling and waste reduction foster mindfulness and discipline, encouraging us to live more consciously in alignment with the values of Earth Stewardship and social responsibility.

Recycling as an Act of Preservation and Renewal

Recycling is a direct way to preserve resources, reduce waste, and minimize our reliance on new materials. By recycling, we participate in a cycle of renewal that mirrors the regenerative processes of nature. In New Universalist thought, recycling can be viewed as a way to restore balance—transforming used items into new resources, much like nature's own cycles of decay and rebirth. This practice reminds us that every item we use has the potential for renewed purpose.

To embrace recycling as a spiritual act, we can begin by learning about local recycling guidelines and ensuring that we're recycling responsibly. Sorting recyclables accurately, cleaning containers, and avoiding contamination contribute to more efficient recycling processes, allowing materials to be reused effectively. As we engage in these steps, we honor our interconnectedness with nature and support systems that renew resources, echoing the natural cycles celebrated in New Universalism.

Reducing Single-Use Plastics and Disposable Items

One of the most impactful ways to reduce waste is to limit the use of single-use plastics and disposable products. Plastic waste is a major environmental issue, polluting oceans, harming wildlife, and contributing to microplastic contamination. By choosing reusable alternatives—such as cloth bags, stainless steel bottles, and glass containers—we actively reduce the demand for plastic and embrace a lifestyle that values sustainability over convenience.

In New Universalism, each decision to opt for a reusable product is a small but meaningful commitment to Earth Stewardship. This simple choice embodies mindfulness, prompting us to consider the long-term impact of our consumption. Every time we say "no" to a disposable item, we affirm our dedication to reducing waste and protecting the planet. Practicing this form of conscious consumption aligns with the New Universalist principles of moderation and intentionality, fostering a balanced approach to resource use.

Composting as a Cycle of Renewal

Composting is a powerful way to transform organic waste into nutrient-rich soil, mirroring the Earth's natural process of decomposition. By composting, we allow food scraps, yard waste, and other organic materials to break down naturally, creating a cycle of renewal that returns nutrients to the soil. Composting reduces the amount of waste sent to landfills, decreases greenhouse gas emissions, and supports healthy soil, making it a practical and spiritually aligned practice within New Universalism.

Starting a compost bin at home or participating in a local composting program invites us to engage with nature's regenerative processes. Composting can be seen as a form of gratitude, recognizing that what we no longer need can still offer value to the Earth. This practice also encourages us to reflect on the importance of all life cycles, even those of decay and rebirth. In New Universalism, composting is a reminder of our interconnectedness with nature, fostering a reverence for Earth's capacity to transform and sustain life.

Practicing "Reduce, Reuse, Recycle" Mindfully

The principle of "reduce, reuse, recycle" is a foundational guideline for waste reduction and sustainable living. In New Universalism, each component of this principle serves as a reminder to make conscious, respectful choices with our resources.

- **Reduce**: Reducing consumption is the first step in waste reduction. This can mean buying fewer items, choosing products with minimal packaging, and avoiding excess wherever possible. By focusing on reducing, we limit the demand on natural resources, and live in closer alignment with the principles of moderation and balance.
- **Reuse**: Reusing items extends their life cycle, reducing the need for new products and conserving resources. This could include repurposing containers, donating gently used items, or finding creative ways to reuse everyday objects. The practice of reusing embodies a New Universalist ethic of resourcefulness, helping us view each item as valuable and capable of multiple uses.
- **Recycle**: Recycling is the final step, capturing materials that can no longer be used in their original form but can be transformed into new products. By recycling effectively, we participate in the cycles of renewal that are central to Earth's natural processes, demonstrating a commitment to responsible resource use.

Practicing Waste Reduction as an Ongoing Journey

Waste reduction is not an all-or-nothing endeavor but an ongoing journey that requires adaptation, commitment, and self-reflection. As we incorporate recycling, composting, and mindful consumption into our lives, we may encounter challenges or moments of convenience that tempt us to revert to less sustainable habits. New Universalism encourages us to approach this journey with patience, recognizing that every step we take toward waste reduction is valuable.

Reflecting on our waste reduction practices can become a form of spiritual introspection, inviting us to evaluate our habits, celebrate our progress, and set new goals. Each effort to reduce waste strengthens our relationship with the Earth, deepens our gratitude for its resources, and aligns us more fully with New Universalism's Earth Stewardship values.

Through recycling, reducing single-use items, composting, and the "reduce, reuse, recycle" principle, we cultivate a lifestyle that honors the Earth's resources and aligns with New Universalism's call to live mindfully, respectfully, and sustainably. In each small step, we affirm our commitment to an interconnected world, knowing that our actions contribute to a healthier planet for present and future generations.

Developing Personal and Community Sustainability Practices

New Universalism encourages each individual to see sustainable living as both a personal and communal commitment, where small, consistent actions contribute to meaningful change. Developing a sustainability practice involves setting intentional goals for reducing environmental impact in our daily lives and joining with others to expand these efforts within the broader community. This journey is an expression of Earth Stewardship—a commitment to honor the planet through mindful and responsible action.

Personal Sustainability Goals: Small Steps for Lasting Impact

Personal sustainability practices start with setting achievable, mindful goals that align with one's values and capacity. Whether it's reducing plastic use, conserving water, or choosing more eco-friendly transportation, these goals allow us to build an intentional lifestyle that respects Earth's resources. For example:

- **Reducing Plastic Use**: Avoiding single-use plastics by carrying reusable bags, bottles, and containers can significantly lower the amount of waste entering our ecosystems. In New Universalist practice, reducing waste is a mindful act of Earth Stewardship, respecting the Earth by choosing sustainable alternatives.
- **Conserving Water**: By taking steps like shorter showers, fixing leaks, and using water-saving devices, we contribute to water preservation, recognizing it as a precious and shared resource. In drought-prone or water-scarce regions, this practice becomes even more vital, honoring the Earth and our shared responsibility to future generations.

- **Supporting Conservation Initiatives**: Volunteering for or supporting conservation organizations allows us to extend our efforts beyond the home, directly contributing to the protection of natural habitats, wildlife, and resources.

Establishing personal sustainability goals provides a foundation for deeper, sustained commitment. These steps serve as an invitation to live in harmony with the Earth, fostering a sense of fulfillment through actions that align with New Universalist values.

Community Initiatives: Building Collective Power

New Universalism views community-based sustainability efforts as a powerful way to amplify positive environmental impact. Working together toward common goals brings people into a shared purpose, where collective action can address larger environmental challenges. Community initiatives may include:

- **Environmental Clean-Ups**: Organizing clean-up events for local parks, rivers, or beaches not only beautifies these spaces but also protects ecosystems from pollution. Community members can work side-by-side, deepening our bonds as we share in the stewardship of natural spaces.
- **Local Gardening Efforts**: Urban gardens, community plots, and reforestation projects bring life back to local areas and provide fresh produce, flowers, and plants that nurture both the soil and the soul. These spaces serve as living expressions of Earth Stewardship, offering nourishment while revitalizing biodiversity.
- **Green Energy Projects**: Community efforts to install solar panels, wind energy, or other renewable energy sources can support a shift toward sustainable energy. Community members might join together in cooperatives, making green energy more accessible and reducing reliance on non-renewable resources.

By engaging in these collective efforts, communities not only reduce environmental impact but also nurture a sense of solidarity. Community sustainability projects embody New Universalist principles by creating spaces for cooperation, respect, and shared responsibility, reflecting the interconnectedness of all life.

Reflecting on the Power of Small, Consistent Actions

New Universalism teaches that profound change is often the result of small, consistent actions carried out by many. Each act of mindfulness, each moment spent in intentional choice, builds toward a lifestyle that respects the Earth and all its inhabitants. When personal commitment to sustainability combines with community efforts, these actions can lead to transformative change, fostering resilient ecosystems and thriving communities.

Practicing sustainability within the framework of New Universalism offers a way to deepen our spiritual relationship with the Earth. Through this lens, every choice made with intention—whether conserving resources, reducing waste, or participating in community efforts—becomes an act of reverence. Together, personal and community sustainability practices remind us that each step taken in respect for the planet contributes to a legacy of harmony, resilience, and honor for generations to come.

8

Practicing Earth-Based Worship

Introduction to Community-Based Earth Worship

In New Universalism, Earth-based worship is an act of sacred devotion, a recognition of our inherent connection to the living planet and the cosmos that birthed us. Community-based Earth worship is more than a gathering; it is a collective honoring of the cycles of nature and an expression of gratitude for the abundant life it sustains. Through these shared practices, New Universalism celebrates the Earth as sacred, affirming the belief that the natural world is not only our home but an integral part of our spiritual being.

Rooted in a theology that views all elements of the Earth—its rivers, mountains, forests, and skies—as infused with divine essence, communal Earth-based worship in New Universalism connects participants to these living forces. Worship is not limited to the observation of nature but actively involves reverence for the seasonal shifts, lunar cycles, and even weather patterns, all seen as expressions of a larger cosmic rhythm. By coming together in worship that honors these cycles, New Universalists deepen our understanding of life's interconnectedness and our responsibility to protect and care for the planet.

Informed by Indigenous and Pagan wisdom, these gatherings are an opportunity to learn from and honor traditions that recognize the Earth as a living entity deserving of respect and care. In this space, New Universalists come together to participate in ceremonies that remind us of our role as stewards of the Earth. This sense of collective reverence extends beyond environmental concern, embodying a deeply spiritual commitment to uphold Earth's balance as both a sacred duty and a path to spiritual enlightenment.

Through Earth-based worship, New Universalists cultivate a shared sense of purpose that transcends individual concerns. We engage in rituals that honor Earth's gifts, from simple offerings of gratitude to the land, to rituals invoking the healing of damaged ecosystems, to sacred rites that incorporate elements of Earth's natural medicines, like cannabis, for healing and connection. Each ritual and act of worship serves as a reminder that human existence is inextricably linked to the health and vitality of the Earth.

In coming together as a community to worship, New Universalists not only foster a sense of unity with each other but also with the vast web of life that sustains us. Earth-based worship becomes a sacred practice through which the collective honors the divine mystery of nature, expressing reverence for the cycles of growth, decay, and rebirth that govern all living things. This communal worship reinforces the theology of New Universalism, reminding all that to care for Earth is to care for oneself, and to honor the cycles of nature is to honor the sacredness of existence itself.

New Universalist Earth-Based Worship

In New Universalism, Earth-based worship practices are not merely rituals; they are central expressions of our theology and an embodiment of our sacred relationship with the Earth and the cosmos. Drawing inspiration from Indigenous and Pagan wisdom, these practices provide a framework for honoring natural cycles, invoking the energies of the elements, and connecting with the spirits that inhabit the land. Through these rituals, New Universalists cultivate a faith rooted in Earth reverence and cosmic interconnectedness, guided by our foundational beliefs in stewardship, respect for all life, and reciprocal relationships with the planet.

Seasonal Celebrations: Embracing the Wheel of the Year as Sacred Worship

In New Universalism, the natural cycles of the Earth are honored through sacred observances aligned with the Wheel of the Year, each marking shifts in the Earth's energies and rhythms. These seasonal celebrations—Winter Solstice, Spring Equinox, Summer Solstice, Autumn Equinox, and the cross-quarter festivals—are foundational in our Earth-based worship. Each gathering serves as a communal act of reverence and an opportunity for spiritual renewal in alignment with the natural world.

During the Winter Solstice, for example, New Universalists gather to honor the return of light on the longest night of the year. This observance is both a celebration and a ritual of hope and renewal, inviting participants to reflect on the light within and our role in illuminating the world. Symbolic acts, such as lighting candles and sharing food, bring warmth and unity to the community, embodying the belief that each person contributes to the light that sustains us.

In contrast, the Summer Solstice is a time of gratitude and celebration, acknowledging the abundance of life and the strength of the sun. New Universalists engage in outdoor gatherings, exchanging blessings, feasting, and participating in nature-based rituals to honor the Earth's bounty. These observances teach us to honor both abundance and humility, recognizing our place within a living ecosystem that provides for all.

By following the Wheel of the Year, New Universalists align our spiritual practices with the Earth's rhythms, cultivating patience, resilience, and a sense of connection with all living beings. Each celebration is an invitation to reaffirm our commitment to Earth stewardship, deepening our bond with the cycles that sustain life.

Reverence for the Elements: Sacred Forces in New Universalist Worship

The elements—Earth, Water, Fire, and Air—are honored as sacred manifestations of the divine, each representing essential qualities that sustain both physical and spiritual life. In New Universalist worship, these elements are invoked not only for their practical benefits but for their spiritual significance, connecting us to the energies that flow through all life. This practice reflects our belief in the interdependence of all things and the need for harmonious relationships between humans and the natural world.

For instance, Earth is honored for its stability and grounding, reminding us of our responsibility to protect the physical world we inhabit. Water, as a symbol of healing and emotional depth, teaches us about compassion and adaptability. Fire represents transformation and vitality, encouraging us to bring passion and purpose to our lives, while Air, as a force of wisdom and communication, inspires us to seek understanding and unity.

During Earth-based rituals, New Universalists invoke each element through specific acts or offerings. To honor Earth, we may offer a handful of soil or stones; to invite Water, a bowl of fresh water will be placed on the altar. Fire can be represented by a candle, while incense or feathers can symbolize Air. These elements become focal points of worship, reminding us of the interconnected web of existence that binds us to the planet and each other. Invoking the elements grounds our rituals in a sense of sacred reciprocity, reflecting the theology of New Universalism by acknowledging the Earth as a dynamic, life-giving force.

Invoking Nature Spirits and Guardians: Honoring the Sacred Presence in Nature

In New Universalism, the Earth is seen as alive with spirits, energies, and guardians who inhabit the natural world. Drawing from Indigenous and Pagan influences, New Universalists engage in practices that acknowledge these beings, recognizing them as integral to the ecosystems we live within. Invoking nature spirits or land guardians is a form of reverence and respect, a way of asking permission to exist within their space and inviting their presence into our worship.

Before beginning a communal ceremony or embarking on a nature walk, a New Universalist gathering opens with an invocation, asking for the blessings and protection of the spirits of the land. This can be as simple as a spoken prayer of gratitude or as elaborate as an offering left at the base of a tree or near a body of water. Offerings may include small tokens such as tobacco, seeds, or fresh flowers, representing a gesture of reciprocity and respect for the beings who share the land with us.

This practice emphasizes the New Universalist belief in interconnectedness and reciprocity. By acknowledging nature spirits and guardians, we affirm our role as respectful visitors and co-inhabitants of the Earth, aware that the world around us is filled with life that deserves honor and consideration. In doing so, we deepen our connection to the divine presence in nature, treating the Earth not merely as a setting but as a sacred partner in our spiritual journey.

Theology of Earth Reverence and Cosmic Interconnectedness

Each of these Earth-based worship practices forms a core aspect of New Universalist theology, inviting us to see ourselves as part of a cosmic web of life, bound by mutual respect and shared purpose. By celebrating seasonal cycles, honoring the elements, and invoking nature spirits, New Universalists cultivate a faith that reveres the Earth as an embodiment of the divine. These practices are not isolated rituals but integral expressions of New Universalism's theology of interconnectedness, which calls us to live in harmony with all beings.

Earth-based worship is, therefore, an act of cosmic unity. By recognizing the sacredness of the Earth and all its inhabitants, New Universalists affirm our commitment to a worldview that honors life in all forms. These rituals ground us in the knowledge that we are participants in a vast, intricate ecosystem, entrusted with the duty of stewardship and the joy of communion. Through Earth-based worship, we celebrate our role within the natural world and strengthen our dedication to nurturing and protecting the life we share.

Cannabis as a Sacred Rite in Earth-Based Worship

In New Universalism, cannabis is embraced as a sacred gift from the Earth—a plant that serves as a bridge between the physical and spiritual realms, offering healing, insight, and a profound connection to the divine. Cannabis, revered for its unique ability to facilitate a heightened state of spiritual and personal awareness, plays a significant role in Earth-based worship, where it is used both individually and communally to deepen spiritual practices. Its sacred nature requires a mindful approach, grounded in reverence, intentionality, and respect for the plant as a powerful spiritual ally.

Cannabis as a Tool for Spiritual Elevation, Healing, and Connection

Cannabis holds a dual role in New Universalist practice as both a healing medicine and a tool for spiritual elevation. Traditionally used across various cultures and indigenous practices, cannabis is respected in New Universalism for its capacity to ease physical discomfort, calm the mind, and open pathways to spiritual exploration. For those in our community, it serves as a natural aid that enhances meditation, prayer, and rituals aimed at self-reflection, healing, and transcendence.

When used as part of spiritual practice, cannabis can help practitioners connect with deeper layers of consciousness, providing insights into personal challenges, relationships, or paths forward. It can also facilitate a sense of unity, allowing individuals to feel more connected to the Earth, the cosmos, and each other. In communal worship, cannabis is used to cultivate a collective sense of peace, openness, and harmony, helping participants enter a shared spiritual space where the boundaries between individuals dissolve, replaced by a feeling of unity and interconnectedness.

Cannabis is seen as a sacred entity in New Universalism not only for its effects but for its role as a gift from Earth. In this light, the plant is viewed as a living entity, one that embodies the Earth's generosity and invites us into a relationship of gratitude and respect. It is treated with the same reverence we would afford any other element of nature, as a spirit in its own right with the power to heal, guide, and connect.

Guidelines for Mindful Use in Worship

As cannabis holds a sacred role in New Universalist theology, its use in worship is approached with great care. When incorporating cannabis into Earth-based worship, we are encouraged to follow a mindful process that aligns with New Universalist principles, honoring the plant as a tool for sacred connection and reflection rather than as a means of escapism or overindulgence.

Guidelines for cannabis use in Earth-based worship include:

1. **Intention Setting:** Before consuming cannabis, we are encouraged to set clear spiritual intentions. Whether seeking clarity, healing, or connection, articulating these intentions frames the experience as a sacred ritual, grounding the mind and heart in purpose. We should begin with a moment of gratitude for the plant itself, acknowledging its role as a healing ally.

2. **Moderation and Respect:** In alignment with New Universalism's principles of balance and moderation, the use of cannabis is approached in a way that respects the plant's potency. We are encouraged to use small, thoughtful amounts that allow for an enhanced experience without overwhelming the senses. This balanced approach honors both the plant and the practitioner's commitment to remaining present, clear-minded, and connected to the Earth.

3. **Personal and Communal Practice:** Cannabis can be incorporated into both personal and communal practices. In personal Earth-based worship, we might integrate cannabis into meditation, nature walks, or rituals, using it as a tool for introspection and connection to the natural world. Communally, it can be included in specific ceremonial gatherings, where participants engage in shared rituals, such as meditative breathing, chanting, or reflection circles, allowing cannabis to foster a sense of shared openness and communion.

4. **Reflection and Integration:** After a cannabis-enhanced spiritual experience, we are encouraged to spend time reflecting on any insights or feelings that emerged, allowing for meaningful integration. Reflective practices, such as journaling, prayer, or quiet time in nature, help ground the experience and reinforce its teachings. Integrating these insights into

everyday life aligns with New Universalist teachings, where the sacred is found not only in worship but in the lived values of daily life.

Cannabis in the Context of Earth-Centered Worship Ceremonies

In New Universalist Earth-centered worship ceremonies, cannabis is used to honor its ancient role in spiritual practices across cultures. When gathered for seasonal celebrations, such as the solstices or equinoxes, or during rites of passage, cannabis may be incorporated into rituals as an offering to the Earth and as a communal practice that unites participants. In these contexts, cannabis serves as both a spiritual tool and a sacred plant to be shared, respected, and acknowledged for its healing powers.

For example, in a Winter Solstice gathering, cannabis might be offered in a ceremonial manner, with a small portion blessed and shared in gratitude for its role in elevating consciousness. This communal sharing fosters a collective atmosphere of peace and unity, creating a sacred space where all participants feel connected to one another and the natural world. During individual moments, participants may find that cannabis deepens their connection to the silence and introspection the season invites, supporting an inner journey of self-awareness and renewal.

In New Universalism, cannabis is not merely a tool but a partner in spiritual practice, one that teaches humility, openness, and respect for the Earth's gifts. By honoring its role within Earth-based worship, New Universalists affirm our commitment to sacred reciprocity, recognizing the gifts of the Earth and responding with gratitude, mindfulness, and a commitment to healing. This relationship reflects a core tenet of our theology: that spiritual connection is cultivated through a respectful, intentional relationship with the Earth and all her offerings.

Community Earth-Based Worship Practices

In New Universalism, community Earth-based worship practices create a shared space for reverence, celebration, and unity. These communal practices are central to the faith, grounding congregants in the cycles of nature and nurturing a collective spirit of stewardship and gratitude. By coming together for seasonal festivals, full-moon gatherings, and weekly sermons, the New Universalist community honors the Earth and its rhythms, reconnecting to the natural world and reinforcing the bond between individuals, community, and the cosmos. These gatherings incorporate music, dance, and storytelling as integral parts of worship, reflecting New Universalism's emphasis on creativity, unity, and sacred expression.

Seasonal Festival Celebrations

The Wheel of the Year provides a sacred structure for New Universalist communities to gather, celebrate, and reflect on the cycles of life and nature. Each of the ten seasonal festivals—ranging from the Winter Solstice to Earth Day and the Autumn Equinox—marks a significant moment in the Earth's annual journey, embodying unique themes and energies. Communal practices for each festival embrace the natural elements and the symbolism associated with the season, bringing the community together to honor Earth's cycles.

For example, during the **Spring Equinox**—a time of balance and renewal—New Universalists gather for rituals of planting, symbolizing new growth and the community's commitment to nurturing life. Rituals may include blessing seeds, planting trees, or creating shared gardens, with participants offering prayers for growth, resilience, and harmony with the Earth. The **Autumn Equinox**, by contrast, celebrates gratitude and harvest, where the community might come together for a shared feast of locally harvested foods. Participants may take turns expressing gratitude for the Earth's abundance and reflecting on the balance between giving and receiving, reinforcing the New Universalist principle of reciprocity.

During each festival, altars adorned with seasonal symbols, such as flowers, fruits, stones, or leaves, serve as focal points for collective worship. Members of the congregation may bring offerings of natural items to place on the altar, symbolizing their connection to the Earth and their shared responsibility for its care. Seasonal festivals thus become immersive experiences of Earth reverence, grounding New Universalist values of unity, gratitude, and interconnectedness in tangible, sacred rituals.

New and Full Moon Gatherings

In New Universalism, the lunar cycle offers sacred moments for reflection and worship. New Moon and Full Moon gatherings bring congregants together to honor the Earth, moon, and cosmos, aligning with the themes each phase represents. Each gathering serves as a powerful reminder of the rhythms that guide both the natural world and our inner lives.

New Moon Gatherings are dedicated to gratitude, intention-setting, and invoking support from natural spirits. As the New Moon marks a time of fresh beginnings, we gather to express thanks for the Earth's ongoing support and to set intentions for the coming cycle. During these gatherings, participants may invoke land spirits, deities, or the moon itself to aid our personal or communal goals. A simple ritual may include lighting candles or incense and silently offering intentions, asking for guidance and strength from the Earth and cosmic forces.

Full Moon Gatherings center around gratitude, release, and drawing wisdom from the Earth and cosmos. The Full Moon represents culmination and insight, making it an ideal time to reflect on what is ready to be released. We may perform rituals that involve writing down burdens or old patterns we wish to let go of, then ceremoniously releasing these by offering them to the Earth or water. We are encouraged to draw on the strength of the moon's light, calling upon its energies to guide us through transition, healing, and renewal. Like New Moon gatherings, Full Moon observances may also include invocations of natural or celestial spirits, enhancing the sacredness of the practice.

Both New and Full Moon gatherings encourage a shared rhythm of worship, grounding congregants in a connection to Earth's cycles and offering moments of reflection, release, and renewal.

Weekly Earth-Based Worship in the New Universalist Church

Weekly services within the New Universalist Church integrate Earth-based worship with traditional New Universalist liturgy, creating a holistic experience that embodies reverence for the Earth, gratitude, and interconnectedness. In these gatherings, ministers lead congregants through prayers, reflections, and rituals that honor the Earth and foster a sense of communal care and responsibility.

A central feature of weekly services is the **Communion of Elements**, where congregants receive a small offering of earth (such as soil or stones), water, air (symbolized through incense or aromatic herbs), and fire (a candle or small flame). This act embodies the interconnectedness of all life and reinforces each person's commitment to honoring the Earth's resources. This ritual aligns with the broader Communion practice in New Universalism, in which we partake in bread and juice as symbols of spiritual nourishment and unity. Communion is a time for us to reflect on our relationship with the Earth, recognizing the sacredness of its gifts.

Inclusivity is a core tenet of New Universalist practice, and weekly gatherings ensure that all members, regardless of ability or disability, can participate fully in Earth-based worship. Dance circles, for instance, may include modifications, allowing individuals with different abilities to join in ways that feel comfortable and meaningful to them. The inclusion of seated dance options or guided hand movements ensures that every member has a place in the shared worship experience, fostering a sense of unity and accessibility within the congregation.

Music, Dance, and Storytelling in Earth-Based Worship

Music, dance, and storytelling enrich communal Earth-based worship, inviting congregants to express reverence for the natural world through creativity and shared sacred experience. These practices draw inspiration from Indigenous, Pagan, and other Earth-centered traditions, where songs, movement, and stories are woven into rituals as ways to honor nature and celebrate life.

Music:

Drumming, singing, and chanting are integral to New Universalist worship. These elements bring congregants together in rhythm, creating a shared heartbeat that resonates with the Earth's pulse. Songs of gratitude and praise for nature's beauty and resilience are common, as they foster an atmosphere of reverence. Music is not only a form of expression but an invocation, a call to the natural and spiritual forces that New Universalists hold sacred.

Dance:

Dance serves as an embodiment of joy, reverence, and connection. Circle dances are a particularly meaningful form of movement in New Universalism, symbolizing the cycles of nature and the unity of all life. In these dances, congregants hold hands and move in sync, embodying a rhythm that reflects life's cyclical patterns. Modified dance practices, such as seated movements, ensure accessibility for all, underscoring New Universalism's commitment to inclusivity. Through dance, each participant experiences a physical, spiritual, and communal bond, reinforcing the New Universalist ideals of harmony and interconnectedness.

Storytelling:

Storytelling remains a cherished practice, enabling congregants to pass down spiritual wisdom, cultural heritage, and values of Earth stewardship. During gatherings, community members may share stories of ancestors, creation myths, or tales of Earth's resilience, creating a tapestry of shared meaning and reinforcing the values central to New Universalism. Through storytelling, the community connects with its collective history and learns to see itself as part of the Earth's larger narrative. Each story brings with it lessons of respect, reciprocity, and renewal, fostering a shared reverence for the planet and its inhabitants.

The Power of Communal Earth-Based Worship in New Universalism

Communal Earth-based worship in New Universalism offers transformative experiences that foster unity, respect, and a deep-rooted commitment to Earth stewardship. Seasonal festivals, lunar observances, and weekly services each serve as invitations to engage meaningfully with the natural world, strengthening participants' connection to both Earth and community. Through collective acts of reverence, New Universalists reaffirm our responsibility to the planet, nurturing a shared purpose that goes beyond the individual.

The use of music, dance, and storytelling in these gatherings adds depth and vibrancy, creating a worship experience that is as dynamic as it is sacred. Each element—whether it's the beat of a drum, the sway of a dance, or the words of an ancient tale—reinforces the communal values of interconnectedness, gratitude, and respect for life. Through these practices, New Universalists find a sense of belonging within the rhythms of nature and the shared journey of our community.

Ultimately, these gatherings remind us that Earth stewardship is not merely a responsibility but a sacred act of devotion. By coming together in Earth-based worship, New Universalists renew our dedication to protecting and honoring the planet, finding strength in our shared commitment and wisdom in the natural cycles that guide us. These communal practices are, at their core, a celebration of life—a testament to the enduring connection between humanity, the Earth, and the cosmos.

Individual Earth-Based Worship Practices

In New Universalism, individual Earth-based worship practices are essential avenues for personal spiritual growth and connection. Through practices like sunrise and sunset meditations, nature walks with blessings, and the creation of personal altars, we deepen our relationship with the Earth and the cosmos. These practices provide sacred moments to honor the natural world, acknowledge the rhythms of the seasons, and strengthen one's inner connection to the principles of New Universalism. The following guidance explores ways to incorporate Earth-based worship into daily life, emphasizing practices that foster reverence, gratitude, and awareness of our place in the larger web of life.

Sunrise and Sunset Meditations

The natural transitions of sunrise and sunset offer powerful opportunities for personal worship. Sunrise marks the renewal of light, inviting gratitude for the day ahead, while sunset embodies the quieting energy of closure and introspection. In New Universalist practice, these times are revered as sacred, symbolizing both beginnings and endings within the cycle of life.

We may incorporate simple meditations during these times to honor the Earth's rhythms and connect with our own spiritual journey. For example, at sunrise, one might sit outdoors or by an open window, facing east, and take a few moments of silent meditation, focusing on breathing in the fresh energy of the morning light. This practice can be accompanied by a spoken or silent prayer of gratitude for the new day and for the energy and strength to fulfill one's purpose.

At sunset, we might face west, reflecting on the events of the day with appreciation and release. A simple prayer of thanks for the lessons learned or a gentle acknowledgment of personal growth aligns with the New Universalist value of intentional reflection. These meditations, practiced with consistency, help foster an awareness of one's connection to the cycles of the Earth, bringing a sense of peace, rhythm, and order to daily life.

Nature Walks with Prayers or Blessings

Nature walks serve as both a grounding practice and a form of moving meditation, connecting us with the living world around us. During these walks, we can attune to the natural environment, observing the elements, plants, animals, and weather with reverence. Walking in nature allows one to practice mindful presence, absorbing the beauty, resilience, and diversity of the Earth.

To enhance these walks as Earth-based worship, we might incorporate simple prayers or blessings for the Earth and its beings. For example, upon encountering a particularly striking tree, one might offer a quiet blessing: "I honor your strength and beauty, and I thank you for the life you bring." If by a river or stream, one might pause to acknowledge the water's journey and offer thanks for its essential role in life. These blessings, though small, cultivate a respectful awareness of each being's role in the ecosystem and deepen our sense of connection to all life.

New Universalists are encouraged to carry small offerings, such as a few seeds or flowers, to leave as tokens of gratitude along the path. In leaving an offering, we symbolize a reciprocal relationship with the Earth, echoing the Indigenous and Pagan principles of giving back. These nature walks become a spiritual act, reaffirming New Universalism's core beliefs in interconnectedness, respect, and Earth stewardship.

Altar Creation with Natural, Spiritual, and Ancestral Items

Creating a personal altar is a foundational Earth-based worship practice, serving as a visual and spiritual focal point for New Universalist beliefs. Altars are personal spaces that reflect an individual's relationship with the Earth, the cosmos, and our own spiritual journey. Typically, altars include natural elements, spiritual items, and ancestral objects, all chosen to represent the connection between oneself, one's lineage, and the Earth.

Natural items, such as stones, shells, flowers, or branches, ground the altar in the natural world and serve as reminders of the beauty and diversity of life. Spiritual items, such as candles, crystals, or images, represent our connection to the cosmic forces and universal energy, fostering a sense of unity with the universe. Ancestral items, like photographs or small heirlooms, honor one's lineage, providing a bridge between the past and present and reinforcing the New Universalist value of filial piety.

We are encouraged to refresh our altars seasonally, aligning with the Earth's cycles and the festivals of the Wheel of the Year. For example, during the autumn season, the altar might include leaves, acorns, or symbols of harvest, reminding us of the themes of gratitude and preparation for rest. At the Winter Solstice, evergreen branches or symbols of renewal might be added, representing the promise of light and the eternal cycle of growth.

Through the mindful arrangement of each item, the altar becomes a place of prayer, meditation, and spiritual reflection. We are invited to visit our altar daily, using it as a place to light candles, reflect on our intentions, or engage in prayer and meditation. This daily practice fosters a steady connection to one's spirituality, reinforcing the values of gratitude, reverence, and personal connection with the Earth.

Reflection on the Spiritual Benefits of Individual Earth-Based Practices

Individual Earth-based worship practices offer pathways for personal healing, self-awareness, and deepening one's understanding of the Earth as sacred. These practices create space for us to honor our personal connection to the natural world and reflect on our place within it. By regularly engaging in these acts of reverence, we embody the principles of New Universalism, nurturing an ongoing relationship with the Earth and cosmos.

These practices are not merely routines; they are acts of spiritual significance that ground us in our faith. Through sunrise and sunset meditations, one is reminded of the cyclical nature of life and gains perspective on daily experiences. Nature walks with blessings enhance one's awareness of the interconnectedness of all beings, reinforcing a sense of compassion and gratitude. Altar creation provides a tangible expression of one's devotion, creating a sacred space that continually invites reflection, reverence, and renewal.

These Earth-based worship practices affirm the New Universalist commitment to seeing the divine in the natural world, honoring life's cycles, and fostering a mindful, grateful existence. We are encouraged to carry these values into our daily lives, finding small ways to honor the Earth, celebrate life's rhythms, and remain rooted in the sacred connection that unites all beings. Through these individual acts, each of us strengthens our role in the New Universalist community, contributing to a collective spirit of Earth reverence, stewardship, and unity.

Personal and Communal Practices

9

⁓

Daily Practices for Spiritual and Personal Growth

Meditation and Mindfulness in New Universalism

Meditation and mindfulness are central to the spiritual practices of New Universalism, offering pathways to self-awareness, spiritual connection, and grounding. These practices serve as bridges between the physical and spiritual realms, fostering harmony within oneself and with the larger interconnected web of life. They emphasize presence, clarity, and balance, allowing us to align our inner experience with the sacred rhythms of the Earth and the cosmos.

At its heart, mindfulness in New Universalism is not merely about observing the present moment but engaging with it deeply and meaningfully. It is a practice of honoring the flow of life and the beauty of existence, recognizing each breath, thought, and interaction as sacred. Meditation, meanwhile, is a tool for reflection and renewal—a space where we can center ourselves, explore inner truths, and cultivate spiritual growth.

These practices are deeply intertwined with New Universalist theology, which prioritizes reason, compassion, and reverence for the Earth. By pausing to breathe, observe, and connect, we embody the core values of New Universalism: Earth Stewardship, Social Responsibility, Filial Piety, and Reasoned Inquiry. Meditation and mindfulness become acts of both personal growth and communal responsibility, fostering inner harmony that radiates outward into compassionate action and environmental care.

Whether through quiet moments of breath awareness, grounding visualizations, or mindful walks in nature, these practices draw attention to the interconnectedness of all things. They encourage us to find stillness amid life's chaos and to carry the insights gained into our daily lives, relationships, and communities.

From breath-focused practices to Earth-based grounding meditations and seasonal reflections, each method offers a unique way to deepen one's spiritual journey. Together, these practices reinforce the idea that mindfulness is both a personal and collective act, nurturing the individual while contributing to the well-being of the broader world.

Mindfulness Techniques for Daily Life

Mindfulness is the art of bringing full attention to the present moment, a practice that bridges the physical and spiritual. In New Universalism, mindfulness is not only a method of finding inner peace but also a profound act of connection—to oneself, to others, and to the Earth. By cultivating presence, we honor the universal truths of interconnectedness, balance, and gratitude.

As we journey through these mindfulness techniques, we will explore how they are more than mere practices; they are spiritual disciplines aligned with New Universalist theology. Each breath, each observation, and each moment of awareness becomes a sacred act of worship, reinforcing our bond with the cosmos and grounding us in the rhythms of the natural world.

Breath Awareness: The Sacred Rhythm of Life

The breath is one of the simplest yet most profound connections between the body, spirit, and the Earth. In New Universalism, breathing is seen as an act of reciprocity with the natural world. As we inhale, we receive life from the trees, the air, and the Earth itself. As we exhale, we give back, a rhythmic expression of gratitude and communion with the interconnected web of existence.

To practice breath awareness is to step into this sacred rhythm. Begin by finding a quiet place where you can sit comfortably. Close your eyes and take a deep, conscious breath, feeling the air as it fills your lungs and nourishes your body. Notice the sensations—how the breath cools as it enters your nostrils and warms as it leaves. Pay attention to the gentle rise and fall of your chest, the rhythm of life flowing through you.

This practice is more than relaxation; it is an act of spiritual alignment. Each breath is a reminder of our dependence on the Earth's cycles and our duty to protect them. Inhale with the awareness that the air is a gift sustained by the trees and ecosystems around you. Exhale with a silent intention of gratitude and a prayer for the well-being of all living things.

In New Universalism, this act of breathing connects us to the theological pillar of **Earth Stewardship**. By becoming mindful of our breath, we are reminded of the sacred responsibility to care for the planet, which sustains not only us but all forms of life. Breath awareness also reflects the principle of **Reasoned Inquiry**, as it encourages a mindful exploration of the present moment, fostering clarity and insight.

As you deepen this practice, let it become a daily ritual. Perhaps you begin your mornings with a few moments of conscious breathing, aligning yourself with the day ahead. Or, in moments of stress, return to your breath as a grounding force, a way to reconnect with your inner stillness and the vastness of the cosmos.

In the simple act of breathing, we discover profound spiritual truth: life is a shared experience, and each breath is a thread in the tapestry of universal connection. With each inhale and exhale, we honor this truth, embodying the values of New Universalism in our daily lives.

Body Scan: Anchoring the Spirit in the Vessel of the Earth

The body is a temple of life, crafted by the same forces that shape mountains, rivers, and stars. In New Universalism, the body is viewed as a sacred vessel, a microcosm of the Earth itself. Through the practice of the **Body Scan**, we nurture a deeper awareness of our physical form while recognizing its intrinsic connection to the greater cosmos.

The Body Scan invites us to honor the Earth's rhythms within our own being. Begin by lying down or sitting comfortably in a quiet space. Close your eyes, take a few deep breaths allowing your awareness to settle into the present moment. Imagine your body as a map of sacred terrain, each part a reflection of the natural world.

Starting at the crown of your head, gently bring your attention to each part of your body, moving slowly downward. Notice the sensations in your scalp, your forehead, and your eyes. Is there tension, warmth, or ease? Simply observe without judgment. As you move through your neck, shoulders, arms, and hands, acknowledge each area as integral to your existence, much like every tree, river, and cloud contributes to the Earth's wholeness.

When you reach your heart, pause to feel the rhythm of its beating. This pulse is a reminder of life's interconnected flow, echoing the cycles of the moon, the tides, and the seasons. Let this awareness fill you with gratitude—for the body that carries you and for the Earth that sustains you.

As you continue the scan, moving through your torso, hips, legs, and feet, envision each part rooting deeper into the Earth. Imagine your feet connecting with soil, anchoring you to the ground below, drawing stability and strength. In this act of mindful attention, you align yourself with the universal rhythm of nature, grounding your spirit within the vessel of your body.

The Body Scan is a sacred act of **Filial Piety**, a way of honoring the gift of life that flows from the Earth and through our ancestors. By tending to our bodies, we acknowledge the sacrifices and efforts of those who came before us and the interconnected lineage of life.

This practice also reflects the principle of **Balance and Moderation**, urging us to care for our physical form without excess or neglect. Just as we must tend to the Earth with care, ensuring its health for future generations, so too must we nurture the body to fulfill its sacred purpose as a vessel of connection and action.

Consider integrating the Body Scan into your evening routine, allowing it to guide you into restful sleep. Or, use it as a midday pause to reconnect with your physical self during moments of stress or fatigue. For those in communal settings, the Body Scan can also be adapted into group meditations, fostering shared awareness and grounding.

Through this practice, we reaffirm our place within the great web of life, where the body is not separate from the Earth but a reflection of its beauty and resilience. Each moment spent honoring the body is a moment spent honoring the sacredness of existence.

Mindful Observation in Nature: Witnessing the Earth's Sacred Story

In New Universalism, nature is a living scripture, its every leaf, stream, and breeze a verse in the eternal hymn of creation. Mindful observation in nature is a practice that transforms the ordinary into the extraordinary, inviting us to bear witness to the sacred essence of the Earth. This practice nurtures humility, interconnectedness, and a profound sense of gratitude for the natural world.

To begin, step outside with an open heart and an intention to listen—not with words, but with your senses. Choose a quiet place, whether it's a forest, park, or even a backyard garden. Pause for a moment, grounding your feet firmly into the Earth, and take a deep breath. As you exhale, release distractions and allow yourself to become fully present.

Start by focusing your gaze on a single element of nature—a tree, a flower, or a stream. Observe its details: the patterns of its bark, the dance of its leaves in the wind, the glint of sunlight on the water's surface. What does it reveal to you about patience, resilience, or beauty? As you observe, let your mind rest from the urge to analyze or label. Simply be with it, as one would with a friend, appreciating its presence.

Extend your awareness to include the sounds around you—the rustle of leaves, the calls of birds, the distant hum of insects. These sounds are the Earth's language, reminding us that we are part of a vibrant, interconnected symphony. Close your eyes if you feel comfortable, allowing the sounds to envelop you, drawing you deeper into communion with the world.

Next, notice the textures and temperatures around you. Run your fingers along the rough bark of a tree or let a cool stream flow over your hands. Feel the warmth of sunlight or the chill of the breeze on your skin. Each sensation connects you to the living Earth, grounding you in the present moment and affirming your place within its cycles.

Mindful observation in nature is a sacred act of **Earth Stewardship**, rooted in the New Universalist belief that the Earth is not a resource to be dominated but a partner to be cherished. By observing its rhythms and intricacies, we cultivate a sense of awe and responsibility for its care.

This practice also embodies the principle of **Reasoned Inquiry**, a cornerstone of New Universalism. Through mindful observation, we approach the natural world with curiosity and reverence, seeking spiritual truths through our direct experiences with creation.

Mindful observation need not be limited to pristine wilderness. A single potted plant, the sky above a busy city, or even a small patch of grass can serve as a portal to the sacred. Consider dedicating a few minutes each day to this practice, whether during a morning walk or while sitting quietly outdoors. For communal worship, mindful observation can be incorporated into seasonal festivals or group meditations, where participants share reflections on the beauty and lessons of the natural world. These shared experiences foster a sense of unity and deepen the collective connection to the Earth.

Through mindful observation, we become both students and stewards of the Earth, learning from its quiet wisdom and carrying its lessons into our lives. In every rustling leaf and flowing stream, the sacred calls us to remember: we are one with this world, and it is one with us.

Earth-Based & Ancestral Meditation Practices

Grounding Meditation: Rooted in the Earth's Embrace

In New Universalism, grounding meditation serves as both a spiritual anchor and a sacred ritual that reaffirms our deep connection to the Earth. It is a practice of rooting oneself—physically, emotionally, and spiritually—into the vast network of life that sustains and nurtures us. By engaging in grounding meditation, we cultivate a sense of stability and support, drawing strength from the Earth's unyielding presence.

To begin, find a quiet place where you can stand, sit, or lie down comfortably. This space could be outdoors on grass, soil, or sand, or indoors with a connection to natural elements such as a potted plant or an open window to the sky. Remove your shoes if possible, allowing your feet to touch the Earth or the floor directly, symbolizing the physical connection to the planet.

Close your eyes and take a deep breath in, feeling the air fill your lungs. As you exhale, imagine the stress and distractions of the day flowing out of you, dissolving into the Earth below. Repeat this breathing pattern several times, letting your mind settle into the present moment.

Now, visualize yourself as a tree with strong, sturdy roots growing downward from your body into the Earth. See these roots extending deeper and deeper, weaving through soil and rock, connecting to the heart of the planet. Feel the grounding energy of the Earth rising through these roots, nourishing and stabilizing you. With each breath, imagine this energy filling your entire being, bringing balance, calm, and a profound sense of belonging.

As you continue, reflect on the Earth as a living entity—a mother who sustains and embraces all life. Offer gratitude for her support, acknowledging the strength and stability she provides. If your mind wanders, gently bring it back to the visualization of your roots and the steady rhythm of your breath.

Grounding meditation is deeply rooted in the New Universalist principle of **Earth Stewardship**, reminding us of our role as caretakers of the Earth. By drawing strength from the planet, we reaffirm our responsibility to honor and protect it. This meditation also embodies the value of **Filial Piety**, where the Earth is revered as a nurturing parent. In rooting ourselves to the planet, we acknowledge our interdependence and express respect for the life-giving energy that sustains us.

Grounding meditation can be practiced at any time but is especially powerful during moments of stress, uncertainty, or disconnection. It serves as a reset, allowing us to find our center and approach challenges with renewed clarity and strength. In communal worship, grounding meditation can be incorporated into seasonal celebrations, where participants join in visualizing collective roots intertwining beneath the Earth. This shared imagery fosters unity and a collective commitment to the planet's care.

Whether practiced individually or as a community, grounding meditation is a sacred act of connection—a reminder that no matter how far we wander, we are always rooted in the embrace of the Earth.

Seasonal Meditations: Aligning the Soul with Nature's Rhythms

In New Universalism, the cycles of nature are not merely external phenomena but sacred reflections of the cosmic dance in which all life participates. These seasonal rhythms mirror the internal journeys of our own lives—birth, growth, harvest, rest, and renewal. By attuning ourselves to these natural cycles, we deepen our connection to the Earth, the cosmos, and the divine principles that guide our faith.

Seasonal meditations serve as a profound practice for aligning with the spiritual lessons offered by each phase of the year. They invite us to reflect, celebrate, and transform in harmony with the Earth's movements. Through these meditations, we embody the New Universalist commitment to **Earth Stewardship** and **Filial Piety**, recognizing the Earth as both teacher and kin. By participating in these guided practices, we honor the interconnectedness of all beings and embrace the opportunity for growth, gratitude, and renewal.

Each meditation is a pathway to the divine, connecting us with the universal truths of New Universalism. These practices not only ground us in the present moment but also provide a framework for living with intention, humility, and awe.

Spring: A Season of Growth and Renewal

Spring heralds the Earth's awakening, a season when dormant seeds stir to life, and the landscape transforms into a canvas of vibrant greens and blossoms. For New Universalists, Spring represents a divine invitation to embrace growth and renewal. This is a time to nurture new beginnings, honor the interconnected cycles of life, and reflect on the potential within ourselves and the world around us.

To engage fully with the energy of Spring, choose a space that resonates with the vibrancy of the season. Ideally, this is outdoors, where you can feel the warmth of the spring sun, hear the soft hum of bees, or smell the freshness of blooming flowers. If indoors, create an altar that reflects Spring's essence: fresh flowers, seeds, or a green candle symbolizing renewal. Prepare your mind and body by sitting comfortably and taking a few deep breaths, allowing yourself to settle into the present moment.

Close your eyes and begin by focusing on your breath. Inhale deeply, drawing in the freshness of Spring and the energy of renewal. Feel this energy filling your body with light and hope. Exhale slowly, releasing the heaviness of winter's rest and the stagnation of what no longer serves you. With each breath, imagine yourself as a seed nestled within the Earth, resting in fertile soil.

As you continue to breathe, visualize the seed responding to the warmth of the sun and the nourishment of the Earth. Roots begin to stretch downward, anchoring you deeply into the soil, while a sprout begins its courageous journey upward, reaching for the light. Reflect on the areas of your life where growth is needed. What intentions or goals do you wish to nurture this season? What dormant potential within you is ready to awaken? Allow these reflections to emerge naturally, holding them gently like seeds ready to take root.

Spring meditation embodies the New Universalist principles of **Reasoned Inquiry** and **Earth Stewardship**, inviting intentional reflection on how to align our lives with universal truths. Just as the Earth renews itself, we are reminded of our capacity for growth and transformation. The act of planting seeds—literal or metaphorical—symbolizes our trust in the divine rhythms of nature and our role as co-creators of a better world. This practice connects us to the cycles of the Earth and the cosmos, reinforcing the sacred partnership between humanity and the natural world.

Conclude your meditation by offering gratitude to the Earth and the cosmos for their guidance and energy. Speak aloud or silently affirm your intentions, committing to nurture the seeds of growth you have planted. If outdoors, consider scattering flower seeds as an offering, symbolizing your partnership with the Earth in fostering renewal. If indoors, light the green candle on your altar, letting its glow remind you of the growth you are cultivating within yourself and in the world.

Spring meditation invites us to awaken alongside the Earth, embracing both the beauty of potential and the responsibility of nurturing it. This season challenges us to move forward with hope, courage, and a deep sense of interconnectedness, honoring the sacred web of life with every thought and action.

Summer: A Season of Abundance and Celebration

As the sun reaches its zenith and the days stretch long, summer envelops the Earth in its warm embrace. It is a season of abundance, vitality, and joy—a time to celebrate the fruits of our labor and to express gratitude for the richness of life. For New Universalists, Summer serves as a sacred reminder to savor the present, honor our achievements, and revel in the unity of creation.

Select a space where you can immerse yourself in the energy of summer. An open field, garden, or even a sunlit room can serve as your sanctuary. If outdoors, allow the warmth of the sun to bathe your skin and the sounds of nature to surround you. Indoors, adorn your altar with symbols of abundance: ripe fruits, summer flowers, and a yellow or gold candle to represent the sun's strength and vitality. Begin with a few centering breaths, releasing any tension and allowing yourself to be fully present. Close your eyes and envision yourself standing in a lush meadow at the height of summer. Imagine the vibrant greens of the grass, the golden rays of the sun casting a warm glow, and the gentle rustling of leaves in the breeze. Inhale deeply, filling your lungs with the vitality of the season, and exhale, releasing any sense of lack or limitation.

As you breathe, reflect on the abundance in your life. What blessings have you received or cultivated this year? Consider the relationships, experiences, and personal growth that have enriched your journey. Allow these reflections to fill you with gratitude and joy, recognizing that abundance is not solely material but also spiritual and emotional. Visualize the sun's rays as threads of golden light, weaving through the meadow and connecting you to all living things. Feel this light infusing you with energy and renewal, strengthening your connection to the Earth and cosmos. With each breath, affirm your readiness to share your abundance with others, embodying the New Universalist principles of **Compassion** and **Social Responsibility**.

Summer meditation reflects the New Universalist teaching that abundance is both a gift and a responsibility. The fruits of the season remind us of the Earth's generosity and the importance of reciprocating this gift through mindful stewardship and acts of kindness. This practice also emphasizes **Reasoned Inquiry**, encouraging us to consider how we use our abundance to support others and foster equity within our communities. By celebrating the interconnectedness of life, we honor the sacred balance of giving and receiving that sustains the natural world.

End your meditation by offering gratitude to the Earth and the sun for their life-giving energy. Speak a prayer or affirmation aloud, expressing your intention to share your blessings and honor the abundance of creation. If outdoors, scatter flower petals or seeds as an offering to the land. If indoors, light the yellow or gold candle on your altar, allowing its glow to symbolize the warmth and vitality you carry within. As you rise from your meditation, carry the joy and gratitude of summer with you. Celebrate the beauty of the present moment, knowing that abundance is not only to be cherished but also to be shared. This season reminds us to bask in the richness of life while remaining mindful of our interconnectedness and our sacred duty to nurture and protect the world around us.

Autumn: A Season of Reflection and Harvest

As the days grow shorter and the air turns crisp, the season of autumn arrives—a time of gathering, gratitude, and letting go. Autumn invites us to reflect on the fruits of our labor, honor the cycles of life, and prepare for the quiet introspection of winter. For New Universalists, autumn serves as a sacred reminder of the interconnectedness of life, the impermanence of all things, and the importance of gratitude and release.

Seek a quiet place, indoors or outdoors, where you can feel the shifting energy of the season. If outdoors, choose a space near trees with changing leaves or a harvested field, allowing the sights and sounds of autumn to surround you. If indoors, create a space with symbols of the season: autumn leaves, pumpkins, apples, or a candle in warm hues like orange or red. Sit comfortably, and begin with a few deep breaths, grounding yourself in the present moment. Close your eyes and envision yourself in a peaceful forest during the height of autumn. Picture leaves in shades of gold, crimson, and amber gently falling to the ground, creating a soft, colorful carpet. Feel the crisp air on your skin and the gentle rustling of leaves in the breeze. Allow yourself to be fully immersed in the scene.

As you breathe deeply, reflect on the personal harvests of your life. What have you cultivated this year? Consider the relationships, achievements, and personal growth that have enriched your journey. Offer gratitude for these blessings, recognizing the effort and care that brought them into fruition. Hold these reflections in your heart, allowing a sense of fulfillment and contentment to wash over you.

Shift your focus to the falling leaves. Imagine each leaf as something in your life that no longer serves you—fears, regrets, or habits you wish to release. With each exhale, visualize a leaf gently falling to the ground, carried away by the wind. Affirm your readiness to let go, creating space for renewal and growth. Repeat silently or aloud: **"I release with grace. I embrace change."**

Autumn meditation is deeply rooted in the New Universalist understanding of **Interconnectedness** and **Reasoned Inquiry**. By reflecting on the harvests of our lives, we honor the cyclical nature of existence, recognizing that all things have their season. The act of letting go embodies the principle of **Filial Piety**, respecting the wisdom of life's transitions and the gifts of past experiences while preparing for what lies ahead. Gratitude, a cornerstone of New Universalist theology, reinforces our spiritual connection to the Earth and the cosmos, reminding us to celebrate abundance while practicing humility.

Conclude your meditation by gathering a natural object, such as a fallen leaf, acorn, or small stone. Hold it in your hands and infuse it with your gratitude and intentions for release. Offer it back to the Earth as a token of appreciation, placing it gently on the ground or in a symbolic location. If indoors, light the candle on your altar, allowing its warmth to symbolize the inner light you carry into the darker months ahead. Speak an affirmation or prayer aloud, such as: **"I honor the gifts of the Earth and the wisdom of change. With gratitude, I release and prepare for renewal."** Rise slowly, carrying the peace and clarity of autumn with you into your daily life.

Winter: A Season of Rest and Renewal

Winter descends with a quiet stillness, blanketing the Earth in frost and offering an invitation to retreat inward. This season is a time for rest, reflection, and renewal—a sacred pause in the wheel of the year. For New Universalists, winter serves as a profound reminder of the cyclical nature of life, the power of stillness, and the promise of rebirth.

Find a space where you feel warm and secure, ideally near a window where you can observe the winter landscape, whether it be bare trees, snow-covered ground, or the gentle gray of the sky. If indoors, light a white or silver candle to symbolize the purity and clarity of winter. Add seasonal symbols to your altar, such as pinecones, evergreen sprigs, or crystals like clear quartz. Wrap yourself in a blanket if needed, creating an environment of comfort and peace. Close your eyes and take several slow, deep breaths. Allow your body to settle into stillness. Imagine yourself standing in a snowy clearing, surrounded by the quiet majesty of winter. Picture the trees, their bare branches reaching skyward, and the soft crunch of snow beneath your feet. Feel the cool, crisp air on your skin and the profound stillness that envelops the landscape.

As you breathe, reflect on the lessons of stillness. Ask yourself: Where in my life can I create space for rest and renewal? What aspects of my being need healing or clarity? Imagine the winter air clearing away mental fog and revealing insights hidden beneath the surface. Allow yourself to rest in this stillness, trusting that the quiet holds wisdom. Shift your focus to the seeds buried beneath the snow—tiny vessels of life that rest and gather strength for spring's awakening. Visualize the seeds within you: your hopes, dreams, and intentions for the coming year. Hold these seeds in your heart, knowing that winter provides the fertile ground for their growth. Repeat silently or aloud: **"In stillness, I gather strength. In rest, I prepare for renewal."**

Winter meditation resonates deeply with the New Universalist principle of **Reasoned Inquiry** and the value of **Restorative Balance**. The stillness of winter invites us to pause and reflect, fostering deeper self-awareness and spiritual connection. By embracing rest, we honor the Earth's rhythms and mirror the cosmic cycles of renewal. This practice also reflects **Filial Piety**, as we respect the wisdom of nature and its guidance for our lives. Winter's emphasis on renewal aligns with the promise of transformation central to New Universalist theology.

When you are ready to conclude your meditation, hold a small token, such as a sprig of evergreen or a clear crystal. Infuse it with your intentions for the coming year, visualizing the strength and clarity you have gathered during your meditation. Place this token on your altar or in a personal space where it can serve as a reminder of your renewal. Speak an affirmation or prayer aloud, such as: **"I honor the stillness and embrace the promise of renewal. In this quiet season, I find peace and prepare for growth."** As you open your eyes, carry the tranquility and clarity of winter into your daily life, honoring the wisdom of rest and the sacred promise of the seasons.

Gratitude Meditation: Honoring the Gifts of the Earth

Gratitude is a foundational practice in New Universalism, inviting us to honor the abundance of the Earth and the interconnected web of life. Through gratitude meditation, we open our hearts to the blessings surrounding us and deepen our reverence for the Earth as a sacred source of life and sustenance. This practice serves as both a spiritual discipline and an act of humility, grounding us in the present and fostering a sense of awe for the gifts we receive daily.

Choose a setting that inspires a connection to nature. This might be outdoors under a tree, beside a stream, or in a quiet garden. If indoors, create a sacred space with elements that represent nature's abundance, such as fruits, flowers, leaves, or stones. Light a green or gold candle to symbolize the Earth's generosity and prosperity. Bring a small journal or piece of paper to note reflections, if desired. Before beginning, take a moment to reflect on specific things, people, or experiences for which you are grateful, allowing these thoughts to guide your practice.

Close your eyes and take deep, steady breaths. With each exhale, release any tension or worry. With each inhale, invite a sense of appreciation to fill your heart. Visualize yourself in a vibrant, lush meadow or a fertile forest, surrounded by the sounds, colors, and fragrances of the Earth. Picture the sun shining warmly, its rays nurturing every living being. Imagine the roots of trees reaching deep into the soil, drawing nourishment from the Earth. Reflect on the countless ways the planet sustains you—through the air you breathe, the food you eat, and the beauty you see. Allow yourself to feel a profound sense of gratitude for these gifts.

As you breathe, silently or aloud, repeat a mantra of gratitude: **"I am grateful for the Earth's abundance. I honor the gifts of life and commit to living in harmony with the natural world."** Let this mantra resonate deeply, aligning your heart and spirit with a sense of reverence.

Visualize your gratitude radiating outward like ripples in a pond, reaching the Earth and all its creatures. Picture this energy nurturing the world, just as the Earth nurtures you. Pause to reflect on how your actions can reciprocate this generosity, considering how you might give back through acts of kindness, conservation, or stewardship.

Gratitude meditation reflects New Universalism's core value of **Filial Piety**, expressing respect and appreciation for the Earth as a sacred mother. It also embodies the principle of **Social Responsibility**, reminding us that gratitude is not passive—it inspires us to act in ways that honor the interconnected web of life. This practice aligns with **Earth Stewardship**, cultivating mindfulness of the Earth's abundance and reinforcing our commitment to preserve and protect these gifts for future generations.

When your meditation feels complete, offer a tangible expression of gratitude to the Earth. This could be as simple as watering a plant, scattering flower petals, or leaving a small token of thanks in nature. Speak aloud a final affirmation: **"With gratitude, I honor the Earth's abundance. With mindfulness, I carry this reverence into my life."**

Write down any insights or commitments from your meditation, keeping them as reminders of your gratitude practice. Carry this sense of appreciation with you, allowing it to shape your interactions, choices, and worship.

Ancestral Meditation: Honoring the Wisdom of Those Who Came Before

In New Universalism, honoring ancestors is a sacred act that connects us to the wisdom, sacrifices, and love of those who came before us. Ancestral meditation offers a pathway to remember and reflect on the lives of our forebears, seeking their guidance and expressing gratitude for their enduring presence. This practice strengthens the bonds between past, present, and future, anchoring us in the continuum of life.

Create an altar or sacred space with objects that represent your ancestors. This might include photographs, heirlooms, candles, or natural items such as stones, leaves, or feathers. Light a candle to symbolize the light of ancestral wisdom, and place it at the center of your space. Consider including items that hold personal significance, such as a favorite food or flower associated with a loved one.

Begin by grounding yourself, taking slow breaths, and setting an intention for your meditation. This might include seeking guidance, expressing gratitude, or simply honoring the presence of your ancestors. Close your eyes and visualize yourself standing in a vast, open field beneath a starry sky. Imagine a line of ancestors stretching behind you, their faces illuminated by the starlight. Feel their presence, strength, and love, as though they are standing beside you, offering support and wisdom.

Begin by silently thanking your ancestors for their sacrifices, resilience, and contributions. Reflect on the lessons they have passed down—through stories, traditions, or the lives they lived. As you breathe deeply, invite a particular ancestor to step forward in your visualization. This may be someone you know or a more distant, unknown forebear whose energy you sense. Picture this ancestor offering you a gift, symbolizing their guidance or wisdom. Hold this gift in your heart, allowing it to inspire and strengthen you. Ask a question or share a concern, trusting that their presence will provide clarity, even if the answer is not immediate.

Spend a few moments basking in this connection, feeling the flow of love and wisdom between you and your ancestor. Repeat silently or aloud: **"I honor those who came before me. Their wisdom guides me, and their strength lives within me."**

Ancestral meditation embodies **Filial Piety**, honoring the relationships that bind us to those who preceded us. It reflects the principle of **Interconnectedness**, showing how each life contributes to the whole and continues to influence the present. This practice also aligns with the New Universalist emphasis on **Gratitude**, recognizing that the blessings of today are built upon the foundations laid by others.

When you are ready to conclude your meditation, offer a prayer or affirmation of thanks: **"I honor my ancestors and the gifts they have given. May their wisdom guide my path, and may my actions honor their legacy."** Place a token from your altar—a flower petal, a pinch of soil, or a small object—outside in nature as an offering to the Earth and your ancestors.

Carry the strength and guidance of this meditation into your daily life, finding ways to honor your ancestors through your actions, words, and choices. By remembering those who came before, you deepen your connection to the continuum of life and the sacred bonds of existence.

Incorporating Eastern Practices: Expanding Horizons of Meditation and Mindfulness

New Universalism embraces the universal truths and wisdom present in all traditions, including the profound teachings of Eastern meditation practices. By integrating elements of Zen meditation, metta (loving-kindness meditation), and other Eastern techniques, we create pathways for greater self-awareness, compassion, and connection to the divine. These practices align with New Universalist values of reasoned inquiry, compassion, and interconnectedness, offering diverse tools for spiritual growth.

Zen Meditation: Finding Stillness in the Present Moment

Zen meditation, or zazen, emphasizes the profound simplicity of sitting in silence and observing the breath. Rooted in the Zen Buddhist tradition, this practice fosters clarity, calm, and the ability to embrace the present moment without judgment. In New Universalism, zazen is a pathway to understanding oneself as part of the greater whole, mirroring the rhythm of the Earth and cosmos.

Find a quiet place to sit comfortably, ensuring your spine is straight but relaxed. Place your hands gently in your lap or on your knees, forming a mudra (a symbolic hand position), if desired. Begin by focusing on your breath, following its natural rhythm as it flows in and out. As thoughts arise, acknowledge them without attachment, letting them pass like clouds in the sky. Return your focus to your breath, finding stillness in the rhythm of your breathing. Imagine yourself as a tree deeply rooted in the Earth, with your breath as the wind moving through your branches. This visualization can deepen your sense of connection to the natural world.

In New Universalism, this practice invites us to align with the principles of **Reasoned Inquiry**—observing thoughts without attachment or judgment—and **Interconnectedness**, as the breath connects us to the life force shared by all living beings.

Metta Meditation: Cultivating Loving-Kindness

Metta, or loving-kindness meditation, is a practice of sending love and goodwill to oneself and others. Originating from Theravāda Buddhism, this meditation resonates with New Universalism's emphasis on compassion and the shared dignity of all beings.

The Practice

Begin by sitting in a comfortable position, closing your eyes, and taking a few deep breaths. Start with yourself, silently repeating phrases such as:

- "May I be happy."
- "May I be healthy."
- "May I live with ease."

Next, extend these wishes to someone you care about, imagining them bathed in light:

- "May you be happy."
- "May you be healthy."
- "May you live with ease."

Gradually widen the circle to include neutral individuals, people with whom you have conflict, and ultimately all living beings, saying:

- "May all beings be happy."
- "May all beings be healthy."
- "May all beings live with ease."

In New Universalism, this practice reinforces the principles of **Compassion** and **Social Responsibility**, cultivating a sense of unity and care that transcends individual differences.

Adaptation to New Universalism

New Universalism encourages the adaptation of Eastern practices to reflect its inclusive theology. We are invited to integrate these techniques into our daily lives, focusing on universal values such as balance, gratitude, and the interconnectedness of all life.

For example, zazen might include a visualization of Earth's cycles, using the breath as a metaphor for the ebb and flow of natural rhythms. Similarly, metta meditation can be expanded to include intentions for the Earth, offering blessings such as:

- "May the Earth be healthy."
- "May the rivers flow clean and free."
- "May all creatures live in peace and safety."

By adapting these practices, New Universalists honor our origins while aligning with the principles of Earth Stewardship, Filial Piety, and universal love.

Theological Integration

Incorporating Eastern meditation practices highlights the **Reasoned Inquiry** central to New Universalism. These techniques invite us to explore inner landscapes and align our spiritual practices with universal truths found in diverse traditions. They also underscore **Earth Stewardship** by fostering mindfulness and respect for all life, reinforcing the interconnected nature of existence.

Through zazen, metta, and other meditative techniques, we deepen our connection to ourselves, others, and the natural world. By incorporating Eastern wisdom into New Universalist practice, we affirm the universal truths shared across spiritual traditions, enriching our collective journey toward wholeness and harmony. Let each meditation be a step closer to the divine unity that binds us to one another and to the cosmos.

Prayer and Affirmations

The Role of Prayer in New Universalism

Prayer in New Universalism is a deeply personal and communal practice that transcends traditional definitions, acting as a bridge between the individual spirit, the broader community, and the interconnected cosmos. Within this framework, prayer is not solely an act of supplication but a sacred dialogue—an expression of gratitude, reflection, and intentionality that aligns us with universal truths.

At its core, prayer in New Universalism is an invitation to unity. It serves as a reminder of our shared humanity and the interconnected web of existence that binds us to one another and the Earth. Whether offered in moments of quiet solitude, communal gatherings, or as part of daily rituals, prayer embodies the values of compassion, humility, and reverence for life that define New Universalist theology.

Prayer as Connection

New Universalism views prayer as a means of connecting with the divine, however one interprets that sacred force—whether as a universal consciousness, the energy of the cosmos, or the spirit of the Earth itself. This connection is deeply rooted in gratitude and respect, fostering a sense of harmony with all living beings and the natural world. Unlike prayer practices that may focus on petitioning for personal gain, New Universalist prayers emphasize unity, collective well-being, and spiritual growth.

Themes of Gratitude, Humility, and Intention

Gratitude is central to the practice of prayer in New Universalism, recognizing the abundance of life and the gifts provided by the Earth and cosmos. Humility emerges as we reflect on our place within the vastness of existence, acknowledging our interdependence with others and the planet. Intention imbues prayers with purpose, focusing energy on values such as healing, justice, and stewardship.

Communal and Individual Practice

Prayer in New Universalism thrives in both individual and communal contexts. For individuals, prayer serves as a moment of personal reflection and grounding, offering clarity and purpose. In communal settings, prayer becomes a unifying act, weaving together the intentions and aspirations of the group in a shared sacred space. These practices reinforce the bonds of community while honoring the unique spiritual paths of each participant.

Prayer as an Act of Filial Piety

In New Universalism, prayer is also an expression of filial piety—respect and reverence for one's ancestors, the Earth, and the larger forces that shape our lives. Honoring these relationships through prayer strengthens the connection between past, present, and future, reminding us of our role as stewards of life's ongoing journey.

Through its focus on gratitude, unity, and intentionality, prayer in New Universalism becomes a transformative practice. It is a pathway to self-awareness, a means of fostering communal harmony, and a sacred act that anchors individuals in the shared pursuit of spiritual and ethical growth.

Prayers Aligned with Universal Truths

Prayer in New Universalism is a practice that reflects the interconnectedness of all beings and the profound values that guide our spiritual lives. Through prayer, we articulate the core principles of compassion, gratitude, unity, and reverence for the Earth and its cycles. Below are examples of prayers aligned with New Universalist theology, each serving as a beacon of universal truth and spiritual reflection.

Prayer for Unity and Compassion

This prayer reflects New Universalism's emphasis on the shared humanity that binds us together, regardless of race, faith, or identity. It is a call for empathy and collective healing.

Prayer:
"Divine force of unity,
May we see the light of compassion in every being we meet.
Let our hearts open wide to embrace the struggles and joys of others,

And may our hands work tirelessly to build bridges of understanding.
Guide us in becoming vessels of peace,
So that we may honor the sacred bond of all life."

This prayer is particularly meaningful when shared during communal gatherings or moments of conflict resolution, emphasizing the need for empathy as the foundation for harmony.

Prayer for Earth and Nature

Rooted in gratitude and Earth Stewardship, this prayer honors the Earth as a living, sacred entity and calls for collective commitment to its care.

Prayer:
"Mother Earth, sacred and alive,
We thank you for your endless gifts—air, food, water, soil, and shelter.
Help us to tread lightly upon your lands,
To cherish and protect the abundance you offer.
May we grow wise in your cycles,
And act with courage to heal the wounds we have caused.
Teach us to love as you love, unconditionally and completely."

Prayer for Personal Growth and Integrity

This prayer invites self-reflection, encouraging us to align their actions with our values and to seek personal growth in harmony with the collective good.

Prayer:
"Infinite wisdom within and beyond,
Guide me as I walk this path of life.
Help me to see my shortcomings with humility,
And my strengths with gratitude.
May my thoughts be pure, my words true, and my deeds kind.

Teach me to grow in integrity and wisdom,
So that my journey reflects the beauty of the interconnected whole."

Prayer for Honoring Our Ancestors

Honoring ancestors is a cornerstone of filial piety in New Universalism. This prayer expresses gratitude to those who came before and recognizes their continued presence in our lives.

Prayer:
"To those who walked this Earth before me,
I offer my deepest gratitude.
Your sacrifices and wisdom have paved the way for my journey.
May your spirits find peace,
And may your lessons guide my steps.
I honor your love, your struggles, and your resilience,
And I promise to carry your light forward for the generations to come."

This prayer is fitting for personal altars or communal ceremonies, particularly during ancestral remembrance rituals, and serves as a bridge between past and present.

Reflections on the Role of Prayer

These prayers are not static recitations but living expressions of New Universalist theology. They serve as tools for transformation, bringing us closer to our inner truth, our community, and the sacred cosmos. Each prayer fosters a connection with the values of New Universalism, grounding spiritual practice in compassion, gratitude, and an unwavering commitment to the well-being of all.

Using Affirmations for Daily Spiritual Growth

Affirmations are sacred tools within New Universalism, fostering a connection between the inner self, the Earth, and the divine cosmos. They serve as beacons of clarity and intention, reminding us of our role in the interconnected web of life. By weaving affirmations into daily life, we align ourselves with the core values of New Universalism—compassion, integrity, Earth stewardship, and personal growth—and cultivate the resilience and grace needed to navigate life's complexities. Through consistent practice, affirmations have the power to shift perspective, inspire action, and anchor us in our spiritual truth.

Interconnectedness: Honoring the Web of Life

The concept of interconnectedness lies at the heart of New Universalism. Recognizing that all beings are intricately woven into the fabric of existence fosters a sense of responsibility and unity. Affirmations centered on interconnectedness encourage mindfulness of our actions and their ripples across the greater whole.

Guided Affirmation Practice:
Affirmation: "I am a vital thread in the fabric of life. My actions ripple across the cosmos with purpose and care."
Reflect on how your daily choices impact the natural world and the lives of others. For example, as you sip a cup of tea, consider the hands that cultivated the tea leaves, the Earth that nourished them, and the water that sustained their growth.
Affirmation: "The Earth and I breathe as one; my heart beats with the rhythm of the universe."
Sit quietly in nature and match your breath to the cadence of the wind or the rustle of leaves. Feel your connection to the larger rhythms of existence.
Affirmation: "I honor the sacred bond I share with all beings and strive to nurture the balance of life."
Use this affirmation to set an intention before engaging in activities such as gardening, cooking, or caring for others. Let it remind you of the unity that binds all living things.
Integrate these affirmations into mindfulness exercises, such as journaling or nature walks. As you practice, visualize the web of connections that sustain life and reflect on how your thoughts and actions contribute to its strength.

Compassion and Integrity: Living with Heart and Truth

Compassion and integrity are foundational to the practice of New Universalism. Compassion calls us to act with kindness and understanding, while integrity ensures that our actions align with truth and ethical principles. Together, these values create harmony within ourselves and with others.

Guided Affirmation Practice:

Affirmation: "I act with compassion and speak with integrity, creating harmony within myself and with others."

Begin your day by reflecting on a specific situation where you can bring more kindness or honesty. Visualize yourself acting with courage and care.

Affirmation: "I honor the truth within me and extend understanding to the truths of others."

Use this affirmation in moments of conflict or misunderstanding, reminding yourself to approach with empathy and authenticity.

Affirmation: "My compassion heals, and my integrity strengthens the bonds of the world."

Repeat this affirmation while placing your hand over your heart, feeling the pulse of life that connects you to the pulse of humanity.

Incorporate these affirmations into your daily interactions. As you practice, take time to pause and ask, "Am I acting from a place of kindness and honesty?" Let this reflection guide your actions.

Earth Stewardship: Reverence for the Natural World

As stewards of the Earth, New Universalists view nature as sacred and essential to spiritual well-being. Affirmations centered on Earth stewardship inspire gratitude for the planet's abundance and encourage thoughtful care for its resources.

Guided Affirmation Practice:

Affirmation: "I honor the Earth as sacred and commit to protecting its beauty for future generations."

Recite this affirmation during rituals, such as planting a tree or tending a garden. Feel the sacred connection between your actions and the Earth's renewal.

Affirmation: "The Earth provides, and I return with gratitude and care."

Use this affirmation as part of a gratitude meditation, visualizing the gifts of the Earth and the ways you can reciprocate through mindful living.

Affirmation: "With each breath, I celebrate the Earth's resilience and pledge to walk gently upon it."

Speak these words while walking in nature, letting each step reaffirm your commitment to sustainability.

Incorporate these affirmations into moments of mindfulness, such as turning off unnecessary lights or reducing waste. Let them inspire actions that reflect reverence for the natural world.

Personal Growth: Cultivating Wisdom and Grace

Personal growth is a journey of continuous learning, self-discovery, and alignment with one's purpose. Affirmations for personal growth encourage resilience, humility, and a commitment to living authentically.

Guided Affirmation Practice:

Affirmation: "Each day, I grow in wisdom and love, walking my path with humility and grace."

Begin each morning by repeating this affirmation, reflecting on the lessons you hope to embrace throughout the day.

Affirmation: "I am a work in progress, guided by the light of my highest self."
Use this affirmation during moments of self-doubt, reminding yourself that growth is a process and that each step is meaningful.

Affirmation: "I release fear and welcome transformation, knowing that change brings strength."
Speak this affirmation aloud during moments of transition, letting its truth bolster your courage.

Make these affirmations a part of your meditation practice or use them to close your day with gratitude for the growth you've achieved.

The Power of Affirmations in New Universalism

Affirmations are not merely words; they are declarations of intention and faith. Within New Universalism, they serve as pathways to personal and communal transformation, uniting thought, action, and spirit in pursuit of universal truth. Whether spoken in solitude or shared in community, affirmations deepen our connection to ourselves, each other, and the sacred whole.

Creating Personal Prayers and Affirmations

The creation of personal prayers and affirmations is both an art and a sacred practice within New Universalism. While our faith offers shared prayers and affirmations as touchstones of unity, crafting personal expressions allows us to deepen our connection to the divine and to our unique path within the spiritual framework of New Universalism. These practices are not only acts of devotion but also profound tools for self-reflection and intentional living.

Crafting Personal Prayers: A Path to Self-Expression

Personal prayers in New Universalism are intimate conversations with the sacred, expressions of gratitude, hopes, and aspirations woven together in reverence for the divine and the natural world. When creating a prayer, consider the following elements:

1. **Start with Gratitude:** Begin your prayer by acknowledging the blessings and abundance in your life. Gratitude creates a foundation of humility and openness, aligning your spirit with universal truths.
   Example:
   "Sacred cosmos and nurturing Earth, I give thanks for the breath of life, the beauty of creation, and the love that connects us all."

2. **Express Your Intention:** Clearly state the purpose of your prayer, whether it is to seek guidance, offer thanks, or find peace. Reflect on how this intention aligns with New Universalist values, such as compassion, integrity, or stewardship.
   Example:
   "Grant me the strength to walk gently upon the Earth, to act with kindness and courage, and to honor the sacred connections that sustain us."

3. **Conclude with Reverence and Hope:** Close your prayer with words that acknowledge the interconnectedness of all things and your place within the grand design.
   Example:
   "With humility and love, I place these words into the currents of the universe, trusting in its wisdom and grace."

Always remember that prayers is a deeply personal practice and intimate conversation. This structure for crafting prayers can serve as a solid guide; but we are always encouraged to realize that at the core, prayer is a conversation like any other. With this acknowledgement, we allow ourselves the freedom to openly express ourselves and commune with the divine.

Creating Affirmations: Anchors for the Spirit

Affirmations are not just declarations; they are touchstones that guide us toward our highest selves. Crafting affirmations in alignment with your personal journey allows you to focus on the qualities you wish to cultivate and the values you hold dear.

1. **Identify a Core Value or Goal:** Reflect on what aspect of your spiritual or personal growth you want to affirm. This could be a desire for greater patience, resilience, or a deeper connection with nature.
   Example: If you seek patience, begin with: "Patience flows through me as naturally as the rivers carve their path through stone."
2. **Phrase Positively and Presently:** Write affirmations as if the desired quality or state is already part of your being. This reinforces a sense of ownership and alignment with your intentions.
   Example: "I embody compassion and extend it freely to myself and others."
3. **Infuse with Meaning:** Include language that connects the affirmation to your spiritual practice, grounding it in New Universalist values.
   Example: "I walk in harmony with the Earth and her rhythms, a steward of her beauty and life."

Incorporating Prayers and Affirmations into Daily Practice

Once created, personal prayers and affirmations become powerful tools for daily spiritual practice. Here are ways to weave them into your life:

Morning Intentions: Begin each day with a personal prayer or affirmation that sets the tone for the hours ahead. Light a candle, face the sunrise, or place your hands over your heart as you recite your words.
Example: "Today, I will act with kindness and courage, honoring the interconnectedness of all life."

Meditative Reflection: During meditation, silently repeat your affirmation as a mantra, allowing it to guide your thoughts and deepen your focus. Visualize its truth becoming a part of your being.

Sacred Spaces: Place written affirmations or prayers on your personal altar or other sacred spaces. Let them serve as visual reminders of your intentions and values throughout the day.

Journaling: Write your prayers and affirmations in a dedicated journal, reflecting on how they resonate with your experiences and growth. Update or refine them as your journey unfolds.

Empowering Spiritual Ownership

The act of creating personal prayers and affirmations is deeply empowering. It allows us to take ownership of our spiritual journey while staying grounded in the shared values and theology of New Universalism. These practices are dynamic, evolving as we grow and deepen our understanding of ourselves and our connection to the world around them. By honoring ones unique path through these sacred expressions, we contribute to the rich tapestry of New Universalism, embodying its commitment to diversity, unity, and personal growth.

Journaling as a Spiritual Practice

In the vast tapestry of spiritual and personal practices embraced by New Universalism, journaling emerges as a profound yet simple tool for introspection and growth. At its heart, journaling is more than a collection of words—it is a sacred dialogue with oneself, a reflective mirror that allows the writer to engage deeply with their thoughts, emotions, and spiritual journey. This practice transcends mere documentation; it becomes an act of spiritual connection and an opportunity to align daily experiences with universal truths.

Journaling as a spiritual practice holds a unique power: it bridges the internal and external worlds, allowing us to explore personal beliefs, observe our relationship with the world, and seek answers to life's most profound questions. Within New Universalist theology, journaling is recognized as a way to embody the values of reasoned inquiry and mindfulness. By dedicating time to intentional reflection, we are guided toward greater self-awareness, emotional clarity, and spiritual alignment.

This practice also serves as a mirror for New Universalism's emphasis on the interconnectedness of all things. When one writes about the world, its natural beauty, and our place within it, we are reminded of our role in the broader cosmic web. Similarly, journaling about struggles and triumphs highlights the shared human experience, fostering compassion and understanding.

In addition to its reflective benefits, journaling becomes a tool for growth. As entries accumulate, they form a living document of one's spiritual evolution, offering a tangible record of insights, lessons, and transformations over time. Revisiting these pages can reveal patterns, illuminate strengths, and even clarify areas for growth, serving as a guide for both personal and spiritual development.

Journaling is not bound by rigid rules or structures. Instead, it is a fluid and personal practice, adaptable to the unique needs and inclinations of each individual. Some may find solace in structured prompts that guide them through introspective exercises, while others may prefer the freedom of unfiltered expression. Both approaches honor the spirit of journaling as a pathway to understanding and connection. From reflective journaling that nurtures self-awareness to gratitude journaling that cultivates a spirit of appreciation, these practices become more than a habit. It transforms into a sacred act of discovery, a daily touchstone for living authentically in harmony with oneself, others, and the cosmos.

Reflective Journaling: A Mirror for the Soul

Reflective journaling is the practice of documenting daily experiences, thoughts, and emotions with the intent of gaining self-awareness and clarity. In New Universalism, this practice is seen as a way to engage deeply with life's moments, celebrating small victories and learning from challenges.

Through reflective journaling, we can ask ourselves meaningful questions: *What did I learn today? How did I act in alignment with my values? Where could I grow further?* By committing these reflections to paper, we gain perspective on our behaviors and choices, enabling intentional growth.

A New Universalist lens encourages us to also explore connections between our reflections and larger universal truths. For example, a challenging conversation might lead to insights about compassion, communication, or shared humanity. Each entry becomes an opportunity to deepen our understanding of self and others, reinforcing New Universalism's emphasis on reasoned inquiry and introspection.

Gratitude Journaling: Cultivating a Heart of Thanks

Gratitude journaling focuses on identifying and recording moments, people, or aspects of life for which one feels thankful. Within New Universalist theology, this practice aligns with the value of mindfulness and the sacred act of acknowledging life's abundance. Each day, we are encouraged to write about three to five things we are grateful for. *These might include personal achievements, the beauty of nature, or the kindness of others.* Over time, this practice fosters a mindset of positivity and appreciation, even during challenging periods.

From a spiritual perspective, gratitude journaling reinforces a sense of interconnectedness. As we note the gifts provided by the Earth, relationships, or our community, we deepen our awareness of the interdependent web of existence. This awareness inspires acts of reciprocity and care, embodying the values of Earth Stewardship and social responsibility.

Nature Journaling: Observing the Earth's Sacred Rhythm

Nature journaling is a practice of mindfulness and reverence for the natural world. It involves documenting observations of the environment—seasonal changes, weather patterns, or encounters with plants and animals—and reflecting on their significance.

In New Universalism, nature journaling is a sacred act, connecting us with the Earth's rhythms and cycles. We may choose to carry our journal on walks, pausing to sketch a leaf, describe the sound of a stream, or write about the emotions evoked by a sunrise. These entries serve as reminders of humanity's deep relationship with nature and the sacred duty to protect it.

This practice also encourages reflection on one's place within the natural order. *How does the changing season mirror personal growth or transformation? What lessons does a forest offer about resilience, diversity, or harmony?* Nature journaling transforms simple observations into profound insights, deepening the spiritual connection to the Earth and cosmos.

These journaling practices offer New Universalists a variety of tools for reflection and growth. Whether through introspection, gratitude, or connection with nature, journaling serves as a bridge between daily experiences and the universal truths that guide us.

Journaling to Explore Spiritual Questions

Journaling is more than a record of thoughts and observations; it is a gateway to profound self-discovery and spiritual growth. In New Universalism, journaling can be a sacred practice to navigate life's most meaningful questions, connecting us with universal truths while fostering deeper understanding of personal beliefs and values.

Exploring Purpose and Values Through Writing

Purpose and values are central to New Universalist theology, which teaches that every individual contributes uniquely to the interconnected web of existence. Journaling provides a space to reflect on these contributions, helping us clarify our life's direction and align our actions with our values.

To begin, we might ask ourselves:

What brings me a sense of fulfillment or peace?

How do my daily choices reflect my commitment to compassion, integrity, and stewardship?

What gifts or talents can I offer to my community and the world?

These prompts encourage introspection and alignment with spiritual principles. Writing about moments of joy, fulfillment, or challenge helps uncover patterns, illuminating the values that guide one's life and areas for growth.

Reflecting on Lessons from Nature and the Cosmos

In New Universalism, nature and the cosmos are sacred teachers, offering lessons in resilience, harmony, and interconnectedness. Journaling allows us to reflect on these teachings, deepening our spiritual connection to the Earth and universe. We might write about how the cycles of the moon influence our emotions or how the changing seasons mirror our personal growth. For example, observing the persistence of a tree in harsh weather might inspire reflections on strength and endurance in one's own life. Similarly, a starry sky can evoke thoughts on humanity's shared origins and the vastness of existence.

Prompts for engaging with nature's wisdom might include:

What did I learn from nature today?

How do I see my life reflected in the cycles of the Earth and cosmos?

What steps can I take to live more harmoniously with the natural world?

Engaging with Spiritual Beliefs and Universal Truths

Journaling provides a space to engage deeply with spiritual beliefs, exploring how they shape one's identity and interactions. In New Universalism, where reasoned inquiry and personal exploration are encouraged, this process is essential for spiritual growth.

We can use our journals to examine questions such as:

What does the concept of interconnectedness mean to me, and how do I embody it in my actions?
How do I balance the spiritual and material aspects of my life?
What experiences have strengthened my faith in universal truths, such as compassion and justice?

By documenting these reflections, we create a record of our evolving beliefs, offering insight into our spiritual journey over time.

Journaling Prompts for Spiritual Exploration

Describe a time when you felt deeply connected to something greater than yourself. What did that experience teach you?

Reflect on a recent challenge. What spiritual lessons can you draw from it, and how can they guide you moving forward?

Write about a moment of kindness or justice you observed or enacted. How does this connect to your understanding of universal truths?

Using journaling to explore spiritual questions offers a pathway to greater self-awareness and alignment with New Universalist theology. Each entry serves as a step toward understanding one's place in the interconnected web of existence, fostering a deeper relationship with oneself, the Earth, and the cosmos.

10

Community Rituals and Celebrations

Community Church Services in New Universalism

Community church services within New Universalism represent far more than gatherings for ritual and worship—they are the heartbeat of a shared spiritual life. These services provide a sanctuary where we can come together to affirm our connection with one another, with the Earth, and with the broader cosmos. They are spaces of mutual support, collective reflection, and vibrant celebration, weaving together the diverse threads of a community into a tapestry of unity and shared purpose.

The theological foundation of these services lies in the New Universalist belief that spirituality is not only a solitary pursuit but a communal journey. By engaging in shared worship, we strengthen our bond with one another and reinforce our commitment to the guiding principles of New Universalism: reasoned inquiry, Earth stewardship, filial piety, and social responsibility. Community services offer a structured opportunity to embody these values in action, grounding us in a sense of collective identity while honoring the diversity that enriches every gathering.

At their core, these services are designed to foster a deep sense of belonging. Whether through shared prayers, storytelling, meditative silence, or acts of service, we are invited to embrace the shared humanity that unites all people. They are spaces where diversity is celebrated as a source of strength, where individuals from varying spiritual paths can find meaning, and where the focus is always on what connects us rather than what divides us.

Furthermore, community services in New Universalism emphasize the integration of spirituality with action. They do not merely serve as moments of reflection but as calls to embody the values of our faith in everyday life. Through rituals that honor the Earth, discussions that explore ethical living, and practices that cultivate mindfulness and compassion, these gatherings encourage us to leave not only inspired but also empowered to contribute to the collective well-being of our communities and the planet.

In this way, community church services become more than rituals; they are living expressions of New Universalist theology. They are opportunities to unite in reverence for the sacred, engage deeply with spiritual truths, and draw strength from the presence of others who share a commitment to living with integrity, purpose, and compassion.

Purpose of Community Church Services in New Universalism

Community church services are central to the practice of New Universalism, offering a sacred space where we can come together to engage in collective worship, reflection, and celebration. Rooted in the principles of unity, reasoned inquiry, and reverence for the Earth, these gatherings transcend mere ritual—they are living expressions of the shared values that bind New Universalist communities together.

The primary purpose of community church services is to create opportunities for us to strengthen our connection to both the divine and one another. In these spaces, worship is not a solitary act but a shared journey, where the collective energy of the congregation enriches the experience of each person. These gatherings foster a sense of belonging, reminding us that our personal spiritual path is interwoven with the broader fabric of humanity and the natural world.

At the heart of these services is the New Universalist commitment to exploring themes that resonate universally—compassion, humility, stewardship, and personal growth. Each service is an opportunity to delve into topics that not only align with the cycles of nature and the rhythms of the cosmos but also address the challenges and aspirations of modern life. Sermons and reflections often weave together insights from diverse traditions, secular philosophies, and contemporary ethical dilemmas, creating a space for reasoned inquiry that honors the shared search for truth.

One key function of community church services is to provide a space for shared rituals that anchor us in the sacred. These rituals—whether they involve lighting candles to honor the seasons, offering prayers of gratitude for the Earth's abundance, or sharing in the symbolic communion of bread and juice—are designed to unite the congregation in a common act of reverence. Through these practices, the teachings of New Universalism come alive, transforming abstract principles into tangible experiences.

Inclusivity is an essential dimension of these services. Recognizing the diversity of its adherents, New Universalism ensures that community gatherings are accessible, welcoming, and meaningful to individuals from all backgrounds. Services are intentionally crafted to reflect the universal themes that connect all people, transcending cultural, spiritual, and philosophical differences. By emphasizing shared values over divisive doctrines, these gatherings celebrate diversity as a source of strength and unity.

The communal nature of these services also reinforces the practice of Earth Stewardship. Held in natural settings whenever possible, or incorporating elements such as plants, stones, or water, New Universalist services honor the Earth as a sacred entity. By grounding worship in the natural world, these gatherings serve as a reminder of humanity's interconnectedness with the environment and the responsibility to protect and nurture it.

Beyond worship and reflection, community church services serve as platforms for action and growth. They inspire us to live out New Universalist values in our daily lives, encouraging acts of kindness, environmental responsibility, and social justice. Themes explored in sermons and rituals often carry practical implications, guiding us in applying spiritual principles to our relationships, work, and community engagement.

Ultimately, the purpose of these gatherings is to offer renewal and inspiration. Whether through the spoken word, shared ritual, or silent reflection, community church services provide us with the spiritual sustenance we need to navigate life's challenges with grace and resilience. They are spaces where the individual and collective meet, where the sacred and the everyday converge, and where the teachings of New Universalism are embodied in the act of coming together.

By fostering connection, celebrating diversity, and grounding worship in universal truths, New Universalist community church services fulfill their purpose as beacons of unity, wisdom, and hope. In these sacred spaces, we find not only a reflection of our own values but also a shared vision for a world that is compassionate, just, and harmonious.

Guiding Principles for Inclusive Church Services

Creating inclusive community church services is both a sacred responsibility and a practical task for New Universalist ministers and leaders. These gatherings are more than assemblies; they are opportunities to weave a spiritual tapestry that reflects the diversity, values, and aspirations of all participants. By embracing inclusivity and intentionality, community church services become spaces of unity, where all feel seen, valued, and inspired to grow.

The foundation of an inclusive service lies in respect and accessibility. Inclusivity begins with recognizing the inherent worth of every individual and extends to creating environments where that worth is honored. Ministers are encouraged to use language and imagery that are universal and welcoming, ensuring that participants from varied backgrounds, abilities, and experiences find resonance in the themes and rituals. Thoughtful consideration of physical spaces—ensuring accessibility for individuals with mobility needs, offering seating that accommodates families, and providing spaces for quiet reflection—also affirms the commitment to inclusivity.

Central to organizing inclusive services is the principle of active participation. New Universalism values the dynamic interplay between personal reflection and communal engagement. Services should include opportunities for attendees to contribute, whether through communal singing, shared prayers, storytelling, or symbolic acts such as planting seeds or lighting candles. These moments of participation transform the congregation from passive observers to active co-creators of the worship experience, fostering a sense of belonging and shared purpose.

Reflection and dialogue are essential components of inclusivity. New Universalist services are not confined to sermons or teachings; they are spaces for collective inquiry and exploration. Incorporating moments for silent meditation, open discussion, or group reflection invites diverse perspectives and deepens the communal bond. This approach aligns with New Universalism's emphasis on reasoned inquiry, encouraging participants to engage thoughtfully with the service's themes and to draw connections between our spiritual journey and the wider world.

Another guiding principle is the intentional integration of Earth-centered values. New Universalism's emphasis on Earth Stewardship provides a rich foundation for community church services. Leaders are encouraged to include natural elements in their worship settings, such as flowers, stones, or bowls of water, and to consider outdoor gatherings where the beauty and rhythm of nature enhance the spiritual atmosphere. Rituals that honor the Earth—such as pouring libations, offering prayers of gratitude to the land, or engaging in symbolic actions like planting—reinforce the sacred connection between humanity and the natural world.

Inclusivity also extends to the thematic focus of services. Topics should reflect universal concerns and aspirations, such as compassion, justice, personal growth, and ecological harmony. By addressing themes that resonate broadly, New Universalist services become spaces where participants from diverse faiths and philosophies can find common ground. For example, a service on compassion might include reflections from various traditions, blending sacred texts with personal anecdotes and practical guidance for embodying compassion in daily life.

Music, art, and storytelling play vital roles in fostering inclusivity and enriching the worship experience. Music selections should span genres and cultural influences, ensuring that the congregation experiences a tapestry of sound that uplifts and inspires. Art, whether through visual displays or participatory activities, can offer another layer of connection, allowing participants to express their spirituality creatively. Storytelling, particularly when drawn from diverse traditions or personal experiences, weaves a narrative of unity and shared humanity.

Finally, inclusivity requires flexibility and openness. Ministers and community leaders are encouraged to adapt services to meet the needs of their specific congregations. This might mean offering multilingual readings, incorporating practices from the local community's traditions, or creating spaces for children and youth to engage meaningfully in the service. By remaining attuned to the evolving needs of the community, leaders ensure that services remain relevant, resonant, and inclusive.

Organizing inclusive community church services in New Universalism is an act of sacred care. It requires attentiveness to the needs and gifts of the congregation, creativity in designing meaningful rituals, and a commitment to honoring the diverse threads that make up the human family. Guided by these principles, ministers and leaders can create worship experiences that reflect the heart of New Universalism: unity, reverence, and a shared commitment to building a compassionate and harmonious world.

Elements of a Community Church Service

The structure of a community church service in New Universalism is designed to create a harmonious flow of reflection, connection, and spiritual enrichment. Each element of the service plays a distinct role in cultivating a shared sacred experience, weaving individual and communal practices into a unified expression of worship. By incorporating meaningful rituals, thoughtful readings, and participatory actions, these services become a testament to the values and theology of New Universalism.

Opening and Welcome

The opening of a service sets the tone, gently inviting participants into a shared spiritual space. A moment of silence often begins the gathering, encouraging individuals to release distractions and center themselves. This silence is not merely a pause but an acknowledgment of the sacred stillness that connects all beings.

After this grounding moment, a spoken welcome follows. Ministers or leaders may offer words of gratitude for the Earth and cosmos, drawing attention to the cycles of nature and the interconnectedness of life. For instance, an opening might reference the day's season, the weather, or a celestial event, grounding the congregation in the present moment. A unifying sentiment such as, **"We gather here as one family, honoring our shared humanity and the Earth that sustains us,"** can further establish an atmosphere of inclusivity and reverence.

Readings and Reflections

The heart of the service often lies in its readings and reflections, which serve as both spiritual nourishment and intellectual engagement. Selections may be drawn from sacred texts, nature poetry, philosophical writings, or personal narratives that align with the day's theme. For example, a service focused on compassion might include a reading from the New Universalist sacred texts, a verse from Buddhist teachings on metta, or an excerpt from environmental literature reflecting the compassion inherent in Earth Stewardship.

Reflections, whether offered as a sermon or a shared dialogue, expand upon these readings. Ministers are encouraged to weave together universal truths with contemporary issues, helping attendees draw connections between our spiritual values and daily lives. For instance, a reflection on justice might explore its theological foundations in New Universalism while addressing modern concerns such as social equity or environmental advocacy.

Transitions between readings and reflections should feel seamless, ensuring that each element builds upon the other. A poetic phrase, a brief moment of silence, or a soft musical interlude can provide a gentle bridge, allowing a moment to absorb the insights shared.

Ritual Actions

Ritual actions bring a tangible, participatory dimension to the service, transforming abstract values into lived expressions. These symbolic acts serve to connect us with the Earth, one another, and our spiritual essence.

For instance, lighting candles can symbolize illumination and unity, with each participant invited to light a flame as an expression of their unique light contributing to the whole. Planting seeds or scattering petals might represent growth and renewal, aligning with themes of seasonal change or personal transformation. Pouring water into a communal vessel could signify shared responsibility, reminding the congregation of their collective role in nurturing life and preserving resources.

These rituals, simple yet profound, provide a shared language of action that transcends verbal expression. They engage the senses and foster a deeper connection to the themes of the service, creating moments that linger in memory long after the gathering concludes.

Music and Creative Expression

Music and art are integral to New Universalist services, providing an avenue for emotional resonance and communal celebration. Songs, whether traditional or contemporary, allow us to join our voices in a shared rhythm, fostering unity and joy. Instrumental interludes, such as the soothing tones of a flute or the grounding beat of a drum, can evoke a sense of connection with nature and the cosmos.

Creative expressions like storytelling, visual displays, or dance can further enrich the service. A congregant might share a personal story that illustrates the day's theme, while visual art created during the service could capture the collective energy of the gathering. These elements ensure that the service engages participants holistically, touching the mind, heart, and spirit.

Closing and Blessing

The conclusion of a service brings the congregation back together, reinforcing the unity and purpose cultivated throughout. A shared blessing or affirmation can serve as a powerful closing act, sending participants forth with renewed inspiration and intention.

A moment of gratitude is often woven into the closing, thanking the Earth, ancestors, or the community itself for their presence and contributions. Ministers might offer a brief prayer or affirmation, such as, **"May we carry the spirit of today's gathering into our lives, walking with compassion, courage, and care for all beings."**

The service might end with a symbolic act, such as the extinguishing of a communal candle, signifying the transition from shared space to individual journeys. This act reinforces the idea that while the gathering concludes, its lessons and connections continue to ripple outward.

Guidance for Ministers and Community Leaders

The role of ministers and community leaders in New Universalism is both a sacred trust and a profound responsibility. As spiritual guides, they create spaces for connection, reflection, and growth, weaving together the principles of Earth Stewardship, social responsibility, and universal compassion into every gathering. Their work requires not only an understanding of New Universalist theology but also the ability to respond to the diverse needs and perspectives of their congregations with wisdom, humility, and creativity.

Preparing and Delivering Sermons

The cornerstone of a New Universalist service is the message conveyed through sermons or reflections. Ministers are encouraged to craft messages that resonate with the shared values of the community, weaving theological insights with practical applications. Sermons should explore themes such as the interconnectedness of life, the importance of justice and equity, or the spiritual call to care for the Earth.

Preparation begins with deep reflection and study. Ministers might draw upon sacred texts, philosophical teachings, or contemporary issues, ensuring that their message is both timeless and relevant. A sermon on Earth Stewardship, for instance, could include reflections on seasonal cycles, insights from Indigenous wisdom, and a discussion of sustainable living practices, connecting spiritual reverence with actionable steps.

The delivery of a sermon should be approachable and engaging, inviting listeners to not only hear the message but to feel inspired by it. Ministers are encouraged to use stories, analogies, or questions to spark thought and dialogue, creating a shared exploration of the day's theme. Maintaining eye contact, varying tone and pace, and incorporating moments of silence for reflection can enhance the impact of their words.

Fostering Participation and Collaboration

Community services thrive when attendees are not merely observers but active participants. Ministers can invite congregants to contribute to the service, whether through sharing personal reflections, leading a prayer or song, or participating in symbolic rituals. This collaborative spirit reinforces the New Universalist value of mutual respect and shared growth.

Creating opportunities for participation requires sensitivity to the diverse abilities and comfort levels of the congregation. Leaders should ensure that all activities are accessible and inclusive, offering modifications or alternatives as needed. For example, a ritual involving movement might include seated options, and communal singing could provide printed lyrics or opportunities for non-vocal participation, such as drumming or clapping.

The inclusion of children and youth is also essential, as their involvement enriches the community's collective experience and fosters a sense of belonging from an early age. Ministers might incorporate storytelling, nature-based activities, or age-appropriate reflections to engage younger members of the congregation.

Addressing Contemporary Issues with Integrity

A defining feature of New Universalist leadership is the ability to connect spiritual values with the challenges and opportunities of the modern world. Ministers are called to address issues such as climate change, social justice, and mental health with thoughtfulness and compassion, demonstrating how the principles of New Universalism can guide responses to these concerns.

For example, a service focused on social justice might include a reflection on the theological foundations of equity, followed by practical steps for advocacy or community support. Similarly, a service addressing mental health might explore themes of resilience and self-care, offering meditative practices or affirmations to nurture well-being.

When engaging with contemporary issues, ministers should prioritize inclusivity and avoid partisanship, framing discussions in ways that invite dialogue rather than division. They are encouraged to model humility and openness, acknowledging the complexity of these issues while offering hopeful and constructive perspectives.

Creating Sacred Atmospheres

The physical and spiritual environment of a service plays a vital role in shaping the worship experience. Ministers are encouraged to create spaces that reflect the values of New Universalism, incorporating natural elements and symbols that honor the Earth and cosmos. Outdoor gatherings can deepen the sense of connection to nature, while indoor spaces might include elements such as plants, stones, or artwork inspired by natural forms. The arrangement of the space should facilitate a sense of community, with seating in circular or semi-circular patterns that emphasize unity and equality wherever possible.

Music, lighting, and intentional use of silence can also enhance the sacred atmosphere. Soft instrumental music or nature sounds might accompany moments of reflection, while the gentle glow of candles can signify light and hope. Silence, used thoughtfully, allows attendees to connect inwardly and with one another in shared reverence.

Rituals in Practice

Rituals are a cornerstone of spiritual expression within New Universalism, offering individuals and communities a means to connect deeply with nature, the cosmos, and one another. Rooted in reverence for the Earth and guided by the rhythms of the Wheel of the Year, these practices reflect the theology and values of our faith, creating spaces for reflection, celebration, and unity. In New Universalism, rituals are not merely symbolic gestures but intentional acts of worship that ground us in the sacred cycles of life and affirm the interconnectedness of all existence.

The practice of rituals aligns with New Universalism's core principles of Earth Stewardship, Social Responsibility, and Filial Piety, honoring our collective responsibility to nurture the Earth and one another. By participating in rituals that are attuned to the seasons and cycles of nature, we are reminded of our place within the broader tapestry of life. These rituals serve as a compass, guiding us through transitions in the year while offering opportunities for introspection, gratitude, and spiritual growth.

At the heart of New Universalist ritual practice is the recognition of both personal and communal needs. Rituals are designed to be inclusive, meaningful, and adaptable, allowing participants from diverse spiritual and cultural backgrounds to engage fully. Whether a simple act of lighting a candle during the Winter Solstice or the vibrant celebration of May Day, these moments create a shared sacred experience that reinforces the bonds of community while honoring individual spiritual paths.

Each practice is a reflection of the unity between humanity and the natural world, fostering a deeper sense of harmony and spiritual fulfillment. From the quiet, reflective practices of All Souls Day to the joyous and exuberant celebrations of the Summer Solstice, these rituals embody the values of gratitude, compassion, and mindfulness. They invite participants to pause, celebrate, and honor the cycles of life and death, growth and rest. As we explore each ritual, may these practices inspire a renewed commitment to the Earth, to community, and to the sacred rhythm of existence.

Importance of Seasonal Rituals in New Universalism

Seasonal rituals are a vital expression of New Universalism, embodying the theology and values that shape our connection to the natural world and one another. These rituals, organized around the Wheel of the Year, serve as sacred markers of time, guiding individuals and communities through the Earth's natural rhythms. Each observance provides a moment to pause, reflect, and engage with the deeper truths of existence, offering a path to spiritual growth and communal harmony.

At the core of New Universalist theology is the belief in the interconnectedness of all life and the sacredness of the Earth. Seasonal rituals reflect this belief by aligning worship practices with nature's cycles, such as the solstices, equinoxes, and midpoints of the seasons. These moments in time are not arbitrary; they mirror the transitions of the natural world, reminding us of the constant ebb and flow of life, growth, and renewal. By participating in these rituals, we ground ourselves in the present while recognizing the continuity and resilience of life's greater patterns.

Seasonal rituals are also profound expressions of gratitude. Each observance invites us to honor the gifts of nature, whether it is the warmth and light celebrated during the Winter Solstice or the abundance of the harvest at the Autumn Equinox. This gratitude extends beyond the immediate moment, fostering a deeper awareness of the Earth's generosity and the responsibility we hold as stewards of the planet. Rituals thus serve as acts of reciprocity, offering thanks to the Earth while committing to its care.

In New Universalism, seasonal rituals also cultivate existing communal bonds and foster new connections. These gatherings provide opportunities for shared reflection and celebration, reinforcing the collective values of compassion, unity, and respect. By participating in symbolic actions—such as lighting candles, planting seeds, or sharing meals—we strengthen our sense of belonging to both our local community and the greater human family. These rituals create a space where differences are transcended, and a shared commitment to spiritual and earthly care is renewed.

The practice of seasonal rituals allows us to embody the theological principles of New Universalism in a tangible way. For example, the balance of light and dark observed during the Spring and Autumn Equinoxes reflects the universal pursuit of harmony, both within ourselves and with the world around us. Similarly, the renewal and growth celebrated in spring rituals inspire personal transformation and hope, echoing the resilience of nature.

Seasonal rituals are not static; they evolve with the needs of the community and the environment. New Universalism encourages creativity and adaptability, allowing each ritual to resonate with the unique cultural, ecological, and spiritual contexts of its participants. This flexibility ensures that rituals remain meaningful and accessible, fostering a deeper connection to both the Earth and the values of New Universalism.

By honoring the cycles of nature through seasonal rituals, we reaffirm our place within the larger web of existence. These practices invite us to slow down, reflect, and engage with the sacred in everyday life. They remind us that, like the Earth, we are part of a living, breathing system that thrives on balance, gratitude, and care. Seasonal rituals are not only acts of worship but also commitments to a life lived in harmony with the natural world and each other.

Seasonal Rites in New Universalism

The Wheel of the Year, central to New Universalist theology, serves as the foundation for these rites. It acknowledges the cyclical nature of life and encourages participants to embrace the interconnectedness of all things. As we move through each season, these rituals remind us of our place in the greater cosmic order and our responsibility to honor and protect the Earth.

Winter Solstice: Return of Light and Inner Renewal

The Winter Solstice, celebrated on or around December 21st, is a sacred moment in New Universalism, a time when the longest night gives way to the returning light. This celestial transition has been observed by countless traditions across time, particularly within Wiccan, Pagan, and other Earth-based spiritualities. For New Universalists, the Winter Solstice is both a community celebration and a deeply personal time of reflection, symbolizing hope, resilience, and the ever-present cycles of nature that connect us to the divine.

In Wiccan and Pagan traditions, the Winter Solstice, often referred to as Yule, honors the rebirth of the sun. Rituals center on themes of light, renewal, and the enduring promise of life even during the darkest times. These ancient observances inspire the New Universalist perspective, which embraces the solstice as a time to honor both the rhythms of the Earth and the spiritual growth that emerges from times of stillness and introspection.

The Community Celebration of Winter Solstice

For New Universalist communities, the Winter Solstice is an opportunity to gather, reconnect, and collectively celebrate the light within and the light returning to the world. The communal celebration begins as dusk falls, with participants gathering in a space infused with the essence of nature—branches of evergreens symbolizing endurance, stones and crystals grounding the circle, and candles or lanterns prepared to honor the return of light. A ceremonial invocation opens the gathering. Led by a minister or chosen community member. This invocation acknowledges the Earth, Sun, and cosmos, expressing gratitude for the cycles that sustain life. Drawing from New

Universalist theology, the invocation speaks to the interconnectedness of all beings and the divine presence inherent in nature's rhythms.

The lighting of candles follows, a deeply symbolic act that invites each participant to bring their own light to the shared circle. As the flame is passed, participants may share reflections of gratitude for the past year or intentions for the season ahead, aligning with the New Universalist value of mindful introspection and personal growth. This act not only illuminates the space but also reinforces the communal strength that emerges when individuals unite their light. The ritual continues with storytelling, a practice rooted in Pagan and Indigenous traditions. Tales of the Winter Solstice's significance, drawn from various cultural and spiritual perspectives, weave a tapestry of shared wisdom. These stories remind us of the enduring cycles of darkness and light, both in nature and within ourselves.

Music and song enhance the celebration, with communal chants and melodies that honor the solstice's themes of renewal and hope. Instruments like drums and bells may be used to create a rhythm that echoes nature's cycles, grounding us in the shared energy of the Earth.

Individual and Family Observances of the Solstice

While the Winter Solstice is richly celebrated in community, it is also deeply meaningful as an individual or family observance. For those observing privately, practices can center on creating a sacred space at home. A family altar adorned with evergreen sprigs, pinecones, candles, and meaningful objects serves as the focal point for reflection and ritual. Lighting a central candle symbolizes the rebirth of light, and families can take turns sharing their reflections or hopes for the season ahead. This practice fosters gratitude and connection, drawing on New Universalist principles of honoring the divine within each person and the interconnectedness of the family unit.

For individuals, a Winter Solstice meditation can offer a profound experience of stillness and renewal. Sitting quietly by candlelight, practitioners can reflect on the lessons of the darker months—patience, introspection, and resilience—while visualizing the light returning to our lives. This practice aligns with New Universalism's emphasis on mindfulness and personal growth, encouraging us to see ourselves as part of the greater cycles of nature and spirit.

Honoring Tradition While Embracing New Universalist Values

The Winter Solstice carries timeless themes, and New Universalism integrates these with its unique theology, doctrine, and practice. Like Wiccan and Pagan traditions, it emphasizes reverence for natural cycles and the sacred connection between Earth and cosmos. Yet it expands on these foundations, framing the solstice as not only a time of personal renewal but also a communal affirmation of shared values.

By honoring the Winter Solstice, New Universalists embrace the sacred responsibility to steward the Earth, cherish the light within us, and support the light in others. Through rituals, storytelling, and quiet reflection, this day becomes a bridge between ancient wisdom and modern spiritual practice, connecting individuals, families, and communities to the timeless rhythms of the world we call home.

Spring Equinox: Renewal, Balance, and New Beginnings

The Spring Equinox, celebrated on or around March 21st, marks the moment when day and night are equal, symbolizing harmony, balance, and renewal. For New Universalists, this seasonal rite is a time to honor the Earth's rebirth and to reflect on personal growth and renewal. Drawing inspiration from Pagan and Earth-based traditions, as well as the agricultural cycles of planting and growth, the Spring Equinox offers an opportunity to realign with nature's rhythms and set intentions for the season ahead.

The Spiritual Foundations of the Spring Equinox

The equinox has been observed across cultures for millennia. In Wiccan and Pagan traditions, this day, often referred to as Ostara, celebrates fertility, balance, and the promise of new life. Symbols such as eggs, seeds, and flowers represent the potential for growth and the cycles of creation. These elements inspire New Universalist theology, which embraces the equinox as a sacred time to nurture the seeds of our intentions, relationships, and communal bonds, while recognizing the balance required to sustain both inner and outer growth.

For New Universalists, the Spring Equinox also resonates with the theological principle of interconnectedness. Just as seeds require light, water, and soil to grow, our lives are deeply interwoven with the Earth and each other. This day calls on us to reflect on how we can cultivate balance and harmony within our own lives, while also contributing positively to our communities and the world.

Community Observances of the Spring Equinox

Spring Equinox celebrations in the New Universalist community are joyous and vibrant, centered on themes of renewal, balance, and hope. Gatherings may take place outdoors, in fields, gardens, or other natural settings that highlight the awakening of the Earth. The altar for the day, adorned with spring flowers, bowls of seeds, and vessels of water, becomes the focal point for the community's rituals. The celebration begins with an invocation led by the minister or a designated community member. This invocation acknowledges the equinox's themes, offering gratitude for the balance of day and night and for the potential that spring brings. Drawing on New Universalist theology, the invocation connects the physical renewal of the Earth with spiritual renewal, emphasizing the importance of balance in our lives and our ecosystems.

A central element of the Spring Equinox ritual is the act of planting. Participants may plant seeds in small pots or directly into the Earth, symbolizing intentions for growth in the coming months. As each participant plants a seed, they may silently or aloud express their personal intentions or hopes for the season. This symbolic act is grounded in New Universalism's values of Earth stewardship and intentional living, reminding us of our responsibility to nurture not only the Earth but also the seeds of change within ourselves.

Rituals of balance are also a hallmark of the Spring Equinox celebration. A communal activity, such as a symbolic balancing of stones or shared movements in a circle to represent the equilibrium of light and dark, helps participants embody the equinox's central theme. Music and chants, reflecting the rhythms of the season, may accompany these rituals, fostering a sense of unity and connection. The gathering often concludes with a shared meal, emphasizing themes of abundance and community. Seasonal foods such as greens, eggs, and breads, symbolizing fertility and growth, are prepared and shared in gratitude for the Earth's bounty. A closing blessing brings the celebration to a reflective end, encouraging participants to carry the spirit of renewal and balance into our daily lives.

Individual and Family Practices for the Spring Equinox

For individuals and families, observing the Spring Equinox can be a deeply personal and meaningful experience. Creating a home altar with symbols of spring—flowers, seeds, eggs, or even a small bowl of soil—can provide a space for meditation and reflection. Lighting a candle to represent the balance of light and dark is a simple yet powerful act that connects us to the day's energy. Engaging in a nature walk offers another way to honor the equinox. Families and individuals can take time to observe the awakening Earth, noticing the budding trees, blooming flowers, and the gentle warmth of the sun. During the walk, a moment of gratitude for the beauty and resilience of nature reinforces the New Universalist principles of Earth stewardship and interconnectedness.

A practice of journaling can also enhance the equinox's themes. Writing prompts such as "What seeds do I wish to plant in my life this season?" or "How can I cultivate greater balance and harmony?" encourage deep self-reflection. Families might adapt this practice by creating a vision board together, outlining shared goals for the season.

Integrating Ancient Wisdom with New Universalist Values

The Spring Equinox invites New Universalists to weave ancient practices into our modern spiritual framework, drawing on the rich traditions of Earth-based spirituality while incorporating New Universalist theology and doctrine. It is a time to honor the balance of light and dark, to celebrate the Earth's renewal, and to commit to nurturing growth in every aspect of life. Through planting seeds, engaging in rituals of balance, or simply reflecting on personal intentions, the Spring Equinox serves as a reminder of life's continual cycles and the promise of renewal inherent in them. Whether observed in community or solitude, this day offers a sacred opportunity to align with the Earth's rhythms and to reconnect with the divine spirit present in all life.

Summer Solstice: Celebrating Light, Abundance, and Community

The Summer Solstice, observed around June 21st, marks the longest day of the year and the peak of sunlight and life's fullness. In New Universalism, this seasonal rite is a celebration of abundance, vitality, and gratitude. It serves as a time to honor the gifts of the Earth and the light within ourselves and our communities. Rooted in traditions that have long celebrated the solstice, this ritual embraces the themes of interconnectedness, joy, and shared purpose.

The Spiritual Significance of the Summer Solstice

The Summer Solstice has been honored across cultures and spiritual traditions for centuries. In Pagan and Wiccan practices, it is often called Litha, a day dedicated to celebrating the sun at its zenith. Rituals focus on joy, abundance, and the recognition of life's blessings. Similarly, Indigenous traditions acknowledge the solstice as a sacred time of connection with the Earth and the cosmos, often integrating storytelling, dance, and offerings to honor the season's energy.

In New Universalism, the Summer Solstice is seen as a moment to reflect on the radiance of the sun and the abundance it sustains. It is a celebration of gratitude, a time to appreciate the fruits of the Earth and the accomplishments of the community. The solstice also encourages us to draw strength from the sun's light, illuminating our path forward with clarity and purpose. This day reminds us of the unity between ourselves, the Earth, and the cosmos, reinforcing the New Universalist principle of interconnectedness.

Community Observances of the Summer Solstice

Summer Solstice celebrations within New Universalist communities are vibrant and joyful, centered on themes of light, gratitude, and abundance. Gatherings often take place outdoors, in open fields, gardens, or near bodies of water, where the sun's warmth and light can be fully experienced. The celebration begins with an invocation, acknowledging the power of the sun and its role in sustaining life. A communal chant or hymn honoring the light and its abundance may follow, creating a unified atmosphere that reflects the shared joy of the day. Drawing on New Universalist theology, the invocation emphasizes the light within each person, symbolizing the collective strength and unity of the community.

One of the central rituals involves creating a communal altar decorated with seasonal fruits, flowers, and symbols of the sun, such as golden candles or sun-shaped ornaments. Participants may be invited to place personal offerings on the altar, expressing gratitude for the season's abundance and their own personal blessings. These offerings might include written notes of gratitude, tokens representing personal accomplishments, or objects that hold spiritual significance.

Another meaningful practice is the "Circle of Light." Community members stand in a circle, each holding a candle or lantern. As the leader lights the central flame, participants take turns lighting their candles from it, symbolizing the spreading of light and the interconnectedness of all beings. This act serves as a reminder that, even at its peak, the sun's light is a shared gift that unites and sustains everyone.

The gathering often incorporates music, dance, and storytelling. Traditional songs and dances that celebrate the sun and the Earth's abundance may be performed, fostering a sense of communal joy and celebration. Stories, drawn from diverse cultural traditions or crafted to reflect New Universalist values, provide moments of reflection and shared wisdom. The solstice concludes with a shared feast, emphasizing gratitude for the Earth's bounty. Foods that represent the fullness of summer—berries, fresh vegetables, and sun-colored dishes—are enjoyed as a community. Before parting, participants may join in a collective blessing, expressing hope for continued abundance and unity in the months ahead.

Individual and Family Practices for the Summer Solstice

For individuals and families, the Summer Solstice offers an opportunity to celebrate the season's abundance and reflect on the light within our lives. Creating a home altar with sun-themed decorations, fresh flowers, and fruits of the season can serve as a focal point for personal reflection and gratitude. Lighting a golden or yellow candle while expressing thanks for the blessings in one's life is a simple yet meaningful act. Nature walks during the solstice can help individuals connect with the Earth's abundance. Observing the lushness of trees, the vibrancy of flowers, or the warmth of the sun can inspire a sense of gratitude and wonder. Families might engage in outdoor activities, such as gardening or creating sun art, to celebrate the day's themes together.

Personal rituals, such as journaling or meditation, can deepen the solstice experience. Journaling prompts like *"What light do I bring into the world?"* or *"How can I share my abundance with others?"* encourage introspection and alignment with New Universalist values. Meditation on the sun's energy, visualizing its light filling the body and illuminating one's path, fosters a sense of strength and clarity.

The Solstice as a Symbol of Gratitude and Unity

The Summer Solstice reminds New Universalists of the interconnectedness of life and the importance of gratitude. It is a day to celebrate abundance—not only in the natural world but also within our communities and ourselves. By honoring the sun's light and its role in sustaining life, the solstice becomes a sacred opportunity to reflect on life's blessings and recommit to sharing light, love, and abundance with the world. Whether observed through community gatherings or personal rituals, the Summer Solstice invites New Universalists to embrace the fullness of life and to recognize the sacred balance that sustains it. Through this celebration, we honor our connection to the Earth, to each other, and to the divine light that shines within all beings.

Autumn Equinox: Gratitude and Balance in the Harvest Season

The Autumn Equinox, falling around September 21st, is a time of equilibrium and thanksgiving. On this day, light and darkness are perfectly balanced, symbolizing the harmony between opposing forces in life. In New Universalism, the equinox is a sacred moment to honor the harvest—both the literal abundance of the Earth and the figurative harvest of personal and communal growth throughout the year. This seasonal rite emphasizes themes of gratitude, balance, and preparation for the inward journey of winter.

The Spiritual Significance of the Autumn Equinox

Across many Earth-centered traditions, the Autumn Equinox is celebrated as a time to express gratitude for the Earth's gifts and to reflect on the cycles of nature. In Pagan traditions, it is known as Mabon, a day to honor the harvest and the changing season. Indigenous cultures often mark this time with ceremonies to thank the Earth for its bounty and to prepare for the coming winter months.

In New Universalist theology, the Autumn Equinox is a time of reflection and thanksgiving, deeply connected to the values of Earth Stewardship and mindfulness. It invites us to pause, express gratitude for the fruits of our labor, and recognize the importance of balance in life. This day also encourages contemplation of the transitions we face, both in nature and within ourselves, as we prepare for rest, renewal, and introspection.

Community Observances of the Autumn Equinox

In New Universalist communities, the Autumn Equinox is celebrated through rituals that combine gratitude, reflection, and shared abundance. Outdoor gatherings in fields, gardens, or near harvest sites create a fitting backdrop for this seasonal observance, connecting participants to the natural world and the harvest season. The celebration begins with an invocation, acknowledging the balance of light and dark and expressing gratitude for the Earth's gifts. This invocation often includes a prayer or chant emphasizing themes of harmony and gratitude, such as:

"We honor the balance of this day, the gifts of the Earth, and the abundance shared among us. May we walk in gratitude and humility, prepared to rest and renew as the Earth teaches us."

A communal altar is central to the ritual, adorned with symbols of the harvest such as autumnal fruits, grains, and vibrant leaves. Participants are encouraged to bring items that represent their personal or communal harvest—perhaps a token of an accomplishment, a written note of gratitude, or offerings of food or flowers. These items are placed on the altar, symbolizing a shared acknowledgment of life's blessings.

One of the most meaningful rituals involves a "Gratitude Circle." Participants gather in a circle and take turns expressing something they are thankful for, whether related to the Earth, their community, or personal growth. This act fosters a sense of unity and shared appreciation, reinforcing New Universalist values of connection and humility.

The equinox is also a time for symbolic actions that represent balance and preparation. For example, participants might create a "Harvest Mandala" using natural items such as leaves, acorns, and fruits, symbolizing harmony and the beauty of diversity. Others may engage in rituals like "Burying Intentions," where seeds are planted in the ground alongside wishes or commitments for the future, symbolizing hope and renewal. Music and storytelling are also integral to the equinox celebration, weaving together themes of harvest and preparation. Songs that honor the season and tales of gratitude or transformation inspire reflection and joy among participants. These elements deepen the sense of community and shared purpose.

The gathering concludes with a shared meal, emphasizing the abundance of the season. Foods such as roasted vegetables, breads, and autumn fruits highlight the harvest theme. Before parting, participants join in a collective blessing, expressing hope for balance and renewal in the months ahead.

Individual and Family Practices for the Autumn Equinox

For individuals and families, the Autumn Equinox offers an opportunity to cultivate gratitude and reflect on the changing season. Creating a home altar with symbols of the harvest, such as pumpkins, wheat, and leaves, provides a focal point for personal meditation and thanksgiving. Lighting a candle and offering a prayer of gratitude strengthens the connection to the season's themes.

Journaling is another meaningful practice for the equinox. Writing prompts such as *"What am I most grateful for this year?"* or *"What lessons have I harvested from my experiences?"* encourage introspection and alignment with the equinox's energy.

Families might engage in activities such as cooking a seasonal meal together or taking a nature walk to collect autumnal items for decoration or craft projects. These practices foster a sense of connection to the Earth and to one another.

Personal rituals, such as meditating on balance or planting seeds as a symbol of renewal, deepen the equinox experience. Visualization exercises, where one imagines balancing the light and dark aspects of life, promote inner harmony and mindfulness.

The Equinox as a Time of Gratitude and Preparation

The Autumn Equinox reminds New Universalists of the importance of gratitude and balance in our spiritual and daily lives. It is a time to honor the Earth's gifts, reflect on the year's growth, and prepare for the inward journey of winter. Through community gatherings and personal rituals, the equinox becomes a sacred opportunity to align with the rhythms of nature and to recommit to the principles of interconnectedness, stewardship, and gratitude. By celebrating the Autumn Equinox, New Universalists affirm our unity with the Earth and each other, recognizing the beauty and harmony of life's cycles. This observance fosters a deeper appreciation for life's blessings and inspires actions that honor and sustain the world we share.

Additional Observance Community and Cosmic Harmony

In addition to the key seasonal rites that mark the rhythms of the year, New Universalism recognizes several additional observances that enrich the spiritual calendar. These occasions offer opportunities to deepen one's connection to the Earth, honor cultural and cosmic cycles, and celebrate themes that resonate with our core values, such as gratitude, renewal, and interconnectedness. While the seasonal rites focus on the balance and transitions of nature, these additional observances highlight specific aspects of our relationship with the Earth, our community, and the divine cosmos. Each additional observance is imbued with unique meaning, combining traditional influences with New Universalist theology, doctrine, and practices. By participating in these celebrations, communities and individuals alike can foster unity, deepen spiritual insights, and affirm our commitment to Earth Stewardship and social responsibility.

Spring Festival - Lunar New Year: A Celebration of Renewal and Purification

The Spring Festival, also known as the Lunar New Year, is one of the most vibrant and spiritually rich observances within New Universalism. Rooted in ancient traditions from Chinese culture and similar practices across various Earth-based and agrarian societies, this festival serves as a sacred bridge between winter's quiet reflection and the dynamic awakening of spring. The holiday heralds the promise of renewal, personal purification, and communal celebration, encapsulating both individual and collective growth.

In Chinese tradition, the Lunar New Year marks a transition not only on the calendar but within the spirit. It is a time to honor ancestors, strengthen familial bonds, cleanse one's home and heart, and prepare for a year of fortune and harmony. Across cultures, similar celebrations occur—such as the Korean Seollal, the Vietnamese Tết, and various agrarian new year observances—each emphasizing purification, gratitude, and the stirring of life's creative energy.

In New Universalism, the Spring Festival takes on added depth. The holiday is celebrated as a time to reflect on the renewal inherent in the cycles of nature and to reaffirm our commitment to growth, both personal and communal. By honoring these traditions, New Universalists embrace a theology that recognizes the interconnectedness of cultural wisdom, the rhythms of the Earth, and the divine energy that animates all life.

Community Ritual and Celebration

The communal observance of the Spring Festival within New Universalism begins with the theme of purification. Held in a shared sacred space—either indoors or within nature—the gathering opens with a symbolic cleansing ritual. This may include participants sprinkling water infused with herbs or flowers, smudging with sacred smoke, or collectively chanting to release negative energy and invite renewal. Central to the celebration is the preparation and dedication of a communal altar. The altar is adorned with elements symbolic of renewal and abundance: blooming flowers, candles to represent the returning light, and tokens such as coins or oranges for prosperity. Participants may contribute personal items, written intentions, or symbols of their hopes for the year to the altar, weaving their individual aspirations into the collective vision.

A core ritual involves the practice of intention-setting. Using strips of biodegradable paper, each participant writes their goals or wishes for the coming year. These papers are then planted alongside seeds in small pots, representing the merging of intentions with the nurturing power of the Earth. Alternatively, these intentions may be burned in a communal fire, symbolizing their transformation into energy for action.

The celebration often incorporates storytelling and communal sharing. Participants are invited to reflect on the themes of renewal and interconnectedness through personal stories, poetry, or traditional tales. Music and dance—often inspired by the rhythmic movements of nature—bring the community together in joy and harmony, while shared songs express gratitude for the bonds of unity and life's endless possibilities.

The communal meal that concludes the ritual reflects the festival's themes of abundance and gratitude. Foods such as rice, dumplings, noodles, and sweet fruits may be served, chosen for their symbolic significance of unity, prosperity, and longevity. Before eating, a collective prayer of thanks for the Earth's sustenance and the community's support sets the tone for the feast.

Individual and Family Observances

For individuals and families, the Spring Festival offers deeply meaningful opportunities for reflection and renewal. The act of cleansing the home—sweeping away old energy and physically cleaning spaces—becomes a sacred practice of releasing burdens and inviting blessings. Family members may engage in this together, blessing each room with intentions of peace and abundance.

The creation of a family altar is another powerful practice. Decorated with fresh flowers, symbolic objects, and written intentions, it becomes a focal point for gratitude and prayer. Each family member contributes to the altar, fostering a shared sense of purpose and unity. Families may light candles together, reflecting on their collective hopes for the year while honoring the interconnectedness of their lives.

A family meal imbued with symbolism is another essential tradition. Foods that represent prosperity, health, and harmony—such as citrus fruits, rice cakes, or long noodles—are prepared and shared with reverence. Before the meal, family members may offer prayers of gratitude for the past year's blessings and ask for guidance and growth in the year ahead.

Nature walks provide another way to celebrate the Spring Festival individually or as a family. Observing the earliest signs of spring—budding trees, birds returning to sing, or the gentle thaw of frozen streams—encourages mindfulness and a connection to the Earth's renewal. Simple meditative practices, such as focusing on breath while walking or silently expressing gratitude for the beauty of nature, deepen this sacred connection.

Honoring Tradition While Embracing New Universalist Values

The Spring Festival in New Universalism honors the deep cultural roots of the Lunar New Year while extending its message to include universal values. Chinese traditions such as cleaning the home, honoring ancestors, and sharing symbolic foods provide a rich foundation. Similar practices from other cultures, such as Korea's Seollal or Vietnam's Tết, emphasize familial bonds, gratitude, and the renewal of spirit, all of which resonate profoundly with New Universalist theology.

By integrating these traditions, New Universalism emphasizes the interconnectedness of cultural wisdom and the divine principles of renewal and harmony. Participants are encouraged to see the Spring Festival as a time to honor both their personal growth and their role within the broader community and natural world. The theology of New Universalism teaches that renewal is a shared journey, one that involves not only individual transformation but also a commitment to collective well-being and Earth stewardship. In blending these influences with contemporary spiritual insights, New Universalism offers a Spring Festival that is both deeply rooted in tradition and dynamically relevant to modern life. It invites all participants to honor the past, celebrate the present, and cultivate hope for the future, creating a sacred bridge between the wisdom of our ancestors and the promise of the year ahead.

Earth Day: Honoring and Protecting the Sacred Earth

Earth Day, observed annually on April 22, is a global call to recognize the interconnectedness of all life and the vital need to protect and heal our planet. Originally established in 1970 as a movement for environmental awareness, Earth Day has since become a sacred observance in New Universalism, transcending its secular origins to embody profound spiritual significance. For New Universalists, Earth Day is not merely a day for activism but a time to reaffirm the sacred duty of Earth stewardship and to celebrate the living Earth as a divine gift.

Drawing from both Indigenous and Earth-based traditions, Earth Day in New Universalism emphasizes reciprocity with the natural world. Indigenous practices of honoring the Earth as a living being inform the holiday's rituals, while Neo-Pagan traditions of seasonal reverence provide a framework for its celebration. By integrating these influences, New Universalism transforms Earth Day into a spiritual observance that fosters both ecological responsibility and cosmic connection. Earth Day reminds us that caring for the planet is an act of reverence and gratitude. The day serves as a sacred pause to reflect on humanity's relationship with the Earth and to engage in meaningful action to heal and protect it. For New Universalists, this holiday is a celebration of life's intricate web, a call to accountability, and a source of hope for the future.

Community Ritual and Celebration

In New Universalist communities, Earth Day is marked by collective rituals that blend spiritual reflection with tangible action. These gatherings often begin with an outdoor opening ceremony, centering participants in the natural world. A communal altar is created in a natural space, adorned with symbolic offerings such as stones, leaves, and water, representing the Earth's elements. Participants may bring personal tokens or written prayers of gratitude and place them on the altar, deepening the sense of shared intention.

The central ritual of Earth Day often involves a symbolic act of Earth healing. This might include planting trees, restoring a local habitat, or conducting a community clean-up. These actions are framed as sacred acts of reciprocity, aligning with the New Universalist theology that sees humanity as caretakers of the Earth. Ritual leaders guide participants through reflective meditations during these activities, encouraging them to connect their physical actions with their spiritual commitments.

Storytelling and shared wisdom are integral to the communal celebration. Elders, spiritual leaders, or environmental advocates may share reflections on the sacredness of the Earth and the importance of stewardship. These moments inspire participants to deepen their understanding of the challenges facing the planet and their role in creating solutions.

The ceremony concludes with a collective blessing for the Earth. Participants may form a circle, holding hands or connecting in symbolic unity, and offer prayers or affirmations of gratitude and hope. A shared song or chant often accompanies this blessing, weaving the community's voices into a collective expression of reverence and commitment.

Individual and Family Observances

For individuals and families, Earth Day is an opportunity to engage in meaningful acts of connection and stewardship. A day spent outdoors—whether hiking, gardening, or simply sitting in stillness—becomes a sacred practice of communion with the natural world. We are encouraged to reflect on our relationship with the Earth, offering silent prayers of gratitude for its beauty and abundance.

Families may observe Earth Day by planting a tree or starting a garden, teaching children the value of nurturing life. Before planting, a moment of reflection or prayer can transform the act into a ritual of hope and renewal. Families may also create a home altar dedicated to the Earth, adorned with natural items collected from outdoor explorations and used as a focal point for daily gratitude.

Journaling is another meaningful practice for individuals, allowing space to reflect on personal commitments to environmental care and the spiritual lessons learned from nature. Families may also engage in shared storytelling, exploring myths or legends about the Earth's creation or balance, weaving cultural traditions into their observance.

Finally, individuals and families can participate in acts of advocacy, such as writing letters to local leaders, donating to environmental causes, or committing to sustainable habits. These actions align with New Universalist values of responsibility and stewardship, connecting personal practice with broader change.

Honoring Tradition While Embracing New Universalist Values

While Earth Day's roots lie in secular environmental activism, New Universalism imbues the holiday with spiritual depth. The observance draws inspiration from Indigenous teachings that emphasize the sacred relationship between humanity and the Earth, as well as Neo-Pagan practices that honor the Earth's elements and cycles. These traditions provide a rich foundation for rituals and actions that elevate Earth Day into a sacred expression of gratitude and accountability. By weaving these traditions into its theology, New Universalism emphasizes that Earth Day is not only a day of awareness but also a holy occasion. We are called to reflect on the divine nature of the Earth and to engage in acts that honor its vitality and resilience. Through this observance, New Universalism fosters a profound connection between spiritual practice and ecological action, uniting personal reflection with collective responsibility.

As New Universalists celebrate Earth Day, we are reminded of the transformative power of unity—both within our communities and with the Earth itself. By honoring tradition while embracing the values of stewardship, compassion, and reciprocity, Earth Day becomes a living testament to the sacred duty to protect and heal the planet.

May Day: A Celebration of Life, Joy, and Fertility

May Day, celebrated on May 1st, is a joyous festival marking the height of spring and the abundance of life. Rooted in ancient Pagan and Earth-based traditions, this holiday celebrates fertility, renewal, and the deep connection between humanity and the natural world. Historically associated with rituals honoring the Earth's fecundity and the blossoming of crops and communities, May Day emphasizes joy, creativity, and unity.

In New Universalism, May Day is recognized as a time to honor the Earth's generative power and to celebrate the beauty of interconnected relationships—between individuals, communities, and the natural world. Drawing inspiration from Celtic Beltane festivities and similar seasonal observances worldwide, New Universalists embrace May Day as a sacred occasion to express gratitude for life's abundance and to affirm the shared bonds that sustain us. This festival encourages participants to reflect on themes of renewal, hope, and balance, as spring transitions into early summer. It is a time to revel in the fullness of life, share in communal joy, and deepen one's spiritual connection to the rhythms of nature.

Community Ritual and Celebration

In New Universalist communities, May Day is celebrated with vibrant rituals and gatherings designed to foster unity and joy. The day often begins with a communal gathering in a natural setting, where participants are greeted with flower garlands and ribbons symbolizing the season's vitality. A Maypole, adorned with colorful ribbons, serves as the centerpiece for the festivities.

The Maypole dance is a cherished ritual that reflects the interconnectedness of life. Participants hold ribbons and weave intricate patterns as they circle the pole, their movements symbolizing the weaving together of community, nature, and shared purpose. This joyous dance is often accompanied by live music or singing, enhancing the celebratory atmosphere.

Offerings to nature play a central role in the ritual. Participants may create an altar with spring flowers, budding branches, and other symbols of fertility and growth. Small offerings—such as seeds, grains, or written blessings—are placed at the altar as tokens of gratitude for the Earth's abundance. Ritual leaders may guide the group in a blessing ceremony, acknowledging the interconnected web of life and offering prayers for continued harmony and balance.

Communal feasting is another highlight of May Day celebrations. A shared meal featuring seasonal foods, such as fresh greens, fruits, and breads, strengthens bonds within the community and reflects gratitude for the Earth's gifts. Storytelling and performances, often centered on themes of renewal and creativity, add depth and meaning to the celebration.

Individual and Family Observances

For individuals and families, May Day provides an opportunity to engage in meaningful rituals that celebrate spring's vitality and the joy of connection. A simple nature walk can become a sacred practice when approached with intention, offering moments to observe the blooming world and reflect on one's relationship with the Earth. Families might celebrate by crafting flower crowns, decorating their homes with fresh blossoms, or planting flowers or herbs together. These activities symbolize growth, beauty, and renewal, while also creating lasting memories. Before planting, a moment of reflection or prayer can transform the act into a ritual of hope and gratitude.

Personal rituals, such as journaling or meditation, can focus on themes of renewal and growth. Individuals might write affirmations or intentions for the coming months, inspired by the season's energy of abundance and potential. Lighting a candle during this practice can serve as a symbolic gesture of illumination and focus.

Solo participants may also create their own altar to honor the season. Using fresh flowers, ribbons, and small offerings, they can create a sacred space for reflection and gratitude. Meditating before the altar or offering silent prayers of thanks can deepen the sense of connection with nature's cycles.

Honoring Tradition While Embracing New Universalist Values

May Day's historical roots in Beltane and similar traditions provide a rich foundation for its observance in New Universalism. By honoring these practices while integrating New Universalist theology, the holiday becomes both a celebration of ancient wisdom and a reflection of modern spiritual values. New Universalists view May Day as a sacred reminder of life's abundance and the importance of nurturing the connections that sustain us. The festival's themes of joy, creativity, and renewal resonate deeply with the faith's emphasis on compassion, community, and reverence for the natural world. Through communal and individual practices, we are encouraged to embody these values in our daily lives.

By celebrating May Day, New Universalists affirm our commitment to living in harmony with the Earth's rhythms and honoring the cycles of renewal that sustain all life. This vibrant festival serves as a joyful expression of gratitude, hope, and unity, inspiring participants to carry its energy into the months ahead.

Harvest Festival: A Celebration of Gratitude and Sharing

The Harvest Festival, celebrated in late summer or early autumn, marks the time when the first fruits of the Earth are gathered and shared. Rooted in agrarian traditions worldwide, this observance reflects humanity's deep dependence on nature's cycles and the importance of community in ensuring survival and abundance.

In New Universalism, the Harvest Festival is a sacred time to express gratitude for the Earth's gifts, recognize the labor that makes sustenance possible, and share abundance with others. Drawing on traditions such as the Wiccan Lammas, Indigenous harvest ceremonies, and thanksgiving practices from diverse cultures, this festival embodies themes of gratitude, generosity, and interconnectedness. The Harvest Festival invites us to reflect on the blessings of the season and to extend those blessings outward through acts of sharing and service. It is a time to honor the Earth, strengthen bonds within the community, and renew commitments to responsible stewardship of nature's resources.

Community Ritual and Celebration

In New Universalist communities, the Harvest Festival is a vibrant and inclusive celebration. The day often begins with a communal gathering in an outdoor space, such as a park, garden, or community farm. Participants are encouraged to bring offerings of food, flowers, or symbols of the harvest, which are arranged on a central altar as an expression of collective gratitude. A central ritual of the Harvest Festival is the sharing of the "Loaf of Unity." This freshly baked bread, often made from locally sourced grains, is blessed by the ritual leader and shared among participants to symbolize the shared labor and interconnectedness of the community. As each person receives a piece, they are invited to silently reflect on their gratitude for the Earth's abundance and their role in nurturing their community and the planet.

Another cherished ritual is the "Circle of Giving." In this practice, participants exchange small tokens or blessings—such as a piece of fruit, a handmade item, or a heartfelt message—with their neighbors in the circle. This act symbolizes the flow of generosity and interdependence that sustains both individuals and the larger community.

Music, storytelling, and dance are integral to the Harvest Festival. Folk songs about the changing seasons, traditional dances celebrating the bounty of the Earth, and stories that convey wisdom about gratitude and sustainability enrich the celebration and strengthen communal bonds. The festival often concludes with a shared meal featuring seasonal dishes prepared from local ingredients. This feast serves as a tangible expression of gratitude and a time for fellowship, allowing us to reflect on the themes of the day and deepen our sense of connection with one another.

Individual and Family Observances

For individuals and families, the Harvest Festival offers opportunities to cultivate gratitude and connection through personal rituals and activities. Families might begin the day by preparing a meal together, using seasonal ingredients and reflecting on the effort and resources that bring food to their table. Before eating, a moment of shared silence or a spoken blessing can transform the meal into a sacred act of gratitude.

Creating an autumn-themed altar at home is another meaningful practice. Individuals and families can gather symbols of the season—such as colorful leaves, grains, fruits, and candles—and arrange them in a space for reflection and meditation. Writing messages of thanks on slips of paper and placing them on the altar can serve as a powerful reminder of the blessings in one's life. Personal reflection through journaling or meditation is also encouraged during the Harvest Festival. Participants might journal about the things they are grateful for, the lessons they have learned in the past year, or the ways they can share their abundance with others. Meditation focused on the themes of gratitude and giving can deepen one's connection to the Earth and community.

Honoring Tradition While Embracing New Universalist Values

The Harvest Festival's historical roots in agrarian and spiritual traditions provide a rich framework for its observance in New Universalism. By incorporating elements from Wiccan Lammas, Indigenous harvest ceremonies, and global thanksgiving customs, New Universalists honor the wisdom of the past while adapting these practices to align with our theology.

New Universalism emphasizes gratitude not only as an individual virtue but as a communal and spiritual act that strengthens the bonds between people and the Earth. Through shared rituals, acts of service, and expressions of gratitude, we embody the faith's core values of stewardship, compassion, and interconnectedness.

The Harvest Festival inspires individuals and communities to recognize the sacredness of the Earth's gifts and to commit to sharing those gifts responsibly and generously. By celebrating this festival, New Universalists affirm our dedication to living in harmony with the planet and supporting one another in a spirit of unity and abundance.

All Souls Day: Honoring the Spirit of Connection and Remembrance

All Souls Day is observed annually on 31 October. In New Universalism this is a deeply spiritual observance rooted in honoring the cycle of life and death, the memory of those who have passed, and the enduring connections that bind us to our ancestors. Drawing inspiration from a rich tapestry of traditions—including the Christian All Souls Day, the Pagan Samhain, Halloween's cultural festivities, the Latin American Día de los Muertos, and the Eastern practice of Tomb Sweeping Day—this holiday serves as a universal expression of remembrance, gratitude, and spiritual continuity.

In New Universalism, All Souls Day is a sacred time for both personal reflection and communal observance, fostering a sense of connection not only with those who came before us but also with the broader cycles of life and the natural world. It is a celebration of legacy, family, and the spiritual threads that connect all beings across time and space.

Community Ritual and Celebration

The communal observance of All Souls Day begins with the preparation of a sacred space. An altar, central to the gathering, is adorned with photographs, mementos, and symbols of departed loved ones. Flowers, particularly marigolds—a nod to Día de los Muertos—are arranged to create a vibrant and sacred atmosphere. Candles are lit to symbolize guiding lights for the spirits, inviting them to join the living in the celebration.

A cornerstone of the New Universalist All Souls Day is the **Ceremony of Remembrance**, where participants share stories, memories, and reflections about those who have passed. This practice fosters community connection and allows us to honor the impact our ancestors and loved ones have had on our lives. This storytelling tradition draws on the spirit of Samhain, where the veil between the worlds is believed to be thinnest, and communication with the dead is most profound.

Another significant ritual is the **Offering of Nourishment and Gratitude**. Drawing from Día de los Muertos and Tomb Sweeping Day, attendees place offerings of food, drink, or symbolic items on the altar to express gratitude to our ancestors. This act acknowledges the interconnectedness of all life and honors the sacrifices and guidance of those who came before. The ceremony may also include the ringing of bells or the recitation of prayers to call forth and honor the spirits.

The evening culminates in a **Procession of Light**. Participants carry candles in a meditative walk, symbolizing the journey of the soul and the enduring presence of light and love in times of darkness. This reflective act unites the community in shared reverence for the cycles of life and death, embodying the New Universalist values of connection and compassion.

Individual and Family Observances

For individuals and families, All Souls Day provides an opportunity for intimate reflection and ritual. Creating a personal or family altar at home allows for a meaningful connection with ancestors and loved ones. Items such as photographs, heirlooms, and offerings are arranged with care, transforming a small corner of the home into a sacred space.

Families may prepare a shared meal, incorporating favorite dishes of their ancestors or loved ones. Before eating, they can pause for a moment of silence, offering gratitude and sharing memories of those who have passed. They may set an empty place at the table or leave a small offering of the meal prepared at the family alter or family cemetery. This practice, inspired by Tomb Sweeping Day's reverence for familial bonds, reinforces the importance of connection across generations.

Another individual or family tradition might include a **Night of Reflection**, where participants light a single candle and meditate on the lessons and legacy of those who have departed. Journaling about the ways ancestors' values, struggles, and triumphs continue to influence the present fosters a deep sense of continuity and gratitude.

For those who wish to engage creatively, making **Remembrance Art**—such as decorating masks, drawing symbolic images, or crafting messages to be placed on the altar—can provide a meaningful way to connect with the spiritual essence of the holiday. Inspired by Halloween's creativity and Día de los Muertos' vibrant artistry, this practice adds a personal touch to the observance.

Honoring Tradition While Embracing New Universalist Values

The celebration of All Souls Day in New Universalism is deeply respectful of its diverse roots. From the solemn prayers of All Souls Day to the joyful creativity of Día de los Muertos, from the introspection of Samhain to the familial connections of Tomb Sweeping Day, this observance weaves together traditions that honor the sacred bonds between the living and the departed.

New Universalism expands these practices by integrating its core theological principles. The act of remembrance becomes not just a ritual but a profound affirmation of interconnectedness, filial piety, and Earth stewardship. Lighting candles symbolizes the eternal flame of unity; sharing stories reinforces the values of compassion and gratitude; and engaging in creative acts honors the enduring legacy of the human spirit. All Souls Day reminds New Universalists of our place in the grand cycle of life and death. By embracing this holiday, individuals and communities affirm our commitment to honoring the past, living mindfully in the present, and preparing a legacy for future generations. It is a time to celebrate life in its fullness and to find peace in the eternal connection that binds all beings.

All Saints Day: A Celebration of Shared Spiritual Heritage

All Saints Day in New Universalism is a vibrant celebration of humanity's shared spiritual heritage, honoring figures of inspiration and wisdom across all faiths, philosophies, and cultures. This observance recognizes the contributions of saints, sages, and exemplary individuals who have embodied universal virtues such as compassion, courage, and integrity.

Drawing its origins from the Christian All Saints Day, this holiday also incorporates elements from Earth-based and global traditions that celebrate those who have lived lives of moral and spiritual excellence. In New Universalism, All Saints Day transcends a single religious tradition, transforming into an inclusive commemoration that uplifts the collective spiritual legacy of humanity. It is a day to reflect on the guiding lights of history, those who have shaped our understanding of universal truths, and the values we strive to embody in our lives.

Community Ritual and Celebration

The communal observance of All Saints Day begins with a **Circle of Honor**, where attendees gather to share the names and stories of individuals they regard as saints, mentors, or guides. These figures may include historical saints from various faiths, spiritual leaders, or even personal role models who exemplify universal values. This practice encourages mutual respect and a recognition of diverse paths to enlightenment.

A key ritual of the day is the **Tree of Virtues Ceremony**, inspired by the universal symbolism of trees as connectors of Earth and heaven. A bare tree or tree-shaped stand is placed at the center of the gathering space. Each participant is invited to write the name of an inspiring figure, along with a virtue they embodied, on a small leaf-shaped card. These leaves are then attached to the tree, symbolizing the flourishing legacy of universal virtues and the interconnectedness of humanity's moral and spiritual heritage.

Music and poetry play a significant role in the celebration. Hymns, chants, or songs from different traditions are shared, emphasizing themes of unity, courage, and spiritual striving. Poetry readings may include verses from Rumi, Tagore, or other global poets who have explored universal truths. This diversity of expression reflects the New Universalist commitment to inclusivity and shared wisdom.

The communal observance concludes with a **Blessing of Aspirations**, where participants join hands and collectively affirm our commitment to living lives of virtue and service. This ritual reinforces the connection between the celebration of saints and the call to embody their values in our daily life.

Individual and Family Observances

For individuals and families, All Saints Day offers an opportunity for personal reflection and intimate ritual. A simple practice is creating a **Personal Shrine of Inspiration**, featuring images, writings, or objects associated with individuals who have profoundly influenced one's spiritual or ethical journey. This shrine serves as a space for meditation and contemplation, encouraging gratitude for those who have illuminated the path.

Families may choose to host a **Shared Storytelling Evening**, where each member recounts the story of a person they admire, exploring the values and lessons that resonate with their lives. This practice not only strengthens familial bonds but also cultivates an appreciation for the diverse ways in which virtue can manifest.

Another meaningful practice is engaging in **Acts of Service** in honor of the day. Whether volunteering, donating to a cause, or offering kindness to a neighbor, these actions embody the spirit of sainthood and demonstrate how individuals can contribute to the common good.

For personal reflection, journaling prompts such as *"Who inspires me to live with greater courage and compassion?"* or *"What virtues do I strive to embody in my daily life?"* can deepen one's connection to the themes of the holiday.

Honoring Tradition While Embracing New Universalist Values

All Saints Day in New Universalism pays homage to its roots while expanding its scope to include the rich diversity of human wisdom. From the Christian tradition of venerating saints to the Earth-based practice of honoring ancestral spirits, this observance weaves together threads of reverence for those who have walked before us on the path of virtue. New Universalism enhances this tradition by emphasizing the universal applicability of sainthood. Saints are not confined to religious figures but include philosophers, activists, scientists, and everyday individuals who inspire others through their lives. This inclusivity reflects the theology of New Universalism, which honors wisdom wherever it is found and recognizes the potential for greatness in every person.

All Saints Day serves as a reminder of the enduring power of virtue and the collective heritage of humanity's moral and spiritual striving. It invites both individuals and communities to reflect on our role in carrying forward this legacy, fostering a spirit of gratitude, unity, and aspiration.

11

Honoring Filial Piety and Intergenerational Bonds

Respect for Elders and Ancestry

In New Universalism, the value of filial piety—the profound respect for elders, ancestors, and those who have shaped our world—is a foundational principle. It serves as both a moral compass and a spiritual mandate, encouraging individuals to honor the wisdom of past generations while fostering intergenerational bonds aspiring to reciprocal respect and care. This concept transcends individual relationships, encompassing a broader commitment to recognizing the interconnectedness of all life and the continuity of human experience.

Honoring elders and ancestors is not merely a passive act of remembrance; it is a living tradition that breathes vitality into personal and communal practices. Within New Universalist theology, these acts are viewed as essential for cultivating gratitude, humility, and a sense of belonging within the great tapestry of existence. By acknowledging the contributions of those who came before us, we affirm our connection to the past while embracing the responsibility to shape a more harmonious future.

New Universalism explores how filial piety is expressed offering insights into its reciprocal nature across varied relationships, including familial, community, and spiritual bonds. Through rituals and meditative practices that enable us to connect deeply with our ancestry and cultural heritage we reflect on how the lessons and values of our forebears inspire personal growth, spiritual understanding, and a shared sense of purpose.

At its heart, the practice of honoring elders and ancestry in New Universalism is an expression of unity. It reminds us that while we are each unique individuals, we are also inextricably linked to the generations before and after us. This continuum of life fosters a sacred obligation: to give reverence to those who came before, to learn from their wisdom, and to pave the way for those yet to come.

The Importance of Honoring Elders and Ancestors

In New Universalism, honoring elders and ancestors is a practice deeply rooted in the theology of interconnectedness and the principle of reciprocity. Filial piety serves as a sacred bond that links generations, fostering gratitude, humility, and a profound sense of belonging. By respecting those who have come before us, we acknowledge the foundation upon which our lives are built and embrace the wisdom they have imparted.

Elders hold a unique position as living repositories of knowledge, tradition, and experience. In honoring them, we affirm their continuing role as guides and caretakers of wisdom. This respect is not unidirectional; it is reciprocal. Elders, too, are called to honor the younger generation by offering support, guidance, and the space to grow into their unique identities. This mutual reverence creates an environment where all members of a community feel valued and heard.

Ancestors, though no longer physically present, remain integral to our spiritual and cultural identities. Within New Universalist theology, ancestors are viewed not as distant figures of the past but as active participants in the ongoing story of life. Their contributions, sacrifices, and teachings resonate in the present, shaping the values, traditions, and aspirations we carry forward. By honoring them, we bridge the temporal gap between past and present, fostering continuity and connection.

Honoring elders begins with simple acts of respect: listening attentively to their stories, seeking their counsel, and creating spaces where they feel valued and included. Community gatherings, whether formal or informal, provide opportunities to celebrate the lives and contributions of elders. These events can include storytelling circles, where elders share their experiences and lessons, fostering a sense of collective wisdom. New Universalist theology emphasizes the role of elders in modeling virtues such as patience, humility, and compassion. By embodying these qualities, elders inspire younger generations to approach life with integrity and purpose. In turn, younger members of the community can honor elders by offering their assistance, showing gratitude through acts of service, and ensuring that their voices are heard in communal decision-making.

Honoring Ancestors: A Bridge Across Time

In New Universalism, the practice of honoring ancestors is a deeply spiritual act that reaffirms the interconnectedness of all life. Ancestors are seen as guardians and guides whose presence can be felt in moments of reflection, prayer, and ritual. Their lives serve as reminders of resilience, strength, and the enduring spirit of humanity. Creating an ancestral altar is one way to honor these connections. Such altars can include photographs, heirlooms, or symbolic items that represent the family lineage or cultural heritage. The act of tending to an altar—cleaning it, adding fresh flowers, or lighting candles—becomes a meditative practice that invites moments of gratitude and remembrance.

Additionally, New Universalists are encouraged to reflect on the broader lineage of humanity, honoring not only our biological ancestors but also the countless individuals who have contributed to the collective progress of society. This perspective fosters a sense of unity and shared responsibility, inspiring actions that benefit the greater good.

Filial Piety: A Living Legacy

The principle of filial piety in New Universalism is dynamic and evolving, emphasizing the reciprocal nature of respect across generations. While younger generations honor the wisdom and sacrifices of their elders, elders reciprocate by nurturing the growth and individuality of the younger members. This balance ensures that the bonds of family and community remain strong, fostering an environment of mutual care and understanding. By honoring elders and ancestors, New Universalists embrace our place within a larger continuum of life, acknowledging the debt owed to the past and the responsibilities carried into the future. This practice becomes a source of inspiration, grounding individuals in a sense of purpose and reminding them of the profound connections that unite all beings.

Rituals for Honoring Ancestors

Rituals for honoring ancestors in New Universalism serve as sacred acts of remembrance and connection. They provide structured yet flexible practices through which individuals and communities can express gratitude for their lineage, celebrate the lives of those who have come before, and draw inspiration from their wisdom. These rituals are both deeply personal and profoundly communal, reflecting New Universalism's emphasis on unity, reciprocity, and reverence. Honoring ancestors is a deeply spiritual practice in New Universalism, rooted in the understanding that our lives are part of a vast and interconnected lineage. This sacred relationship with those who came before us forms the foundation of filial piety, encouraging gratitude, reflection, and reverence for the wisdom and sacrifices of previous generations. Across cultures and traditions, the act of honoring ancestors has been expressed in rituals that bridge the realms of the living and the departed, and New Universalism draws from these practices to create meaningful and inclusive ways of engaging with our heritage.

Ancestral Altar

At the heart of ancestral reverence in New Universalism is the creation of an ancestral altar. This sacred space serves as a tangible connection to the past, a focal point for reflection, remembrance, and spiritual dialogue. The ancestral altar is a practice with deep historical roots, appearing in numerous cultures around the world. In Chinese traditions, altars often hold photographs, incense, and offerings of food or drink, reflecting respect and ongoing familial ties. In Latin America, the vibrant altars of Día de los Muertos are adorned with marigolds, candles, and mementos of the deceased, inviting their spirits to join the living in celebration and remembrance. African traditions similarly incorporate symbolic objects, such as textiles or sacred items, to honor lineage and cultural identity.

In New Universalism, the ancestral altar is a dynamic and personal expression of spiritual practice. A typical altar might include photographs of ancestors or loved ones who have passed, heirlooms or objects representing family traditions, and natural elements such as stones, flowers, or branches. The use of candles or lanterns adds a sacred dimension, symbolizing the eternal light of memory and connection. Each item placed on the altar carries intention, creating a space that feels alive with the presence of those who came before. Tending to the altar—whether by lighting a candle, arranging fresh flowers, or simply pausing in quiet reflection—becomes a ritual of gratitude and continuity.

Seasonal Remembrance Rituals

Seasonal observances, such as those during All Souls Day or other ancestral holidays, provide communal opportunities to honor ancestors. During these times, New Universalist communities are encouraged to integrate remembrance into existing seasonal rites. For example:

- **Lighting Candles:** Participants may light candles for specific ancestors, sharing their names and a memory or lesson associated with them.

- **Sharing Stories:** Community members can gather to recount stories of their loved ones, weaving a collective narrative of wisdom, resilience, and love.
- **Symbolic Actions:** Activities like planting trees or creating communal altars offer tangible expressions of remembrance and continuity.

These rituals are deeply connected to the cycles of nature, symbolizing the interconnectedness of life and death, growth and renewal.

Offerings and Prayers

Making offerings and saying prayers for ancestors are integral aspects of honoring their presence. Offerings reflect gratitude and acknowledgment of the continuing influence of those who have passed. Some common offerings in New Universalist practice include:

- **Food and Drink:** Representing sustenance and hospitality, these offerings acknowledge the nourishment provided by one's lineage.
- **Incense or Herbs:** Burning incense or herbs, such as sage or cedar, symbolizes purification and the lifting of prayers to the spiritual realm.
- **Handwritten Notes or Symbols:** Writing letters of gratitude or drawing symbols that represent personal or family values allows for a creative and intimate expression of connection.

In New Universalism, these offerings are accompanied by prayers that reflect gratitude, honor, and a request for guidance.

Prayer of Honor and Remembrance:

"With deep reverence, we honor the spirits of those who came before us.
Ancestors, we remember your wisdom, your strength, and your love.
You are the roots that ground us, the foundation of our being.
May your lessons guide us as we walk our paths,
And may your memories remain eternal within our hearts."

Prayer of Gratitude and Offering:

"To those who paved the way before us, we offer our deepest thanks.
These offerings are given in gratitude.
For your sacrifices, your dreams, and your love, we are forever grateful.
May this token of our thanks reach you across the veil,
And may your spirits find peace and joy in our remembrance."

Incorporating these prayers into ritual observances fosters a sense of dialogue with the spiritual world, allowing individuals and communities to engage with their heritage on a deeper level. For those seeking guidance or support, the Prayer for Guidance and Evocation provides a framework for connection:

Prayer for Guidance and Evocation:

"Beloved ancestors, guardians of our lineage, I call upon you.
Grant me your wisdom, as I navigate the challenges of this life.
Let your strength and courage flow through me,
That I may honor your legacy with my words and deeds.
Be present with me in this sacred moment,
And guide me as I seek harmony, justice, and truth."

These prayers are not only expressions of reverence but also affirmations of the enduring presence of our ancestors in our lives. They remind us that we are part of an unbroken chain of existence, a lineage that connects us to the past and propels us toward the future.

Integrating Ancestral Rituals into Daily Life

While formal rituals are significant, daily acts of remembrance can also honor ancestors. Simple practices, such as saying a silent "thank you" before meals or carrying a symbolic token of an ancestor, reinforce the connection between past and present. Journaling about lessons learned from family stories or meditating on the values passed down through generations can deepen one's understanding of their lineage and role within it.

Daily practices, such as lighting a candle on the altar help weave ancestral reverence into the fabric of everyday life. On a communal level, storytelling sessions, shared meals, or collaborative rituals provide opportunities for communities to come together in remembrance and gratitude. These acts of collective memory not only strengthen bonds but also affirm the shared values and traditions that unite us.

In honoring ancestors, New Universalism emphasizes the interconnectedness of all life, the importance of remembering our roots, and the responsibility to carry forward the wisdom and values of those who came before us. This sacred practice serves as a reminder that while we are individuals, we are also part of a vast and eternal tapestry, woven together by love, memory, and shared purpose

Meditative Practices to Connect with Ancestry

Connecting with ancestry through meditation is a powerful way to deepen one's understanding of self, heritage, and place in the continuum of life. Within New Universalism, meditative practices centered on ancestry foster a sense of unity with one's lineage and cultural heritage, serving as a spiritual bridge to those who have come before. These meditations are grounded in the belief that our ancestors are a source of strength, guidance, and wisdom, and that by connecting with them, we can better understand our own values, paths, and roles within the larger tapestry of life.

One foundational practice is the **Guided Visualization of Ancestral Connections**, designed to create a vivid sense of communion with those who have passed. This meditation begins by finding a quiet, sacred space, such as near an ancestral altar or in a place of natural beauty. We are encouraged to sit comfortably, close our eyes, and focus on our breath, drawing our awareness inward. The visualization unfolds by imagining a golden thread extending from the heart, connecting to the ancestors who came before. This thread, shimmering with light, symbolizes the shared life-force that flows across generations. As the visualization deepens, we are invited to picture a gathering of our ancestors in a sacred space—a forest clearing, a circle of stones, or beneath a starry sky. These ancestors may appear as familiar faces or as symbolic figures representing the strength and resilience of the lineage. We are encouraged to greet our ancestors with gratitude, expressing thanks for their sacrifices, wisdom, and love. This visualization can conclude with a moment of stillness, allowing messages, emotions, or insights to emerge from the shared spiritual connection.

A complementary practice is the **Reflection Exercise on Ancestral Values and Strengths**, which helps us explore the traits, lessons, and traditions passed down through our family line. Using a journal or simply sitting in quiet contemplation, practitioners are encouraged to reflect on questions such as:

- *What values did my ancestors hold dear, and how do I see those values in myself?*
- *What challenges did they face, and what strengths did they cultivate to overcome them?*
- *How can I honor their legacy in my daily actions and choices?*

This reflective practice not only deepens appreciation for the lineage but also fosters a sense of responsibility to carry forward the best qualities and lessons into the present and future.

For those seeking a more somatic and grounded connection, **Ancestral Root Meditation** offers a way to feel physically and spiritually connected to the Earth and one's lineage. In this practice, participants imagine themselves as a tree, with roots extending deep into the soil. These roots intertwine with the roots of their ancestors, creating a vast and interconnected network beneath the ground. As participants breathe, they visualize drawing strength, wisdom, and support from this network, feeling anchored and empowered by the enduring presence of their lineage.

Another practice that resonates deeply within New Universalism is the **Cultural Remembrance Meditation**, which focuses on honoring one's cultural heritage through sensory experiences. This meditation may involve lighting incense with a scent associated with the homeland of one's ancestors, listening to traditional music, or holding an object of cultural significance. These sensory anchors serve as portals to memories and emotions tied to one's heritage, deepening the connection to both individual ancestors and the broader cultural narrative.

In all these meditative practices, the emphasis is not only on honoring the past but also on integrating its wisdom into present life. By cultivating a sense of connection to one's lineage, we can draw strength from the resilience of our ancestors, find guidance in their values, and develop a deeper understanding of our place within the flow of time and existence.

New Universalism encourages the inclusion of ancestral meditative practices in both personal and communal settings. Individually, these practices offer moments of quiet reflection and spiritual nourishment. Communally, they provide opportunities to share stories, celebrate shared heritage, and foster a sense of unity across generations. These meditations remind us that while we are shaped by the past, we also hold the power to shape the future—a sacred responsibility and a profound privilege.

Community Values and Leadership

Community is the foundation upon which New Universalism thrives, serving as a dynamic space where individuals connect, share wisdom, and grow together. Rooted in the principles of filial piety, New Universalism emphasizes a reciprocal relationship between the individual and the collective, recognizing the unique contributions each person brings to the shared fabric of life. In this context, community values and leadership are not merely tools for organization but sacred practices that embody the mutual respect, responsibility, and care that define the New Universalist faith.

Within a New Universalist framework, leadership is not a hierarchical imposition but a shared and fluid practice, where both elders and youth play vital roles in guiding the community. Elders, with their wisdom and experience, provide a stabilizing presence, preserving traditions and offering insight into life's challenges and joys. Simultaneously, younger members bring energy, creativity, and fresh perspectives, ensuring that the community remains adaptable and forward-thinking. This harmonious interplay exemplifies the spiritual principle of balance, a cornerstone of New Universalist doctrine.

Community is also the space where values are nurtured and reinforced. It is in the collective that members learn to embody compassion, integrity, and responsibility. Through active participation in communal life, we find opportunities to reflect on our place within the whole, recognizing our interdependence and the importance of mutual care. Leadership, in this context, is not about authority but about service, with leaders acting as facilitators who inspire, guide, and support the collective growth of the community.

New Universalism believes in the essential role of community in passing down wisdom, the importance of encouraging youth participation in leadership, the creation of opportunities for intergenerational learning, and the promotion of mutual respect and understanding. Together, these elements illustrate how New Universalism fosters a culture of inclusion, collaboration, and shared growth, demonstrating that strong communities are built not through division but through unity and reciprocity.

Role of Community in Passing Down Wisdom

In New Universalism, the community is more than a gathering of individuals; it is a sacred space where the collective wisdom of generations converges to nurture, guide, and inspire. Community life is viewed as an interwoven tapestry, with each thread representing the contributions, experiences, and perspectives of its members. This interconnectedness reflects New Universalist theology's emphasis on reciprocity, mutual care, and the shared responsibility of passing down values, knowledge, and traditions.

Communities serve as living archives of cultural and spiritual wisdom. Through storytelling, rituals, and daily interactions, they preserve the essence of lived experiences, ensuring that future generations can draw from a wellspring of guidance. Elders play an especially significant role in this process. Their lived experiences embody resilience, adaptability, and insight into life's complexities. In New Universalism, filial piety emphasizes not only respecting elders but actively engaging with their knowledge, seeking their counsel, and valuing their stories as sacred teachings.

However, this flow of wisdom is not unidirectional. Younger members of the community are equally vital to its vibrancy and growth. They bring curiosity, creativity, and innovation, challenging traditions when needed and ensuring that the community evolves in response to a changing world. In this way, New Universalism envisions the relationship between generations as a dynamic exchange rather than a rigid hierarchy. This reciprocity enriches the collective experience, fostering a culture where learning is a lifelong endeavor and wisdom is a shared treasure.

Rituals and practices in the New Universalist community emphasize this intergenerational connection. For example, storytelling circles are often held as sacred gatherings where members of different ages come together to share experiences, dreams, and insights. These circles honor the contributions of elders while inviting younger participants to share their hopes and visions. Through such practices, the community celebrates the diversity of perspectives that each generation brings, reinforcing the idea that every voice matters.

New Universalism also highlights the importance of cultural and spiritual traditions in community wisdom. Members are encouraged to learn about and honor their heritage while remaining open to the lessons that other cultures and practices offer. This approach fosters inclusivity, recognizing that wisdom transcends boundaries and is enriched by diversity. By creating spaces where traditions are celebrated and adapted, communities become not only preservers of the past but innovators of the future.

The role of community in passing down wisdom is not solely about preserving knowledge but about nurturing a sense of belonging and continuity. It reminds individuals of their place within the larger story of humanity, grounding them in shared values while encouraging growth and transformation. Through the collective effort of sharing, learning, and honoring one another, New Universalist communities exemplify the sacred practice of interdependence, ensuring that wisdom flows like a river—endlessly replenished and ever connected to its source.

Encouraging Youth Participation in Leadership

In New Universalism, the engagement of youth in community leadership is not just encouraged—it is essential. Leadership is seen as a collective responsibility, one that must include voices from every generation to ensure the community's resilience and adaptability. This reciprocal relationship between established leaders and emerging voices reflects the core New Universalist value of filial piety, emphasizing mutual respect, responsibility, and shared growth.

Youth participation in leadership begins with creating meaningful opportunities for involvement. In New Universalist communities, young people are invited to take active roles in decision-making, event planning, and service initiatives. By being included in these processes, they develop a sense of responsibility and ownership over the community's direction. This approach reinforces the belief that leadership is not confined to age or status but is a shared endeavor rooted in service to the greater good.

Mentorship is a key practice for fostering youth leadership. Elders and experienced members of the community are encouraged to serve as mentors, guiding younger members with wisdom and care. These relationships are more than educational; they are partnerships where both mentor and mentee benefit from the exchange of ideas and perspectives. For example, a seasoned leader might guide a younger member in organizing a seasonal festival, offering practical advice while allowing space for creative input. This collaboration not only strengthens the younger member's confidence but also revitalizes traditional practices with fresh insights.

Collaborative projects and discussions further deepen youth engagement. Community forums, for instance, provide a space where younger members can present ideas, share concerns, and participate in shaping communal goals. These discussions exemplify the New Universalist principle of inclusivity, demonstrating that every voice is valued. Such practices also help bridge generational divides, fostering understanding and mutual respect.

Leadership opportunities for youth often align with the community's spiritual and ethical commitments. For example, young members might lead environmental clean-ups, organize food drives, or host educational workshops on social justice. These activities allow them to embody New Universalist values, such as Earth Stewardship and Social Responsibility, while building essential skills in collaboration, empathy, and organization. By connecting leadership roles to these values, the community ensures that its leaders remain grounded in its core principles.

Celebrating youth contributions is another vital aspect of encouraging leadership. Public recognition of their efforts, whether through ceremonies, acknowledgments during services, or symbolic gestures, reinforces the community's appreciation for their role. These moments of recognition are not just about individual achievements; they are collective affirmations that the community thrives on the energy and dedication of its younger members.

Through these practices, New Universalism seeks to cultivate leaders who are not only competent but deeply connected to the community and its values. By empowering youth to take on leadership roles, the community ensures its continuity and growth, fostering a culture where every member feels seen, heard, and essential to the whole. Leadership, in this sense, is not a position but a shared journey, one where generations walk side by side toward a common purpose.

Creating Opportunities for Intergenerational Learning

In New Universalism, the bond between generations is considered sacred, a living thread that weaves wisdom, experience, and vitality into the fabric of the community. Opportunities for intergenerational learning are central to this vision, serving as a way to honor the reciprocal nature of filial piety while fostering a culture of mutual respect and shared growth. By bringing together elders and youth, these opportunities celebrate the balance of tradition and innovation, ensuring that both heritage and new ideas are cherished.

One of the most impactful ways to encourage intergenerational learning is through community gatherings that emphasize shared storytelling and wisdom exchange. Storytelling circles, for instance, allow elders to recount life experiences, cultural teachings, and ancestral stories, providing younger members with insights into the values and history that have shaped the community.

These gatherings are not one-sided; youth are encouraged to share their perspectives, questions, and creative ideas, creating a dynamic dialogue that enriches all participants. The exchange is deeply aligned with New Universalist theology, which values every individual's voice as a unique expression of the universal spirit.

Workshops and skill-sharing events are another powerful tool for intergenerational learning. These events might involve traditional crafts, environmental practices, or even modern skills like technology use, allowing participants to both teach and learn. For example, an elder skilled in sustainable farming techniques might guide a younger group in creating a community garden, while a tech-savvy youth could help elders navigate digital tools to connect with the wider world. These collaborative experiences highlight the strength of community bonds, reinforcing the idea that every generation has something valuable to offer.

Seasonal celebrations also serve as fertile ground for intergenerational learning. During these gatherings, rituals often incorporate elements that require participation from all ages, such as creating shared altars, planting trees, or performing symbolic actions together. These rituals provide a space for elders to guide and teach while inviting youth to infuse the traditions with their energy and creativity. The act of participating in these ceremonies fosters a deeper understanding of the community's spiritual practices and strengthens the collective identity.

Educational initiatives, such as mentorship programs or cultural workshops, further deepen intergenerational ties. Mentorship provides a structured way for elders to pass on their wisdom while nurturing the growth of younger members. In return, youth mentors can offer fresh perspectives, bridging traditional knowledge with contemporary challenges. Cultural workshops, on the other hand, might focus on exploring diverse spiritual practices, histories, and ethical principles, inviting both elders and youth to reflect on their shared and individual journeys.

A particularly meaningful practice in New Universalist communities is the inclusion of reflective activities that honor both past and future generations. A community might host an event where members plant a tree together, symbolizing the continuity of life and the shared responsibility for nurturing it. During such events, participants could reflect on the lessons they have received from their ancestors while considering the legacy they wish to leave for those yet to come. These practices embody the core New Universalist value of interconnectedness, reminding all participants of their place within a larger, ongoing story.

In fostering intergenerational learning, New Universalism also emphasizes the importance of balance—celebrating the wisdom of elders without romanticizing the past and honoring the vitality of youth without overlooking the need for guidance. This balance reflects the dynamic, evolving nature of the community itself, which thrives on the interplay of tradition and innovation. Ultimately, intergenerational learning within New Universalism is more than a transfer of knowledge; it is a sacred exchange that deepens relationships, enriches understanding, and builds a resilient, compassionate community. By providing opportunities for elders and youth to learn from and support one another, the community ensures that its values are not only preserved but continually renewed and expanded for the benefit of all.

Promoting Mutual Respect and Understanding

Mutual respect and understanding form the cornerstone of a harmonious New Universalist community. These principles transcend mere tolerance, creating a culture where every individual—regardless of age, background, or experience—is valued as a unique contributor to the collective. In the context of intergenerational bonds, mutual respect is not only a moral imperative but a sacred expression of the New Universalist virtue of filial piety, which emphasizes reciprocal care, honor, and acknowledgment between individuals and their communities.

To nurture mutual respect, the community must actively create spaces where elders feel cherished for their wisdom and experiences, while youth are empowered to contribute their energy and perspectives. In practice, this begins with fostering a culture of listening. For elders, it means being open to the fresh ideas and innovative thinking that younger generations bring, recognizing their role as torchbearers of the future. For youth, it means honoring the life lessons and guidance of elders, understanding that their insights are invaluable in navigating life's complexities.

Community gatherings and rituals serve as essential platforms for cultivating this culture. For instance, a shared meal can become an intentional act of respect when each participant is encouraged to share a thought or reflection, creating an atmosphere where every voice is heard. Similarly, intergenerational discussions can be woven into seasonal celebrations or workshops, allowing participants to explore topics of mutual interest—from spiritual practices to environmental stewardship. These exchanges not only build understanding but deepen the bonds of trust and collaboration within the community.

Practical steps can also be taken to ensure that respect and understanding are consistently demonstrated. For example, elders might be invited to lead workshops on traditional skills or ethical teachings, while youth could spearhead initiatives that integrate technology or address contemporary issues. By creating opportunities for collaboration, the community highlights the unique strengths of each generation, promoting a sense of shared purpose and unity.

Another powerful tool for fostering mutual respect is storytelling. Inviting elders to share their life experiences, cultural knowledge, and spiritual insights provides youth with a profound sense of connection to the past, while also affirming the elders' significance in the present. Conversely, encouraging youth to share their aspirations, challenges, and visions for the future allows elders to see their legacy in action, fostering a sense of hope and continuity. These exchanges are particularly meaningful when paired with rituals, such as lighting candles for shared intentions or planting seeds as symbols of growth.

New Universalist theology also emphasizes humility as an essential component of respect. Members are encouraged to approach intergenerational relationships with a spirit of humility, acknowledging that learning is a two-way street. Elders may hold deep reservoirs of wisdom, but youth often embody the courage to question, adapt, and innovate. Both perspectives are vital, and the interplay between them strengthens the community as a whole. At its core, promoting mutual respect and understanding is about recognizing the sacredness of every individual's journey. This recognition is reflected in the rituals, teachings, and daily interactions that define New Universalist practice. For instance, during community rituals, it is common to see symbols of balance—such as the yin-yang or a paired set of candles—used to represent the harmony between past and future, wisdom and innovation, elder and youth. These symbols remind participants of the interdependence that defines their shared existence.

In practical terms, mutual respect also involves addressing challenges or conflicts with compassion and a commitment to growth. For example, if misunderstandings arise between generations, the community is encouraged to engage in dialogue circles, where participants can express their feelings and concerns openly, guided by a mediator or minister who upholds New Universalist values. These practices reinforce the idea that respect is not just a passive attitude but an active process of understanding, reconciliation, and connection.

Ultimately, mutual respect and understanding are not merely ideals within New Universalism; they are living practices that sustain the community's spirit and integrity. By valuing each individual's contributions and fostering genuine connections, the community creates an environment where every generation feels seen, heard, and supported—a true testament to the sacred bonds that unite us all.

Honoring Oneself- Inner Harmony & Spiritual Growth

In New Universalism, the concept of filial piety is a multifaceted expression of respect and reverence that extends to relationships with elders, communities, and the divine. Yet, its reciprocal nature calls for equal attention to one's relationship with the self. To truly honor others, we must first honor ourselves, nurturing our inner lives and affirming our inherent worth. This balance is not only foundational to personal and communal well-being but also central to living in harmony with New Universalist principles. Turning inward, we explore the spiritual and practical dimensions of honoring oneself, reflecting the deep interplay between autonomy, divine expression, and ethical living.

The Importance of Self-Respect and Integrity in New Universalism

In New Universalism, the concept of self-respect is not merely an individual pursuit but a foundational spiritual value, intricately tied to the recognition of one's divine essence. At its core, self-respect is the practice of affirming one's inherent worth, a reflection of the universal truth that every life carries unique purpose and sacred significance. This acknowledgment is a vital first step in fostering personal well-being and authentic connection with others. When we honor ourselves, we also honor the divine spark within, affirming our place in the intricate web of life.

Self-respect begins with the recognition that each individual is an expression of the cosmos, uniquely created yet universally connected. This perspective invites us to view our lives as sacred, treating our minds, bodies, and spirits as gifts to be cherished and nurtured. This isn't an act of selfishness or egotism; rather, it is a humble acknowledgment of one's responsibility to oneself as a steward of divine energy. Self-respect encourages us to see our worth not as something to be earned but as an intrinsic quality, cultivated through intentional living and self-compassion.

Integrity, closely interwoven with self-respect, is the guiding principle that ensures alignment between one's values, actions, and words. In New Universalism, integrity is viewed as a spiritual commitment to authenticity—a promise to oneself to live in accordance with truth and to uphold principles of compassion, justice, and responsibility. To live with integrity is to embody the doctrine of "harming none, do what you will," striking a harmonious balance between personal autonomy and ethical responsibility. This principle requires consistent self-awareness and intentionality. Integrity invites us to evaluate our choices regularly, ensuring that our actions reflect our deepest values. This practice isn't about perfection but about striving toward alignment, even in the face of challenges or mistakes. It requires a willingness to reflect, to learn, and to grow—qualities that are deeply embedded in New Universalist theology as part of the lifelong journey of spiritual and personal development.

Honoring oneself in this way extends beyond internal reflection; it manifests in the outward choices we make. For instance, maintaining physical health through balanced nutrition, rest, and exercise is an act of respect for the vessel that carries one through life. Caring for one's emotional well-being by setting boundaries, fostering healthy relationships, and addressing stressors is equally essential. And nurturing spiritual health through practices like meditation, prayer, or time in nature reaffirms one's connection to the universal divine. The practice of self-respect and integrity also creates a ripple effect within our communities. When we live with authenticity and honor ourselves, we set an example that inspires others to do the same. This communal reinforcement of self-worth and ethical living strengthens the collective bonds of the New Universalist community, fostering an environment of mutual care, understanding, and support.

Honoring oneself is an act of gratitude—gratitude for the life one has been given and the opportunities for growth, connection, and creativity it offers. By valuing oneself, we affirm our place in the cosmos and recognize our ability to contribute meaningfully to the greater good. This perspective transforms self-respect and integrity from personal virtues into acts of spiritual service, reflecting the interconnectedness of all life and the divine presence within. Through self-respect and integrity, New Universalists honor the sacred within ourselves, embracing a path of authenticity and alignment that deepens our spiritual journey and enhances our ability to live in harmony with others and the Earth.

Practices for Nurturing Self-Respect and Inner Growth

Nurturing self-respect and fostering inner growth are central to the spiritual practices of New Universalism. These practices affirm the sacred nature of the individual and promote a harmonious balance between self-awareness, personal well-being, and the interconnected responsibilities we hold within our communities and the world. In New Universalism, cultivating these virtues is not merely a personal endeavor but a spiritual act that aligns the self with universal truth and the divine.

The Power of Reflection

Self-reflection is the cornerstone of nurturing self-respect. This practice invites us to pause, observe, and assess our actions, values, and emotions with honesty and compassion. Reflective practices might include journaling, meditation, or simply dedicating quiet time to introspection at the start or end of each day. Reflection helps us identify areas of growth while recognizing and celebrating our strengths and accomplishments. In New Universalism, reflection is seen as a dialogue with the divine within. By considering questions like, *"Am I living in alignment with my values?"* or *"How can I better honor my needs and those of others?"* we deepen our understanding of ourselves and our spiritual purpose. This ongoing practice of self-inquiry nurtures integrity, as it encourages alignment between one's inner truths and outward actions.

Setting Healthy Boundaries

Respecting oneself also means protecting one's well-being through the establishment of healthy boundaries. In New Universalism, setting boundaries is viewed as an act of compassion—both for oneself and for others. By clarifying limits, we preserve our energy and maintain our ability to engage meaningfully with the world. For instance, boundaries might take the form of managing time effectively to ensure rest and rejuvenation, or they may involve saying no to commitments that conflict with one's values or well-being. In relationships, boundaries foster respect and mutual understanding, as they create a framework for authentic connection without overextension or resentment. When we honor our boundaries, we not only safeguard our inner peace but also model respect and balance within our communities.

Self-Care as a Sacred Ritual

In New Universalism, self-care is elevated to a spiritual practice—a deliberate act of honoring the divine essence within oneself. This perspective transforms ordinary self-care routines into rituals of reverence. Whether it is through nourishing meals, regular physical activity, or mindful rest, self-care becomes a way of sustaining the body, mind, and spirit.

For example, a morning meditation might be paired with affirmations of gratitude, aligning the day's intentions with universal principles. An evening bath infused with natural oils or salts might be accompanied by a silent prayer of release and renewal. These moments of care are not indulgent; they are vital acts of maintaining the vessel through which one experiences and contributes to life.

Connecting with Nature for Inner Growth

Nature is a profound teacher, offering lessons of resilience, growth, and interconnectedness. Spending time in nature, whether through walks in the forest, observing the cycles of the seasons, or simply sitting in a garden, reconnects us to the Earth and the larger cosmos. These practices foster a sense of grounding and humility, reminding us of our place within a greater whole. Grounding meditations, where one visualizes roots extending into the Earth, can be a powerful way to draw strength and stability from the natural world. Similarly, practicing mindfulness during nature observation—focusing on the intricate details of a leaf, the sound of water, or the feeling of the breeze—enhances present-moment awareness and fosters a sense of gratitude for the beauty and abundance of life.

Embracing the Lifelong Journey of Growth

Inner growth is a lifelong journey, and New Universalism encourages individuals to view each stage of life as an opportunity for learning, adaptation, and self-discovery. Growth is not linear, nor is it without challenges, but it is through these experiences that one gains strength, wisdom, and resilience.

By setting personal goals and aspirations, we can create a sense of direction and purpose, while remaining open to the unexpected lessons that life offers. Periodically revisiting one's values and achievements can provide perspective, affirm progress, and inspire renewed commitment to the path of growth. In honoring self-respect and inner growth, New Universalists deepen our connection to the divine within, fostering harmony in our relationships and the world around us. These practices, grounded in reflection, care, and intentionality, create a foundation for living authentically and with integrity.

Commitment to Personal Growth

In New Universalism, personal growth is regarded as both a spiritual mandate and an ongoing journey of self-discovery. This commitment reflects the theology that each individual is a dynamic expression of the divine, capable of evolving in harmony with the broader interconnected cosmos. Growth, in this sense, is not merely about achieving personal success but about aligning oneself with universal principles of compassion, integrity, and purpose. Growth is sacred, an unfolding process that mirrors the rhythms of nature. Just as the Earth moves through cycles of renewal, abundance, and rest, individuals navigate periods of learning, reflection, and transformation. Each stage of life presents unique opportunities to deepen self-understanding, refine values, and contribute meaningfully to the world.

This perspective encourages us to approach growth with humility and patience. Challenges are not seen as failures but as necessary elements of transformation. The difficulties encountered along the way offer valuable lessons, fostering resilience and expanding one's capacity for empathy and wisdom.

Setting Goals with Purpose and Intention

To honor the sacredness of growth, New Universalists are encouraged to set personal goals that reflect our values and aspirations. These goals act as guiding stars, providing direction while allowing space for flexibility and adaptation. For instance, a goal might involve cultivating a specific virtue, such as patience or kindness, or developing a skill that enhances one's ability to serve others. Goal setting in New Universalism is not about rigid achievement but about intentional living. We might begin by reflecting on our core values and asking questions such as, *"What do I hope to contribute to the world?"* or *"How can I align my daily actions with my highest principles?"* These reflections lead to goals that are deeply meaningful and grounded in the individual's spiritual journey.

Growth requires patience, both with oneself and with the process. In a world often focused on immediate results, New Universalism emphasizes the importance of slowing down, trusting the journey, and appreciating incremental progress. We are encouraged to embrace the idea that growth unfolds in its own time, much like a seed germinating beneath the soil before sprouting into the light. Challenges, too, are integral to growth. They serve as opportunities for introspection, adaptation, and the development of inner strength. For instance, a conflict might teach the importance of active listening and compromise, while a period of uncertainty might inspire deeper trust in oneself and the divine. By viewing challenges as teachers, we can approach them with curiosity and courage rather than fear or resistance.

An essential aspect of personal growth is the practice of celebration and reflection. Acknowledging progress, no matter how small, reinforces a sense of accomplishment and gratitude. Whether it is through journaling, sharing milestones with a community, or creating a ritual of thanksgiving, these moments of recognition affirm the effort and intention invested in the journey. Reflection is equally vital. Revisiting past experiences and lessons offers perspective, helping us to identify patterns, clarify priorities, and refine our path forward. For example, rereading old journal entries or meditating on previous challenges can reveal how much one has grown, fostering a deeper appreciation for the journey.

A Communal Perspective on Personal Growth

While personal growth is inherently individual, New Universalism recognizes its communal dimension. By sharing our journeys with others, we contribute to a collective culture of learning and support. Community gatherings, mentorship relationships, and collaborative projects provide spaces where we can inspire and be inspired, enriching our own growth while fostering interdependence.

Ultimately, commitment to personal growth in New Universalism is an expression of reverence for life itself. By striving to become more compassionate, intentional, and authentic, we honor our divine nature and our interconnectedness with all beings. Growth is not a destination but a continuous process of becoming, one that enriches the individual and contributes to the harmony of the whole.

Aligning with One's Values and Purpose

In New Universalism, aligning with one's values and purpose is a profound spiritual practice, rooted in the belief that every life is inherently valuable and interconnected with the broader tapestry of existence. This alignment not only fosters personal fulfillment but also serves as a pathway to living harmoniously with others, the Earth, and the divine.

Purpose as a Reflection of the Divine

At the heart of New Universalist theology is the understanding that all beings are expressions of the divine. This belief imbues every life with inherent worth and a unique potential for contributing to the world. Purpose, therefore, is not a rigid or singular concept but a dynamic and evolving journey. It begins with the foundational truth that one's existence alone is meaningful and expands into the discovery of how individual talents, passions, and experiences can serve the greater good.

For some, purpose may be found in creative expression, nurturing relationships, or acts of service. For others, it may involve exploring the mysteries of the cosmos or advocating for justice and equity. Whatever form it takes, purpose in New Universalism is deeply personal yet universally connected, reflecting the balance between individuality and unity.

The process of aligning with one's purpose begins with identifying core values—those guiding principles that shape one's actions and aspirations. Values such as compassion, integrity, and humility often emerge from self-reflection and lived experience. We are encouraged to spend time exploring questions like, *"What matters most to me?"* and *"How do I want to contribute to the world?"* Practices such as journaling and meditation, offer tools for uncovering these values. For instance, a guided meditation might invite us to envision a life lived in full alignment with our highest principles, noting the emotions and imagery that arise. Similarly, reflective journaling prompts, such as *"Write about a time when you felt most true to yourself,"* can illuminate the values that resonate most deeply.

Living a Purpose-Driven Life

Once core values are identified, the next step is integrating them into daily life. This practice requires intention and mindfulness, as each decision and action becomes an opportunity to reflect one's values. For example, a commitment to environmental stewardship might inspire someone to adopt sustainable habits or advocate for conservation initiatives. A value of kindness might manifest in small, thoughtful acts, such as offering support to a friend or volunteering in the community. New Universalism also recognizes the importance of flexibility and adaptation in living a purpose-driven life. As we grow and evolve, our understanding of purpose may shift, leading to new insights and directions. Embracing this fluidity ensures that purpose remains authentic and aligned with one's current values and circumstances.

Living in alignment with one's values and purpose is not without challenges. There may be times when external pressures or conflicting priorities create tension. In these moments, New Universalist teachings encourage us to return to our foundational truths, seeking guidance through reflection, prayer, or dialogue with trusted mentors and community members. Challenges are viewed not as obstacles but as opportunities for growth and deeper understanding. By approaching difficulties with a spirit of inquiry and resilience, we can reaffirm our commitment to our values and find creative ways to navigate complexity.

A meaningful practice in New Universalism is the regular review of one's values and purpose. Life's rhythms and experiences often bring new perspectives, making it essential to revisit core principles and aspirations. Seasonal meditations, personal retreats, or community gatherings can provide spaces for this reflection, allowing us to celebrate progress, reassess goals, and refine our paths forward.

The Ripple Effect of Living with Purpose

When we align our lives with our values and purpose, the impact extends far beyond ourselves. Our actions inspire others, strengthen communities, and contribute to the collective harmony envisioned by New Universalism. Whether through acts of kindness, creative endeavors, or dedicated service, living with purpose becomes a testament to the interconnectedness of all life. In the New Universalist perspective, the journey of aligning with one's values and purpose is a sacred act, a way of honoring both the self and the divine. It is a practice that not only enriches the individual but also radiates outward, creating a world rooted in compassion, respect, and unity.

Honoring Others as Oneself

In New Universalism, the act of honoring others is not merely a moral imperative but a profound spiritual practice. It reflects the interwoven nature of our existence, where the dignity we extend to others mirrors and reinforces the dignity we hold for ourselves. This reciprocal dynamic aligns with New Universalism's theology of interconnectedness, which emphasizes that every person is a reflection of the divine, and by honoring one, we honor the whole.

To honor others as oneself requires more than outward acts of politeness; it is a deeper commitment to inclusivity, empathy, and mutual respect. This practice extends beyond personal interactions to encompass advocacy for justice, equity, and the celebration of diversity. By fostering such values, we strengthen not only our connections with others but also our own sense of purpose and self-respect, reinforcing the foundational virtue of filial piety as it manifests in the broader community.

We are called to explore the theological and ethical underpinnings of honoring others as oneself by engaging in practical measures for nurturing inclusiveness, cultivating empathy and compassion, and recognizing diversity as a source of collective strength. These practices, rooted in both ancient wisdom and contemporary understanding, serve as a pathway to creating harmonious and compassionate communities while deepening one's spiritual growth within New Universalism.

Honoring Others: An Extension of Self-Respect

In New Universalism, the principle of honoring others is rooted in a profound recognition of interconnectedness: the understanding that each individual reflects a fragment of the divine and contributes to the collective harmony of existence. Honoring others is not simply an act of kindness; it is a sacred practice that reinforces one's own sense of self-respect and integrity. When we respect the dignity and worth of others, we affirm the same truths within ourselves, creating a cycle of mutual growth and spiritual elevation.

At its heart, this practice is an embodiment of the New Universalist belief that justice, compassion, and respect are essential for nurturing both personal and communal well-being. To honor another person is to see them fully—not as an abstraction or an obstacle but as a being of inherent value, shaped by their own experiences, struggles, and aspirations. This recognition calls on us to cultivate empathy and engage with others in ways that are patient, kind, and deeply respectful.

The act of honoring others begins with the acknowledgment that all individuals are imbued with sacred value. This theological cornerstone of New Universalism asserts that the divine resides within all life. As such, treating others with dignity and fairness is not only a social obligation but a spiritual one. Each interaction becomes an opportunity to honor the sacred within another person while strengthening one's own moral and spiritual clarity. Consider, for instance, a conversation where you actively listen to another person's perspective without judgment or interruption. This simple act of respect affirms their voice and creates a space for connection and mutual understanding. It demonstrates both humility and empathy, qualities that align with New Universalism's teachings on integrity and compassion. By valuing another's experiences, we reaffirm our shared humanity and deepen our own character.

The Reciprocal Nature of Respect

New Universalist theology also emphasizes the reciprocal nature of honoring others. Just as we are called to treat others with kindness and respect, we are also reminded that these acts enrich our own lives. To honor others is to strengthen the bonds of community and affirm the values that guide us—justice, compassion, and the pursuit of unity. These values, when practiced outwardly, reflect inwardly, enhancing one's sense of purpose and self-respect.

This reciprocity extends to recognizing and challenging our own biases. To truly honor others, we must confront the prejudices and assumptions that limit our ability to connect. This requires humility, courage, and a commitment to continuous growth. In doing so, we not only expand our capacity for empathy but also uphold the New Universalist vision of an inclusive and equitable society.

Honoring others is not a passive act but an active engagement with the world around us. It manifests in countless ways, from small gestures of kindness to steadfast commitments to justice and equity. Holding the door for a stranger, advocating for marginalized communities, offering a genuine apology when wrong, or simply smiling at someone who may need it—all these actions reaffirm the sacred bonds we share. One particularly transformative practice is the cultivation of mindful interactions. When we engage with others, we should aim to do so fully, setting aside distractions and preconceived notions. Whether it is through a heartfelt conversation, a shared meal, or collaborative work, these moments of genuine connection allow us to honor the uniqueness of those around us while strengthening our collective spirit.

In honoring others, we are also called to honor ourselves. This reciprocity lies at the core of New Universalist theology, reminding us that our relationships with others mirror our relationship with the divine. Treating others with dignity and respect reaffirms our own self-worth and underscores the sacred interconnectedness of all life. It is a practice that nurtures both the individual and the community, fostering a sense of unity that transcends differences.

Ultimately, the practice of honoring others as oneself is a testament to the universal truths at the heart of New Universalism: that all life is sacred, all beings are interconnected, and the way we treat others reflects the values we hold dear. In this light, each interaction becomes an opportunity to create a world rooted in compassion, justice, and mutual respect.

Practices to Nurture Inclusiveness and Equity

Inclusiveness and equity are cornerstones of New Universalism, rooted in the understanding that every individual holds inherent value and deserves to be treated with fairness and dignity. These practices are not merely ideals but deliberate, daily actions that build bridges across differences and create a culture of mutual respect. To honor these principles is to actively seek understanding, dismantle biases, and foster environments where all voices are heard and valued. Through intentional practice, inclusiveness and equity become transformative forces in our communities and within ourselves.

Active Listening as a Foundation for Inclusiveness

One of the simplest yet most profound ways to nurture inclusiveness is through the practice of active listening. This involves giving undivided attention to others, seeking to understand their perspectives without interruption or preconceived judgment. Active listening honors the speaker's voice, affirming their worth and creating a safe space for open dialogue. In New Universalism, active listening is a sacred act that reflects our commitment to honoring the inherent dignity of others. It transforms conversations into opportunities for connection and mutual growth. Imagine sitting in a community discussion where each participant feels truly heard. The act of listening becomes the bridge, fostering empathy and cultivating respect for diverse viewpoints.

Inclusivity in Daily Interactions

Inclusivity begins with a conscious effort to recognize and address biases that may hinder genuine connections with others. This practice requires self-reflection and a willingness to confront the prejudices we hold, whether implicit or explicit. New Universalism calls on us to approach each interaction with an open heart and mind, embracing the richness of diversity in culture, belief, and experience.

For example, inclusivity can be practiced by learning about the traditions and customs of others, ensuring accessibility in shared spaces, or inviting someone who may feel excluded to participate in a group activity. These small but meaningful actions weave inclusivity into the fabric of daily life, creating a world that reflects the New Universalist ideals of equity and mutual respect.

Advocacy for Justice

Inclusiveness and equity extend beyond personal interactions to encompass broader societal responsibilities. Advocacy for justice is a natural expression of these values, calling on each of us to stand against discrimination, inequality, and intolerance. New Universalism teaches that justice is not only an ethical imperative but a spiritual one, rooted in the belief that all life is interconnected. Advocacy can take many forms, from supporting equitable policies to participating in community initiatives that uplift marginalized voices. For instance, attending a local meeting to advocate for environmental justice, volunteering at a shelter for underserved populations, or donating to organizations that promote human rights are all ways to embody the principles of inclusiveness and equity in tangible ways.

Creating Welcoming Spaces

Inclusiveness also involves cultivating spaces—physical, emotional, and spiritual—where all individuals feel safe, valued, and respected. This may involve organizing community events that celebrate diversity, ensuring that language and symbols used in worship or meetings are inclusive, or creating opportunities for everyone to contribute meaningfully.

In a New Universalist gathering, inclusiveness might be reflected in shared rituals that honor multiple traditions, meals that accommodate diverse dietary needs, or accessible seating arrangements for individuals with disabilities. These practices affirm the sacred interconnectedness of all participants, reinforcing the values of respect and equity.

The Transformative Power of Inclusiveness and Equity

Nurturing inclusiveness and equity transforms both individuals and communities. When we listen actively, honor differences, and stand for justice, we create an environment where everyone has the opportunity to thrive. These practices strengthen the bonds between people, fostering resilience, compassion, and a shared commitment to the greater good. Inclusiveness and equity are not static goals but ongoing journeys. Each act of kindness, every moment of understanding, and all efforts toward justice contribute to a world that reflects the highest ideals of New Universalism. By embracing these practices, we honor the divine within each individual and affirm the sacred unity of all life.

Cultivating Empathy and Compassion for Others

Empathy and compassion lie at the heart of New Universalist theology, reflecting our deep connection to one another and to all forms of life. These virtues are not abstract ideals but tangible practices that transform relationships, communities, and the self. By cultivating empathy and compassion, we honor the sacredness of each individual, foster unity, and uphold the New Universalist commitment to living with integrity and care.

Empathy is the ability to understand and share the feelings of another, to place oneself in their situation and view the world from their perspective. It is the foundation of meaningful connection, allowing individuals to bridge differences and create relationships built on mutual respect and understanding.

In New Universalism, empathy is seen as an act of spiritual alignment with the interconnected nature of existence. When we empathize with others, we acknowledge our shared humanity and the threads that bind us together. For example, listening to the struggles of a friend or stranger with an open heart not only validates their experience but deepens our own sense of connection to the larger human story.

Practicing empathy begins with attentiveness and a willingness to be present for others. A simple but effective technique is to imagine oneself in another's position, considering their emotions, challenges, and perspectives. For instance, when witnessing someone's frustration or sorrow, we might ask ourselves, *"How would I feel in this situation?"* This mental shift opens the door to greater understanding and a compassionate response. Another technique involves recognizing shared experiences and emotions. Although the specifics of each person's journey are unique, many emotions—joy, fear, love, grief—are universally felt. By focusing on these commonalities, we can connect with others in a profound and authentic way.

While empathy is the recognition of another's feelings, compassion is the desire to alleviate their suffering and contribute to their well-being. In New Universalism, compassion is both a spiritual and ethical mandate, rooted in the belief that every act of care reflects the divine within us and strengthens the bonds of community. Compassion can be practiced in both small and significant ways. Offering a kind word to a colleague, supporting a neighbor in need, or volunteering for a cause that uplifts others are expressions of compassion that ripple outward, creating a culture of care. These actions are particularly powerful when undertaken with intention, reflecting New Universalism's emphasis on mindful living.

Compassionate action requires self-awareness and reflection. By taking the time to examine our intentions, we ensure that our efforts to help others are genuine and respectful. For example, when offering support, it is important to consider the other person's autonomy and preferences, honoring their dignity and agency.

Mindfulness also plays a key role in sustaining compassion over time. It helps us remain present and engaged, even in the face of challenges. A daily meditation or reflection on compassion can serve as a reminder of our commitment to living with kindness and integrity.

In New Universalism, the practice of empathy and compassion is not one-sided; it benefits both the giver and the receiver. When we extend care to others, we strengthen our own sense of purpose and self-worth. Likewise, when we experience the empathy or compassion of others, we are reminded of the inherent goodness and interconnectedness of life. This reciprocity is particularly evident in community settings, where acts of empathy and compassion inspire a collective spirit of mutual support. A New Universalist gathering, for example, might include moments of shared reflection on the importance of caring for one another, followed by practical actions, such as organizing support for a member in need or addressing a social issue together.

Practicing empathy and compassion deepens our spiritual journey by aligning us with the values of New Universalism. These virtues remind us that we are not isolated beings but integral parts of a larger whole. They encourage us to live with humility, gratitude, and a sense of responsibility for the well-being of all. As we cultivate these qualities, we not only transform our relationships but also embody the ideals of New Universalism in our daily lives. Empathy and compassion become the threads that weave together our shared humanity, creating a tapestry of unity, care, and hope.

Recognizing Diversity as a Source of Strength

In New Universalism, diversity is celebrated as an expression of life's richness and a reflection of the interconnected beauty of existence. Recognizing and honoring diversity—of cultures, beliefs, experiences, and identities—not only strengthens communities but also broadens individual perspectives, fostering mutual respect and understanding.

Diversity as a Reflection of Universal Truths

Diversity is not an obstacle to unity but an essential component of it. Just as ecosystems thrive through the balance and interplay of varied species, human communities flourish when they embrace the unique contributions of each individual. In New Universalist theology, diversity is seen as an expression of the divine, manifesting through the myriad forms of human and natural life. By honoring these differences, we affirm the sacredness of every being and uphold the principles of inclusivity and equity.

Diverse communities offer a wealth of perspectives, skills, and traditions that enrich collective life. For example, a multicultural gathering provides opportunities to learn from one another's stories, foods, rituals, and histories, deepening our appreciation for the world's complexity and beauty. In this way, diversity broadens understanding, challenges assumptions, and fosters a culture of curiosity and openness. In practice, this might take the form of a New Universalist service that includes readings from varied spiritual traditions, musical performances from different cultural backgrounds, or communal meals celebrating global cuisines. Such acts of inclusion not only strengthen communal bonds but also highlight the interconnectedness of human experience.

Cultivating Respect for Different Beliefs and Identities

A key aspect of honoring diversity is cultivating respect for others' beliefs, identities, and experiences, even when they differ from one's own. In New Universalism, this respect is grounded in the principle of mutual dignity: every person is inherently worthy of honor and kindness. Practicing respect requires a willingness to listen, to approach others without judgment, and to remain open to learning from their perspectives. For instance, a New Universalist leader might invite members of their community to share their personal traditions or beliefs during a gathering, creating a space where all voices are valued. This approach not only fosters mutual respect but also deepens the community's collective understanding of the world.

Celebrating Diversity in Rituals and Practices

Incorporating diverse elements into rituals and practices is a powerful way to honor and celebrate the richness of human experience. A New Universalist celebration of the spring equinox, for example, might draw from various cultural traditions, such as the Iranian Nowruz, Pagan fertility rites, and Japanese cherry blossom festivals. By weaving together these threads, the ritual becomes a tapestry that reflects both individual uniqueness and shared humanity.

Similarly, personal practices might include exploring art, literature, or spiritual teachings from different traditions, fostering a sense of connection to the broader world. Community leaders can also organize events like storytelling circles, intercultural workshops, or collaborative art projects that celebrate the contributions of diverse voices.

Diversity as a Catalyst for Personal Growth

Engaging with diversity is not just an external act—it is also a profound opportunity for personal growth. By encountering and appreciating differences, we challenge our own biases, expand our understanding, and cultivate humility. These experiences encourage self-reflection and empathy, aligning with New Universalism's emphasis on continual learning and spiritual development. For example, a New Universalist might attend a cultural festival, listen to the stories of immigrants in their community, or read texts from unfamiliar philosophical traditions. These acts, while seemingly small, are transformative, planting seeds of connection and respect that grow over time.

Building Bridges Across Differences

In a world often divided by misunderstandings and prejudices, New Universalism calls for building bridges across differences. This requires intentional efforts to foster dialogue, collaboration, and solidarity. It might involve reaching out to marginalized groups, advocating for policies that promote equity, or simply extending a hand of friendship to someone with a different background. The New Universalist community might hold interfaith dialogues, support local initiatives that address systemic inequalities, or organize cultural exchange programs. These actions not only demonstrate a commitment to justice and compassion but also embody the belief that diversity is a source of strength rather than division.

A Vision for Inclusive and Unified Communities

Recognizing diversity as a source of strength is not merely an ideal—it is a vision for creating inclusive and unified communities. By honoring the unique contributions of each person and embracing the richness of human experience, New Universalists affirm our commitment to equity, respect, and shared growth. This vision inspires not only personal transformation but also collective progress, paving the way for a world where differences are celebrated and unity thrives.

Reflections and Path Forward

12

The Journey of New Universalism

Becoming a Pillar of Truth and Stewardship

New Universalism invites us to reflect deeply on the teachings, values, and practices that have shaped our exploration of truth, connection, and purpose. Turning our attention to the profound call to action embedded in the New Universalist path: to embody the principles we hold dear and to live as pillars of truth, stewardship, and unity, we set a foundation of continued growth not only as individuals, but as a larger interconnected community.

The *Journey of New Universalism* is both a reflection on what has been learned and an invitation to step forward with intention. It encourages each of us to weave the threads of reason, Earth stewardship, social responsibility, and filial piety into the fabric of our daily lives, becoming a living testament to these guiding principles. By embracing this path, we not only deepen our personal spiritual journey but also contribute to the creation of a world illuminated by compassion, equity, and harmony. Through these reflections and aspirations, we are reminded that the journey of New Universalism is ongoing, vibrant, and collective. As we delve into its themes, let us envision a future where the values of this faith are a beacon for all who seek to live with integrity, purpose, and interconnectedness.

To become a pillar of truth and stewardship in New Universalism is to embody the faith's guiding principles in thought, word, and action. A pillar, by its nature, provides strength, stability, and support, standing firm not only for itself but also for the structures and communities it upholds. In the context of New Universalism, this metaphor extends to individuals whose lives reflect the virtues of Reason, Earth Stewardship, Social Responsibility, and Filial Piety. These pillars are not static ideals but dynamic principles, calling each person to live with integrity and purpose.

At the heart of New Universalism is the belief that the self and the world are interconnected expressions of the Divine. This sacred interconnection forms the foundation for the four pillars, guiding us toward lives of meaningful engagement. Becoming a pillar is not merely about personal achievement; it is a spiritual journey that aligns one's actions with universal truths, promoting harmony between the individual, community, and cosmos. This alignment begins with an understanding that truth is not rigid but ever-evolving, discovered through reason, dialogue, and reflection. Truth in New Universalism is a shared pursuit, one that grows richer through compassion, inclusivity, and collective wisdom. Likewise, stewardship extends beyond environmental care to encompass the nurturing of relationships, community, and justice, recognizing that the act of giving sustains the world.

The Path to Becoming a Pillar

The journey to becoming a pillar of truth and stewardship begins with self-awareness and a commitment to growth. We are encouraged to reflect deeply on our values, choices, and aspirations, recognizing how these elements shape our impact on others and the world. This process requires cultivating habits of mindfulness, accountability, and resilience, aligning daily actions with the broader goals of New Universalism. For example, embodying Reason calls for thoughtful engagement with complex questions, fostering curiosity, and resisting dogmatic thinking. It encourages us to explore diverse perspectives, embracing the humility required to learn and grow. Earth Stewardship, on the other hand, emphasizes tangible actions such as reducing waste, supporting conservation efforts, and advocating for sustainable practices within one's community.

A pillar does not seek recognition but instead inspires through quiet strength and consistent action. In communities, a pillar of truth and stewardship models the values of New Universalism, creating spaces where dialogue, collaboration, and mutual respect flourish. This leadership extends beyond formal roles, inviting each of us to see ourselves as agents of change, capable of influencing our families, neighborhoods, and societies.

To be a pillar is also to recognize the reciprocal nature of giving and receiving. Just as a pillar supports a structure, it is held firm by the ground upon which it stands. We are encouraged to find strength in our communities and spiritual traditions, drawing upon these sources to sustain our journey. This reciprocity reflects the interdependence celebrated in New Universalism: by nurturing others and the world, one finds nourishment for the self.

Ultimately, becoming a pillar of truth and stewardship is about leaving a legacy of compassion, wisdom, and care. Each act of kindness, each thoughtful decision, and each moment of reflection contributes to a world guided by justice and unity. This legacy is not measured in grand achievements but in the everyday commitment to living in alignment with the values of New Universalism. It is a call to transcend individual limitations, embracing a shared purpose that uplifts and inspires.

Embodying the Pillars in Daily Life

The four pillars of New Universalism—Reason, Earth Stewardship, Social Responsibility, and Filial Piety—offer a roadmap for living a meaningful and principled life. Embodying these pillars in daily life is not a rigid checklist but a dynamic process, inviting us to integrate these values into our thoughts, actions, and relationships. By doing so, we become living embodiments of New Universalist theology, demonstrating the power of these principles to create harmony and purpose.

Living by Reason: Illuminating Truth Through Thoughtful Action

Reason is the compass guiding us toward truth and understanding. It invites a thoughtful approach to life, one that embraces inquiry, dialogue, and discernment. In practice, living by reason means cultivating habits of critical thinking, asking questions that challenge assumptions, and seeking knowledge with humility. It is about balancing the head and the heart, ensuring that reason serves the greater good over personal gain.

For example, we might use reason to navigate ethical dilemmas, weighing the potential consequences of our actions with empathy and clarity. In daily interactions, this could manifest as listening with an open mind, seeking common ground in disagreements, or engaging in conversations that build bridges rather than walls. Reason is not about intellectual superiority but about fostering understanding, curiosity, and connection.

Earth Stewardship: Honoring the Sacred Balance of Nature

Earth Stewardship calls for an active reverence for the natural world, recognizing the interconnectedness of all life. In daily life, this principle encourages us to adopt sustainable practices, from reducing waste and conserving energy to supporting local environmental initiatives. Beyond practical actions, Earth Stewardship is a spiritual commitment to seeing the Earth as a living entity deserving of respect and care. For instance, a family might choose to celebrate seasonal changes with rituals that honor the rhythms of nature, such as planting a tree during the Spring Equinox or offering gratitude for the harvest during the Autumn Equinox. These acts, both practical and ceremonial, reinforce the idea that caring for the Earth is a sacred duty. By integrating stewardship into daily routines, we affirm our role as caretakers of a shared world.

Social Responsibility: Fostering Compassion and Equity

Social Responsibility emphasizes the importance of contributing to the well-being of others and creating a more just and compassionate society. It asks us to extend our care beyond personal circles, recognizing the inherent worth of every individual. This principle comes alive through acts of service, advocacy, and solidarity with marginalized communities.

In practice, living with social responsibility might involve volunteering at a local shelter, mentoring a younger community member, or supporting policies that promote equity and inclusion. On a smaller scale, it could mean offering a kind word to someone in distress or standing up against harmful behavior. By embracing social responsibility, we demonstrate that our faith is not confined to personal growth but extends to the collective betterment of humanity.

Filial Piety: Honoring Relationships and Heritage

Filial Piety speaks to the reciprocal relationships we hold with family, community, and those who have come before us. It calls for respect, gratitude, and care in these relationships, encouraging us to honor the wisdom of elders and the contributions of ancestors while also nurturing bonds with peers and future generations. In daily life, filial piety might be expressed through small gestures of care, such as checking in on an elderly neighbor, sharing stories with children, or creating a family altar that honors ancestors. It could also involve participating in communal rituals that celebrate intergenerational bonds or advocating for policies that support families and communities. By living with filial piety, we strengthen the connections that sustain and enrich our lives.

Building a Life of Integrity and Purpose

Embodying the four pillars in daily life is not about perfection but about intention. It invites us to approach each day with mindfulness, asking how our choices reflect the values we hold dear. It is about weaving these principles into the fabric of life, creating a pattern of integrity, purpose, and unity. By doing so, we not only enrich our own lives but also inspire others, becoming beacons of truth and stewardship in a complex and interconnected world.

Practical Ways to Live the Pillars

Living as a Pillar of Truth and Stewardship means embodying the principles of New Universalism in a way that not only enhances personal growth but inspires others. This practice involves aligning daily actions with the four guiding pillars—Reason, Earth Stewardship, Social Responsibility, and Filial Piety—and moving from individual practice to broader leadership within one's community. By doing so, we become active participants in shaping a compassionate and sustainable future, fulfilling the promise of New Universalism.

Reason: Leading with Clarity and Open Inquiry

To live by reason is to approach life with intellectual curiosity, humility, and a commitment to universal truth. Beyond personal decision-making, this pillar invites us to become advocates for critical thinking and constructive dialogue in our communities. A New Universalist leader might organize discussion groups or workshops that explore philosophical, ethical, or spiritual questions. These gatherings can encourage collective exploration of ideas, fostering an environment where diverse perspectives are welcomed and understood. Additionally, we can lead by example in moments of conflict, modeling patience and a rational approach to resolving disputes.

Reason also calls for lifelong learning. Whether through formal education, self-study, or communal teaching, expanding one's understanding strengthens one's ability to guide others. Sharing insights with humility and a willingness to learn from others ensures that leadership remains grounded in collaboration, not ego.

Earth Stewardship: Championing Environmental Leadership

Earth Stewardship moves beyond personal sustainability practices to embrace advocacy and community engagement. We are called to become leaders in environmental preservation, uniting others in efforts to protect and restore the planet. For example, a New Universalist leader might organize community clean-ups, tree-planting events, or educational campaigns about sustainability. They might advocate for environmental policies at the local or national level, using their voice to amplify the urgent call for climate action. Hosting seasonal celebrations or rituals that honor the Earth can also inspire a deeper connection to nature within the community.

Leading by example in this pillar involves not only action but also consistency. Whether choosing eco-friendly options, reducing waste, or supporting sustainable businesses, we demonstrate how small, intentional choices can contribute to collective environmental health.

Social Responsibility: Advocating for Equity and Justice

Social responsibility challenges us to extend our compassion and care to the broader community. Leaders in this pillar actively work to create spaces where everyone feels valued, safe, and respected. One way to embody this pillar is by organizing or participating in community service projects, such as food drives, tutoring programs, or initiatives to support marginalized groups. Leaders can also engage in advocacy, speaking out against injustice and promoting equitable policies. Whether addressing systemic inequalities or supporting individual well-being, social responsibility calls for a balance of empathy and action.

Practicing social responsibility as a leader also involves creating opportunities for others to engage. By mentoring young people, facilitating group discussions on social issues, or collaborating with diverse organizations, leaders foster a culture of inclusivity and shared responsibility.

Filial Piety: Building Bridges Across Generations

Filial Piety asks us to honor the relationships that sustain our lives, particularly those with family, community, and ancestors. Leadership in this pillar involves creating spaces where these connections can flourish. A New Universalist leader might establish intergenerational programs, such as storytelling circles where elders share their experiences or workshops where younger members teach technological skills. These gatherings not only build community but also emphasize the reciprocal nature of learning and respect.

Leaders can promote rituals that honor ancestry and heritage, such as creating communal altars or organizing events that celebrate cultural traditions. By fostering a sense of continuity and shared history, they remind their community of the strength and wisdom rooted in their collective past.

Inspiring the Next Generation of Leaders

Becoming a Pillar of Truth and Stewardship involves nurturing leadership in others. We are encouraged to mentor, support, and uplift those around us, recognizing that everyone has a role to play in advancing New Universalism. Whether through formal roles, such as serving in a New Universalist congregation, or informal actions, such as guiding a friend through a challenge, every act of leadership contributes to the collective good.

By embodying the pillars in tangible, inspiring ways, we show that leadership is not about authority but about service. It is a commitment to living with integrity, compassion, and a vision for a better world. This practice invites others to join in the journey, expanding the reach and impact of New Universalism with every step.

Creating a Legacy of Faith and Reason

The concept of legacy is one of the most profound ways we leave our mark on the world. In New Universalism, creating a legacy is not solely about material achievements or worldly accolades; rather, it is about the enduring impact of our values, actions, and connections. It is an invitation to participate in something greater than oneself—a collective journey shaped by faith, reason, and a commitment to universal truths. This legacy is rooted in the idea that each individual is both a recipient of the wisdom passed down through generations and a steward of that wisdom for those yet to come. Within New Universalism, the intertwining of faith and reason allows for a legacy that is not only spiritually fulfilling but also intellectually and ethically robust. Faith provides the foundation for compassion, hope, and reverence for the divine interconnectedness of all life, while reason offers the tools for discernment, inquiry, and the pursuit of truth.

Each person plays a role in shaping the story of New Universalism. Individual lives, filled with purpose and guided by universal values, ripple out to shape families, communities, and the world at large. By living intentionally and sharing our wisdom, we contribute to a legacy that honors the pillars of New Universalism—Reason, Earth Stewardship, Social Responsibility, and Filial Piety. This legacy is not fixed or final but is an evolving testament to humanity's shared aspiration for a more harmonious and just world.

The Role of Individuals in Shaping New Universalism's Legacy

In New Universalism, the individual is seen as a vital thread in the larger tapestry of existence. Each person's actions, decisions, and beliefs contribute to the ongoing story of this faith, weaving a narrative that is deeply personal yet intrinsically tied to the collective journey. The legacy of New Universalism is not constructed in grand gestures alone but is built upon the everyday choices that reflect its core values—Reason, Earth Stewardship, Social Responsibility, and Filial Piety.

Every action we take, no matter how small, ripples outward, influencing those around us and shaping the world we leave behind. When individuals embody New Universalist principles in their daily lives, they create a foundation for others to do the same. A simple act of kindness, a moment of reflection, or a thoughtful decision can inspire those in our families, communities, and beyond. For example, practicing Earth Stewardship by cultivating a garden not only nurtures the planet but also demonstrates a deep respect for the interconnectedness of life. Similarly, living with social responsibility—whether through volunteering at a local shelter or advocating for equitable policies—models a commitment to justice and compassion. These actions, though rooted in personal choices, contribute to a collective legacy that uplifts humanity and honors the Earth.

Living with purpose is a cornerstone of creating a meaningful legacy within New Universalism. This does not require grand ambition or extraordinary circumstances. Instead, it asks for intentionality and alignment with universal values. When we approach our lives with a sense of purpose—recognizing our inherent worth and our potential to contribute to the greater good—we become living examples of New Universalism's teachings. The legacy of New Universalism is not limited to the present moment but extends into the future, shaping the lives of those who will come after us. When we live in alignment with New Universalist principles, we leave behind a legacy of wisdom, love, and resilience that can inspire generations.

Looking to the Future: A Vision for New Universalism

The teachings of New Universalism invite us to look forward with a shared vision of hope, unity, and stewardship. As individuals, communities, and a global collective, our role is not only to embody the values of this faith in our daily lives but to nurture our impact on future generations. New Universalism can be a force for transformative change in a world yearning for compassion, equity, and sustainability.

Looking to the future, we envision a world where reason and faith coexist harmoniously, where Earth stewardship is seen as a sacred duty, and where compassion and justice define the fabric of human interaction. Each of us is encouraged to consider how our life and choices ripple outward, contributing to a legacy of hope and care. Together, we can move toward a future that honors the interconnectedness of all life, ensuring that the principles of New Universalism serve as a guiding light for personal growth, collective progress, and planetary healing.

Envisioning a Future Guided by New Universalism

The future shaped by New Universalism is one rooted in harmony, compassion, and sustainable progress. Imagine a world where individuals live with integrity, communities flourish in mutual support, and humanity as a whole respects the sacred balance of life on Earth. This vision is not distant or unattainable; it begins in the hearts and minds of those who choose to embody New Universalist principles.

A future guided by New Universalism is one where reason and spirituality converge to foster understanding and cooperation. The pillar of reason calls us to explore universal truths with curiosity and humility, empowering us to approach global challenges with thoughtful solutions. In this future, decision-making is guided by rationality tempered with compassion, recognizing that the wellbeing of one is tied to the wellbeing of all.

Central to this vision is the principle of Earth Stewardship. A world guided by New Universalism would see communities embracing practices that honor the Earth as a sacred entity. Renewable energy, sustainable agriculture, and the restoration of natural habitats become not just initiatives but shared commitments, ensuring the health of our planet for generations to come. Through these acts, humanity expresses gratitude for the interconnected web of life that sustains us all.

Social responsibility also plays a pivotal role in shaping this future. In a world aligned with New Universalism, equity and justice are not ideals but realities. Communities would prioritize the eradication of poverty, the promotion of inclusive education, and the protection of human rights. Compassion-driven policies would foster environments where everyone has the opportunity to thrive, and diversity is celebrated as a source of collective strength. The principle of filial piety enriches this vision by reminding us of our place within an intergenerational legacy. Respect for elders, gratitude for ancestors, and the nurturing of the next generation create a society where wisdom and innovation coexist. The values passed down through generations form the foundation for continuous growth, allowing humanity to adapt to new challenges while remaining grounded in timeless truths.

This envisioned future is both a collective aspiration and an individual responsibility. Each person has the power to contribute to this reality through their choices and actions. By living with purpose, honoring the interconnectedness of life, and embracing the teachings of New Universalism, we take meaningful steps toward a world defined by truth, stewardship, and unity.

The Importance of Collective Progress and Care

At the heart of New Universalism lies the understanding that progress is not the journey of individuals alone but a shared endeavor. Collective progress, rooted in care and mutual respect, is essential to creating a world where justice, equity, and sustainability are not merely aspirations but realities. As we look toward the future, this emphasis on collective responsibility and cooperative action takes on profound significance.

New Universalism teaches that we are bound by the threads of interconnection. Every action, whether personal or communal, ripples outward, influencing the lives of others and shaping the larger world. Recognizing this truth, New Universalism calls us to embrace collective progress as a sacred duty, where shared values guide our efforts toward common goals. This is not a matter of altruism alone but of mutual thriving, as the well-being of the individual is intrinsically tied to the well-being of the community and the Earth.

Communities practicing New Universalism hold the power to drive meaningful societal change. By fostering equity, they challenge systemic inequalities, ensuring that every individual, regardless of background, has the opportunity to live with dignity and purpose. This commitment to justice is reflected in actions both grand and humble: from advocating for inclusive policies to creating welcoming spaces where diverse voices are heard and valued.

The principle of Earth Stewardship amplifies this commitment to collective care. Communities united under New Universalist values understand the urgent need to restore balance to the natural world. Collaborative initiatives—such as local conservation projects, reforestation efforts, and community-supported agriculture—become expressions of reverence for the Earth. These actions are not merely practical responses to ecological challenges but deeply spiritual practices that honor the interconnected web of life.

Social responsibility also manifests through acts of compassion and support within communities. Caring for one another, whether through volunteer efforts, mentorship, or providing aid to those in need, strengthens the fabric of society. These shared acts of kindness embody the spirit of New Universalism, demonstrating that true progress arises from cooperation, not competition. Intergenerational collaboration enriches the pursuit of collective progress. Elders bring wisdom and perspective, while younger generations infuse energy and innovation. By working together, communities weave a tapestry of knowledge and action, ensuring that progress is both grounded in experience and responsive to emerging challenges.

The path to collective progress is not always easy, but it is deeply rewarding. When we choose to act with care for one another and the world, we align ourselves with the highest ideals of New Universalism. In doing so, we not only build a better present but also lay the foundation for a future where shared values lead to enduring harmony and unity.

Fostering Hope and Vision in Times of Change & Challenge

In a world defined by rapid change and frequent challenges, the principles of New Universalism serve as a beacon of hope and vision. They remind us that, even in the face of uncertainty, our values and collective efforts can create a foundation for resilience and transformation. Fostering hope is not a passive act but an intentional practice of envisioning a better future and taking meaningful steps to bring that vision to life. New Universalism acknowledges the inherent difficulty of living in an era marked by ecological crises, social inequities, and global upheaval. Yet, it offers a framework that encourages optimism and courage. At its core is the belief that every challenge is an opportunity to reaffirm our commitment to universal truths: respect, wisdom, care, and unity. By embodying these values, individuals and communities can navigate adversity with clarity and purpose.

Hope in New Universalism is deeply intertwined with action. It is not merely the anticipation of better times but the active pursuit of change rooted in our shared ideals. Communities are encouraged to embrace initiatives that align with these principles, whether through sustainability projects, advocacy for justice, or fostering inclusivity within their own circles. These actions become tangible expressions of hope, demonstrating that progress is possible, even in the most trying circumstances.

Vision plays a complementary role in fostering hope, as it allows us to imagine the world not only as it is but as it could be. In New Universalism, vision is cultivated through reflection, dialogue, and a willingness to dream beyond the constraints of the present. It invites us to ask critical questions: *What kind of future do we want to create? How can our actions today pave the way for a more compassionate and sustainable tomorrow?* Cultivating vision also involves recognizing the interconnectedness of all life. When we understand that our struggles are shared and that our actions impact others, we gain a greater sense of purpose and accountability. This perspective transforms individual efforts into collective movements, reinforcing the idea that no one is alone in the pursuit of a better world.

During times of change and challenge, it is essential to remain anchored in the present while looking toward the horizon. Practices such as meditation, community rituals, and personal journaling can help us reconnect with our inner strength and align our actions with our values. These practices foster resilience, offering a sense of stability even when external circumstances are uncertain. New Universalism also emphasizes the importance of adaptability. Change is an inevitable part of life, and those who embrace it with openness and flexibility are better equipped to thrive. By viewing challenges as opportunities for growth and transformation, we can approach them with a mindset of curiosity and determination.

Fostering hope and vision requires celebrating small victories and progress along the way. Each step, no matter how small, contributes to the larger journey. By acknowledging these achievements, we remind ourselves of the power of perseverance and the impact of collective effort.

In times of change and challenge, New Universalism calls us to be both dreamers and doers, envisioning a brighter future while taking practical steps to make it a reality. Hope and vision are not merely ideals to aspire to but tools to guide us through uncertainty, ensuring that we remain steadfast in our pursuit of a world grounded in compassion, wisdom, and unity.

Inspiring Action for Future Generations

The legacy of New Universalism is not only about the present but also about the world we leave behind for future generations. Each individual's actions, however small, contribute to a larger narrative of care, wisdom, and unity, shaping the foundation upon which future generations can build. By inspiring action today, we ensure that the principles of New Universalism endure, serving as a beacon for those who come after us.

At the heart of this inspiration is the recognition that every generation inherits both the challenges and the opportunities left by those before them. New Universalism calls us to take responsibility for this inheritance by acting as stewards of truth, justice, and the Earth. This stewardship requires a proactive commitment to living in alignment with our values, demonstrating by example how a life grounded in compassion and integrity can create ripples of positive change. Inspiring future generations begins with education. Sharing the teachings, values, and practices of New Universalism with younger members of our communities fosters a deep understanding of their own potential to contribute meaningfully. This education need not be formal; it can occur through storytelling, mentorship, or simply engaging in open, respectful dialogue about the importance of universal values in navigating life's complexities.

Community rituals and shared practices play an essential role in connecting generations. Events such as seasonal celebrations, intergenerational storytelling circles, and collaborative service projects provide opportunities for individuals of all ages to come together, share wisdom, and create lasting memories. These gatherings not only strengthen the bonds between individuals but also reinforce a sense of shared purpose, reminding participants that they are part of something greater than themselves.

For individuals, inspiring action means leading by example. This leadership can take many forms: a quiet commitment to sustainable living, active advocacy for social justice, or dedicated mentorship of younger community members. Each act of integrity and compassion serves as a powerful model, demonstrating to others the tangible ways in which New Universalism's principles can be lived out in daily life. In practical terms, this might involve engaging in projects that directly benefit future generations, such as environmental conservation initiatives, educational outreach, or the creation of inclusive community spaces. Planting a tree, for example, is more than an environmental act—it is a symbol of faith in the future and a gift to those who will come after us. Similarly, advocating for equitable policies and practices ensures that the next generation inherits a world more just and inclusive than the one before it.

Reflection also plays a critical role in inspiring action. Taking time to consider the impact of our choices and the legacy we wish to leave behind encourages a sense of purpose and intentionality. Journaling, meditation, or community discussions can help individuals align their actions with their values, fostering a deeper connection to the principles they seek to embody.

New Universalism also emphasizes the importance of hope as a driver of action. When individuals are inspired by a vision of what is possible, they are more likely to take the steps necessary to bring that vision to life. Cultivating hope in younger generations means empowering them to see themselves as agents of change, capable of shaping the future through their decisions and contributions. Inspiring action for future generations requires humility. It is an acknowledgment that we are part of an ongoing journey, one that began long before us and will continue long after we are gone. By embracing this perspective, we recognize the importance of nurturing not only the present but also the seeds of possibility for those yet to come.

New Universalism invites each of us to view our lives as part of a larger tapestry, one woven from the threads of countless generations. By taking thoughtful, intentional action today, we not only honor the legacy of those who came before but also ensure that the principles of truth, stewardship, and unity continue to guide and inspire for years to come.

Blessing for Unity and Peace

This blessing serves as both a moment of gratitude and a call to action, inspiring us to carry forward the principles of our faith into our daily lives and into the broader world. It is a unifying meditation that bridges the personal and the collective, honoring the connections we share with humanity, the Earth, and the divine essence present in all things.

The blessing is more than words—it is an invocation of hope and purpose. It acknowledges the challenges of the present while affirming our collective potential to shape a world that embodies peace, equity, and stewardship. It celebrates the journey we have taken together, inviting each of us to feel the presence of unity and peace not just as ideals, but as lived experiences that begin within and ripple outward into the world.

Blessing for Unity and Peace

We give thanks for the Earth beneath our feet, steady and enduring, offering its endless gifts to sustain us. May we walk upon it with reverence, cherishing the beauty and abundance it provides.

We give thanks for the air we breathe, carrying the whispers of generations before us and the promise of those yet to come. May we speak words of kindness and truth, carried by the winds to uplift and inspire.

We give thanks for the waters that flow, nourishing life and teaching us the power of renewal. May we move through our days with grace and resilience, finding strength in the currents of change.

We give thanks for the fire of the sun, warming and illuminating our paths. May we kindle our inner light, sharing its warmth and brilliance with those around us.

To humanity, we extend our deepest hopes:

May we walk together in unity, celebrating the beauty of our differences while honoring the common threads that bind us.

May we act with courage and compassion, uplifting one another in the face of challenge and adversity.

May we nurture the seeds of peace within ourselves, allowing them to bloom into actions that heal and transform the world.

To the Earth, we offer our unwavering commitment:

May we protect its forests, its oceans, and all its creatures, recognizing our responsibility as stewards of its well-being.

May we tread lightly and live mindfully, preserving its gifts for future generations.

To the divine essence that flows through all creation, we express our gratitude:

May we always be guided by its light, finding within ourselves the strength to live with integrity, purpose, and love.

Let this blessing be a beacon for all who seek unity and peace. May it remind us that we are not alone, that we are part of a sacred whole, and that together, we hold the power to shape a world that reflects our highest ideals.

So may it be.

Listed Holidays and Descriptions

- **Winter Solstice - December 21**
    - Marks the return of light on the shortest day of the year, symbolizing hope, rebirth, and inner reflection.
    - Themes of inner warmth, community gathering, and renewal of spirit.
    - Rituals could include candle lighting, storytelling, and shared meals to foster warmth and unity.
- **Spring Festival / Lunar New Year - Late January to Mid-February**
    - Celebrates the stirring of life beneath winter's surface, a time of new beginnings and personal purification.
    - Emphasis on setting intentions, preparing for growth, and nurturing potential.
    - Traditional activities could involve clearing spaces, planting seeds, and engaging in rituals of renewal.
- **Spring Equinox - March 20**
    - The day of equal light and dark, symbolizing balance, growth, and the return of life and color to the Earth.
    - Celebration of creativity, fertility, and harmony with nature.
    - Rituals may include planting flowers, painting eggs, or engaging in community gatherings to honor life's reawakening.
- **Earth Day – April 22**
    - The day dedicated to celebrating the Earth and raising awareness of various environmental challenges our planet faces.
- **May Day - May 1**

- A vibrant celebration of life, fertility, and sensuality as spring reaches full bloom.
- Emphasis on joy, community, and the interconnectedness of all beings.
- Customs may include dancing around the maypole, feasting, and offering gratitude for life's abundance.

◦ **Summer Solstice (Midsummer) - June 21**
- The longest day of the year and peak of the sun's strength, a time for gratitude, joy, and personal fulfillment.
- Reflection on achievements, expressing gratitude, and celebrating life's fullness.
- Rituals could involve sun-watching, gathering flowers, and honoring light with bonfires or light-filled ceremonies.

◦ **Harvest Festival - August 1**
- The first harvest, celebrating the fruits of one's labor and the abundance of the Earth.
- Themes of sharing, gratitude, and communal support.
- Traditional practices may include sharing harvest meals, honoring community bonds, and giving thanks for sustenance.

◦ **Autumn Equinox - September 21**
- A time of equal light and dark, inviting reflection on balance, gratitude, and preparation for the inward journey of winter.
- Emphasis on letting go, acknowledging life's transitions, and focusing on inner harvest.
- Rituals may include creating altars with autumn fruits, sharing stories of gratitude, and giving thanks for the year's blessings.

◦ **All Souls Day - October 31**
- Marks the end of the harvest and the start of winter, honoring ancestors and reflecting on life's cycle.
- Themes of remembrance, mortality, and connection with those who came before.

- Observances could involve lighting candles for loved ones, sharing stories, and setting up ancestral altars.
- **All Saints Day - November 1**
  - Celebrates humanity's shared spiritual heritage, honoring notable figures across faiths and philosophies.
  - Focus on inclusivity, respect for diverse spiritual paths, and recognizing universal values.
  - Activities might include storytelling, reading passages from sacred texts, or quiet reflection to honor unity across human experience.

Rev. Brandon Arroues, M.Ed.
Founder of New Universalism | Ordained Minister | Educator & Consultant

Brandon Arroues is the founder of **New Universalism**, a faith tradition centered on unity, ethical responsibility, and reverence for truth. As an **ordained minister**, educator, and consultant, he has dedicated his life to fostering **spiritual growth, intellectual inquiry, and community empowerment**. With a deep commitment to bridging the wisdom of diverse traditions, Brandon has guided the formation of a faith that honors both **reason and spirituality**, embracing universal truths that unite all people.

Holding a **Master's in Instructional Design**, Brandon has received numerous awards for **excellence in research, classroom engagement, and educational leadership**. His academic journey is marked by continuous research in **educational & counseling psychology, phenomenology, and evidence-based coaching**. His scholarship informs his approach to **spiritual leadership**, integrating **psychological insight, ethical philosophy, and human development** into New Universalist teachings.

Brandon's work spans continents, beginning in **international education** in 2013 in Shandong, China, and expanding across **the United States, Europe, Eastern Asia, and Southeast Asia**. His experiences in **education, administration, counseling, and special education** have deepened his commitment to inclusivity, personal transformation, and social responsibility—**core tenets of New Universalism**.

In 2018, he founded **Brilliant Consulting & Advocacy**, where he has helped individuals and institutions navigate education and mental wellness. His **consultative and ministerial work** focuses on **empowering individuals to embrace personal growth, ethical leadership, and global interconnectedness**.

Beyond his professional and ministerial work, Brandon is deeply engaged in **spiritual practice, cultural exploration, and the arts**. He finds joy in **nature, writing, creative expression, and deep conversations on philosophy and faith**. He welcomes the opportunity to connect with seekers, scholars, and spiritual communities, continuing the lifelong journey of **learning, service, and sacred inquiry**.